FRIENDS, NEIGHBOURS, SINNERS

Friends, Neighbours, Sinners demonstrates the fundamental ways in which religious difference shaped English society in the first half of the eighteenth century. By examining the social subtleties of interactions between people of differing beliefs, and how they were mediated through languages and behaviours common to the long eighteenth century, Carys Brown examines the graduated layers of religious exclusivity that influenced everyday existence. By doing so, the book points towards a new approach to the social and cultural history of the eighteenth century, one that acknowledges the integral role of the dynamics of religious difference in key aspects of eighteenth-century life. This book therefore proposes not just to add to current understanding of religious coexistence in this period, but to shift our ways of thinking about the construction of social discourses, parish politics, and cultural spaces in eighteenth-century England.

CARYS BROWN is a Research Fellow at Trinity College, University of Cambridge. She has published articles in *The Historical Journal*, *British Catholic History*, *Journal for Eighteenth-Century Studies*, and *Cultural and Social History*.

CAMBRIDGE STUDIES IN EARLY MODERN BRITISH HISTORY

SERIES EDITORS

MICHAEL BRADDICK
Professor of History, University of Sheffield

KRISTA KESSELRING
Professor of History, Dalhousie University

ALEXANDRA WALSHAM
*Professor of Modern History, University of Cambridge,
and Fellow of Emmanuel College*

This is a series of monographs and studies covering many aspects of the history of the British Isles between the late fifteenth century and the early eighteenth century. It includes the work of established scholars and pioneering work by a new generation of scholars. It includes both reviews and revisions of major topics and books which open up new historical terrain or which reveal startling new perspectives on familiar subjects. All the volumes set detailed research within broader perspectives, and the books are intended for the use of students as well as of their teachers.

For a list of titles in the series go to
www.cambridge.org/earlymodernbritishhistory

FRIENDS, NEIGHBOURS, SINNERS

SINNERS

Religious Difference and English Society, 1689–1750

CARYS BROWN

University of Cambridge

 CAMBRIDGE
UNIVERSITY PRESS

CAMBRIDGE
UNIVERSITY PRESS

Shaftesbury Road, Cambridge CB2 8EA, United Kingdom

One Liberty Plaza, 20th Floor, New York, NY 10006, USA

477 Williamstown Road, Port Melbourne, VIC 3207, Australia

314–321, 3rd Floor, Plot 3, Splendor Forum, Jasola District Centre, New Delhi – 110025, India

103 Penang Road, #05–06/07, Visioncrest Commercial, Singapore 238467

Cambridge University Press is part of Cambridge University Press & Assessment, a department of the University of Cambridge.

We share the University's mission to contribute to society through the pursuit of education, learning and research at the highest international levels of excellence.

www.cambridge.org
Information on this title: www.cambridge.org/9781009221337

DOI: 10.1017/9781009221375

First published 2022
First paperback edition 2024

A catalogue record for this publication is available from the British Library

ISBN   978-1-009-22138-2   Hardback
ISBN   978-1-009-22133-7   Paperback

Contents

Figures

Acknowledgements

The research upon which this book is based was first undertaken for my PhD thesis, which would have been impossible without the generous support of the Arts and Humanities Research Council and St John's College, Cambridge. I have been subsequently very fortunate to hold a research fellowship at Trinity College, Cambridge, which has given me the intellectual space and financial means to develop this research into a book. My gratitude goes to Cambridge University Press for the publication of this manuscript, and in particular to Ethan Shagan and Michael Braddick, whose comments were invaluable in helping me frame my argument as well as tackle the details. I am also very grateful to Liz Friend-Smith for cheerfully and patiently directing me through the publication process.

The archive and library trips that underpinned this research were made more productive and enjoyable by the expertise of the staff of the Angus Library and Archive, Berkshire Record Office, Bodleian Library, British Library, Cambridge University Library, Cambridgeshire Archives, Cheshire Archives and Local Studies, Coventry History Centre, Devonshire Archives and Local Studies, Dr Williams's Library, Essex Record Office, Gloucestershire Archives, Hertfordshire Archives, Huntingdonshire Archives, Hull History Centre, Lancashire Archives, Lambeth Palace Library, Library of the Society of Friends, Manchester Archives, Norfolk Record Office, Somerset Heritage Centre, Surrey History Centre, the John Rylands Library, West Yorkshire Archive Service, and Wiltshire and Swindon History Centre.

Gabriel Glickman's comments on early and late stages of this project were invaluable to both the PhD thesis and my subsequent rethinking of it. I am also grateful to my other examiner, Jonathan Barry, for his close and expert reading of my thesis. The audiences of seminars and workshops at Cambridge, Warwick, Newcastle, the Institute of Historical Research, Manchester, and Tübingen were generous in sharing comments and questions, and helped me to clarify my argument. I have benefitted greatly from the support and ideas of other scholars, including Jens Åklundh, Helen Berry, Pippa Carter, Simone Hanebaum, Charmian Mansell, Patrick McGhee, Jonah Miller, Anthony Milton, Adam Morton, Kate Peters, Naomi Pullin, Fred Smith, Alice Souliex-Evans, and Rebecca Whiteley. The ten months I spent at the University of Manchester working on the project 'Faith in the Town' with Hannah Barker, Jeremy Gregory, and Kate Gibson were of enormous intellectual value and were made very enjoyable by generous and supportive colleagues. At Trinity College I have been encouraged in my efforts by Alex Freer, Sachiko Kusukawa, Samita Sen, Richard Serjeantson, Hannah Shepard, Partha Shil, Jitka Štollová, George Roberts, Tessa Webber, and Luca Zenobi. Allison Neal and Tim Heimlich have been fantastic friends; I am so glad our arrivals at Trinity College coincided.

My biggest intellectual debt is to Alex Walsham, without whom I am not sure I would have pursued graduate study, let alone an academic career. It is difficult to exaggerate her generosity, patience, care, and immense insight, all of which have been instrumental not just when she was supervising my doctoral thesis but at every subsequent stage. Among the innumerable ways she has helped and supported me, I dread to think of the precious time she has spared to read not-quite-there iterations of the chapters of this book, and she has never ceased to encourage. I cannot thank her enough.

Harriet Lyon has contributed to this book through her intellectual insight and invaluable friendship in equal parts, and I don't know where I'd be without her. Ed and Rhoda Brown have provided both support and healthy scepticism about this academic tome; I'm sorry I didn't use any of your suggested titles. Sophie Brown, I can't say you contributed much in the way of intellectual content, but you are excellent. Fiona and Melvin Brown have gone above and beyond the call of parental duty in their interest in my project and have been relentless in their encouragement. They are both inspiring people.

Tom Smith has been, and will always be, wonderful both as a wise scholar and as an unspeakably great husband. I may be closing the cover on this book, but I'm looking forward to filling the blank pages of whatever comes next.

Note on the Text

Original spelling, punctuation, and capitalisation have been retained in all quotations, except that the use of i and j, u and v has been modernised. Standard contractions and abbreviations have been silently expanded and superscript characters silently lowered. All dates given in this book are given in the Old Style (Julian Calendar), but with the year taken to begin on 1 January rather than 25 March.

Abbreviations

ALA	Angus Library and Archive
BL	British Library
Bod.	Bodleian Library
BRO	Berkshire Record Office
CA	Cambridgeshire Archives
CALS	Cheshire Archives and Local Studies
CHC	Coventry History Centre
CUL	Cambridge University Library
DALS	Devonshire Archives and Local Studies
DWL	Dr Williams's Library
ERO	Essex Record Office
Friends' Lib.	Library of the Society of Friends
GA	Gloucestershire Archives
HA	Huntingdonshire Archives
HeA	Hertfordshire Archives
HHC	Hull History Centre
LA	Lancashire Archives
Lambeth Lib.	Lambeth Palace Library
MA	Manchester Archives
NRO	Norfolk Record Office
SHC	Somerset Heritage Centre
SuHC	Surrey History Centre
UoMSC	University of Manchester Special Collections
WSHC	Wiltshire and Swindon History Centre
WYAS	West Yorkshire Archive Service, Wakefield

Introduction

On the afternoon of 22 July 1722, seven young ladies were sitting in the drawing room of a house somewhere near Rochdale, Lancashire. Two of them were engaged in needlework; the rest were playing cards. This was a pleasant but unremarkable scene, at least to the casual observer. From the perspective of one of the women, however, the occasion was a cause of considerable consternation. Anne Dawson, the 26-year-old daughter of a Presbyterian minister from Rochdale, recorded later that day in her diary that she had found the five hours spent at the house deeply uncomfortable. She had arrived there with her sister, hoping for 'agreeable conversation', and had been appalled when instead 'there came out a Pack of Cards'. She and her sister had both refused to play, and while she admitted that 'my thoughts was not well imployed', she believed she was 'imploying my hands much better with my nedle than they were, And when I came home and Vewed my work I was well pleased at it ... whereas had I spent my time as they did I durst not reflect on it for if I did it must be with trouble & regret'. She concluded her diary entry by imploring God that she 'be spur'd on by other people's negligence'.[1]

Dawson's social discomfort is intriguing. She looked for 'agreeable conversation', but it is unclear what she expected this to be. Given her objection to card-playing – a common contemporary social activity – did she equally reject conversational norms? We hear Dawson's side of the story, but how was her behaviour received? And how might it have affected her long-term social relationship with the other ladies? Dawson was hoping to 'be spur'd on' in her piety by viewing the idleness of others; this sense of spiritual and moral difference can hardly have oiled the wheels of friendship. So what was her relationship with the other people in that room, and how did she square this with her particular understanding of pious social

---

[1] Diary of Anne (Dawson) Evans 1721–22, Add MS 71626, fol. 38r-v, British Library (BL), London.

practice? Presented with a social scene in which she evidently wished to take part, but felt unable, she was left to seek a balance between religious integrity and her desire for social participation. From her own admission that her 'thoughts was not well imployed', it seems that this balance was not easy to strike.

The layer of social tension hovering over that Rochdale drawing room bore some resemblance to that present in English society more broadly in the half century that followed the passage of the so-called 'Toleration' Act of 1689. This legislation marked a significant change in the legal status of religious minorities in England. While providing no toleration for Catholics, it allowed Protestants who dissented from the Established Church to worship separately in their own registered meeting houses for the first time in the nation's history. However, a single piece of limited and contested legislation was insufficient to erase completely over a hundred years of religious strife.[2] Many contemporaries remained hostile to perceived competitors to the Established Church, a hostility that crept into multiple aspects of social and cultural life. The toleration of 1689 was not so much an end point as the start of a process by which English society worked out how to manage – rather than attempt to remove – religious differences previously denied legitimacy by the legal exclusion of Dissent.

This process was not linear; neither was it frictionless. Protestant Dissenters, many of whom had, under the persecutions of the Restoration, maintained group identities that placed a strong emphasis on solidarity in suffering, now had to work out what it meant to Dissent under a legal framework that was considerably more favourable. Grateful for their increased liberty, and hopeful that it might be extended, Dissenters in this context had good reason to demonstrate their ability to integrate within contemporary society. At the same time, however, the very fact of their Dissent from the Established Church was a claim to difference. In order to justify this Dissent, and to meet the expectations of their religious professions, Dissenters were obliged to distinguish themselves. Like Anne Dawson, who entered a room in expectation of social interaction but quickly found herself unable to share fully in the sociability of those therein, Dissenters in general were left teetering between integration and separation. The Toleration Act theoretically placed them within a shared Protestant interest united against the perceived threat of popery, but it by

---

[2] Ralph Stevens, *Protestant Pluralism. The Reception of the Toleration Act, 1689–1720* (Woodbridge: Boydell & Brewer, 2018), p. 6.

no means guaranteed that their conception of Protestant society would chime wholly with that of staunch supporters of the Established Church.

The scene from Rochdale is also telling in another respect. Polite culture – including activities such as sitting and playing cards – has generally been regarded by scholars as a discourse that rejected and smoothed over the religious divisions of the past. In fact, the eighteenth century as a whole has been seen by some historians as an 'Age of Tolerance', meaning that work emphasising the widespread impact of religion, and particularly religious difference, on everyday life in this period has been slow to gain traction.[3] Approaches to the eighteenth century which do emphasise the role of religion in shaping cultural developments tend to characterise new conversational norms and sociable venues as reactions to religious division, rather than products of it.[4] By such accounts, eighteenth-century society was decisively and somewhat deliberately moving away from the troubles of a previous age. Yet Dawson's experience shows how senses of religious difference could be deeply embedded within even the most innocent of social activities. As many other incidents in this book demonstrate, brazen persecution decreased across English society after the Toleration Act, but this was accompanied by a move towards more insidious forms of social exclusion.

With this in view, this book throws into relief the extensive cultural impact of England's new and unstable religious settlement. The Toleration Act of 1689, despite its apparently innovative nature, failed to resolve in full the country's religious problems, and instead forced religious and social issues into closer conversation. Recent scholarship has demonstrated decisively the sense of uncertainty created by this ambiguous legislation.[5] This book shows how in a period when prejudices remained ingrained but were no longer fully facilitated by the law, contemporaries sought social means to manage living with religious difference. The result was that as new social modes and cultural venues developed, assumptions about religious differences were embedded into the norms of social interaction in a way that sustained distinctions without necessarily spilling into immediate conflict.

---

[3] The challenges of this descriptor are discussed in Ourida Mostefai, 'Dissensus and Toleration: Reconsidering Tolerance in the Age of Enlightenment', *Studies in Eighteenth-Century Culture*, 47 (2018), pp. 269–73.

[4] Lawrence E. Klein, 'Politeness and the Interpretation of the British Eighteenth Century', *Historical Journal*, 45, 4 (2002), p. 890; Alison E. Hurley, 'Peculiar Christians, Circumstantial Courtiers, and the Making of Conversation in Seventeenth-Century England', *Representations*, 111, 1 (2010), p. 41; Brian Cowan, '"Restoration" England and the History of Sociability', in Valérie Capdeville and Alain Kerhervé (eds.), *British Sociability in the Long Eighteenth Century: Challenging the Anglo-French Connection* (Woodbridge: Boydell & Brewer, 2019), pp. 22, 24.

[5] Stevens, *Protestant Pluralism*.

In 1689 both High Church opponents to toleration and some Protestant Dissenters were attempting to manage religious difference by eliminating it outright. However, an increasing recognition of the impossibility of this over the period resulted in a shift in emphasis towards the management of religious difference through social and cultural means. By 1750 religious difference was no longer so frequently a cause of violent conflict, but it had been deeply woven into English culture. This process – and its effect on daily life – lies at the heart of this book; by these means religious difference was a formative principle of English culture and society after 1689.

By examining the social terms in which religious differences were framed, the contestation of ideas about 'public religion', and the places and spaces in which religious differences were subtly reinforced and managed through social behaviour, this book demonstrates the mutually constitutive relationship between religious difference and English society in the first half of the eighteenth century. In doing so, it makes two principal contributions to our understanding of this period. First, through examining the social subtleties of interactions between people of differing beliefs, and how they were mediated through language and behaviour common to the period, it moves beyond binaries of assimilation and separation to examine the graduated layers of religious exclusivity that shaped everyday existence. Secondly, it points towards a new approach to the social and cultural history of the eighteenth century, one that acknowledges the integral role of the dynamics of religious difference in shaping key aspects of eighteenth-century life. This book therefore proposes not just to add to current understandings of religious co-existence in this period, but also to shift our ways of thinking about the construction of social discourses, parish politics, and cultural spaces in eighteenth-century England.

Eighteenth-Century Cultural Change

Historians have given substantial attention to the impact of England's religious settlement on the Established Church clergy, and on contemporary religious and political developments.[6] The work of Ralph Stevens

---

[6] Nicholas Tyacke, 'The "Rise of Puritanism" and the Legalizing of Dissent, 1571–1719', in Ole Peter Grell, Jonathan I. Israel, and Nicholas Tyacke (eds.), *From Persecution to Toleration: The Glorious Revolution and Religion in England* (Oxford: Oxford University Press, 1991), pp. 17–51; Brent Sirota, 'The Occasional Conformity Controversy, Moderation, and the Anglican Critique of Modernity, 1700–1714', *Historical Journal*, 57, 1 (2014), pp. 81–105; Stevens, *Protestant Pluralism*; Hugh Trevor-Roper, 'Toleration and Religion after 1688', in Grell, Israel, and Tyacke (eds.), *From Persecution to Toleration*, pp. 389–408.

in particular has drawn attention to the practical challenges of religious plurality for Established Church clergy as they adapted to a 'new religious reality' after 1689.[7] More generally, over the past two decades the importance of religious developments in the eighteenth century has been given considerable scholarly attention in accounts of what has been termed the 'long Reformation'.[8] It is now widely understood that England 'did not go into the eighteenth century complacent about its post-confessional stability', and that senses of instability had widespread religious, political, and intellectual consequences.[9] However, the implications of the religious settlement of 1689 for England's social and cultural development have been little considered.

This is symptomatic of a lack of conversation between religious, social, and cultural histories of this period.[10] With the advent of a social history that predominantly took a materialist view of religion in the 1960s and 1970s, social historians were reluctant to emphasise the role of religion in shaping English society.[11] The influence of this approach is to some degree still evident today. Histories of politeness, sociability, commerce, and many other key themes of the period have been written with religion either on the margins or discussed in isolation.[12] This is in spite of earlier work that recognised the necessity of a more integrated approach to the

---

[7] Stevens, *Protestant Pluralism*, p. 1.

[8] See for example Jeremy Gregory, 'The Making of a Protestant Nation: "Success" and "Failure" in England's Long Reformation', in Nicholas Tyacke (ed.), *England's Long Reformation, 1500–1800* (London: UCL Press, 1998), pp. 314, 324; Lucy Bates, 'The Limits of Possibility in England's Long Reformation', *Historical Journal*, 53, 4 (2010), p. 1051; Robert G. Ingram, *Reformation Without End. Religion, Politics, and the Past in Post-Reformation England* (Manchester: Manchester University Press, 2018), pp. xi–xii.

[9] Sarah Apetrei, *Women, Feminism, and Religion in Early Enlightenment England* (Cambridge and New York: Cambridge University Press, 2010), pp. 24–5.

[10] Jeremy Gregory, 'Introduction: Transforming the "Age of Reason" into an "Age of Faiths:" or, Putting Religions and Beliefs (Back) into the Eighteenth Century', *Journal for Eighteenth-Century Studies*, 32, 3 (2009), *passim*.

[11] See for example Eric Hobsbawm, 'Methodism and the Threat of Revolution in Britain', *History Today*, 7 (1957), pp. 115–24; Peter Laslett, *The World We Have Lost* (London: Methuen, 1965); Keith Wrightson, *English Society, 1580–1680* (London: Routledge, 1993); E. P. Thompson, *Customs in Common* (London: Penguin, 1993). The problems of separating social, religious, and political history were described in Dan Beaver, 'Religion, Politics, and Society in Early Modern England: A Problem of Classification', *Journal of British Studies*, 33, 3 (July 1994), pp. 314–22.

[12] This problem is outlined in B. W. Young, 'Religious History and the Eighteenth-Century Historian', *Historical Journal*, 43, 3 (2000), pp. 857, 859. See for example Peter Borsay, *The English Urban Renaissance. Culture and Society in the Provincial Town 1660–1770* (Oxford: Clarendon Press, 1989); Paul Langford, *A Polite and Commercial People. England 1727–1783* (Oxford: Clarendon Press, 1989); H. T. Dickinson (ed.), *A Companion to Eighteenth-Century Britain* (Oxford: Blackwell, 2002); Maxine Berg, *Luxury and Pleasure in Eighteenth-Century Britain* (New York: Oxford University Press, 2005).

eighteenth century.[13] J. C. D. Clark's *English Society*, while controversial in its emphasis on the hegemony of the Church of England in tandem with the state, undoubtedly demonstrated the need for attention to religion in histories of this period.[14] However, perhaps partly because Clark's work focused primarily on political and ecclesiastical matters, paying little attention to the central interests of social and economic historians, this work had a frosty reception in these fields.[15] In addition to this, there has been a considerable strand of scholarship that while rejecting the notion that the eighteenth century was the beginning of an inexorable march towards 'secular' modernity, suggests that religious pluralism diluted the influence of religion over public life.[16] The result is that historians have not considered religious differences to be of primary importance for understanding eighteenth-century society and culture.

It is fair to say that many of the social and cultural developments of this period did, at least superficially, turn away from a century of religious and political division. Although controversial in the Restoration period, urban venues such as coffeehouses were by the eighteenth century an accepted part of social life, allowing contemporaries (principally men) to exchange news and conversation, drink coffee, and debate ideas in a genial fashion.[17] Other venues – such as pleasure gardens, assembly rooms, and spas – were new in the eighteenth century, and themselves facilitated the display of fashionable consumption.[18] Alongside this emerged new modes of behaviour, such as politeness – a form of moderate, decorous, agreeable social interaction that has become a 'key word' for historians of the eighteenth century.[19] Politeness was by no means the only social mode of the period,

---

[13] See for example Jonathan Barry, 'The Cultural Life of Bristol, 1640–1775' (Unpublished DPhil thesis, University of Oxford, 1985), p. 3.

[14] J. C. D. Clark, *English Society 1688–1832: Ideology, Social Structure and Political Practice during the Ancien Regime* (New York: Cambridge University Press, 1985; 2nd edn 2000).

[15] Frank O'Gorman, 'Review of English Society 1688–1832: Ideology, Social Structure and Political Practice During the Ancien Regime', (review no. 41b) https://reviews.history.ac.uk/review/41b, accessed 15 October, 2019.

[16] Blair Worden, 'The Question of Secularization', in Alan Houston and Steve Pincus (eds.), *A Nation Transformed. England After the Restoration* (Cambridge: Cambridge University Press, 2001), p. 24; Penelope Corfield, '"An Age of Infidelity": Secularization in Eighteenth-century England', *Social History*, 39, 2 (2014), pp. 229, 231; Brad S. Gregory, *The Unintended Reformation. How a Religious Revolution Secularized Society* (Cambridge, MA: Harvard University Press, 2012), pp. 368–9, 373–4, 376.

[17] Brian Cowan, *The Social Life of Coffee. The Emergence of the British Coffeehouse* (New Haven and London, Yale University Press, 2005), p. 100.

[18] Hannah Greig, '"All Together and All Distinct": Public Sociability and Social Exclusivity in London's Pleasure Gardens, c. 1740–1800', *Journal of British Studies*, 51, 1 (2012), pp. 70–1.

[19] Paul Langford, 'The Uses of Eighteenth-Century Politeness', *Transactions of the Royal Historical Society*, 12 (2002), p. 311; Klein, 'Politeness and the Interpretation of the British Eighteenth Century', p. 875.

and it could take many different forms, but is particularly important here because it has been understood to be significant in its apparent rejection of divisive religious politics.[20] This stemmed from the fact that the Civil Wars and Interregnum of the 1640s and 1650s had witnessed a violent mix of religious conflict and social prescription, denounced by contemporaries as fanatical 'enthusiasm'. This experience, along with the fresh memory of the religious and political dilemmas of the Restoration, resulted in the emergence of new social practices in the late seventeenth and early eighteenth centuries which, by discouraging fanaticism, sought to limit the potential for religious divisions to cause damage.[21]

Supporting these cultural changes was an economy that appeared to be (and in some places literally was) steaming ahead. This was a period of expanding national wealth, commercialisation, and increased material possession, in which many households, urban and rural, had greater access to luxury goods and new consumables.[22] Better communication and an expanding print trade allowed greater national economic and cultural integration than ever before.[23] Improvements in agriculture had by the beginning of the eighteenth century enabled structural adjustments in the workforce that underpinned the country's ability to produce goods for export.[24] This engagement in global commerce facilitated the increased domestic purchase and consumption of goods such as tea, coffee, sugar, and hot chocolate – staples of eighteenth-century social life.[25] Against the backdrop of much that seemed innovative about the eighteenth century, it

---

[20] Nicholas T. Phillipson, 'Politics and Politeness in the Reigns of Anne and the Early Hanoverians', in John Pocock (ed.), *The Varieties of British Political Thought, 1500–1800* (Cambridge: Cambridge University Press in association with the Folger Institute, Washington, DC, 1993), p. 215; Klein, 'Politeness and the Interpretation of the British Eighteenth Century', p. 890; Markku Peltonen, 'Politeness and Whiggism, 1688–1732', *Historical Journal*, 48, 2 (2005), p. 396.

[21] Cowan, '"Restoration" England and the History of Sociability', pp. 22, 24.

[22] Klein, 'Politeness and the Interpretation of the British Eighteenth Century', p. 898; Langford, *A Polite and Commercial People*, pp. 2–3; Lorna Scammell, 'Town Versus Country: The Property of Everyday Consumption in the Late Seventeenth and Early Eighteenth Centuries', in Jon Stobart and Alastair Owens (eds.), *Urban Fortunes: Prosperity and Inheritance in the Town, 1700–1900* (Aldershot: Ashgate, 2000), pp. 27, 35; John Brewer, '"The Most Polite Age and the Most Vicious": Attitudes Towards Culture as a Commodity, 1600–1800', in Ann Bermingham and John Brewer (eds.), *The Consumption of Culture, 1600–1800: Image, Object, Text* (London and New York: Routledge, 1995), p. 345.

[23] Dror Wahrman, 'National Society, Communal Culture: An Argument About the Recent Historiography of Eighteenth-Century Britain', *Social History*, 17, 1 (1992), p. 44.

[24] Patrick Wallis, Justin Colson, and David Chilosi, 'Structural Change and Economic Growth in the British Economy before the Industrial Revolution, 1500–1800', *The Journal of Economic History*, 78, 3 (2018), p. 864.

[25] Patrick K. O'Brien, 'Inseparable Connections: Trade, Economy, Fiscal State, and the Expansion of Empire, 1688–1815', in P. J. Marshall and Alaine Low (eds.), *The Oxford History of the British Empire. Volume II: The Eighteenth Century* (Oxford: Oxford University Press, 1998), pp. 56–7.

is in some ways unsurprising that social and cultural historians have paid little attention to the effect of religious divisions in this period.

As much as early eighteenth-century England may look like the prelude to an 'Age of Improvement', the universality of the effects of economic expansion, commerce, and fashionable consumption has been questioned in recent scholarship. The acquisition of new 'luxury' goods, for instance, was not necessarily always motivated by a desire for fashionable display as an end in itself, but rather by the role of display in establishing a credit-worthiness increasingly based not so much on an individual or household's accrual of possessions, but on their purchasing power.[26] Those of middling social status – a group often associated with the increased purchase of consumer luxuries in this period – were also prey to considerable financial insecurity that made their status difficult to maintain.[27] Participation in eighteenth-century consumer culture was precarious, and for a range of reasons some individuals abstained from embracing the cultural trends of the day. As Helen Berry's study of 'the pleasures of austerity' has highlighted, there were multiple different ways of engaging with contemporary culture, including abstinence from it. In focusing on those who did not participate fully in the cultures of luxury and pleasure, either through choice or necessity, we can 'develop a new and more expansive understanding of Georgian England'.[28]

This book proposes that exploring the impact of religious difference on the first half of the eighteenth century is important for creating this wider view of eighteenth-century society and culture. An understanding of the dynamics of religious difference is not, it suggests, merely an addition to our knowledge of the eighteenth century, but rather is fundamental to our interpretation of the social and cultural developments of the period. By exploring the religious ideals inherent in ideas such as politeness, and in the social interactions that took place in a wide range of locations, such as the alehouse, the assembly room, and the street, it shows the lingering and evolving impact of religious difference in social discourses and venues that were idealised by contemporary writers as rejecting a divisive religious past. Religious difference, it shows, is an essential lens for understanding eighteenth-century life.

---

[26] Alexandra Shepard, 'Crediting Women in the Early Modern English Economy', *Historical Workshop Journal*, 79, 1 (2015), pp. 17–19.

[27] Tawny Paul, *The Poverty of Disaster: Debt and Insecurity in Eighteenth-Century Britain* (Cambridge: Cambridge University Press, 2019), pp. 4–5.

[28] Helen Berry, 'The Pleasures of Austerity', *Eighteenth-Century Studies*, 37, 2 (2014), p. 263

The 'Toleration' of 1689

The nature of the religious settlement of 1689 was crucial in creating the conditions in which religious difference shaped English society. It is not simply the case that the eighteenth century had more of a hangover from the poisonous disputes of the Reformation than we first thought. The reconfiguration of England's religious landscape created new headaches – and cures – that are especially illuminated when we examine religious changes in tandem with social and cultural developments.

There is no doubt that the Toleration Act was a highly significant departure from state insistence on religious conformity. In addition to its unprecedented resignation to the existence of worship outside of the Established Church, it acknowledged all nonconformists who subscribed to the doctrine of the Trinity, including Quakers, to be part of a wider Protestant cause. This was clear from the preamble to the Act, which stated that 'some ease to scrupulous Consciences in the Exercise of Religion may be an effectuall meanes to unite their Majesties Protestant Subjects in Interest and Affection'.[29] This represented a substantial change in mind-set from the 1662 Act of Uniformity, which had made it clear that any deviation from the Established Church was contrary to the interests of the nation.[30] Thus, the 1689 Act was vastly different in its sentiment from the legislation that had been brought in just twenty-seven years previously. However, born of political expediency, this measure was also highly limited.[31] The Act was open to differing interpretations, and the result was that Protestant Dissenters and stalwarts of the Established Church alike battled to define the religious settlement in ways that promoted their interests.

These definitional battles took place amidst ideological shifts in attitudes towards the management of religious difference in the later seventeenth century. Although the view that persecution was a just means of

---

[29] 'William and Mary, 1688: An Act for Exempting their Majestyes Protestant Subjects Dissenting from the Church of England from the Penalties of Certaine Lawes' [Chapter XVIII. Rot. Parl. pt. 5. nu. 15.]', in John Raithby (ed.), *Statutes of the Realm* (s.l, 1819), vol. VI, pp. 74–6. *British History Online*, http://www.british-history.ac.uk/statutes-realm/vol6/pp74-76.

[30] 'Charles II, 1662: An Act for the Uniformity of Publique Prayers and Administrac[i]on of Sacraments & Other Rites & Ceremonies and for Establishing the Form of Making Ordaining and Consecrating Bishops Priests and Deacons in the Church of England.', in Raithby (ed.), *Statutes of the Realm* (s.l., 1819), vol. V, pp. 364–70. *British History Online*, http://www.british-history.ac.uk/statutes-realm/vol5/pp364-370.

[31] Trevor-Roper, 'Toleration and Religion after 1688', p. 391; David L. Wykes, 'Quaker Schoolmasters, Toleration and the Law, 1689–1714', *Journal of Religious History*, 21 (1997), p. 186; Martin Hugh Fitzpatrick, 'From Natural Law to Natural Rights? Protestant Dissent and Toleration in the Late Eighteenth Century', *History of European Ideas*, 42, 2 (2016), p. 199; Stevens, *Protestant Pluralism*, pp. 8–9.

saving erroneous consciences persisted, during the Restoration an increasing number of contemporary thinkers promoted the idea that persecution of conscience might itself produce immorality, encouraging only outward conformity while facilitating inward error.[32] Most famously, John Locke's *Letter Concerning Toleration* (1689) argued that it was possible to win over consciences only through persuasion, rather than coercion, and that the jurisdiction of the magistrate extended only over civil matters. Dissenters were therefore to be tolerated.[33] Locke was not alone in promoting such ideas. In his 1687 Declaration of Indulgence, James II had argued that constraint of conscience 'has ever been directly contrary to our inclination, as we think it is to the interest of government'.[34] While James had plenty of self-interested reasons to promote toleration, such as a desire for his fellow Catholics to be able to serve in political office, he may also have genuinely supported the principle of liberty of conscience.[35] The Toleration Act was passed at a time when the idea of indulgence to tender consciences was becoming more current.

However, the Act itself did not represent acceptance of the idea of liberty of conscience. In fact, the measure was something of a last resort. Initially, attempts to achieve a religious settlement following the landing of William III in 1688 had been focused on the comprehension of moderate Dissenters within the Established Church. Proposals for the indulgence eventually enacted in 1689 were brought to the fore of negotiations of England's settlement only when the recalcitrance of many in the Church, combined with Dissenting concern about the Church's sincerity, resulted in the rejection of comprehension.[36] This was, then, a 'politique religious settlement', and not one that could erase the memory of the past century.[37]

The difficult circumstances in which the Act was passed were reflected in its detail – or lack thereof. As recent histories of this period have

---

[32] Mark Goldie, 'The Theory of Religious Intolerance in Restoration England', in Grell, Israel, and Tyacke (eds.), *From Persecution to Toleration*, pp. 334; Ethan Shagan, *The Rule of Moderation: Violence, Religion and the Politics of Restraint in Early Modern England* (Cambridge: Cambridge University Press, 2011), p. 302.

[33] John Locke 'A Letter Concerning Toleration [2nd edn, 1960]', in Mark Goldie (ed.), *John Locke: A Letter Concerning Toleration and Other Writings* (Indianapolis: Liberty Fund, 2010), pp. 8, 11–12.

[34] 'Declaration of Indulgence of James II, 4 April 1687', in Andrew Browning (ed.), *English Historical Documents, 1660–1714* (London: Eyre & Spottiswoode, 1953), p. 399.

[35] Scott Sowerby, *Making Toleration. The Repealers and the Glorious Revolution* (Cambridge, MA: Harvard University Press, 2013), p. 3.

[36] John Spurr, 'The Church of England, Comprehension, and the Toleration Act of 1689', *English Historical Review*, 104, 413 (1989), pp. 943–4.

[37] Stephen A. Timmons, 'From Persecution to Toleration in the West Country, 1672–1692', *The Historian*, 68, 3 (2006), p. 461.

emphasised, the permanence of the Act was uncertain, its wording ambiguous, and its coverage limited.[38] The Toleration Act only suspended rather than removed permanently the penal legislation against Protestant Dissent, thereby creating room for ambiguity about the extent to which Dissenters really were included as part of a national Protestant interest. The Test and Corporation Acts (1673 and 1661 respectively), which prevented anyone who did not take communion in the Church of England from taking public office, still remained in force. The legislation of 1689 also failed to mention a number of key issues, including the legality of Dissenters' education and political involvement. This created confusion about its practical implications, and allowed for an ungenerous interpretation of its terms.[39] This was important. While all parties wished to avoid a repeat of the Civil Wars of the mid-seventeenth century, deeply held religious prejudices that had been fostered and refined across generations did not dissolve overnight.[40] Furthermore, those who had previously suffered social exclusion and punishment at the hand of the magistrate on account of their religious affiliation were unlikely to abandon their sense of difference at the first sign of legislative change.

Protestant Dissenters – the main 'beneficiaries' of the Act – were therefore in the immediate aftermath of 1689 left in a somewhat uncomfortable and vulnerable position. Many supporters of the Established Church promoted a narrow interpretation of this ambiguous toleration, seeing it merely as a temporary indulgence, and Dissenters were left fearful that their liberty might be withdrawn.[41] Anxious to hold onto this liberty, however limited it was, they sought to show a degree of conformity with the expectations of contemporary society. At the same time, however, this liberty complicated Dissenters' status. Until the late 1680s, they could unequivocally oppose a persecutory regime, but the Toleration Act partially undermined their outsider identity.[42] In the face of a partial and

---

[38] Stevens, *Protestant Pluralism*, pp. 6–7, 8–9.

[39] Ibid., p. 11.

[40] Tim Harris, 'The Legacy of the English Civil War: Rethinking the Revolution', *The European Legacy*, 5 (2000), p. 503; Gabriel Glickman, 'Political Conflict and the Memory of the Revolution in England, 1689-c.1745', in Tim Harris and Stephen Taylor (eds.), *The Final Crisis of the Stuart Monarchy: The Revolutions of 1688–91 in Their British, Atlantic, and European Contexts* (Woodbridge: The Boydell Press, 2013), pp. 244–5.

[41] Tyacke, 'The "Rise of Puritanism" and the Legalizing of Dissent, 1571–1719', p. 48; Wykes, 'Quaker Schoolmasters', p. 186; Andrew Thompson, 'Contesting the Test Act: Dissent, Parliament and the Public in the 1730s', *Parliamentary History*, 24, 1 (2005), p. 61.

[42] John Seed, 'History and Narrative Identity: Religious Dissent and the Politics of Memory in Eighteenth-Century England', *Journal of British Studies*, 44, 1 (2005), p. 47.

ambiguous toleration, Dissenters had to find new ways of building up their Churches and defining their places in society.[43]

The situation of those who opposed or disliked the toleration granted under the 1689 Act was also awkward. Previously, legal measures had provided a clear means of excluding Dissenters from English society, and indeed defenders of Established Church interests sought to continue to use legal means to keep Dissent on the margins. The occasional conformity controversy of the first decade of the century, and the passage of the Schism Act in 1714, which aimed to secure Dissenters' exclusion from political office and educational provision, respectively, illustrated the determination of some to keep the toleration as limited as possible. However, as the political influence of the Tories diminished, it was increasingly apparent that they were unlikely to achieve the permanent marginalisation of Dissent that they sought. This left some defenders of the Established Church deeply concerned that the ecclesial nature of society would be lost as the Church and its norms ceased to play such a prominent role.[44] They reacted by attempting to secure the Church's position at the centre of society in other ways, extending existing stereotypes of Dissenters as fanatical, over-zealous, and hypocritical, to fit new situations and social scenarios. The Toleration Act had introduced a degree of voluntarism in English religious life: people 'had to be persuaded' to attend the Established Church 'for they could no longer be coerced'.[45] The exclusion of Dissenters through social means was an important persuasive strategy.

Thus, legal tolerance undoubtedly represented a considerable change, providing Protestant Dissenters with greater freedom of worship and substantial relief from persecution. However, religious discrimination remained a potent fact of life in the first half of the eighteenth century. Where the law no longer excluded Dissenters comprehensively, some defenders of the Established Church sought extra-legal means to place them beyond the social pale. At the same time, Protestant Dissenters, fearful that even this limited toleration would be revoked, faced the challenge of demonstrating their integration into contemporary society while also maintaining a sense of group identity within their Churches. The peculiar

---

[43] Doreen Rosman, *The Evolution of the English Churches, 1500–2000* (Cambridge: Cambridge University Press, 2003), p. 129.

[44] Sirota, 'The Occasional Conformity Controversy', p. 85; Alex W. Barber, 'Censorship, Salvation and the Preaching of Francis Higgins: A Reconsideration of High Church Politics and Theology in the Early 18th Century', *Parliamentary History*, 33, 1 (2014), pp. 116–17.

[45] Mark Goldie, 'Voluntary Anglicans', *Historical Journal*, 46, 4 (2003), p. 979. See also Stevens, *Protestant Pluralism*, p. 9.

social effects of this situation are apparent throughout this book, demonstrating how England's religious divisions, rampant throughout the sixteenth and seventeenth centuries, were, in a different way, a structural feature of the eighteenth.

The Anatomy of Religious Difference

The anatomy of religious difference was complex in this period, more so than contemporary polemicists let on. Labels applied to others were a tool for argument; terms such as 'fanatic', 'High Church zealot', and 'papist' were used to reduce a broad range of positions to single categories to be reviled. Such epithets obscured distinctions between individuals while also suggesting that the lines of religious difference were much more sharply and plainly drawn than was necessarily the case. The fact that, as the Whig politician John Hampden recalled in a letter to his former tutor, the Presbyterian minister Francis Tallents, one person might variously be called 'Papist, an Atheist, a Socinian' highlights the mutability of religious labels.[46] The complexity and diversity of contemporary interpretations of religious inclusion after 1689 was both a cause and product of the long negotiation of the meanings, boundaries, and implications of religious difference.

There were some broad categories of religious affiliation which most people could agree on. These were apparent in the 1689 Act, the full title of which was 'An Act for Exempting Their Majestyes Protestant Subjects Dissenting from the Church of England from the Penalties of Certaine Lawes'. This title, and the preamble, which made it clear that 'Papists or Popish Recusants' were excluded from the benefits of the Act, identified three broad religious alignments: Protestant Dissenters, Roman Catholics (or 'papists'), and the majority who remained loyal to the Established Church, whether by default or active choice.[47] Outside of these groupings was an unknown quantity of heterodox thinkers, unbelievers, and blasphemers labelled by many contemporaries as 'deists' and 'atheists' – and feared by them too.[48] These were distinctions around which debates about

[46] John Hampden, Jun., to Rev. [Francis] Tallents, London, 27 May 1693, Stowe MS 747, vol. V., fol. 16, British Library, London.
[47] 'William and Mary, 1688: An Act for Exempting their Majestyes Protestant Subjects Dissenting from the Church of England from the Penalties of Certaine Lawes'.
[48] Richard H. Popkin, 'The Deist Challenge', in Ole Peter Grell, Jonathan Israel, and Nicholas Tyacke (eds.), *From Persecution to Toleration: The Glorious Revolution and Religion in England* (Oxford: Oxford University Press, 1991), p. 195; David Berman, *A History of Atheism in Britain: From Hobbes to Russell* (Routledge: London and New York, 1990), pp. 35–6.

the relationship between Church and state, and about the role of religion in public life, were formed.

However, in 1689 these alignments did not represent homogenous groups. Under the umbrella of Protestant Dissent were Presbyterians, Independents, Baptists, and Quakers; arguably, there were more differences between these groups than similarities. Many Presbyterian and some Independent Meetings had come into being when ministers and their flocks had felt painfully unable to conform to the Restoration Church settlement in 1662; many of them therefore fought for comprehension within the Established Church, and continued to hope for it for some time after 1689.[49] In contrast, Quakers and Baptists were deliberate separatists, and had never had any desire to be part of the existing national communion.

This matters to our understanding of how religious difference affected English society in this period, because the differences between the varieties of Protestant Dissent had a potentially critical impact on the nature of their engagement with those beyond their profession. Many in the Established Church who had Low Church leanings were inclined to be more sympathetic towards good and pious people whose consciences prevented them from conforming in 1662 than they were towards principled separatists. On the other hand, the associations that other contemporaries made between the danger of Dissent and the ravages of the Civil Wars led some to fear that Presbyterians in particular might, if given the opportunity, seize control of the Established Church, an accusation that did not apply in the same way to Quakers or Baptists.[50]

The significant differences between Dissenting groups were not just confined to how they related to the Established Church. They also had differing ecclesiologies that affected the nature of their social obligations towards their congregations and the wider community. Presbyterians believed in a Church organised on a parochial basis with communion open to all but those who had been excluded as unfit.[51] Presbyterian ministers therefore had a direct responsibility for the entire parish rather than their congregation alone, and this was evident in their form of ordination. Whereas in most Independent Churches the minister was ordained

---

[49] John D. Ramsbottom, 'Presbyterians and "Partial Conformity" in the Restoration Church of England', *Journal of Ecclesiastical History*, 43, 2 (1992), pp. 251, 270.

[50] See for example Phillip Collier, *The Duty and Advantages of Promoting the Peace and Prosperity, Both of Church and State. A Sermon* (Exeter, 1712), p. 18.

[51] Roger Thomas, 'Parties in Nonconformity', in C. G. Bolam, Jeremy Goring, H. L. Short, and Roger Thomas, (eds.), *The English Presbyterians. From Elizabethan Puritanism to Modern Unitarianism* (London: George Allen and Unwin, 1968), p. 93.

to serve a particular congregation, Presbyterian ministers held their titles from their fellow ministers. Ultimately their duty was therefore to the Universal Church rather than one particular congregation.[52] By contrast, 'gathered' Churches were more closed communities, holding to the view that each Church was a group of individuals gathered by God to make up the visible Church. For Baptists and many Independents, the responsibility of members of the congregation for one another's spiritual and physical well-being was solidified through subscription to a covenant agreement. These agreements emphasised the congregation's unity under God, and their commitment to the duties of the Church.[53] This did not necessarily make these Churches insular, or mean that they felt no responsibility to the community at large.[54] However, it did mean that members had a particular commitment to those of their own profession.

Different again were Quakers, who believed that, in contrast to the visible Church constructed according to man-made rights, the only true Church was a community created by God, who kindled the light of the spirit in human hearts. Thus, Quaker meetings were constituted of those who responded to the grace of God by coming to faith through turning towards the Light.[55] This involved separation from the unholy structures of the world, a matter made especially urgent by the fact that holiness was taken as a sign of the inner light working in an individual's heart. On the basis of their ecclesiology, Quakers might be expected to be the most socially exclusive of the Dissenting groups. However, they also believed that the inner light was available to all who turned to Christ, and this gave them a need to proselytise. As such, their faith demanded regular contact with non-Quakers.[56] These differing ideas about how the community of the faithful was constituted undoubtedly shaped Dissenters' perception of those not within their communion.

There were also significant theological distinctions, particularly when it came to the question of salvation. On the whole, both Presbyterians and Independents held to Calvinist principles of limited atonement (whereby only the elect would be saved), but some Presbyterians accepted the

---

[52] H. S. Ross, 'Some Aspects of the Development of Presbyterian Polity in England', *Journal of the Presbyterian Historical Society of England*, 13 (1964), p. 14.

[53] Karen E. Smith, 'Baptists', in Andrew Thompson (ed.), *The Oxford History of Protestant Dissenting Traditions, Volume II: The Long Eighteenth Century* (Oxford and New York: Oxford University Press, 2018), pp. 56–7.

[54] Ibid., p. 55.

[55] Donald S. Nesti, 'Early Quaker Ecclesiology', *Quaker Religious Thought*, 47 (1978), p. 8.

[56] Ibid., pp. 12, 20, 28.

possibility of universal atonement.[57] There were also differences in beliefs about redemption among Baptists. While General Baptists believed in the principle of universal atonement, available to all through believers' Baptism, Particular Baptists subscribed to the doctrine of limited atonement.[58] Quakers, by contrast, believed that salvation was open to all who accepted God in their hearts.[59] Theological differences between these groups led in some cases to active conflict. Most famously, during the Salters' Hall debates of 1719, Presbyterians, Independents, and Baptists were divided over the necessity of subscription to the doctrine of the Trinity, an issue that was particularly controversial because of the perceived link between Arian views and the threat of deism.[60]

Theology and ecclesiology mattered to contemporaries – they even talked about these ideas in the alehouse – and these differences cannot be ignored.[61] And yet these groups themselves recognised the inescapable fact that the Toleration Act had lumped them together under the category of Protestant Dissent. Thus, while there were numerous disputes and differences in organisation and doctrine, on a national level Dissenters frequently recognised their common interests. This was seen in the attempt to unite Presbyterians and Congregationalists in the 'Happy Union' of 1691, in the development of the Committee of Three Denominations (made up of four Presbyterians, three Congregationalists, and three Baptists) to combat the Tory threat to Dissent on the accession of Queen Anne in 1702, and in the establishment of the Protestant Dissenting Deputies to fight for the repeal of the Test Act and ensure the integrity of Dissenters' legal rights in cases of local persecution from 1732.

Although these formal organisations did not include Quakers, and there was often tension between groups, there is substantial evidence that Presbyterians, Independents, and Baptists also co-operated with Quakers for their mutual benefit. In 1705, for instance, there was an attempt to organise the electoral interests of Dissenters of all varieties: the Presbyterian minister John Evans wrote to a fellow minister, Matthew Henry, inclosing

[57] Alan P. F. Sell, *Dissenting Thought and the Life of the Churches. Studies in an English Tradition* (San Francisco: Mellen Research University Press, 1990), p. 149.
[58] John H. Y. Briggs, 'The Changing Shape of Nonconformity, 1662–2000', in Robert Pope (ed.), *T&T Clark Companion to Nonconformity* (London: Bloomsbury, 2013), p. 7.
[59] Nesti, 'Early Quaker Ecclesiology', pp. 7, 8–10.
[60] Joseph Waligore, 'Christian Deism in Eighteenth Century England', *International Journal of Philosophy and Theology*, 75, 3 (2014), pp. 216–7. For a detailed analysis of the events at Salters' Hall, see R. Thomas, 'The Non-Subscription Controversy Amongst Dissenters in 1719: The Salters' Hall Debate', *Journal of Ecclesiastical History*, 4, 2 (1953), pp. 162–86.
[61] See discussion of 'Alehouses, Taverns, and Intoxication' in Chapter 4.

'a paper agreed upon by all the denominations of Dissenters, Presbyterians, Independents, Anabaptists & Quakers to be sent to their friends in the Countrey as their Agreed sense about the next Election', and instructing him to 'communicate it to any active & prudent persons as what is the agreed sense of the Protestant Dissenters here. Those of each denomination undertake to send it to their brethren all over the Kingdom'.[62] Furthermore, when uniting to campaign for the extension of their liberty, Presbyterians, Independents, and Baptists looked explicitly to Quaker examples of political organisation as a model, in clear acknowledgement of the similarity of their circumstances under the law.[63] In terms of their national position, Dissenters of all varieties recognised they were on common ground.

The Toleration Act therefore cemented the shared status of Presbyterians, Independents, Baptists, and Quakers in relation to Church and state under a now legally defined category of Protestant Dissent. It is with this in mind that the term 'Dissenters' used in this book usually refers collectively to Protestants who did not conform to the Established Church. It was under this same category that, despite their differences, all these groups had to work to negotiate their place within society and culture; it was also through the lens of 'Dissent' that some supporters of an exclusive Established Church attempted to limit the social, political, and religious influence of these groups. There was an inherent tension in contemporary uses of this term, between a recognition of the divisions between different forms of Dissent and an acknowledgement of their common position. This tension is crucial to this book: it was symptomatic of the difficulty of working out the relationship between Church, Dissent, and society in the wake of a religious settlement that had reconfigured their legal status.

Of course, 'Church' and 'Dissent' were not the only categories through which contemporaries tried to delineate religious differences. As has been discussed extensively elsewhere, there were considerable differences within the Established Church itself. Some latitudinarian adherents to established religion may have had more sympathy for Dissenters who were engaged in promoting moral improvement than they did for High Church Anglicans who placed a strong emphasis on Church hierarchy and sacramental

---

[62] John Evans, London, to Matthew Henry, Chester, 23 Jan. 1705, MS Eng. lett. e. 29/220, Bodleian Library, Oxford.

[63] N. C. Hunt, *Two Early Political Associations. The Quakers and the Dissenting Deputies in the Age of Sir Robert Walpole* (Oxford: Clarendon Press, 1961), p. 117.

theology.[64] Equally, some High Church Anglicans more or less equated Low Church standpoints with Dissent.[65] The clearest dividing line was – as the 1689 Act made clear – between Protestants and 'papists'. But for all that Protestants agreed that popery was bad, they disagreed on to whom the label applied: for some Dissenters and their sympathisers, High Church versions of the Established Church could look distinctly popish; to the High Church-inclined, Dissent from the Church of England perpetuated just the sort of divisions that acted as a back door to popery.

A group to which the term 'popery' could be unambiguously applied was Roman Catholics. Their experiences, and the broader culture of anti-Catholicism, provide an integral point of comparison in this story. It is well acknowledged that anti-Catholicism was a significant feature of eighteenth-century English society, even to the extent that Catholics have been regarded as the structural 'other' against which local and national identities could be constructed.[66] Yet at the same time, the social and cultural engagement of many Catholics bore a strong resemblance to that of their conforming Protestant counterparts. Eighteenth-century English Catholicism did not necessarily demand clear social differentiation from its participants, and Catholics embraced hunting, dancing, dining, and drinking as much as their Protestant neighbours.[67] The Toleration Act of 1689 did not change the legal status of Catholics; they remained potentially subject to considerable penal legislation. In the light of this, social integration remained one of the most significant ways that Catholics could defend their faith, because they often relied heavily on the charity of Protestant neighbours to protect them from the worst excesses of the law.[68]

---

[64] Jeffrey S. Chamberlain, 'The Limits of Moderation in a Latitudinarian Parson: Or High-Church Zeal in a Low Churchman Discover'd', in Roger D. Lund (ed.), *The Margins of Orthodoxy. Heterodox Writing and Cultural Response 1660–1750* (Cambridge and New York: Cambridge University Press, 1995), pp. 200, 208; Robert D. Cornwall, 'The Church and Salvation: An Early Eighteenth-Century High-Church Anglican Perspective', *Anglican and Episcopal History*, 62, 2 (1993), pp. 177–8.

[65] Robert Cornwall, 'Charles Leslie and the Political Implications of Theology', in William Gibson and Robert G. Ingram (eds.), *Religious Identities in Britain, 1660–1832* (Aldershot: Ashgate, 2005), p. 40.

[66] Linda Colley, *Britons. Forging the Nation, 1707–1837* (London: Pimlico, 1992), p. 5; Colin Haydon, '"I Love My King and My Country, but a Roman Catholic I Hate": Anti-Catholicism and National Identity in Eighteenth-Century England', in Tony Claydon and Ian McBride (eds.), *Protestantism and National Identity. Britain and Ireland, c. 1650–c.1850* (Cambridge: Cambridge University Press, 1998), pp. 34, 36.

[67] Leo Gooch, '"The Religion for a Gentleman": The Northern Catholic Gentry in the Eighteenth Century', *Recusant History*, 23, 4 (1997), p. 565

[68] See especially William Sheils, 'Catholics and their Neighbours in a Rural Community: Egton Chapelry, 1590–1780', *Northern History*, 34, 1 (1998), pp. 109–30; Malcolm Wanklyn, 'Catholics in the Village Community: Madeley, Shropshire, 1630–1770', in Marie B. Rowlands (ed.), *English Catholics of Parish and Town, 1558–1778* (London: Catholic Record Society, 1999), pp. 210–36; Sarah

The social and cultural impact of religious difference between Catholics and Protestants was therefore potentially divergent from that caused by differences between Established Church and Protestant Dissent. The latter are the central subjects of this book because of the clear change in their position after 1689, and the partial configuration of their religious identity in social and cultural terms. However, comparisons between Protestant Dissenters and Catholics, and between stereotypes of each, usefully highlight aspects of the specific social and cultural impact that the Toleration Act had on the groups that were affected by it.

This comparative element is important, because it underlines the fact that while Dissenters' experiences and the wider social and religious contexts that shaped them lie at the centre of this book, tracing these experiences is not its principal end. Until very recently, there has been an historiographical tendency to study Dissent from a denominational perspective. Early histories of individual denominations were generally undertaken by adherents of these groups, seeking to trace the roots of their own tradition in the actions of their forefathers.[69] The result was, as Patrick Collinson's important essay on this subject highlighted, a neglect of 'the horizontal and lateral relationships of early protestant dissent' from the early seventeenth century onwards.[70] Work that has avoided explicit celebration of the historical lineage of Dissenting Churches has nevertheless commonly retained a focus on the fortunes and development of particular groups or denominations, rather than exploring their impact on each other and on society more generally.[71] There are notable exceptions to this denominational tendency, including in the most recent scholarship, and this is a promising sign for the future examination of these groups.[72] Nevertheless,

L. Bastow, *The Catholic Gentry of Yorkshire, 1536–1642: Resistance and Accommodation* (New York: Edwin Mellen Press, 2007), pp. 152, 156–9.

[69] Andrew Thompson, 'Introduction', in Thompson (ed.), *The Oxford History of Protestant Dissenting Traditions*, p. 6.

[70] Patrick Collinson, 'Towards a Broader Understanding of the Early Dissenting Tradition', in C. Robert Cole and Michael E. Moody (eds.), *The Dissenting Tradition. Essays for Leyland H. Carlson* (Athens, OH: Ohio University Press, 1975), pp. 3, 10, *passim*.

[71] Bolam, Goring, Short, and Thomas (eds.), *The English Presbyterians*; Adrian Davies, *The Quakers in English Society, 1655–1725* (Oxford: Clarendon Press, 2000); Simon Dixon, 'Quakers and the London Parish, 1670–1720', *The London Journal*, 32, 3 (2007), pp. 229–49; John Miller, '"A Suffering People": English Quakers and Their Neighbours, c. 1650-c. 1750', *Past and Present*, 188, 1 (2005), pp. 71–103; Jon Mackenzie, '1689 and All That. An Exploration of the Function and Form of the Second London Baptist Confession of Faith', *Baptist Quarterly*, 42, 8 (2008), pp. 555–68.

[72] Thompson, 'Introduction', pp. 6, 7; Bill Stevenson, 'The Social Integration of Post-Restoration Dissenters, 1660–1725', in Margaret Spufford (ed.), *The World of Rural Dissenters, 1520–1725* (Cambridge: Cambridge University Press, 1995), p. 385; Michael Watts, *The Dissenters. From the Reformation to the French Revolution* (Oxford: Clarendon Press, 1978).

studies of Dissent still often retain the propensity to trace the development of the 'culture of nonconformity' rather than viewing that culture as a piece in the puzzle of contemporary social and cultural change.[73]

Many aspects of this scholarship are highly important for this present study. The changes that took place within denominations can throw significant light on broader trends in the roles that religion played in daily life. It is worth acknowledging, for instance, that as Dissent became more hereditary and formalised in the eighteenth century, Dissenters showed a greater concern both with the education and upbringing of the next generation, and with their place in society more broadly.[74] Dissenters had to make choices about social and cultural behaviours that defined their religious profession, and this is undoubtedly significant for understanding how Dissenters worked out their place in English society after 1689.

However, the intra-denominational developments and cultural changes that have been explored in histories of Dissent are not the principal subject of this book: it is not an overview of the social life of Dissent. Rather, it seeks to throw into relief the extensive cultural impact of England's unstable religious settlement. This impact was underpinned not so much by the experience of individual denominations as by the tendency of groups to view religious difference variously according to their precise vision of the religious inclusivity of civil society. This book therefore focuses not primarily on the 'vertical' denominational history of the experiences of one group, but on points of contact: on how individuals and groups within both Church and Dissent tried to draw lines of inclusion and exclusion relative to one another in their daily lives; on how they dissected the anatomy of religious difference and stitched it back together again to create a functioning society. It is this emphasis that distinguishes the contribution of this work from highly valuable studies that seek to understand the Dissenting experience, and this that makes it pertinent not just to the religious but also the social history of the eighteenth century.

---

[73] N. H. Keeble, *The Literary Culture of Nonconformity in Later Seventeenth-Century England* (Leicester: Leicester University Press, 1987); David L. Wykes, 'Religious Dissent and the Penal Laws: An Explanation of Business Success?', *History*, 75, 243 (1990), pp. 39–62; Christopher Durston and Jacqueline Eales (eds.), *The Culture of English Puritanism, 1560–1700* (Basingstoke: Macmillan, 1996); George Southcombe, *The Culture of Dissent in Restoration England: The Wonders of the Lord* (Woodbridge: The Boydell Press, 2019).

[74] Watts, *The Dissenters*, pp. 388–9, 392; Mark Burden, 'Dissent and Education', in Thompson (ed.), *The Oxford History of Protestant Dissenting Traditions*, pp. 394–5, 402–4, 409. This did not always take the form of closer accommodation with the norms of society – see Michael Mullett, 'From Sect to Denomination? Social Developments in Eighteenth-Century English Quakerism', *Journal of Religious History*, 13, 2 (1984), pp. 168–191.

Social Dynamics and Religious Boundaries

Understanding where the boundaries of religious difference were drawn is one thing; unpicking the social dynamics of inter-confessional relations across these fluid lines is quite another. The ambiguous, uncertain, and partial toleration created by the 1689 Act left Dissenters in an awkward position when it came to interacting and socialising with their Established Church brethren. Legally tolerated to a degree, but by no means universally accepted, they were forced to walk a tightrope between assimilation and differentiation. The path they chose proved to be an unstable compromise, one that ensured that religious differences continued to be noticed and to matter in social interactions well into the eighteenth century.

This was because, despite adjustments in their legal status, Protestant Dissenters still found themselves the subjects of suspicion, with attacks on their persons and property occurring at moments of particular national political tension across the period. During the Sacheverell crisis of 1710–11, at the time of the accession of George I to the throne in 1714, and during the Jacobite disturbances of 1715 and 1745–6, for instance, Dissenters across the country saw their meeting houses and other property smashed by rioters. This was accompanied in some instances by physical attacks on Dissenters themselves, with one Bristol Quaker killed during the coronation riots.[75] In between more widespread episodes of popular violence against Dissenters and their property, local tension also led to instances of verbal and physical abuse.[76]

It is difficult to square such episodes of violence between Protestant Dissenters and members of the Established Church with apparently functional everyday relationships. In order for daily life to function in communities with mixed religious affiliations, latent tensions over religious difference had to be managed. One way to understand how this was possible is through an analysis of the pragmatic motivations for co-existence; this is an approach that has been used extensively to understand Catholic–Protestant relations across Europe in the same period.[77] Many studies of the

---

[75] Paul Kléber Monod, *Jacobitism and the English People, 1688–1788* (Cambridge and New York: Cambridge University Press, 1993), p. 174.

[76] Wykes, 'Quaker Schoolmasters', pp. 178–9.

[77] Gregory Hanlon, *Confession and Community in Seventeenth-Century France. Catholic and Protestant Coexistence in Aquitaine* (Philadelphia, PA: University of Pennsylvania Press, 1993), pp. 8–11; Martin Ingram, 'From Reformation to Toleration: Popular Religious Cultures in England, 1540–1690', in Tim Harris (ed.), *Popular Culture in England, c. 1500–1850* (Basingstoke: Macmillan, 1995), p. 123; Bob Scribner, 'Preconditions of Tolerance and Intolerance in Sixteenth-Century Germany', in Ole Peter Grell and Bob Scribner (eds.), *Tolerance and Intolerance in the European Reformation*

everyday realities of living with confessional difference in this period have found that theoretical intolerance and abstract prejudice were tempered by the practical necessities of daily life.[78] A number of works – particularly those relating to the Dutch Republic – have observed the importance of the distinction between public religion (as established by law) and private religion (as followed discreetly by individuals).[79] Benjamin Kaplan in particular has argued that the 'distinction between public and private supplied the key to religious toleration'.[80] In areas where it was theoretically illegal to deviate from the state religion, a framework of relative tolerance of religious difference could be constructed around the distinction between public and private.

However, while such frameworks can be applied to Catholics in England during the eighteenth century, they are not so easily applicable to Protestant Dissenters. Many Catholics lived relatively peaceably with their neighbours, engaging together in social activities while using their local social status to defend their religious practice from prosecution.[81] However, unlike Catholics, whose legal status was left unchanged by the Toleration Act, Dissenters were now explicitly included as part of the national interest, and their worship made legal. Consequently, few Dissenters appeared willing to settle for mere co-existence; they wished to demonstrate that they were integral to their communities and to the nation. In fact, as the second chapter of this book discusses, Dissenters increasingly built meeting houses in more prominent and in some cases more provocative locations, and sought positions in public office and involvement in the local affairs of their communities.[82] Many Dissenters – particularly those such

---

(Cambridge: Cambridge University Press, 1996), p. 39; Sheils, 'Catholics and Their Neighbours in a Rural Community', pp. 109–33; Willem Frijhoff, *Embodied Belief. Ten Essays on Religious Culture in Dutch History* (Hilversum: Uitgeverij Verbren, 2002).

[78] Nadine Lewycky and Adam Morton, 'Introduction', in Lewycky and Morton (eds.), *Getting along? Religious Identities and Confessional Relations in Early Modern England: Essays in Honour of Professor W. J. Sheils* (Farnham: Ashgate, 2012), pp. 9, 12.

[79] See Benjamin Kaplan, 'Fictions of Privacy: House Chapels and the Spatial Accommodation of Religious Dissent in Early Modern Europe', *American Historical Review*, 107, 4 (2002), pp. 1031–64.

[80] Benjamin Kaplan, *Divided by Faith. Religious Conflict and the Practice of Toleration in Early Modern Europe* (Cambridge, MA: Belknap Press, 2007), p. 171; Jesse Spohnholz, *The Tactics of Toleration. A Refugee Community in the Age of Religious Wars* (Newark, DE: University of Delaware Press, 2011), pp. 61, 68, 73; Frijhoff, *Embodied Belief*, pp. 65.

[81] Carys Brown, 'Militant Catholicism, Interconfessional Relations, and the Rookwood Family of Stanningfield, Suffolk, c. 1689–1737', *Historical Journal*, 60, 1 (2017), p. 44.

[82] Judith J. Hurwich, '"A Fanatick Town": The Political Influence of Dissenters in Coventry, 1660–1720', *Midland History*, 4, 1 (1977), pp. 28–9; James E. Bradley, *Religion, Revolution, and English Radicalism: Nonconformity in Eighteenth-Century Politics and Society* (Cambridge: Cambridge University Press, 1990), p. 85.

as Presbyterians and Independents who had always sought comprehension within the Church – were unwilling to accept a co-existence based on religious quietism, and instead sought integration and active participation in society.

At the same time, however, the survival of Dissenting professions was to a degree dependent on their self-identity as different and separate from others, not just in religious terms but in social behaviour. Prominent Dissenting writers such as Phillip Doddridge and Isaac Watts suggested that Dissenters should be distinguished not only by their different worship, but also by their pious social interactions.[83] As a result, Dissenters, unlike most Catholics, were sometimes reluctant to engage in the ordinary social activities of their neighbours because of concerns about betraying their pious integrity. This was perhaps most clearly demonstrated in Dissenters' debates about whether or not they should engage in polite cultural forms, such as dancing.[84] Dissenters wished to participate fully in key aspects of contemporary society, but they could not afford to lose their religious integrity in the process.

The relationship between Protestant Dissenters and members of the Established Church during this period was therefore somewhat more unstable than a pragmatic co-existence. Dissenters sought full acceptance within English society, but in the face of tension between integration and separation, pious Dissenters balanced different priorities, often engaging with contemporary cultural forms and venues but not embracing them wholly, or maintaining relationships with their neighbours but not establishing firm friendships.[85] This balancing act meant that religious difference continued to be an obvious fact of daily life, not just for Dissenters, but for the broader structure of social relations. The endurance of contemporary stereotypes of Dissent meant that even occasions of integration and conviviality had the potential to be read through a lens of religious difference.

By exploring the problems that Dissenters faced, and how supporters of the Established Church reacted to them, this study makes a contribution

---

[83] Philip Doddridge, *Free Thoughts on the Most Probable Means of Reviving the Dissenting Interest* (London, 1730), p. 38; Isaac Watts, *An Humble Attempt Toward the Revival of Practical Religion Among Christians, and Particularly the Protestant Dissenters* (London, 1731), p. 236.

[84] See for example Strickland Gough, *An Enquiry into the Causes of the Decay of the Dissenting Interest* (London, 1730), p. 43; Abraham Taylor, *A Letter to the Author of an Enquiry into the Causes of the Decay of the Dissenting Interest* (London, 1730), p. 4.

[85] For an exploration of diverse experiences of inclusion and exclusion in early modern England, see Naomi Pullin and Kathryn Woods (eds.), *Negotiating Exclusion in Early Modern England, 1550–1800* (London and New York: Routledge, 2021).

to how we understand the multi-faceted ways in which inter-confessional relations can operate beyond a framework of co-existence. Whereas most research on inter-confessional relationships focuses on pragmatic reasons for their peaceful operation, such as economic and social necessity, this book highlights numerous instances where individuals *chose* to interact socially with those who did not share their religious outlook.[86] It demonstrates that by analysing the specific language contemporaries used to describe their social relationships, we can see how they retained varying degrees of social distance depending on religious affiliation. By investigating the social languages employed by Protestant Dissenters when they described their relationships with their co-religionists and with members of the Established Church, and vice versa, we are able to see beyond the fact of pragmatic co-existence to understand the range of elective social relationships that underpinned ostensibly peaceful inter-confessional relations.

Tracing Religious Tension

Social relationships and perceptions of cultural change are not always obvious in archival records, or in print. Research on religious difference frequently faces the problem that conflict is more likely to be recorded than concord, while archival silence can indicate apathy or confusion as much as it does tolerance.[87] This study is not immune to these problems. Printed polemic frequently made recourse to polarising language, while interactions between Dissenters and their Established Church neighbours in court records and meeting books were often recorded because of the occurrence of conflict or unacceptable behaviour. Furthermore, the formulaic nature of many printed stereotypes of Dissent tends to stress continuity rather than change in the dynamics of religious tension. The use of similar language over time can obscure the ways in which its meaning changed. In a book that argues that religious difference contributed significantly to the shape of English society, these issues require particular consideration.

To some degree, the prominence of conflict in these records is tempered by the attention the book also gives to records of quotidian interactions,

[86] See for example Brown, 'Militant Catholicism', pp. 21–45; Lewycky and Morton, 'Introduction', in Lewycky and Morton (eds.), *Getting Along?*; William Sheils, '"Getting On" and "Getting Along" in Parish and Town: Catholics and their Neighbours in England', in B. Kaplan, B. Moore, H. Van Nierop, and J. Pollman (eds.), *Catholic Communities in Protestant States. Britain and the Netherlands, c. 1570–1720* (Manchester: Manchester University Press, 2009), pp. 67–83; Kaplan, *Divided by Faith*.
[87] Alexandra Walsham, 'Cultures of Coexistence in Early Modern England: History, Literature and Religious Toleration', *The Seventeenth Century*, 28, 2 (2013), p. 123.

particularly in Dissenters' life-writings, but also in the diaries and letters of defenders of the Established Church. Individual Dissenters who chose to write diaries as a form of spiritual practice had a tendency to record moments of tension and conflict, thereby bolstering their religious identity by emphasising their embattled minority status. This appears a significant possibility when we consider that diaries and journals were not necessarily the 'private' documents which we might presume them to be, but rather were often passed around families, or intended for the edification of future generations.[88] However, the chapters of this book pay careful attention to the more incidental details recorded by diarists and epistolary correspondents: daily routines, visits, church attendance, drinking habits. They also analyse the specific language through which Dissenters and their opponents described their social interactions, and in doing so attend to how individuals responded to both religious tension and sociability. Life-writings are used here less to examine particular instances of conflict or amity between religious groups (although these certainly feature) than to understand the social frameworks available to individuals of different religious professions as they managed their daily interactions.

Sensitivity to the inevitable prominence of conflict in the archival record is also reflected in the way meeting house records are used in this book. The records that Independents, Baptists, and Quakers kept of their meetings are often formulaic in their language, and place a strong emphasis on discipline and misdemeanour. However, read against the grain, accounts of members' frequent failures to live up to the pious expectations of their religious professions can often give detailed glimpses of the types of inter-confessional sociability in which Dissenters were in fact engaged. It is evident, for instance, from the rebuke that Elizabeth Mollineux of Maghull, Lancashire, received from her Friends' Meeting for allowing visitors to her house to dance and play music, that she was on reasonably friendly terms with those who did not share her religious standpoint.[89] So frequent are pious lapses among congregations that they should not be taken as an indication of a lack of faith or commitment among believers, but rather as manifestations of the different ways Dissenters chose to negotiate the religious culture and society in which they lived. Meeting house records are used here to inform understandings of how Dissenters managed a degree

---

[88] Cynthia Aalders, "'Your Journal, My Love": Constructing Personal and Religious Bonds in Eighteenth-Century Women's Diaries', *Journal of Religious History*, 39, 3 (2014), p. 395.

[89] Society of Friends, Hardshaw Monthly Meeting Book, M85/1/11, fol. 48r, Manchester Archives, Manchester.

of integration after 1689, rather than to highlight their separation from or antagonism with the rest of society. Along with the approach taken to other sources used in this book, these records are read with close consideration of the potentially misleading prominence of conflict in both archival and printed sources.

Even setting aside issues over the typicality of what has been recorded, the question of who is represented in these sources remains. Extant manuscript materials relating to Protestant Dissent are but a tiny fragment of what was produced by contemporaries. In their very survival the materials used here are unusual; their presence in the archive is a reflection of a past judgement about their worth, a judgement that may have been skewed towards preservation of the records of those considered most pious. This may be one reason why the surviving life-writings used in this book were produced by individuals of middling or greater wealth, and often by families of significance within their local communities. The social homogeneity of these sources should not be exaggerated: there is some range in the social status of the historical actors discussed here. The material life of the Presbyterian Hoghton family of Hoghton Towers, Lancashire, for instance, was very different from that of John Croker, Exeter Quaker and fuller. In recording incidents involving a wide range of members of a community, the records of meetings and Quarter Sessions papers give voice to a far wider social spectrum than do life-writings, but in many ways still support the conclusions drawn from diaries and letters. Nevertheless, it must be acknowledged that the conclusions of this study are primarily based on records produced by those of relatively comfortable means, who may have been particularly likely to be concerned with emerging cultures of politeness and consumption.

This book deliberately takes a nationwide approach in order to explore more fully the complex interplay between religious, social, and cultural developments. For this reason, care has been taken to use records from all corners of England. Inevitably, relations between Church and particular types of Dissent in some regions are better represented than others: Presbyterianism in the north-west and south-west, Quakerism in the south-west, and Baptists and Independents in the south-east and East Anglia. It is, furthermore, important to acknowledge the urban focus of much of the printed work examined here, and in particular of conduct literature. At points in the book where printed literature is most prominent, particularly in Chapter 3, this urban focus takes precedence. Greater attention to the effects of regional difference on the cultures of Dissent, and especially the urban–rural divide, would no doubt be illuminating, but this is not the main emphasis of this work.

Nevertheless, the significance of geographical difference should not be overplayed. Dissenters shared enough common ground to sometimes organise on a national scale; individuals were also often willing to travel between town and country in search of edifying meetings or preaching, or to visit other Dissenters. Because of this, the divide between town and country may have been more porous for Dissenters than it was for others.[90] What is evident in the sources used here is a surprising consistency in the experiences recorded by Dissenters across England, and in the language they used to describe them. Local incidents and pressures shaped the day-to-day lives of Dissenters, but the interpretive frameworks through which they understood their lives, and their reactions to issues of national concern, appear strikingly similar from region to region. On this basis, it appears reasonable to suggest that the conclusions of this work highlight patterns pertinent to understanding the impact of religious difference across eighteenth-century England.

The book is formed of five chapters. Chapter 1 highlights how legal changes in the status of Dissent in 1689 encouraged both Dissenters and their opponents to focus on social behaviours as a means of defining the place of Protestant Dissent within – or outside of – English society. Debates about the meaning and implications of the Toleration Act reframed seventeenth-century associations between social behaviour and religious affiliation; the social and cultural implications of religious difference were viewed as integral to the viability of toleration.

Chapter 2 argues that these complex legacies of the Toleration Act stimulated significant disagreements about the relationship between religion, authority, and public space in English society which transcended any straightforward distinction between public and private. Considering disputes about the extent to which Dissenters could be regarded as contributors to the public religious communities of nation and parish, it shows how concepts of what constituted 'public religion' were contested and were changing over this period, and how these ideas were manifested in daily life. This is significant not just for understanding the social and political positions of Dissenters, but also for examining the role of the Toleration Act in the eventual acceptance of religious pluralism in England.[91]

---

[90] Carl Estabrook, *Urbane and Rustic England: Cultural Ties and Social Spheres in the Provinces 1660–1780* (Manchester: Manchester University Press, 1998), pp. 227–8.

[91] This engages with and builds on earlier criticisms of secularisation, such as J. C. D. Clark, 'Secularization and Modernization: The Failure of a "Grand Narrative"', *Historical Journal*, 55, 1 (2012), p. 163, *passim*; Tony Claydon, *William III and the Godly Revolution* (Cambridge: Cambridge University Press, 1996), pp. 5, 39–40, 44; Gregory, 'Introduction: Transforming "the Age of Reason" into "an Age of Faiths"', pp. 289–90.

The violent and grotesque language of some printed debates was not consistent throughout the period. As the century progressed, there was an increasing emphasis on more moderate forms of discourse and behaviour that rejected the divisive social and religious attitudes of the previous century.[92] Yet, as Chapter 3 demonstrates, these ostensibly more inclusive social norms and discourses belied patterns of exclusion. Focusing on the idea of politeness, and how it interacted with the accusation of Dissenting hypocrisy, it highlights how this discourse did not wholeheartedly reject the religious divisions of the previous century, but rather re-configured them for a new era of supposed moderation.

Religious differences were also framed through the common social practices of the eighteenth century. Chapter 4 looks at some of these practices – drinking, dancing, and coffeehouse culture – through the lens of Dissenting engagement with them in a context of continuing religious stereotyping. Although Dissenters were not excluded from the social practices of the eighteenth century, religious affiliation was an important determinant of how contemporaries interpreted their own, and others', social interactions. Looking at Dissenters' differing engagements with contemporary culture, and how others reacted to them, helps us to recognise the diverse ways in which contemporaries could approach and make meaning from the common cultural modes and spaces of eighteenth-century England. In particular, it shows how religious difference shaped the assumptions, expectations, and actions which framed the cultural and social experiences of both Church and Dissent.

The everyday impact of religious difference on social interaction is further explored in Chapter 5. While the previous chapter underscores how social norms were shaped by religious expectations in this period, this chapter looks specifically at the social dynamics of inter-confessional relations after 1689. In particular, it emphasises that the way contemporaries mentally framed different types of social relationship may have helped them to navigate the contradictory impulses to foster both group identity and integration with others after 1689. Close attention to social language reveals the graduated layers of social interaction that lay between religious inclusion and exclusion, layers that are revealed only by conversation between religious and social history.

---

[92] Klein, 'Politeness and the Interpretation of the British Eighteenth Century', p. 9; Mark Knights, 'Occasional Conformity and the Representation of Dissent: Hypocrisy, Sincerity, Moderation and Zeal', *Parliamentary History*, 24, 1 (2005), p. 43; Sirota, 'The Occasional Conformity Controversy', p. 82.

The Conclusion begins by exploring the impact that social and cultural responses to the problem of religious difference had by the middle of the century. Drawing on examples of anti-Methodism, and incidences of inter-confessional violence in the second half of the eighteenth century, it emphasises that while religious pluralism had become an irrevocable fact of society, religious difference continued to shape contemporary social and economic interactions. There was greater capacity for mutual tolerance between different denominations by the end of the century, but contemporary examples of deep intolerance show that the ease with which prejudice could prevail should not be underestimated. The need to manage, but also to maintain, religious differences had been inextricably woven into the fabric of English society; it would take a long time for those threads to wear thin.

CHAPTER I

Reframing Religious Difference

Son Rad[clif]f ... shewes mee the new Act of Indulgence, directed to you, concerning which I say, as wee us'd to say at school, when a whole play-day was expected & wee could have but an afternoon, *est aliquid prodire renus, si non datur ultra* [it is something to proceed thus far, if it be not permitted to go further (Horace)].

Phillip Henry to Matthew Henry, 1 June 1689

The Toleration Act of 1689 provided a new legal framework for the management of England's religious differences. It allowed both considerable relief from persecution for Protestant Dissenters and closer regulation by the Established Church of forms of nonconforming worship that had in many places already been occurring illicitly. There was, then, scope in this legislation to please elements of both Church and Dissent.

Undeniably, there were individuals and groups who viewed this legislation in a very positive light. It was not, however, by any means universally regarded as satisfactory. Neither Dissenters nor staunch defenders of the Established Church were completely reassured that the 1689 Act had set up a clear and suitable framework for a stable religious settlement; they also disagreed on what a stable religious settlement should look like. As the comments of the Presbyterian minister Phillip Henry to his son in the epigraph indicate, Dissenters were pleased with the liberty they had been given, but the fact that they were still subject to the terms of the Test and Corporation Acts (1673 and 1661) meant that the fight was not over.[1] In contrast, their opponents viewed even the allowance of Dissent that was given under the Act as an appalling prospect that threatened to unravel Church, state, and society. For all parties, the new relationship with state and society that the Act created for Church and Dissent required considerable adjustment.

---

[1] Phillip Henry to Matthew Henry, 1 June 1689, MS Eng. lett. e. 29/89, Bodleian Library (Bod.), Oxford.

This chapter explores the process of adjusting to toleration and the broader impact that this process had on the way that religious differences were discussed. It does so by seeking answers to two questions. Firstly, why was the legislation of 1689 an inadequate framework for managing religious difference? Secondly, how did contemporaries seek to overcome these perceived inadequacies? Through exploring these questions, it becomes apparent that adaptation to toleration involved the development of rhetorical strategies that set up oppositions between Church and Dissent not just in political or religious terms, but in terms of social status and behaviour. As the process of coming to terms with toleration unfolded, therefore, religious difference came to shape the developing social and cultural norms of the period.

The Limitations of Liberty

In December 1709, the Suffolk Independent minister Samuel Say wrote in some distress to his friend John Paris. He reported that he had heard that some lords and gentlemen were meeting daily in London to take 'steps toward the Rescinding the Act of Tol-----n'. Reflecting on this, he asked 'why shou'd a Man think of a Wife & Children who knows not but in a Month or two more He shall be rendered in capable of providing for 'em, & be defeated of the very Rights to which He thought himself born'?[2] At the height of a period of particular tension between Church and Dissent, Say's fear that toleration would not last was deeply affecting how he thought about his future family life.

As Say's concerns exemplify, one of the reasons for the continuing resonance of problems associated with religious difference in the first half of the eighteenth century was that the permanence of the legislation of 1689 was uncertain. Many Dissenters quite reasonably feared that the improvements in their position provided by the 1689 Act would be taken away. This was a product of the fraught political and religious context into which the Act was born. The passage of the 1689 legislation was an act of political expediency in the wake of revolution, and it suspended rather than removed the penal laws, with the result that in the immediate aftermath of the Act it was by no means clear or inevitable that it would mark the beginning of a more permanently plural religious landscape.[3] Rather, contemporaries'

---

[2] Samuel Say, Lowestoft, to John Paris, London, 21 December 1709, 12.107(63), Dr Williams's Library (DWL), London.
[3] Scott Sowerby, *Making Toleration: The Repealers and the Glorious Revolution* (Cambridge, MA: Harvard University Press, 2013), p. 251; Gordon J. Schochet, '"The Tyranny of a Popish Successor" and the Politics of Religious Toleration', in Gordon J. Schochet, with Patricia E. Tatspugh and

competing visions of the Act made its potential impact highly uncertain.[4] This resulted in sustained 'instability in English religious life', with extensive consequences for the clergy of the Established Church.[5]

This uncertainty was also a critical factor as Dissenters attempted to define themselves in relation to Church and society. Dissenters' fear of losing their liberty highlighted how acutely they felt the need to demonstrate loyalty to the Protestant interest, and display a non-threatening stance towards the Established Church; it compelled them to balance any distinctiveness and exclusivity with a desire to be considered part of a broader Protestant society. The endurance of this problem for Dissenters contributed to the evolving discursive significance of religious difference after 1689 as they, along with supporters of the Established Church, tried to work out how to negotiate around religious differences that had previously been denied legal legitimacy.

Given the recent example set by French religious policy, it was unsurprising that Dissenters were concerned about the potential impermanence of the liberty granted under the Toleration Act. The Revocation of the Edict of Nantes in France by Louis XIV in 1685 had brought to an end eighty-seven years of royal indulgence of Protestantism under an officially Catholic regime, with the result that thousands of French Huguenot Protestants were forced to seek refuge from persecution by flight to England. Set against this context, the extent of Dissenters' concern that their liberty might be withdrawn appears particularly understandable. Indeed, some Dissenters directly compared their situation to the French context, even reading small local incidents in this light. In a letter to the Independent minister and county historian William Holman, for instance, Nicholas Jekyll lamented the refusal of the parish minister at Halsted, Essex, to bury a child whose parents were Dissenters, calling it 'an unchristian practice' comparable with how 'the Laws allow in France to deny a Protestant Christian buriall'.[6]

Carol Brobeck (eds), *Restoration, Ideology, and Revolution* (Washington, DC: The Folger Institute, 1990), p. 96; Michael Mullett, 'From Sect to Denomination? Social Developments in Eighteenth-Century English Quakerism', *Journal of Religious History*, 13, 2 (1984), pp. 180–1.
[4] David Wykes, 'Quaker Schoolmasters, Toleration and the Law, 1689–1714', *Journal of Religious History*, 21 (1997), p. 186; Andrew Thompson, 'Contesting the Test Act: Dissent, Parliament and the Public in the 1730s', *Parliamentary History*, 24, 1 (2005), p. 61.
[5] Ralph Stevens, *Protestant Pluralism: The Reception of the Toleration Act, 1689–1720* (Woodbridge: The Boydell Press, 2018), p. 7, *passim.*
[6] Nicholas Jekyll to William Holman, 8 April 1715, D/Y 1/1/III/31, Essex Record Office (ERO), Chelmsford.

Comparisons with France were also made by Dissenters in a more general sense, both in private correspondence and in published material. When Samuel Say voiced his concerns about a potential revocation of the Toleration Act he suggested that those involved were 'pursuing the very same steps … that once a great Prince in a Nation South of England thought fitt to take before the final & fatal Revocation of that famous Edict … which at the same time He promis'd once and again he wou'd inviolably maintain'.[7] Say was gloomily reading domestic events through the lens of the French example, which provided, in the eyes of Dissenters, an alarming precedent.

Dissenters' concerns about the permanence of the Toleration Act were most clearly manifest in an unwillingness, at least in private, to presume that the suspension of the penal laws would continue into the future. This was particularly the case in the first decades after the Act, when proposals such as the Occasional Conformity Bill – a measure intended to stop Dissenters qualifying for office by occasionally taking communion within the Established Church – presented a direct challenge to the breadth of its application. The Cheshire Presbyterian minister Matthew Henry wrote to his father in 1692 that there were 'Many that wish ill to us & our peace yet', and to his mother following elections in 1701, 'I perceive wise men are apprehensive of some great Designs on foot against our Peace.'[8] The Toleration Act had not removed Henry's sense that their cause was under threat.

This sentiment was not, however, confined to the years immediately following the Act. It was evident in the wills of members of Matthew Henry's Chapel congregation in Chester throughout the eighteenth century. Mrs Mary Young, for instance, made a will in 1732 in which she gave £10 in trust to the meeting house 'so long as the Toleration or Liberty now allowed to Protestant Dissenters shall be Continued but if the said Tolleration shall at any time hereafter be taken away' then the money was to be put to charitable uses as the trustees saw fit.[9] Such a stipulation was common to wills made by members of this congregation even in the second half of the century; they lacked confidence that their meeting was securely protected under the law.[10] Neither did the Derbyshire

---

[7] Say to Paris, 21 December 1709, 12.107(63), DWL.

[8] Matthew Henry to Phillip Henry, 21 October 1692, MS Eng. lett. e. 29/103, Bod.; Matthew Henry to Katherine Henry, 8 January 1701, Add MS 42849, fol. 34r, British Library (BL), London.

[9] Matthew Henry's Chapel Church Book, 1687–1928, p. 116, D/MH/1, Cheshire Archives and Local Studies (CALS), Chester.

[10] Ibid., pp. 150, 152.

Presbyterian Minister James Clegg take the legal position of Dissenters for granted, even when nearly forty years had passed without the toleration legislation being withdrawn. At the end of December 1727 he found 'great cause thankfully to acknowledge the goodness of God to me and mine. No breach hath been made among us, our Civil and Religious liberties are continued.'[11] Dissenters were unwilling to take the permanence of the 1689 Act as a given, and this uncertainty informed their thought and action well into the eighteenth century.

Indeed, Dissenters' private fears that the laws might be revoked were further demonstrated by their anxiety to show in public that they were obedient to the law and grateful for their existing liberty. During a dispute in 1699 between Baptists and Quakers in Burnham, Essex, for instance, Thomas Upsher (Quaker) reported that he did not desire a dispute 'being Tumultuous as Disputes are Offensive to the Government and counted an abuse of our Present Liberty, with which wee as well as they & other Dissenters are Privilged'.[12] Upsher may have had other reasons to avoid entering into debate with the Baptists, but the fact that he framed his reasoning in terms of retaining their liberty suggests that he believed that this was a concern common to both congregations. Dissenters of all stripes had to be on guard against putting their freedom in jeopardy by exposing themselves to charges of sedition and unrest.

However, at the same time as they were concerned about retaining the liberty they had secured, many Dissenters felt the remaining discriminatory legislation to be unjust. They wanted to continue campaigning for an extension of, and greater security for, their privileges, and this required that they maintain some level of opposition to the established order. Even as Dissenters publicly celebrated in 1689, Phillip Henry had reservations about the true significance of the Act, stating to his son that 'The quarell is, wil you let my people goe, that they may serve mee; wee wil, but let them not goe very far away, the men but not the women & children; the women & children but not the cattle.' Henry was clear that the toleration was incomplete, and that 'our Business is not done'.[13]

This view was sustained and strengthened as Dissenters were buffeted by the repeated attempts of defenders of the Established Church to

[11] Vanessa S. Doe (ed.), *The Diary of James Clegg of Chapel en le Frith, 1708–1755, Part 1* (Derby: Derbyshire Record Society, 1978), p. 24.
[12] The Sum and Substance of a Dispute Between William Couch an Elder of the Baptist Congregation, and Thomas Upsher, One of Those in Scorn Called Quakers at Burnham in Denge Hundred, 1699, MS Add.106, fol. 2r, Cambridge University Library (CUL).
[13] Phillip Henry to Matthew Henry, 1 June 1689, MS Eng. lett. e. 29/89, Bod.

define more closely the legal limits of toleration. Because the Toleration Act suspended rather than removed penalties against Dissenters, and did not explicitly establish means for Dissenting participation in education or political life, those who wished to limit the influence of Dissent insisted on the narrowest possible interpretation of toleration provided by the Act.

This was most clearly reflected in the repeated attempts of High Church Tories in 1702–5 to outlaw the practice of occasional conformity. This issue was reignited to violent effect in 1709, when a sermon preached by High Churchman Henry Sacheverell on 5 November suggested that the means of bringing about the revolution of 1688–9 were unjustifiable, the Toleration 'unwarrantable', and that the Church and State were in danger under the current administration. The resulting impeachment of Sacheverell saw riots break out in the city of London in support of his cause, and the vast debate in the pamphlet press resulted in a landslide victory for the Tories in 1710 and the passage of the Occasional Conformity Act in 1711.

This attempt to ensure that the scope of toleration was as limited as possible was further demonstrated by the passage of the Schism Act in 1714, which sought to restrict the control Dissenters had over the education of their youth. The Act rendered Dissenting academies illegal by stipulating that anyone who wanted to keep a school, or act as a tutor, had to have a licence from a bishop. Queen Anne died on the day the legislation was due to come into force, with the result that the measure was ineffective, and it was repealed in 1719 – along with the Occasional Conformity Act. This did not, however, prevent the alarm that either of these measures caused to Dissenters. The Schism Act was indicative of the continuing attempts of High Church interests to limit the influence of Dissent, and it represented a serious threat to Dissenters' existing liberty. It was, furthermore, demonstrative of the failure of the legislation of 1689 to satisfactorily reconcile differing views about what England's religious settlement should look like.

Unsurprisingly, the attempts of some supporters of the Established Church to exclude Dissenters as far as the law could allow fed into the latter's pre-existing fears about the insecurity of their positions. In the wake of the passage of the Schism Act, Daniel Defoe warned Dissenters against complacency over their liberty in 'believing that they had so far convinc'd the Church of *England*, that they were no way Dangerous to their Constitution … and believing they had so far obliged the Church, as that there could not possibly be any Civil breaches between them hereafter'.[14]

---

[14] Daniel Defoe, *The Weakest Go to the Wall, or the Dissenters Sacrific'd by All Parties: Being a True State of the Dissenters Case* (London, 1714), p. 22, emphasis original.

In his view, the Schism Act was an inevitable consequence of Dissenters' failure to continue to demonstrate that they were worthy of and grateful for liberty in the eyes of the Church of England.

This Act was also interpreted with the French example in mind. Writing in 1717, the Huguenot author Abel Boyer warned that 'The Extirpation of the Reformed Religion in *France* was introduced by the Prohibition of their Schools …', and that regardless of any royal reassurance that liberty would be preserved, 'when we see such Infringements and restrictions one after another put upon our Liberty, we cannot be without very afflicting Apprehensions'.[15] The Schism Act, and the debates that surrounded it, not only kept disputes about the meaning of the 1689 Act alive, but also fed into Dissenters' insecurity about the gains they had made.

The Toleration Act represented significant changes in the relationship between Dissent, Church, State, and society, and marked a considerable break with many of the persecutory impulses of the Restoration. However, the impact of this for Dissenters was complicated by uncertainty about the permanence of toleration and resentment at the Act's limited nature. Desirous of greater liberty, but anxious not to lose what they already had, Dissenters could afford neither to demonstrate discontent with their lot, nor to destroy their interest by ceasing to voice their views. Those who saw toleration as a threat to the Established Church were extremely reluctant to adjust to a tacitly pluralistic religious settlement, and tried to use further legislation to define the Act of 1689 in its narrowest possible terms. Both the fraught context into which this legislation was born, and the room it left for ambiguity in its meaning, meant that the settlement of 1689 was a flimsy tool for the management of religious difference.

The Problem of Popery

On top of tensions between Church and Dissent that made it difficult for all parties to adjust to the new settlement created by 1689, there was a further issue that repeatedly ignited the fires of religious tension: the problem of popery. By fundamentally shifting the relationship between Protestant Dissent and the Established Church, the legislation of 1689 posed a significant challenge to existing discursive connections between Dissent and Roman Catholicism. This was in many ways beneficial for Protestant

[15] Abel Boyer, *An Impartial History of the Occasional Conformity and Schism Bills* (London, 1717), pp. 90–1, emphasis original.

Dissenters. While popery had always been seen as the ultimate threat, the 1689 Act set out in clearer terms than previous legislation that Protestant Dissent should be firmly included within the fight against Catholicism, rather than treated, as in some polemic, as an aid to the popish cause. However, there remained aspects of anti-popish rhetoric that implicated Dissenters in the threat of popery. Much like the legislation of 1689 itself, changes in the language of anti-popery after 1689 to a degree improved the lot of Dissenters, but nevertheless left behind substantial vestiges of exclusion. The continued expression of differences between Dissent and the Established Church through anti-Catholic rhetoric is demonstrative of one of the outlets through which tensions within the 'Protestant interest' found expression. And as long as 'popery' remained a perceived threat to contemporaries, the rhetoric of anti-popery would remain a complicating factor in the management of religious difference.

Anti-popery was, by all accounts, an important unifying discourse in the eighteenth century. Throughout the seventeenth century it had been a Protestant way of 'dividing up the world between positive and negative characteristics'.[16] By seeking to unite 'their Majesties Protestant Subjects in Interest and Affection', the Toleration Act set down in legislation that Protestant Dissenters were on the right side of the divide.[17] However, Dissenters had not always been considered unambiguously part of the Protestant cause. Anti-Catholic and anti-nonconformist polemic during the Restoration period had consistently made links between popery and non-conformity, often suggesting that the two were working together to bring down the establishment. This was particularly the case during the Popish Plot crisis, when rabid anti-Catholicism was accompanied by Tory accusations that Whigs and Dissenters were using the plot to undermine Church and State.[18] It was often alleged that Protestant Dissenters were in fact papists in disguise who, in pretending to be committed Protestants, were able to unravel the Church and State from within.[19] This was exemplified clearly

---

[16] Peter Lake, 'Anti-Popery: The Structure of a Prejudice', in Richard Cust and Ann Hughes (eds.), *Conflict in Early Stuart England: Studies in Religion and Politics, 1603–1642* (London and New York: Longman, 1989), p. 74.

[17] 'William and Mary, 1688: An Act for Exempting their Majestyes Protestant Subjects Dissenting from the Church of England from the Penalties of Certaine Lawes [Chapter XVIII. Rot. Parl. pt. 5. nu. 15.]', in John Raithby (ed.), *Statutes of the Realm* (n.p., 1819), vol. 6, pp. 74–6: British History Online, www.british-history.ac.uk/statutes-realm/vol6/pp74-76.

[18] John Miller, *Popery and Politics in England, 1660–1688* (Cambridge: Cambridge University Press, 1973), p. 177.

[19] Ibid., p. 86.

Figure 1.1   *The Fetter Lane Loyalist or a Description of a True Sonne of Rome* (London, 1681), etching on paper; 331 × 403 mm.
Source: British Museum no. 1849,0315.88, © The Trustees of the British Museum.

in a pamphlet, published in 1680, encouraging Dissenters to conform to the Church of England. Suggesting that the Jesuits had been particularly successful in converting people during the Civil Wars and Interregnum, the author wrote that 'the [Jesuit] Knave lurked under the shape of an Anabaptist, of a Quaker, of a Fifth Monarchy man, and sometimes for his Interest he would appear amongst the Presbyterians and Independents'.[20] Similarly, *The Fetter Lane Loyalist* (Figure 1.1) satirised Presbyterians by implying that their real loyalties lay with the Pope. The Presbyterian's status as a 'true sonne of Rome' was made particularly evident in the top left panel, in which the Presbyterian consorts with the Pope and the Devil. In this view, Presbyterians were unequivocally on the wrong side of the divide between the Protestant interest and its enemies.

---

[20] M. D., *Friendly Advice to Protestants, or, An Essay Towards Comprehending and Uniting of all Protestant Dissenters to the Church of England* (London, 1680), p. 5.

Even when they were not portrayed as actual papists, Restoration Dissenters were often accused of deliberately collaborating with them. This was demonstrated in verse form in The Dissenter Truely Described, which summarised its critique of Dissent with the lines 'In fine, they are the foes of Royal State, /... They'd Undermine the Churches Harmony, / And Ride a full Carier to Popery.'[21] Equally, while the bitterly anti-Dissenting clergyman Thomas Long acknowledged in his 1689 defence of the Church of England that Catholics and Dissenters held opposing ideas, he argued that they were working together, stating that after accusations against the Established Church 'of Superstition and Popery, by Fanaticks, and of Schism and Heresy, by the Papists, the opposite Factions did agree to charge her with the horrible Crime of Persecution'.[22] Tacitly alluding to the favour that Dissenters had received alongside Catholics under James II's 1687 Declaration of Indulgence, Long suggested that the Church of England was besieged by popery and Dissent working in harmony with one another. This idea could hardly have been more obviously portrayed than in the 1680 broadside Popery in Masquerade (Figure 1.2). Led by a Presbyterian, a variety of Interregnum sects were shown sitting around a table under the banner of the Solemn League and Covenant, while a bust of Charles I, the Magna Carta, and various remnants of the Established Church (the surplice, the Book of Common Prayer) lay scattered on the floor. Crucially, however, the author made a clear link between this and a strengthened Catholic interest: the Pope looks down on the scene from a window in the top right of the image, and is described in the explanation of the image as 'Heart'ning on' those at the table 'Who, while they talk of Union, Bawl at Rome; / Revolt, and set up Popery at Home'. Protestant Dissent was letting popery in through the back door.

This tendency to group popery and Protestant nonconformity together appears to have become less common by the early eighteenth century. This is unsurprising given the Toleration Act's legislative expression of the idea that unity between different elements of the Protestant cause might aid the fight against popery. The shifts in polemical language were, how-ever, subtle, and by no means eliminated the issue of popery as a cause of tension between Church and Dissent. Before the 1689 Act, supposed plots against the monarchy were often framed in terms of a collaboration between popery and Dissent. During the Popish Plot, for instance, Tory

---

[21] *The Dissenter Truely Described* (London, 1681), p. 2.
[22] Thomas Long, *The Case of Persecution, Charg'd on the Church of England, Consider'd and Discharg'd, in Order to Her Justification, and a Desired Union of Protestant Dissenters* (London, 1689), pp. 1–2.

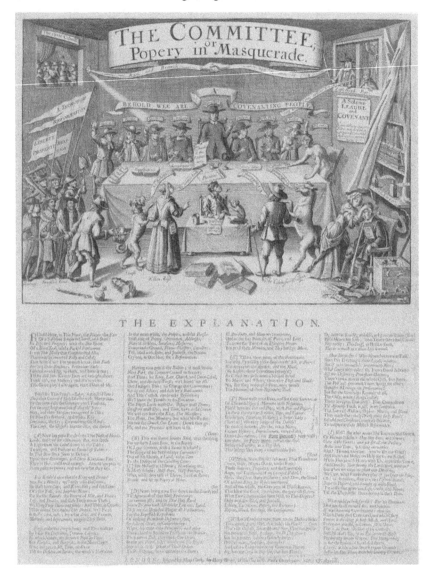

Figure 1.2   *The Committee, or Popery in Masquerade* (London, 1680), engraving
on paper; 554 × 417 mm.
Source: British Museum no. 1849,0315.82, © The Trustees
of the British Museum.

satirists sought to undermine the Whig cause by suggesting connections between 'papists' and Puritan 'fanatics', emphasising that both were acting outside the law to destroy the state.[23] In the eighteenth century, however, such plotting was more commonly portrayed as solely the domain of Jacobite Catholics. A call in 1689 for Dissenters and members of the Established Church to unite behind the revolutionary government spoke of 'the Plots and Conspiracies which have bin promoted by the Roman Catholicks in *England*, since the Reformation ... and have caused such dreadful Convulsions both in Church and State'.[24] Catholics were a useful scapegoat even when plots had clear Protestant involvement. When in 1722 the High Church Bishop of Rochester, Francis Atterbury, launched a plot to restore the Stuart monarchy, Robert Walpole responded by levying a tax on Catholic estates, despite there being no evidence of Catholic participation. Fed by the lurking presence of the Jacobite court in France, treason was now perceived to be even more so a Catholic domain.

This was, in some ways, a positive development for Dissenters. Even when eighteenth-century authors accused them of encouraging popery, the suggestion was now usually that Dissenters' actions were inadvertent rather than the product of deliberate collaboration. The author of the highly critical *Grand Designs of the Dissenting Teachers Discover'd and Exposed to Publick View* framed their attack on Dissenters in terms of failure to see the damage they were causing, rather than as a result of malicious intent. 'Let them learn what weak Supports they have been', he wrote, 'Let them remember, they have always declin'd the Combat with the proper Enemy: They have weakened the Protestant Interest by their unreasonable Divisions, they never strengthen'd it by their Writings.'[25] There was no doubt for this author that the Dissenters intended to support a broader Protestant cause. His criticism was that they failed to see that in their zeal they were undermining it.

This was set out even more plainly in a 1715 pamphlet which, at first glance, suggested a collaboration between Jesuits and Dissenters. The title page depicted Jesuits alongside Protestant reformers and Interregnum leaders, and acknowledged that while they have different titles, forms, and means, they all look to defraud the people and destroy the cause of God

---

[23] Susan Owen, *Restoration Theatre and Crisis* (Oxford: Clarendon Press, 1996), pp. 144–5.
[24] *The Absolute Necessity of Standing by the Present Government, or, a View of What Both Church Men and Dissenters Must Expect if by Their Unhappy Divisions Popery and Tyranny Should Return Again* (London, 1689), sig. A2v.
[25] *The Grand Designs of the Dissenting Teachers Discover'd and Exposed to Publick View* (London, 1710), p. 24.

through iron and fire.[26] However, the main text of the piece made it clear that while 'to encourage the Dissenters of whatever Denominations ... is in Effect the same as to encourage Popery', this was the result of Dissenting ignorance rather than a secret loyalty to Rome: 'For, how disagreeable and frightful ... the Sound of Popery is to the Generality of such simple and well-meaning deluded Dissenters of all kinds', who were being tricked into its propagation.[27] In these texts, Dissenters were no longer presented as crafty collaborators with popery, or Jesuits in disguise. Instead, they were a well-meaning, but ultimately foolish, element of the Protestant interest who needed to recognise the damage they were causing by perpetuating divisions.

Writings from a variety of political angles after 1689 stressed the urgent need to repair the fractures in the Protestant interest for the sake of fighting the Catholic cause, but they disagreed on the whether that meant binding the interests of Church and Dissent together. One Established Church writer who showed a great deal of sympathy towards Dissent was concerned about the 1714 Schism Bill, 'however it may be intended by many Well-wishers to our Church', because 'it will, by dividing us among our selves, and setting us one against another, weaken our Hands, and make us an easy Prey to the Common Enemy'. Referring to 'the Severities of our Church towards Dissenters' during the Restoration, and the danger those severities caused to the Church, he advocated a continuation of 'the Lenity of our Church towards 'em' as a guarantee of the security of the Church and Protestant cause.[28] The association of the Toleration Act with the Protestant revolutionary regime allowed avowed opponents of Jacobitism and supporters of the Dissenting interest to equate popery with attempts to limit toleration. This is clearly demonstrated in the 1745 anti-Jacobite and anti-Catholic print *The Procession or the Pope's Nursling Riding in Triumph* (Figure 1.3). Not only was the French-driven popish carriage of the Pretender depicted as riding roughshod over the Magna Carta and the Bible (discarded in a manner reminiscent of the 1680 image *Popery in Masquerade* (Figure 1.2)), but it was also shown to be running over the Act of Toleration. Thus the artist makes a very clear distinction between the Catholic cause, associated with popish France and the Pretender, and the

---

[26] *Popery and Schism Equally Dangerous to the Church of England, as by Law Establish'd* (London, 1715), frontispiece.
[27] Ibid., p. ii.
[28] A. B., *A Church of England Man's Serious Thoughts upon the Bill against Dissenting School-Masters* (London, 1714), pp. 5, 9.

Figure 1.3   *The Procession or the Pope's Nursling Riding in Triumph* (London, 1745),
etching and engraving on paper; 253 × 276 mm.
Source: British Museum no. 1868,0808.3768, © The Trustees
of the British Museum.

broader Protestant cause in which Dissenters were included by virtue of
the Toleration Act. The Toleration Act, and its association with the regime
which had overthrown a Catholic monarch, set Dissenters more firmly
on the right side of the divide between the Established Church and its
enemies. Interpreted in this fashion, the best means of collectively resisting
the popish threat was to tolerate Dissent.

However, this sentiment was not universal. For those who wished to
ensure the exclusion of Dissenters, the supposed link between Dissent
and popery was a sharp tool. Stalwarts of the Established Church suggested that Dissenters were deliberately trying to create divisions among
the Protestant cause in order to take control for themselves. Even if their

actions were not deliberate, the refusal of Dissenters to conform would, it was argued, always undermine the integrity of Protestantism. This view was particularly prominent during the occasional conformity controversy of 1709–10. Patrick Drew, a clear supporter of the Established Church, suggested that Dissenters and Catholics drew on the same ideological roots to create deliberate divisions that undermined Church and State. His view that 'A Popish Maxim it is, that Ignorance is the Mother of Devotion: This is a Maxim belonging to the Dissenters also' was accompanied by the accusation that Dissenters 'are much of the Roman Catholick Temper in the Way of planting their Schism by Blood … They have poison'd the Corporations of England with their Principles of Schism and Rebellion.'[29] Significantly, he used this to argue against any extension of toleration for Dissenters, stating that 'While they enjoy the Serenity of a Toleration to Preach Resistance, the Church Ministers Mouths shall be Stopt from preaching Non-Resistance.'[30] Toleration here did not signify the unification of the Protestant interest, because Dissenters were continuing to exploit it for their own popish ends.

The theme of Dissenting collaboration with Catholics can also be seen in visual and material culture in this period. The later Stuart period saw the market for printed visual media flourish, and in particular the beginning of the practice of transferring designs in print onto consumer items such as fans, handkerchiefs, playing cards, and ribbons. Through their use in a social context, these objects weaved together contemporary politics with the material fashions of sociability. Clear examples of this can be seen from the period of the Sacheverell crisis.[31] An emblematic fan printed 'in honour of the Church of England' and in support for Henry Sacheverell in 1711 (Figures 1.4 and 1.5), for instance, included the image of a boat, containing both a Dissenter and a Jesuit and steered by the Pope, misfiring a cannon at church and monarch.[32] The message that Dissenters were in league with the popish threat could hardly have been more obviously presented; neither could the interaction between religious tension and sociability be

[29] Patrick Drew, *The Church and England's Late Conflict With, and Triumph Over the Spirit of Fanaticism* (London, 1710), pp. 5–6, 38.
[30] Ibid., p. 8.
[31] For exploration of the materiality and development of these objects, see Mark Knights, 'Possessing the Visual: The Materiality of Visual Print Culture in Later Stuart Britain', in James Daybell and Peter Hinds (eds.), *Material Readings of Early Modern Culture: Texts and Social Practices, 1580–1730* (Basingstoke: Palgrave Macmillan, 2010), pp. 116, 105–6.
[32] *An Historical Emblematical Fan in Honour of the Church of England* (London, 1711), etching on paper; 162 × 480 mm; British Museum no. 1868,0808.3449.

Figure 1.4   *An Historical Emblematical Fan in Honour of the Church of England*
(London, 1711), etching on paper; 162 × 480 mm.
Source: British Museum no. 1868,0808.3449, © The Trustees of the British Museum.

Figure 1.5   *Dr Sacheverell – An Emblematic Fan* (England, *c.*1710), 26 cm, paper,
ivory, and tortoiseshell.
Source: © The Fan Museum, Greenwich.

more clearly demonstrated than through the representation of religious
dispute on a polite object such as a fan. Particularly during periods such as
the occasional conformity controversy, when opponents of Dissent were
politically powerful, the message sent out in the wording of the Toleration

Act that Dissenters were part of the Protestant interest was rivalled by the clamour of the High Church cause, and this could seep into all aspects of social life.

The revolution of 1688–9 and the Toleration Act which accompanied it did, at least theoretically, place Dissenters' claims to be supporting the Protestant interest against the threat of popery on firmer ground. It is clear from general shifts in the way Catholics and Dissenters were presented in relation to one another in print that many writers and artists adopted this idea. This was, however, a fragile alliance. Use of the accusation of popery against Dissenters by many stalwarts of the Established Church meant that if Dissenters showed any signs of distinction or exclusivity these could still be interpreted as a means of letting popery in through the back door.

The continuing resonance of anti-popery in this period made a vital contribution to the protracted process of negotiation between parties who held conflicting interpretations of the settlement of 1689. The Toleration Act gave Dissenters a place within the national interest, but it had not secured it sufficiently that they were immune to accusations of popery; anti-popery was a powerful channel through which continuing Established Church discontent could be expressed. The result was that as Dissenters tried to carve out a place for themselves in post-Toleration society, they found themselves walking a tightrope between accepting the limited view of toleration propounded by High Church interests, and taking the risk of reinforcing the association of Dissent with the popish threat by opposing further restrictions to their liberty. In this context, it was very difficult for the legal settlement of 1689 to put issues of religious difference to bed.

Fanaticism and Social Abnormality

As we have seen, in the years after 1689 the Toleration Act was interpreted in divergent ways in the context of continued religious stereotyping and differing political aims. It was apparent that religious differences could not be peacefully managed through simple recourse to the legislative frame-work. What alternative strategies, then, did contemporaries use to carve out a place for their interests, and what impact did they have on wider society? In the absence of comprehensive legislative support for the exclusion of Dissenters, the rhetoric of those who sought to limit the toleration of Protestant Dissent instead emphasised the abnormality of Dissenters' social behaviour. In doing so, it framed religious differences in social and cultural terms, a strategy that contributed to the continuing resonance of issues of religious difference through English society for years to come.

One of the contexts in which the strategy of labelling Dissenters as social outsiders was most clearly apparent was during the occasional conformity controversy. The outpouring of printed sermons, pamphlet literature, and other polemic surrounding this issue not only emphasised the precarious political position of Dissenters, but also fabricated justifications for their social exclusion. By highlighting their vulnerability to charges of sedition, madness, and social abnormality, discussions of occasional conformity limited the ways in which Dissenters were able to assert their roles and positions in contemporary society.

Controversy over the practice of occasional conformity reached its height in 1709–11, when the country was in the grip of a 'print fever'. Pamphlets and broadsides advanced vitriolic arguments in support and derision of High Churchman Henry Sacheverell and his extremely critical attitude towards occasional conformity.[33] Underpinning this debate were fundamentally different interpretations of the Toleration Act.

The historiography of the occasional conformity controversy has tended to focus on its immediate political impact.[34] Recent scholarship, however, has recognised the importance of the controversy for understanding the role of the Established Church in the wake of the 1688–9 revolution.[35] This has included an acknowledgement of the significance of the occasional conformity controversy in reinforcing discourses of politeness, moderation, and sincerity, in opposition to the enthusiastic and hypocritical zeal of the years 1709–12.[36] The following discussion situates the occasional conformity controversy within wider attempts to fix particular interpretations to the Toleration Act. Seen within this context, the discourses surrounding the controversy appear more broadly symptomatic of the need to work out the religious inclusivity of civil society after 1689.

The encouragement of 'moderation' prevalent in discourse in this period was, at least theoretically, a rejection of the immoderate extremes that had

---

[33] Mark Knights, *The Devil in Disguise: Deception, Delusion, and Fanaticism in the Early English Enlightenment* (New York and Oxford: Oxford University Press, 2011), p. 166.

[34] W. A. Speck, 'The Current State of Sacheverell Scholarship', *Parliamentary History*, 31, 1 (2012), pp. 16–17; Lee Horsley, '"Vox Populi" in the Political Literature of 1710', *Huntingdon Library Quarterly*, 38, 4 (1975), p. 340, *passim*.

[35] Knights, *The Devil in Disguise*, p. 143; Brent M. Sirota, 'The Occasional Conformity Controversy, Moderation, and the Anglican Critique of Modernity, 1700–1714', *Historical Journal*, 57, 1 (2014), pp. 82, 84. See also Alex W. Barber, 'Censorship, Salvation and the Preaching of Francis Higgins: A Reconsideration of High Church Politics and Theology in the Early 18th Century', *Parliamentary History*, 33, 1 (2014), pp. 114–39.

[36] Mark Knights, 'Occasional Conformity and the Representation of Dissent: Hypocrisy, Sincerity, Moderation and Zeal', *Parliamentary History*, 24, 1 (2005), pp. 56–7; Knights, *The Devil in Disguise*, pp. 186–9.

caused so much division and strife in the previous century.[37] However, there was more than one way to be moderate, and High Churchmen advocated a specific definition of moderation that placed Dissenters beyond its reach.[38] In sixteenth- and seventeenth-century uses of the terms, 'governance, restraint, repression and control' had been viewed as central to finding a middle way between excess and deficiency; by the early eighteenth century more emphasis was being placed on the individual's exercise of reason.[39] Nevertheless, High Church arguments promoted a partisan view of moderation which justified the restraint of erring consciences. Within this interpretation, any actions that were antithetical to the interests of Church and State could be regarded as immoderate, and were to be treated with zealous opposition rather than tender accommodation.

This view was reflected in the words of leading nonjuring clergyman Samuel Grascome in 1704: 'I desire to know what more intemperate Zeal and fierce Biggotry there can be; and consequently what more Opposite to Moderation, than to fly in the Faces of their Governours.'[40] Similarly, Phillip Collier, a rector in Cornwall, argued in a 1712 sermon that however much Dissenters represented their deviations from the Established Church as 'Harmless and Moderate Errors', 'there are no Causes more productive of publick Troubles, than Different Judgements and Persuasions in Matters of Religion'.[41] By High Church logic, Dissenters had demonstrated through their historic disruptive opposition that they were unable to govern themselves through reason. Against such anarchical reprobates the use of zealous argument and restraining action was the necessary moderate course of action.

The view that a divisive and impolite excess of enthusiasm was typical of Dissenters was set out clearly in an anonymous octavo pamphlet of thirty

---

[37] Nicholas Phillipson, 'Politeness and Politics in the Reign of Anne and the Early Hanoverians', in J. G. A. Pocock, Gordon J. Schochet, and Lois Schwoerer (eds.), *The Varieties of British Political Thought, 1500–1800* (New York and Cambridge: Cambridge University Press, 1993), pp. 215, 223; Lawrence E. Klein, 'Politeness and the Interpretation of the British Eighteenth Century', *Historical Journal*, 45, 4 (2002), p. 890.

[38] Knights, 'Occasional Conformity and the Representation of Dissent', pp. 51–2; Markku Peltonen, 'Politeness and Whiggism, 1688–1732', *Historical Journal*, 48, 2 (2005), p. 396; Andrew Lincoln, 'War and the Culture of Politeness: The Case of *The Tatler* and *The Spectator*', *Eighteenth-Century Life*, 36, 2 (2012), p. 65.

[39] Ethan H. Shagan, *The Rule of Moderation. Violence, Religion and the Politics of Restraint in Early Modern England* (Cambridge: Cambridge University Press, 2011), pp. 15–16.

[40] Samuel Grascome, *The Mask of Moderation Pull'd Off the Foul Face of Occasional Conformity* (London, 1704), p. 7.

[41] Phillip Collier, *The Duty and Advantages of Promoting the Peace and Prosperity, Both of Church and State. A Sermon* (Exeter, 1712), p. 15.

pages, entitled *The Fanatick Feast*, printed at the height of the occasional conformity controversy in 1710.[42] In the context of the discussion at hand, it provides a useful case study for how opponents framed arguments about the meaning of toleration and the threat of Dissent with reference to specific social contexts. In particular, it suggests some of the ways in which senses of religious difference were maintained through social language after the Toleration Act.

The pamphlet describes the farcical wedding of the son and daughter of 'the chief elders of two different Sects', who chose to invite among others 'the principal Leaders, the P[reache]rs and Pedagogues of the several Sects amongst 'em'.[43] Unable to agree on anything, the preachers descended into dispute over seating, table manners, and material wealth.[44] They also fought over food, and one of them attempted to pay a waiter-boy for sex.[45] Eventually, the increasingly drunken company started brawling, during which food and tableware was liberally thrown, one of them lost an eye and half his nose, and another two of his teeth.[46] The story ends by leaving it to the reader's judgement 'whether these mighty Pretenders to Self-denial, have not been guilty of as much Irregularity and Debauchery, as even a profess'd Libertine'.[47]

Highly polemical and clearly pro-Tory, there is no circumstantial evidence to suggest that the pamphlet is based on a real series of events, and it seems more likely that it was a rhetorical device. The image of Dissent it projects, however, cuts to the core of concerns about where Dissenters would fit into English politics and society in the wake of toleration. The support given by the pamphlet to Sacheverell and Tory opposition to occasional conformity is evident throughout, and it draws directly on some of the arguments and language used in the illegal printed edition of Sacheverell's sermon *The Perils of False Brethren*. Sacheverell's characterisation of Dissenters as ostentatiously pious and 'Holier than Thou', for instance, is resoundingly taken up in *The Fanatick Feast*.[48] Sectarianism was linked with morally questionable behaviour throughout the text,

---

[42] *The Fanatick Feast. A Pleasant Comedy. As It Was Acted at a Wedding-Dinner in Gr------* (London, 1710).

[43] Ibid., pp. 6–7.

[44] Ibid.

[45] Ibid., pp. 8–10.

[46] Ibid., p. 30.

[47] Ibid., p. 31.

[48] Henry Sacheverell, *The Perils of False Brethren, Both in Church, and State: Set Forth in a Sermon…5 November 1709* (London: 1709), p.17.

with the guests of the wedding feast behaving themselves contrary to their claims to piety. The cumulative disorderly conduct of the company by the end of the tale was sufficient for the narrator to report that 'For all those Reverend P----rs that were at the Table, I could not see one that was exempt from the ordinary Frailties of Mankind; but made himself a Jest to the Standers by, either for some indecent thing that he did, or something worse that he spoke.'[49] In its emphasis on the hypocrisy of Dissenters, *The Fanatick Feast* stuck closely to the narrative woven by Sacheverell.

Sacheverell's arguments are further present in the pamphlet's focus on the tendency of Dissenters towards the division and destruction of the Church established by law. Sacheverell's references to the responsibility of Dissenters for the ills of 30 January (the date of the execution of Charles I in 1649), and the extreme disruption of the Interregnum, tie Dissenters to division and treason.[50] Thus Sacheverell bellowed that to create an inclusive Church would be to 'render it the most Absurd, Contradictory, and Self-Inconsistent Body in the World', filled with 'such Unhallow'd, Loathsome, and Detestable Guests, as would have Driv'n out the Holy Spirit of God with Indignation'.[51] *The Fanatick Feast* directly addresses these ideas, sarcastically commending the father of the bride for 'picking out the Sages and Virtuosoes of all Sects to adorn his Daughter's Wedding Dinner', who then proceed to drag the occasion entirely away from any focus on love or marriage by fighting among themselves.[52] Crucially, the author chose to make their point by focusing primarily on the social behaviour of those present. The slights given by the guests to each other throughout the text and the descent into complete anarchy by the end can be interpreted as a metaphor for the future fortunes of the Church under the practice of occasional conformity. For contemporaries, immoderate social behaviour and immoderate religion were natural bedfellows.

The presence of the theme of disorder also places *The Fanatick Feast* firmly within a category of critiques of broader Whig ideology, including their support for the principle of resistance and the validity of public opinion, and the expression of the crowd as a force in politics. As Lee Horsley has highlighted, the fact that the crowd turned out in 1710 to support the Tory cause presented a problem not only for the Whigs, who had claimed ownership over the vox populi, but also for many Tories,

---

[49] *The Fanatick Feast*, p. 21.
[50] Sacheverell, *The Perils of False Brethren*, pp. 3, 21.
[51] Ibid., pp. 28, 29.
[52] *The Fanatick Feast*, p. 8.

who claimed to support passive obedience. Some Tory writers chose to blame the disorderly behaviour of rioters not on their ideology but on the fact that the Whigs had sown the seeds of disorderly behaviour among the populace, and were therefore getting their comeuppance.[53] In *The Fanatick Feast*, the Whigs are represented by the father of the bride, who undermined the civility of his own feast by a poor choice of guests. Finding them quarrelsome, he only made matters worse by attempting to divert them from their disagreements 'by putting the Glass merrily about'.[54] Just as Tories claimed that Whigs had stoked disorder and then lost control, so the father of the bride, in attempting to control the company, merely exacerbated the problem.[55] The disorder that resulted can thus be read not only as highlighting the danger of occasional conformity to the integrity of the Church, but also as an attack on Whig principles of resistance. If allowed within the communion feast of the Church, Dissenters would undermine both Church and State from within.

The parallels drawn in *The Fanatick Feast* between the wedding celebration and the feast of communion are important. By suspending other legislation against Dissenters, the Toleration Act had made communion one of the last legal barriers to their full integration within civil society. The integrity and role of communion within the Church was at the heart of debates about occasional conformity, spanning not just the issue of political office but also questions of inclusion and belonging within a spiritual community. Scripture made it clear that only those who had prepared themselves spiritually should partake in communion. The parable of the wedding banquet in Matthew 22: 2–14 highlights the necessity of spiritual preparation, with the guest who arrived without wearing wedding clothes being tied up and thrown out into the darkness, 'For many are invited, but few are chosen.' In *The Fanatick Feast*, the father of the bride was insufficiently scrupulous about who he invited and how he managed the behaviour of his guests, with the result that his feast ended in a chaos that far from mimicked a heavenly banquet. The implication, therefore, was that the very integrity of communion would be undermined if it were not kept to some extent exclusive. In broader terms, this suggested that the social inclusion of Dissent would undermine the integrity of society. Given the apparent resonance of these views, it is unsurprising that Dissenters felt socially insecure under the so-called toleration of the 1689 Act.

---

[53] Horsley, '"Vox Populi" in the Political Literature of 1710', pp. 336, 343–4.
[54] *The Fanatick Feast*, p. 10.
[55] Horsley, '"Vox Populi" in the Political Literature of 1710', p. 344.

The immoderate and impolite nature of Dissent was not only made clear by the behaviour of the Dissenters at the feast, but also by the language in which it was described. Labelling Dissenters as 'fanaticks' associated them with the immoderate excesses of the Interregnum. The term was first used in the early 1600s, but it was not until the 1650s, with the multiplication of religious sects, that it appeared more frequently in print. Strikingly, for the years immediately following the Restoration, the frequency with which the term appears in surviving printed works almost doubles, before falling away again, reaching similar peaks in usage around the time of the Test Act (1673) and in the aftermath of the Popish Plot (1678–81).[56]

This term was strongly linked to criticism of Dissenters as responsible for the disruption and bloodshed of the Civil Wars.[57] During the process of Restoration, General Monck was eager to demonstrate the opposition of the monarchical interest to what had gone immediately before, warning the loyal gentry to 'be carefull neither Cavalier nor Phanatique party have yet a share of your Civil or Military Power; of the last of whose impatience to Government, you have had so severe experience'.[58] Printed celebrations of the Restoration also sought to associate the ruling party of the Interregnum with fanaticism. One broadsheet poem wrote 'Of England's joy to see her Prince at home' when the country had been reduced to 'ruinous streights' and 'Torn by the fury of Phanatick winds'.[59] If this was not enough, other authors spelt out the association of fanaticism with Dissent and the Interregnum regime more clearly, describing fanatics as 'those who kick against the present constitution of a regulated Church and State'.[60]

Labelling Dissenters as 'fanatics' was therefore much more than mere personal slander. Early eighteenth-century critics of Dissent and occasional conformity drew on the association of Dissent with the excesses of the mid-seventeenth century to point to the immoderate enthusiasm of Dissenting groups. Phillip Collier was convinced that past example

---

[56] Based on an analysis of word frequency in the *Early English Books Online* corpus using the 'EEBO N-gram browser', created by Anupam Basu for *Early Modern Print. Text Mining Early Modern English* (Washington University, St Louis: 2014), https://earlyprint.wustl.edu/tooleebospelling-browser.html, accessed 3 July 2020.

[57] Matthew Neufeld, *The Civil Wars After 1660: Public Remembering in Late Stuart England* (Woodbridge: The Boydell Press, 2013), p. 2.

[58] *A Collection of Several Letters and Declarations, Sent by General Monck Unto the Lord Lambert, the Lord Fleetwood, and the Rest of the General Council of Officers in the Army* (London, 1660), p. 17.

[59] *Anglia Rediviva: A Poem on His Majesties Most Joyfull Reception into England [sic]* (London, 1660), single sheet.

[60] *The Character of a Phanatique* (London, 1660), single sheet. See also *A Brief Description or Character of the Religion and Manners of the Phanatiques in Generall* (London, 1660).

showed that, given the opportunity, Dissenters would destroy both Church and State, pointing out that 'when this National Church maintain'd its Authority, the Prince sate secure upon the Throne; but no sooner was the first overturn'd, but the latter was shaken; Rebellion appeared bare-fac'd and open; and this whole Land was laid wast with such Barbarous Cruelty and Unparallell'd Violence'.[61] A similar argument was made by the staunch Anglican writer Mary Astell, who wrote that 'it is neither Hard nor Untrue to affirm, that Dissenters never want the Will when they have Power to destroy the Church and State, since they have given us too sad and too full a Demonstration of it'.[62] The use of the term 'fanatic' to char-acterise the Dissenters at the feast was a strategy with political resonance, reminding readers that despite the liberties that the Toleration Act pro-vided, Dissenters were still associated with previous enthusiasm and the destruction of Church and State.

The Fanatick Feast thus used a combination of social and political criti-cism to place Dissenters outside of the bounds of a functioning civil soci-ety. In doing so, it represented a strand of argument that still baulked at the idea of accepting the existence of religious difference within English society. In order to combat the creeping threat of Dissent represented by toleration and the practice of occasional conformity, High Churchmen used the influential tropes of the day to argue that even if Dissenters were legally tolerated, they were socially disqualified from playing a role in a state and society that they wholeheartedly believed should be under the monopoly of the Established Church. The occasional conformity contro-versy was a debate in which, against the context of newly inclusive defini-tions of legal Protestant worship, social norms were used as a measure for the limits of toleration.

Languages of Social Exclusion: 1714 and Beyond

The exclusion of Dissenters through the language of social disqualifica-tion took a particularly biting tone during the occasional conformity controversy, and established recourse to accusations of social abnormality as a strategy for religious argument. This discursive connection between religious affiliation and social behaviour continued to be made by oppo-nents of Dissent after the first decade of the century, even as disputes

---

[61] Collier, *The Duty and Advantages of Promoting the Peace and Prosperity*, p. 18.
[62] Mary Astell, *Moderation Truly Stated* (London, 1704), p. 88.

caused by religious difference became less heated. The temperature of debate had cooled significantly by the mid-1720s, when a Tory loss of power and increasing anti-clericalism in parliament and beyond had, it seemed, significantly weakened the 'High Church' cause.[63] The apparent decline of Dissent and the reconciliation of many of the clergy to Whig rule decreased the sense that Dissent was an urgent threat to the integrity of the Church.[64]

Nevertheless, it seems that discourse connecting social and religious behaviours evolved and embedded itself, rather than straightforwardly declining. There is considerable evidence that religious controversies affected contemporary politics well into the middle of the century, and that many of these disputes couched the exclusion of Dissent in social terms. A substantial portion of printed polemic retained a concern with the unresolved religious disputes of the previous century.[65] Furthermore, 'starkly contrasting accounts of the past' held by Dissenters and defenders of the Established Church fed into divergent interpretations of the present.[66] 'High Church' opinions did not simply disappear, even if their interests were poorly represented at court and in parliament. Jeffrey Chamberlain has gone so far as to suggest that whatever their political colours, 'the majority of parochial clergymen in early Georgian England' maintained High Church views in relation to 'piety and churchmanship ... They were traditionalists trying to keep their religious foundations secure amidst the shifting sands of government and society.'[67] Beyond the clergy, by the 1720s the experience of the previous seventy years and more had ensured that fear of the effects of religious difference was well embedded. While violent persecution of Dissent was no longer on the agenda, prejudice against Dissenters had considerable cultural cachet.

Anti-Dissenting rhetoric in the second quarter of the century therefore framed the exclusion of Dissent in social as well as political and religious

[63] Stephen Taylor, 'Whigs, Tories, and Anticlericalism: Ecclesiastical Courts Legislation in 1733', *Parliamentary History*, 19, 3 (2000), p. 329; Jeffrey S. Chamberlain, 'Portrait of a High Church Clerical Dynasty in Georgian England: The Frewens and Their World', in John Walsh, Colin Haydon, and Stephen Taylor (eds.), *The Church of England, c.1689–c.1833: From Toleration to Tractarianism* (Cambridge: Cambridge University Press, 1993), p. 299; Stevens, *Protestant Pluralism*, p. 153.
[64] Stevens, *Protestant Pluralism*, pp. 156–7.
[65] Robert G. Ingram, *Reformation Without End. Religion, Politics, and the Past in Post-Revolutionary England* (Manchester: Manchester University Press, 2018), p. 12.
[66] Jeremy Black, *Charting the Past: The Historical Worlds of Eighteenth-Century England* (Bloomington, IN: Indiana University Press, 2019), p. 129.
[67] Chamberlain, 'Portrait of a High Church Dynasty in Georgian England', p. 315.

terms. Many arguments were not particularly new. Objections to Dissent raised during the 1730s, when defenders of the Church hierarchy felt threatened by both anti-clericalism and by Dissenters' campaigns for the repeal of the Test and Corporation Acts, sometimes mirrored those expressed during the occasional conformity controversy. This is particularly clear in *A Looking-Glass for the Fanaticks*, which was published anonymously in 1730. Drawing a parallel 'between the Fanaticks and the Pharisees', the anonymous author wrote that 'The Fanaticks ... will not eat with Publicans and Sinners, pretending to a superabundance of Purity; their Fasts are made publick to the World, and leavened with disfigured Countenances.' He went on to highlight their 'strange, uncouth and affected Postures and Gestures in Prayer' and, crucially, the fact that 'they scorned to call others Brethren who were not of their godly Party'.[68] Dissenters were, once again, being portrayed as unmannerly, anti-social, and divisive.

Almost imperceptibly, however, the tone of such arguments was changing. Sacheverell had sought to stir with his words; in the 1730s pamphleteers and preachers against Dissent were frequently professing to pacify. Responding to the printed sermons and polemical contributions of the London Presbyterian minister Samuel Chandler, the author of *A Scourge for the Dissenters: Or, the Fanatic Vipers* complained that it was incumbent on such figures to keep 'within the Bounds of Decency and Good-Manners', rather than preaching sermons that endeavoured to 'break ... Harmony and Agreement'.[69] In fact such was the 'Discord and Disunion' caused by the preaching and publications of Dissenters that they were tantamount to a sedition that would lead to 'Corruption of Manners ... Revenge, Forgetfulness of Consanguity, Parentage and Friendship, Violence, Robberies, Confiscations, savage Murders, infinite Excesses, and intolerable Miseries'.[70] The author concluded that the Dissenters would not 'meet with better Treatment from me, till they shew better Manners, and become better Christians, and Better Subjects'.[71] This publication presented Dissenters' rhetoric as a breach of the peace and a threat to the integrity of civil society. In a similar vein, John Dudley, the Archdeacon of Bedford, published a sermon in 1736 against the repeal of the Test and Corporation Acts which intimated that Dissenters 'desert their own Pastor out of Spite and Ill-will, and purely to gratify

---

[68] *A Looking-Glass for Fanaticks* (London: 1730), pp. 3, 4, 13, 14.
[69] *A Scourge for the Dissenters: Or the Fanatick Vipers* (London: 1735), pp. 2, 18.
[70] Ibid., p. 19.
[71] Ibid., p.47.

their ill-grounded Resent'.[72] Once again, Dissenters' separation from the
Church was being characterised in terms of ill-manners, anti-social attitudes, and deep-seated grudges. But whereas in 1710 few could have argued
that Dissenting polemic violated an otherwise peaceful religious culture,
by the 1730s unmannerliness was presented as antithetical to a harmonious
and inclusive Established Church.

Some of these attitudes still surfaced in 1745–6, when a flurry of print
discussed the relationship between Church and Dissent in the light of
the Jacobite Rebellion. *A Brief Account of the Methods Used to Propagate
Popery*, for example, highlighted that national divisions left Church and
State vulnerable to the misfortune of popish invasion. The author laid
the blame for this squarely at the feet of Dissenters, who sustained an
'innate Principle of Division'.[73] This divisiveness was, other authors suggested, characterised by Dissenters' unmannerly and vituperative preaching. In a printed letter to the eccentric Dissenting preacher John 'Orator'
Henley, particular attention was given to Henley's 'Railery, Virulency and
personal false Reflections' in his preaching of 'Discourses calculated chiefly
to keep up a Spirit of Sedition in a superstitious Sect of People'. Labelling
Henley's style as 'clamourous Billingsgate Rhetoric', the author suggested
that 'Want of Decency is Want of Sense'.[74] In these publications, we again
see a tendency to link the divisiveness of Dissent with their social manners.

In some other works published in the 1740s, however, there is evidence
of an increased acknowledgement of Dissenters' good behaviour under
the toleration they had enjoyed for the previous fifty years. *A Defense of
Set or Prescribed Forms of Prayer*, written by John Downes the rector of St
Michael, Woodstreet (Cripplegate) in 1746, for instance, praised 'the good
Temper and Moderation which at present is presev'd betwixt those of the
established Church, and those who dissent from it'.[75] Nathaniel Ball, the
curate of Chelmsford, put forward an equally charitable interpretation of
the behaviour of Dissenters, describing how 'their Persons and Characters
are blameless, and they live like faithful Subjects, good Neighbours, and in

---

[72] John Dudley, *A Charge to the Clergy Within the Archdeaconry of Bedford: In Which are Some Remarks
Concerning the Late Application of the Dissenters for a Repeal of the Test Act. Delivered at a Visitation
Held at Ampthill, April 30th, 1736* (London, 1736), pp. 29–30.

[73] *A Brief Account of the Methods Used to Propagate Popery, in Great Britain and Ireland; Ever Since the
Reformation, to the Present Rebellion* (London, 1745), p. 4.

[74] *An Epistle to O------r H----nl--y; Containing, Some Remarks on the Discourses Set Forth at the
Conventicle the Corner of Lincoln's-Inn-Fields* (London, 1746), pp. 3, 4.

[75] John Downes, *A Defence of Set or Prescribed Forms of Prayer; Being an Answer to Mr Phelps's Remarks
Upon a Sermon Preached on that Subject* (London, 1746), p. iii.

all Respects Friends to Society'.[76] This was a far cry from the heated accusations of social abnormality, unneighbourliness, and sedition embedded throughout *The Fanatick Feast* and other publications. Dissenters were in some quarters perceived as better integrated into society, and as less of a threat than they had been at the beginning of the century.

However, while the violence of accusations against Dissent undoubtedly reflected a greater degree of acceptance, even these publications maintained the understanding that social misdemeanours could be interpreted as a religious and political threat. For all his support of tolerance towards moderate Dissenters, Ball framed his argument in such a way as to highlight that unmannerly Dissent could still be dangerous, stating that 'mere Opinions can hurt no Body, unless they are rudely propagated'.[77] In his condemnation of the objections of Dissenter John Phelps to set forms of prayer, John Downes equally recognised the potential for the ill behaviour of Dissenters to foment divisions, describing Phelps as a 'rude and turbulent Writer, who by rifling into old Sores, and raising up former and almost forgotten Quarrels from their dying Embers, is labouring to subvert that good Harmony which now subsists'.[78] Similar warnings that although peace and moderation currently reigned, intemperate behaviour could very quickly allow old tensions to rise to the surface, were expressed by the Bishop of Chichester, Matthias Mawson, in a sermon preached before the House of Lords in 1746. Alluding to the contention and animosity that occurred during the Civil Wars, 'When the established Church was thrown down', he claimed that his aim was 'not to revive the Memory of past Animosities, or cast any oblique Reflexions on any Bodies of Men now living in a State of Separation from the Church of England', but rather to remind his hearers 'how difficult it is for all Parties when fired with intemperate Zeal … to practice … Forbearance and Moderation'.[79] While past contentions had undoubtedly lost their momentum, and were in their 'dying Embers', they had not been forgotten.[80]

There was, then, a shift in printed discussions of religious conflict across the first half of the eighteenth century. In the first few decades after the

---

[76] Nathaniel Ball, *Sermons on Several Important Subjects* (London, 1745), p. 8.
[77] Ibid., p. 9.
[78] Downes, *A Defence of Set of Prescribed Forms of Prayer*, p. viii. Downes was responding to John Phelps's *A Vindication of Free and Unprescribed Prayer: In Some Remarks Upon Dr Newton's Sermon on the Liturgy of the Church of England* (London, 1746).
[79] Matthias Mawson, *The Mischiefs of Division with Respect Both to Religion and Civil Government. A Sermon Preach'd Before the House of Lords* (London, 1746), pp. 7–8.
[80] Downes, *A Defence of Set of Prescribed Forms of Prayer*, p. viii.

Toleration Act, High Church opponents of Dissent could reasonably hope that toleration might be withdrawn or, at the very least, limited, and this was reflected in the tone of their criticism. As the century wore on, however, the violent expression of religious exclusivity began to be regarded as unacceptably immoderate. The emphasis was now on the idea that Dissenters were stuck in an unmannerly past, seeking to drag society backwards by opening up old wounds when these were barely healed.

The material threat of these later arguments against Dissent was less substantial than earlier arguments against toleration and occasional conformity. Appeals to Dissenters to let bygones be bygones implicitly accepted that religious pluralism was there to stay: by the 1740s the core message of some arguments against Dissenting campaigns for further freedoms was that Dissenters should join the rest of society in moving on from ruminating over divisive religious issues. Yet this was rhetorical wizardry, because accusations of Dissenting divisiveness were themselves a tool for marginalisation. The link between overzealousness, social nonconformity, and the threat of Dissent, entrenched by the middle of the seventeenth century and reiterated ever since, remained resonant. Because of this, the stereotype that Dissenters were more wont to act immoderately or in an unmannerly fashion was difficult for society to unlearn. This stereotype was important, because, as is shown throughout the rest of this book, it formed the basis for the subtle social exclusion of Dissenters that was embedded in the emergent social modes and venues of the first half of the eighteenth century.

The Rhetoric of Suffering

We have seen that opponents of Dissent responded to the removal of many concrete legal means of persecution by making recourse to languages of social exclusion. The impact of this was somewhat enhanced by Dissenters' own reactions to a religious settlement that did not go as far in providing relief as some would have liked. Dissenters responded by campaigning for measures that would increase their security under the law, by emphasising both the suffering they had previously received under Restoration persecution, and the unjust suffering that they still had to endure after the Act. This served the double purpose of reinforcing a sense among Dissenting groups of solidarity in suffering, and of illustrating the case for further measures for the relief of Dissenters. However, this rhetoric of suffering also had the unhelpful effect of setting Dissenters up as social outsiders, thereby embedding senses of difference that underpinned stereotypes of Dissent. The rhetoric of suffering was a useful tool for sustaining support for their cause, but it put Dissenters at greater risk of accusations of social abnormality and exclusivity. The vulnerability of Dissenters to social and political stereotyping was thus exacerbated by the fact that they continued to perceive and portray themselves as subject to exclusion.

Not all Dissenters chose to emphasise continued suffering after 1689. Despite their uncertainty over its permanence, many Dissenters demonstrated gratitude for toleration, and described their suffering as firmly in the past. This interpretation emphasised the hope that the Toleration Act would be a distinct break, a measure that would usher in a new era in which Dissenters could finally take their rightful places within society. In reflection of this, and in spite of his apparent fears that toleration would be withdrawn, Matthew Henry recalled in an account of the establishment of his Dissenting Chapel in Chester that

> In the month of May 1689 the Act of Parliament was pass'd for the establishing of our Liberty, Jun. 6 I Kept a Day of Thanksgiving for it, and preach'd on Hos. 11. 4. 'I was unto them in one that taketh up the yoke in their jaws, and I laid meat into them' and at the next Quarter sessions after held for this City Mr Harvy and I qualified ourselves for the Benefit of the Toleration.[81]

Henry's choice of Bible verse was significant. Chapter 11 is a turning point in the Book of Hosea: having judged and punished an unrepentant Israel, God demonstrates his love for its people, and promises not to give them up entirely, declaring 'My heart is changed within me; all my compassion is aroused.'[82] In his *Complete Commentary* (1708–10), Henry emphasised how in this part of Hosea God took the Israelites 'by the arms, to guide them, that they might not stray, and to hold them up, that they might not stumble and fall' and 'eased them of the burdens they had long groaned under'.[83] In using this as the subject of his Thanksgiving sermon, Henry was interpreting the Act as a sign of God's mercy and a shift from a past of sin and punishment to a future of repentance and forgiveness. The yoke of Dissenters' suffering was being removed and left behind.

This view of the 1689 Act as a distinct break that allowed Dissenters to throw off the shackles of the past is in evidence elsewhere. The autobiographical account of the Essex Congregationalist Mary Churchman,

---

[81] Matthew Henry's Chapel Church Book, 1687–1928, fol. 8r, D/MH/1, CALS.
[82] Hosea 11:8 (New Standard Version).
[83] Matthew Henry, *An Exposition of All the Books of the Old and New Testament* (London, 1721–1725), vol. 4, p. 642.

transcribed by her daughter in *c.*1732–4, recalled in detail her suffering following her rejection of the Established Church during the Restoration, but
made it clear that that this changed with the Revolution: 'Now nothing but
goodness & Mercy followed me all the days of my life when we enjoyed our
liberty under our great Deliverer from Popery & Slavery King Wm.'[84] The
introduction of a degree of liberty of conscience in 1689 was here interpreted
as distinct from what had gone before. A similar sentiment was expressed
in striking terms in an eighteenth-century manuscript account of the life of
the Worcester Dissenting minister Chewning Blackmore, which stated 'He
Entred upon the Ministry in those dark Times, a little before the Revolution
In the beginning of the year 1688 (when it pleased God very mercifully &
seasonably to save our Land from Ruin).'[85] In both accounts the darkness of
the pre-Toleration era was contrasted with the brighter times that followed.
In social terms, this represented a distinct rejection of the outsider status
created by Restoration persecution in favour of a picture of a Protestant
society in which Dissenters had a deserved place codified in law. This ran
directly contrary to print that emphasised connections between an unmannerly Dissent and the religious divisions of the previous century.

However, at the same time as it was prudent for Dissenters to put
the past behind them in order to enjoy the degree of toleration they
had gained, there were also reasons for them to resurrect the rhetoric of
suffering for the present. As decades passed without their liberty being
fully secured, Dissenters became more assertive in publicly campaigning for its extension. Thus in 1712, the Presbyterian historian Edward
Calamy complained that 'tho' we had at last a Legal Toleration granted
us, for which we are very Thankful to God, and our Governours … are
not Protestant Dissenters now cast out from all Places of Profit and
Trust, unless they'll quit their Principles, and entirely fall in with the
Publick Establishment?'[86] It was this sentiment that saw Presbyterians,
Independents, Baptists, and Quakers launch concerted campaigns to
repeal the Test and Corporation Acts in the early 1730s, filled with 'a
very deep Sense of the Unreasonableness of the Sacramental Test and
Corporation Acts'.[87] This was not only the concern of the Protestant

---

[84] Commonplace Book: 'John Churchman His Book', 1749, fol. 14r, D/DQs 22, ERO.
[85] An Account of the Rev. Chewning Blackmore by George Bewson copied by Rev. Fr. Blackmore, fol.
4r, 12.40/61, DWL.
[86] Edmund Calamy, *Comfort and Counsel to Protestant Dissenters* (London, 1712), p. 24.
[87] *A Narrative of the Proceedings of the Protestant Dissenters of the Three Denominations; Relating to the
Repeals of the Corporation and Test Acts* (London, 1734), p. 3; Thompson, 'Contesting the Test Act',
pp. 58–70.

Dissenting Deputies (an alliance of Presbyterians, Independents, and Baptists) campaigning in London. It was also an issue that played on the minds of individual Dissenters in the provinces, including James Clegg's congregation in Chapel-en-le-Frith, Derbyshire. Clegg wrote in his diary in May 1732 that he was 'with Ms James Clegg at Breakfast, Mr Butterworth, Mr Walker, Mr Winder and Mr Mottershead there, the subject of our conversation was the most proper method for procuring the Repeal of the Test act etc'.[88] Even while they might be grateful for the substantive improvements that the 1689 Act represented, Dissenters wanted to work for the continuation of their cause. Unfortunately, this gave potential fuel to accusations that Dissenters were ungrateful, divisive social outsiders.

An emphasis on suffering was a way for Dissenters to ground their identities in the recent past in a period when they felt uncertain about the long-term implications of the 1689 settlement. The persecutory legislation of the Restoration period had been an important means of fostering political unity among Dissenters.[89] Historians examining Puritanism and Protestant nonconformity in the seventeenth century have recognised that a sense of shared suffering was essential for maintaining the integrity of Dissenting groups in opposition to the Established Church. This has been regarded as particularly the case for Quakers, for whom undergoing persecution was 'a necessary, even a somewhat welcome element of their being'.[90] As a result, the toleration granted under the 1689 Act was a challenge to the essential identity and visibility of Quakers, even as it provided some relief.[91] This was also apparent among Restoration nonconformists more generally, who drew on the 'stimulus of persecution' under the Clarendon Code to create unity and deepen personal religion.[92] This emphasis on suffering under

---

[88] Doe (ed.), *The Diary of James Clegg*, p. 145.

[89] James E. Bradley, *Religion, Revolution, and English Radicalism: Nonconformity in Eighteenth-Century Politics and Society* (Cambridge: Cambridge University Press, 1990), pp. 50, 87–8.

[90] Richard L. Greaves, 'The "Great Persecution" Reconsidered. The Irish Quakers and the Ethic of Suffering', in Muriel C. McClendon, Joseph P. Ward, and Michael MacDonald (eds.), *Protestant Identities. Religion, Society, and Self-Fashioning in Post-Reformation England* (Stanford, CA: Stanford University Press, 1999), p. 212. See also Naomi Pullin, *Female Friends and the Making of Transatlantic Quakerism, 1650–c.1750* (Cambridge: Cambridge University Press, 2018), pp. 6–7, 76.

[91] Richard C. Allen, 'Restoration Quakerism, 1660–1691', in Stephen W. Angell and Pink Dandelion (eds.), *The Oxford Handbook of Quaker Studies* (Oxford and New York: Oxford University Press, 2013), pp. 44–5.

[92] Horton Davies, *The English Free Churches* (London: Oxford University Press, 1952), p. 104; Alexandra Walsham, *Charitable Hatred. Tolerance and Intolerance in England, 1500–1700* (Manchester: Manchester University Press, 2006), p. 308.

persecution built on a broader Puritan tradition in which 'a sense of being despised and hated by the impious and unregenerate' was vital.[93]

Given that the Act of 1689 removed most of the tools that underpinned this persecution, toleration in some ways presented 'a psychological threat to the identity and hence survival of religious minorities'.[94] In the eighteenth century, references to historic suffering thus took on a particularly important role in bringing together disparate groups of Protestant Dissenters.[95] The published sermon *Christian Sufferers*, preached during Dissenters' joint campaigns to remove the Test and Corporation Acts in the early 1730s, for instance, made strong appeals to senses of suffering among Dissenters. It acknowledged that the 'badges of dishonour' against Dissent had been removed and 'a redress of their grievances' had been 'done, as far as the prudence of many wise men has judged it, at this time, proper', but stressed that Dissenters were 'still left to suffer under the complain'd of hardships'.[96] In the light of this, the author recommended that Dissenters bear the burden of suffering with pride, stating that 'Taunts and cruel mockings; invidious marks of infamy; fines and imprisonments, are the honours and privileges or rewards you are to look for in this world.'[97] To reinforce this point, he made reference to the 'much greater trial' of previous generations, questioning whether his readers were 'worthy of the honour of being descended from them, if you are impatient and murmuring under much lesser burdens'.[98] His viewpoint was clear: the suffering of Dissenters was not simply the symptom of past injustice. It was a mark of distinction to be borne until God saw fit to remove it.

Daniel Defoe also advocated the idea that Dissenters should suffer zealously rather than capitulate to their self-interest through actions such as occasional conformity. Alleging that 'the Dissenters have lost Ground by Toleration', which served to 'cool that blessed Fervour which carried our Fathers into Prisons ... and kept them Company to the Grave', he suggested that the only way to maintain the Dissenting cause was to adhere

---

[93] Alexandra Walsham, 'The Godly and Popular Culture', in John Coffey and Paul C. H. Lim (eds.), *The Cambridge Companion to Puritanism* (Cambridge: Cambridge University Press, 2008), p. 277.

[94] Walsham, *Charitable Hatred*, p. 315.

[95] Bracy V. Hill II, 'Suffering for Their Consciences: The Depiction of Anabaptists and Baptists in the Eighteenth-Century Histories of Daniel Neal', *Welsh Journal of Religious History*, 5 (2010), pp. 84–113; Bradley, *Religion, Revolution, and English Radicalism*, pp. 50, 53, 87–8.

[96] *Christian Sufferers: Or, Seasonable Advice to Protestant Dissenters, Relating to Their Behaviour, Under Their Present Disappointment. A Sermon Preach'd in the Country, January 28 1732–3* (London: 1732–3), pp. 4–5.

[97] Ibid., p. 11.

[98] Ibid., pp. 33–4.

'steadily to the Principles of a Dissenter, in Contempt of Honours, Profits, Trusts, and Temporal Advantages'.[99] Dissenters of all varieties could undoubtedly find common ground through re-living the sufferings of the past, while still pleading for clemency.

In different ways, the occasional conformity controversy, the Schism Bill, and the continuation of the Test and Corporation Acts all allowed Dissenters to perpetuate a narrative of suffering. The pressure these legislative issues put on Dissenters meant that at the same time as some praised the glorious effects of liberty of conscience, others continued to harness the rhetoric of suffering to advance their present agenda. This was most famously evident in Daniel Neal's *History of the Puritans*, in which he used the example of past suffering caused by intolerance to demonstrate the necessity of the repeal of the Test and Corporation Acts.[100] It was also a tactic consistently employed in other works, such as Defoe's 1711 *Essay on the History of Parties*, which tackled what he presented as the injustice of the intention in the Occasional Conformity Bill to prevent Dissenters from choosing to take communion occasionally in the Established Church. He emphasised the extent of Dissenters' suffering by stating that 'It would be too tedious a thing to undertake here, what all our Histories are full of,' before drawing a line between a persecutory past and the disputes of the present. For Defoe, the promise of toleration inherent in the 1689 Act had been 'reduc'd' by the enemies and oppressors of Dissent who wanted to act 'contrary to the Intent and Meaning of the whole Legislature at the time of its making' by excluding Dissenters 'from the common Privileges in Society with their Fellow-Subjects'.[101] Defoe acknowledged that 1689 had brought change; he alleged that Dissenters' suffering was being prolonged by those who refused to acknowledge the true meaning of this legislation.

This view that High Church interpretations of the legislation of 1689 were unreasonably perpetuating the sufferings of Dissenters can similarly be seen in a 1717 pamphlet which stated that Dissenters had 'not only been long deny'd their Liberty, but all the while, been bely'd by their Oppressors, as an unsettl'd, unreasonable sort of People that can never be pleas'd'. 'For those who honour the Revolution in 1688', the author argued, 'they cannot

---

[99] Daniel Defoe, *Wise as Serpents: Being an Enquiry Into the Present Circumstances of the Dissenters, and What Measures They Ought to Take in Order to Disappoint the Designs of Their Enemies* (London, 1712), pp. 16, 17, 44.

[100] Daniel Neal, *The History of the Puritans or Protestant Non-Conformists* (London, 4 vols. 1732), vol. I, p. viii. See Ingram, *Reformation Without End*, pp. 202–4; Black, *Charting the Past*, pp. 135–41.

[101] Daniel Defoe, *An Essay on the History of Parties, and Persecution in Britain* (London, 1711), pp. 7, 20, 34.

in Reason, but be for the utmost Liberty to Dissenters'.[102] Dissenters did express gratitude for the 1689 Act and marked it out as an end to suffering, but for these authors its promise had not been fully fulfilled. The rhetoric of suffering needed to be resurrected and adapted to the present.

Such a stance was not held consistently across different groups of Dissenters, and the denominational affiliation of Dissenters does appear to have been a significant factor in how they represented the suffering of their members. The organisational structure of Quakerism ensured that narratives of suffering remained at the forefront of the movement. Meetings for Sufferings, first established in 1675 to aid imprisoned Friends, continued after the Toleration Act, and the emphasis of these meetings was very clearly on Quaker suffering in the present and the inadequacy of the law in redressing their grievances. A letter from the London Yearly Meeting in 1749 complained that although an Act had been passed under William III to relieve Quakers from the obligation to swear oaths, 'we find by Experience, that divers of those Claimants (either ignorantly or vexatiously) do continue to prosecute Friends ... to their great Expence, and to the Imprisonment of some of them'. However, as much as they sought relief from this persecution, such trials were interpreted as an opportunity to demonstrate the faith of believers: the letter also declared 'We have however firm Faith (if Friends remain faithful) the Lord will in his Time work a Deliverance.'[103] Among Quakers an emphasis on suffering after the Toleration Act not only served to help them to make practical moves towards removing the remaining obstacles to practising their faith, but also allowed them to re-emphasise their status as a beleaguered minority faithful to the Lord.

This position was perhaps more necessary for Quakers, who still suffered regular violence and persecution on a local level as a result of their failure to pay tithes, than for Presbyterians, Independents, and Baptists. These groups did face prejudice, but they were not as widely ostracised as Quakers. Given that Dissenters were vulnerable to accusations of fanaticism, immoderation, and divisiveness, it was perhaps more in the interests of Presbyterians, Independents, and Baptists to protect the liberty they already had than to campaign for its extension. Indeed, such was

---

[102] Impartial Pen, *What the Dissenters Would Have. Or, the Case of the Dissenters Briefly yet Plainly Stated*, (London, 1717), pp. ii, 9.

[103] Society of Friends, London Yearly Meeting, *Advice to Friends Under Prosecution, Either in the Temporal or Ecclesiastical Courts, for Their Christian Testimony Against the Payment of Tithes* (London, 1749), pp. 1, 3.

the desire of the Baptist historian Thomas Crosby to avoid accusations of self-interest during campaigns against the Test Act that he criticised the movement, stating that he could not 'see, that the Dissenters or rather the English Dissenters, who desire only their liberty to worship God, according to their own consciences, have any reason to be discontented ... Is it not better to content ourselves (having our civil and religious liberties secured unto us) with the will and pleasure of the state'?[104] Crosby's stated aim was to show the long-standing loyalty of Baptists and their desire for peace.[105] He therefore viewed continued complaints about the suffering of Dissenters as unhelpful to the cause of his profession.

Baptists, Independents, and Presbyterians alike may have particularly felt the need to prioritise demonstrating loyalty and gratitude for their liberty over discussion of their suffering because they still faced charges that their disloyalty and tendency to rebellion was responsible for the outbreak of the Civil Wars of the previous century.[106] The Presbyterian lawyer and theologian John Shute Barrington showed awareness of the need to combat this problem in the dedication of his *Rights of Protestant Dissenters* to Queen Anne in 1704. 'Some former Reigns indeed have been jealous of the Dissenters, and thought 'em dangerous', he wrote, 'But your Majesty's Glorious Predecessor, who having nothing so much at heart as Liberty and the Protestant Religion, chang'd the private Maxims of the Court for the general Good and Inclinations of his People.' Indeed, he continued, 'the Dissenters are equally secure against such Trial of their suffering Vertues now, both by your Majesty's Penetration into the false Policys of former Reigns, your Knowledge of their ill Success, and your Royal Promise, that no such Methods shall be made use of in Yours'.[107] This was rhetoric that sought to use suffering in the past to emphasise Dissenters' gratitude and loyalty in the present, rather than complaining of suffering with the hope of an extension of their liberty in the wake of a limited toleration.

We should be wary of over-emphasising any denominational pattern in how Dissenters employed the rhetoric of suffering to serve their interests. Quakers did not always choose to highlight their continued suffering. The

---

[104] Thomas Crosby, *The History of the English Baptists, from the Reformation to the Beginning of the Reign of King George I* (London, 1738), vol. 4, pp. xxxii–xxxiii, xxxiv.

[105] Ibid., vol. 1, sig. A2v.

[106] Neufeld, *The Civil Wars After 1660*, pp. 2, 160, 249; Burke W. Griggs, 'Remembering the Puritan Past: John Walker and Anglican Memories of the English Civil War', in McClendon, Ward, and MacDonald (eds.), *Protestant Identities*, pp. 162, 170.

[107] John Shute Barrington, *The Rights of Protestant Dissenters. In Two Parts* (London, 1704–5), pp. viii–ix, x.

historian William Sewel, for instance, chose the start of the reign of Queen Anne as the temporal end point of his *History of the Rise, Increase, and Progress of the Christian People Called Quakers*, because 'in the Reign of King William III they [moderate supporters of the Established Church] promoted a general Liberty of Conscience, by which the People called Quakers at length obtained Liberty to perform their publick Worship without Molestation. Thus far the Limits of this History are extended'.[108] Conversely, as we have seen, Presbyterians sometimes deployed the rhetoric of suffering, particularly during times of political disruption, to reinforce a sense of the group identity of congregations and to reassure Dissenters that they had taken the right path against temptation.[109] Emphasis on Dissenters' continued sufferings in the present could be a useful reminder not to become complacent in their faith; a sense of embattlement could helpfully stoke zeal in a time of generally greater liberty.

The utility of the rhetoric of suffering for Dissenters was therefore ambiguous after the Toleration Act. On the one hand, some used the suffering of their forefathers under a persecutory Restoration regime as a means of reinforcing the idea that 1689 should represent liberation from oppression and a final unification of the Protestant interest. On the other hand, others (Quakers in particular) took a more pessimistic view that recognised the limitations of the 1689 Act and used narratives of the suffering of Dissenters to reinforce a much more exclusive identity that emphasised continuity with the past.

While the rhetoric of suffering was a powerful tool for eighteenth-century Dissenters, it was also dangerous. As long as opponents of Dissent maintained past stereotypes of Dissenters as seditious social misfits, it was risky for Dissenters to emphasise their difference. While recalling former and present sufferings was one of the principal ways in which Dissenters could foster a sense of unity, this had to be balanced against the hope that 1689 did represent a real break with the past, as well as the danger that an overemphasis on suffering could exacerbate the exclusion and separation of Dissenters from the rest of society. The difficult balance that Dissenters tried to achieve was one manifestation of the process by which contemporaries tried to negotiate the meanings of the changed dynamics of religious difference brought about by 1689.

---

[108] William Sewel, *The History of the Rise, Increase, and Progress of the Christian People Called Quakers, Intermixed with Several Remarkable Occurrences* (London, 1722), sig. B2r.
[109] William Tong, *A Funeral-Sermon on the Much Lamented Death of the Late Reverend Mr. John Shower, Preach'd at Old-Jury, July 10 1715* (London, 1716), p. 6.

Conclusion

In the complex aftermath of the 1689 Toleration Act, Dissenters were faced with a new set of political and social problems, while their opponents wrestled with alternative ways to challenge Dissent within the social framework of the eighteenth century. The changed legal position of Dissenters relative to Church and State brought them immense relief from violent persecution, but it also meant that they could no longer safely portray themselves as suffering outsiders. Instead, they had to show that they were important contributors to a shared Protestant interest, while still attempting to gain greater liberty under the law. This was set against the continuing suggestions of their opponents that Dissenters would, through their immoderate, seditious, and ungracious behaviour, unravel the very fabric of society from within.

This chapter has demonstrated the multiple discursive means by which controversy over religious difference evolved across the first half of the eighteenth century. It has also highlighted some of the ways in which religious difference was framed in social terms. The ambiguity of the 1689 Act ensured that the debate over the effects of religious difference on English society could not be put to rest. Instead, both Church and Dissent stoked controversy over occasional conformity, education, and the continuation of the Test and Corporation Acts. Crucially, the uncertainty of their position under the law put tight constraints on the ways in which Dissenters could argue for an extension of their liberty. As the occasional conformity controversy demonstrated, vigorous objection to the limitations of the Toleration Act risked accusations of fanaticism and enthusiasm, which opponents of Dissent linked to sedition and social abnormality. Furthermore, appealing to the historic and present suffering of Dissenters was no longer an unequivocally helpful argument for greater toleration. While it was a tactic that could serve to highlight the common interests of Dissenters and the injustices they faced, it also risked emphasising both Dissenters' differentiation from wider society and their association with the religious divisions of the previous century. This was something they particularly wanted to avoid, given that accusations of division were yet another route to the re-association of Dissent with popery. The legal ambiguity of 1689 thus created a long legacy of political negotiation and polemical discussion that represented challenges for Protestant Dissenters well into the eighteenth century.

With this in mind, it is impossible to ignore the degree to which, even as it in many ways eased the lives of Dissenters, the Toleration Act both perpetuated and reframed the problem of religious difference in English society. Adjustments in the relative positions of Church and Protestant Dissent after 1689 raised key social questions that would remain unresolved for much of the following century. What did it mean to have a shared Protestant cause? Could Dissenters use a compliant and integrative stance to fight accusations of seditious and divisive conduct, and avoid social ostracism, while still maintaining their distinctive identity? For those who genuinely saw Dissenters as a threat to society, were there practical measures beyond the legal framework that they could use to perpetuate the exclusion of Dissent? And how would the potential solutions to these problems be played out in varied local contexts? Far from being a matter of private conscience, religious affiliation continued to be a central issue for governance and everyday life. These were questions that forced contemporaries to consider where and whether religious differences could be accommodated within the social and cultural landscape of eighteenth-century England. In examining their answers, we may, as the following chapters show, be able to see that landscape in fuller colour.

CHAPTER 2

Public Religion

The year 1689 saw a radical shift in the legal status of Dissenting worship, creating a framework in which Dissenting meetings could be viewed as direct rivals to the Established Church. The Toleration Act's eye-catching promise of 'ease to scrupulous Consciences in the Exercise of Religion' represented a significant change in the state's management of religious difference.[1] Implicit in this was the first legislative acknowledgement that individual consciences could not be coerced, and that religious difference would be accommodated within the state, albeit to a limited extent. Liberty of conscience was not, however, considered an end in itself. Rather, it was, as the preamble to the Act stated, 'an effectuall meanes to unite their Majesties Protestant Subjects in Interest and Affection'.[2] This second phrase was at least as important as the first. By recognising Protestant Dissenters as part of England's Protestant interest, the Toleration Act gave them a potential share of public religious life. Along with the legalisation of meeting houses for Dissenters, and the recognition of Dissenting meetings as a form of public worship, it unintentionally created the opportunity for Dissenters to stake a claim in politics and society.

Such an emphasis on uniting Protestant subjects by easing their tender consciences significantly improved the situation of Dissenters. However, for those who saw 1689 as merely a temporary indulgence, this was highly concerning, and it was vital that the influence of Dissent over public religious life was kept to a minimum. The changed status of Dissent under the Act meant that Dissenting meetings could be viewed as direct rivals to the Established Church's role in the everyday life of the nation.

---

[1] 'William and Mary, 1688: An Act for Exempting their Majestyes Protestant Subjects Dissenting from the Church of England from the Penalties of Certaine Lawes. [Chapter XVIII. Rot. Parl. pt. 5. nu. 15.]', in John Raithby (ed.), *Statutes of the Realm* (n.p., 1819), vol. VI, pp. 74–6: *British History Online*, www.british-history.ac.uk/statutes-realm/vol6/pp74-76.
[2] Ibid.

The fact that Dissenters lost no time in building meeting houses, or in emphasising their essential contributions to English society, considerably aggravated opposition to them. This chapter explores the manifestations of this tension, arguing that at the same time as the Toleration Act provided significant legal protection that made the lives of Dissenters much easier, it also sparked a new and difficult process whereby differing parties jostled to secure their place in public religious life. The greater confidence of Dissenters in expressing their religion publicly, combined with the desire of Church interests to limit Dissenting influence, stimulated contests over religion on a local level.

This was evident in several ways. First, printed and local disputes over the extent to which the Toleration Act considered Dissenters to be contributors to the public religious communities of nation and parish underpinned many of the tensions between the Established Church and Dissent. These were further stimulated by the changing physical presence of Dissent – in the form of meeting houses – in public space; Established Church attitudes to these physical manifestations of Dissent emphasised the increased sense of religious competition facilitated by the Act. This friction is further apparent from court records of disputes over funerals and burials. The greater security that the Act gave to Dissenting ministers appears to have increased their confidence in asserting their influence over such occasions, to the great chagrin of their Established Church counterparts. Ultimately, disputes over the place of Dissent within the public religious landscape resulting from the settlement of 1689 acted to keep issues of religious difference alive in new ways, even as the embers of Restoration persecution burned out. As the concluding section of this chapter emphasises, considering the prominence of such dispute may help us to reconsider the place of the first half of the eighteenth century within longer narratives of the privatisation of belief.

Dissent and Public Life

The Toleration Act was initially understood by many to be a temporary measure. Failure to comprehend moderate nonconformists within the Established Church in 1689 had reflected the continuing belief among many members of the Church that association with or inclusion of Dissent would be highly damaging to Protestantism in England.[3] Ironically, the

---

[3] John Spurr, 'The Church of England, Comprehension and the Toleration Act of 1689', *English Historical Review*, 104, 413 (1989), pp. 942–4.

resulting alternative to comprehension – the 1689 Act – unwittingly gave Dissenters of all varieties a much more public role in the religious life of the nation than they would have received under a narrower comprehension. The terms of the Act reconfigured notions of public and private in relation to Church and State by acknowledging the status of Dissent within public life. The result was that disputes about toleration, previously centred around the validity of private conscience, now gave even greater emphasis to the struggle to define the meaning of public religion.

'Public religion' as it is used here refers in a general sense to the observable expressions of religion within communities, both national and local, and the associated authority to exercise power and organise others in the name of religion. As later sections of this chapter demonstrate, contemporary uses of this phrase show that there was disagreement over how to define the limits of this in the wake of clear changes to the public position of Dissent inherent within the legislation of 1689.

There were several important ways in which the terms of the 1689 legislation facilitated an increased public status for Protestant Dissent. First, by placing them under the umbrella of 'Protestant Subjects', the Act tacitly recognised the contribution that Protestant Dissenters could make to both parish and national interest.[4] It thus suggested that toleration was not primarily a matter of easing private consciences, but rather was for the benefit of the wider public Protestant cause in the fight against the spectre of popery.

More subtly, the Act also recognised the pastoral role of Protestant Dissenting ministers within the parish. It stipulated that Dissenting ministers would be exempt from jury service and parish office, thereby putting them on a par with ministers of the Church of England, whose office and responsibilities for the spiritual and pastoral care of parishioners already exempted them from such duties.[5] This gave Dissenting ministers a recognised public role, the significance of which did not escape them. In a letter by the Presbyterian minister Phillip Henry to his son discussing the Act, for instance, he noted that 'There are severeal things in it very acceptable, particularly Freedom from Juryes & Offices – &c.'[6] Henry evidently saw this recognition of the status of Dissenting ministers as important. In both

---

[4] 'William and Mary, 1688: An Act for Exempting their Majestyes Protestant Subjects Dissenting from the Church of England from the Penalties of Certaine Lawes'.

[5] Ibid.

[6] Phillip Henry to Matthew Henry, 1 June 1689, MS Eng. lett. e. 29/89, Bodleian Library (Bod.), Oxford.

its framing of the national interest, and its reference to the position of Dissenting ministers on a parish level, the 1689 Act contained an implicit recognition that the Established Church was not the only source of spiritual and pastoral support.

Furthermore, the conditions under which the law was to be applied gave Dissenting worship itself a recognised public status. This was apparent in the stipulation that 'if any Assembly of persons dissenting from the Church of England shall be had in any place for Religious Worship with the doores locked barred or bolted dureing any time of such Meeting', the penalties against Dissent would continue to apply.[7] This stipulation was a means of minimising the perceived risk that seditious Dissenters would plot from behind closed doors, but it also inadvertently changed the status of Dissent. Far from being confined to private practice, gathered Dissenting worship in England under the 1689 Act was only to be allowed if it was made public by keeping the doors unlocked. In addition, Dissenters' meetings had to be registered and certified by a bishop. While this was a restriction on freedom to worship, the successful registration of a meeting house was also, paradoxically, a public legitimisation of the validity of worship therein.

The idea that Dissenting meetings were a form of public worship was also positively reinforced by improvements in the status of Dissenting worship under the Act. This was especially apparent in the parity given to parish church services and Dissenting meetings in terms of qualifying for the requirement under the law for 'the frequenting of Divine Service on the Lords Day commonly called Sunday'.[8] Furthermore, disruptions to parish services and registered Dissenting meetings were, at least theoretically, treated with equal severity under the terms of the Act. Although it did not provide (or intend) a complete or permanent toleration, the 1689 Act changed the status of Dissenting meetings from hidden conventicles to venues for public worship on a legal footing approaching that of the Established Church.

The legislative changes of the Toleration Act had, perhaps unintentionally, opened up the opportunity for Dissenters to assert their role in public religious life. In the wake of the Act, Dissenters sought to show their loyalty and participation in the interests of the nation. Unsurprisingly, however, this was not a vision shared by those who sought to preserve the primacy of the Established Church. The result was that the very nature of 'public

---

[7] 'William and Mary, 1688: An Act for Exempting their Majestyes Protestant Subjects Dissenting from the Church of England from the Penalties of Certaine Lawes'.
[8] Ibid.

religion' lay at the heart of debates about the management, or suppression, of religious difference after the Toleration Act.

Contesting Authority over Public Religion

The acceptability of the changed public status of Dissent after the Toleration Act rested on how contemporaries defined 'public religion', and who they believed could legitimately exercise power and authority in the name of the religious interests of community and nation. This was a highly contested area of debate, the heat of which changed over the sixty years under discussion. The first decades of the eighteenth century were fraught with partisan rancour and cries for moderation that were seldom matched by action. While the idea that these years were followed by a sustained period of 'stability' has been substantially modified, it has long been acknowledged by historians of contemporary politics that the temperature of debate cooled from the 1720s onwards.[9] Nevertheless, the negotiation of the meaning and implications of the Toleration Act was an ongoing process, and contentious religious and political issues continued to be discussed. Building on earlier scholarship that stressed the continuing political importance of religious concerns in the 1730s and 1740s, Robert Ingram has recently underlined that questions connected with the Reformation were debated by the 'revolution-haunted' English into the second half of the eighteenth century.[10] The memory of the 1688–9 Revolution fed a sustained concern that although religious tensions were less prominent, there could easily be a collapse 'into a state of chaos and bloodshed', and this was reflected in the printed polemic of contemporary divines.[11]

---

[9] For challenges to the idea of political stability in this period see Linda Colley, *In Defiance of Oligarchy. The Tory Party 1714–1760* (Cambridge: Cambridge University Press, 1982); Kathleen Wilson, *The Sense of the People: Politics, Culture and Imperialism in England, 1715–1785* (Cambridge: Cambridge University Press, 1995), pp. 84–122; Gabriel Glickman, 'Political Conflict and the Memory of the Revolution in England, 1689-c.1750', in Tim Harris and Stephen Taylor (eds.), *The Final Crisis of the Stuart Monarchy* (Woodbridge: The Boydell Press, 2013), pp. 243–5. For explorations of stability in this period see Geoffrey Holmes, *Politics, Religion and Society in England, 1679–1742* (London and Ronceverte: The Hambledon Press, 1986), pp. 182, 211–2; Richard Connors, 'The Nature of Stability in the Augustan Age', *Parliamentary History*, 28, 1 (2009), pp. 32–3, 35–6.

[10] Stephen Taylor, 'Sir Robert Walpole, The Church of England, and the Quakers Tithe Bill of 1736', *Historical Journal*, 28, 1 (1985), p. 52; Robert G. Ingram, *Reformation Without End. Religion, Politics and the Past in Post-Revolutionary England* (Manchester: Manchester University Press, 2018), pp. xii, 10.

[11] Ibid., p. 16. See also Robert G. Ingram, 'The Church of England, 1714–1783', in Jeremy Gregory (ed.), *The Oxford History of Anglicanism, Volume II* (Oxford and New York: Oxford University Press, 2017), pp. 50–67.

Taken in its broadest sense, the term 'public religion' could be used to indicate any religion that was protected by civil authority, and not just the established religion of the state.[12] Early Quaker leaders such as William Penn had supported this definition in the 1670s when arguing not for a completely unrestrained conscience, but rather for a broadly Christian civil society.[13] Penn saw toleration as important not just for individual salvation, but also for the collective good of society because, as he put it, 'by seeking an Unity of Opinion [through persecution] ... the Unity requisit to uphold us, as a *Civil Society*, will be quite destroy'd'.[14] His solution to the problem of public religion within a religiously pluralistic society was to create a civil religion with Christianity at its root, in which the government enforced particular virtuous behaviour, thereby guaranteeing the morality and safety of society while allowing individual conscience and limited religious plurality to flourish. Although coming from a very different standpoint, similar ideas were seen in the work of John Locke. In his *Letter Concerning Toleration*, he emphasised that public worship of God, while it should not be in a prescribed form, was a precondition of toleration and essential for the function of civil society.[15] Writing that 'All men know and acknowledge that God ought to be publickly worshipped ... and perform such other things in Religion as cannot be done by each private Man apart,' Locke stipulated that the magistrate should treat such religious assemblies as the same whether part of the Established Church or not.[16] In this view 'public religion' was not defined by a particular denomination, but rather entailed any form of collective worship of God that benefitted society as a whole.

It was within this framework that Dissenters argued that they were important contributors to the public religious life of the nation. The Baptist minister Daniel Turner argued for the crucial social importance of religion as the basis for stability and order in government and society. Writing that

---

[12] *An Inquiry Into the Miracle Said to Have Been Wrought in the Fifth Century Upon Some Orthodox Christians* (London, 1730), p. 7; *Of the Relation Between Church and State: Or, How far Christian and Civil Life Affect Each Other; Being a Translation of a Book of Baron Puffendorf's, Upon this Important Subject* (London, 1719), p. 155.

[13] Sally Schwartz, 'William Penn and Toleration: Foundations of Colonial Pennsylvania', *Pennsylvania History*, 50, 4 (1983), p. 288–9.

[14] William Penn, *The Great Case of Liberty of Conscience Once More Briefly Debated & Defended ... Which May Serve the Place of a General Reply to such Late Discourses as Have Oppos'd a Tolleration* (n.p., 1670), pp. 29–31, emphasis original.

[15] John Locke, 'A Letter Concerning Toleration [2nd edn, London, 1690]', in Mark Goldie (ed.), *John Locke: A Letter Concerning Toleration and Other Writings* (Indianapolis, IN: Liberty Fund, 2010), p. 32; Elissa B. Alzale, 'From Individual to Citizen: Enhancing the Bonds of Citizenship Through Religion in Locke's Political Theory', *Polity*, 46, 2 (2014), pp. 226–7, 230.

[16] Locke, 'A Letter Concerning Toleration', p. 32.

careful individual choice of Church was compatible with broader Christian unity, he suggested that 'Instead of violently compelling one another to uniformity in lesser matters', society could 'learn to differ in opinions, without dividing in affection'.[17] On the basis of this inclusive public religion, his argument suggested, the Protestant nation would thrive.

Turner's vision of a broad religion, published in 1758, had its basis in half a century of Dissenting arguments about public religion that had sought to stake out a place for Dissent in the wake of the changes of 1689. Dissenting authors had repeatedly suggested that immoderate attitudes towards Dissent risked undermining the entire Protestant cause.[18] This was a stance particularly evident in the arguments of the Independent ministers Philip Doddridge and Isaac Watts.[19] Doddridge identified himself with a Dissent that was active in the interests of the nation, and condemned divisions that prevented it.[20] In a sermon preached on a royally appointed day of public humiliation in aid of the war against Spain in January 1740, he included a prayer 'for those, that preside in Religious Assemblies of all Denominations … May their Hearts and Hands be united in that good Work which is committed to them! May God deliver them from the Shame and Folly of employing the Solemn Seasons of Publick Worship, in reproaching their Brethren, and animating the Hearts of professing Christians against each other!'[21] In the same sermon he prayed for the Spanish enemy, that 'their Eyes might be opened to see the Delusions of Popery'.[22] In calling for shared prayer against the popish enemy, Doddridge could hardly have argued more clearly for the importance of uniting 'their Majesties Protestant Subjects in Interest and Affection', as spelled out in the 1689 Act.[23]

---

[17] Daniel Turner, *A Compendium of Social Religion, or the Nature and Constitution of Christian Churches* (London, 1758), p. xviii.

[18] See for example Isaac Gilling, *A Sermon Preach'd at Lyme Regis in the County of Dorset, at a Quarterly Lecture, Appointed for the Promoting the Reformation of Manners* (Exeter, 1705), p. 23.

[19] Isabel Rivers, *Reason, Grace, and Sentiment. A Study of the Language of Religion and Ethics in England, 1660–1780* (Cambridge: Cambridge University Press, 1991), vol. 1, p. 172; J. F. Maclear, 'Isaac Watts and the Idea of Public Religion', *Journal of the History of Ideas*, 53, 1 (1992), pp. 34–5. Maclear uses the term 'public religion' in the specific sense of a particular concept of official religion designed to provide a basic level of religious consensus (p. 25).

[20] Robert Strivens, *Philip Doddridge and the Shaping of Evangelical Dissent* (Farnham: Ashgate, 2015), p. 149.

[21] Philip Doddridge, *The Necessity of a General Reformation in Order to a Well-Grounded Hope of Success in War: Represented in a Sermon Preached at Northampton, January 9 1739–40* (London, 1740), pp. 33–4.

[22] Ibid., p. 37.

[23] 'William and Mary, 1688: An Act for Exempting their Majestyes Protestant Subjects Dissenting from the Church of England from the Penalties of Certaine Lawes'.

These arguments were possible only because of wider shifts in attitudes to liberty of conscience. Restoration theories about the duty of the state to control the religious beliefs and practices of their subjects had rested heavily on the principle of St Augustine that 'it is better to love with severity than to deceive with indulgence'.[24] Most seventeenth-century Protestants saw religious coercion as a necessary and indeed virtuous middle way between 'licentious tolerance of sin and cruel intolerance of human imperfection'.[25] However, by the beginning of the eighteenth century the view that the use of religious coercion had been responsible for the excesses and disruption of the seventeenth century had become more current.[26] Liberty of conscience could now be seen as the moderate position for a state to take, and this principle was reflected in the mention of 'scrupulous Consciences' in the 1689 Act.[27] It was in this context that Dissenters could argue for an inclusive public religion.

However, as defenders of the Established Church were particularly keen to emphasise, this did not mean that temporal law could be abandoned in the name of obedience to godly authority. Even the staunchest Dissenting advocates of liberty of conscience recognised that within a society men could be kept free to submit to the will of God in religious matters only if there was a social framework within which they operated.[28] 'Liberty' in the eighteenth century did not have the secular connotations that it does today. Although John Locke wrote in the preface to his *Letter Concerning Toleration* that 'Absolute Liberty, Just and True Liberty, Equal and Impartial Liberty, is the thing we stand in need of,' this was a liberty that had to be sustained in the name of Christianity and obedience to God's authority.[29] Only through this could civil society function. This type of liberty, as supporters of a broad-based toleration argued, aided a peaceful and lawful society, which was obstructed 'when Men usurp a Power over other People's Consciences, and deny them the Liberty of judging for themselves *in Matters of Religion*'.[30]

[24] Mark Goldie, 'The Theory of Religious Intolerance in Restoration England', in Ole Peter Grell, Jonathan Israel, and Nicholas Tyacke (eds.), *From Persecution to Toleration: The Glorious Revolution and Religion in England* (Oxford: Clarendon Press, 1991), p. 337.

[25] Ethan H. Shagan, *The Rule of Moderation: Violence, Religion, and the Politics of Restraint in Early Modern England* (Cambridge: Cambridge University Press, 2011), p. 297.

[26] Ibid., p. 329.

[27] 'William and Mary, 1688: An Act for Exempting their Majestyes Protestant Subjects Dissenting from the Church of England from the Penalties of Certaine Lawes'.

[28] Alzale, 'From Individual to Citizen', pp. 229–30; John Dunn, 'The Claim to Freedom of Conscience: Freedom of Speech, Freedom of Thought, Freedom of Worship?', in Grell, Israel, and Tyacke (eds.), *From Persecution to Toleration*, p. 186.

[29] Locke, 'A Letter Concerning Toleration', p. 4; Goldie, 'Introduction' in Goldie (ed.), *John Locke*, p. xi.

[30] Nathaniel Ball, *Sermons on Several Important Subjects* (London, 1745), p. 6, emphasis original.

Those who expressed concern that liberty of conscience threatened the security of society reminded their opponents that 'Men incorporated in Civil Societies, have by their own Consent, bounded their Liberty in relation to the Publick, and their Neighbours, and are no longer free to act, but as the Law of the Land in such Cases shall direct.'[31] Eighteenth-century debates about religious liberty were thus concerned not with how to allow individuals to be autonomous, but with what civil restraints best enabled them to be free to submit to godly authority without interfering with the state.

Unsurprisingly, therefore, defenders of the Established Church sought to discredit the broader definitions of public religion put forward by Dissenting groups. The sense that the Established Church was threatened by the status of Dissenting meetings as forms of public worship was particularly prominent during the heated controversies of the 1700s and 1710s, but opponents of Dissent reiterated arguments against the Toleration Act at moments of political tension across the first half of the century. This was particularly the case during the 1730s, when increasing parliamentary anti-clericalism was accompanied by Dissenting campaigns for the repeal of the Test and Corporation Acts.[32] One important argument presented by those who opposed such measures was that allowing public office to Dissenters would undermine stable government because Dissenters would inevitably seek to promote their own interests. One author, writing in 1735, interpreted toleration as the dangerous creation of a religious marketplace, arguing that 'The distributing publick Encouragements to Preachers of all Sorts, would no more promote Truth and sound Doctrine, than the Opening of a Mart, where all Commodities, both good and bad, should be sold at the same Price, would promote Honesty and Fair Dealing.'[33] Public toleration of a variety of sources of religious authority would not, in this author's view, promote piety and public good through a broad Protestant interest. Instead, it would create a competitive religious marketplace in which parties would unfairly and divisively jostle with one another. Where most Dissenters argued that toleration could bring a charitable Protestant unity and improved morality, their opponents saw only division.[34]

---

[31] *Civil Security, Not Conscience, Concern'd in the Bill Concerning Occasional Conformity* (London, 1702), p. 3.

[32] Ingram, *Reformation Without End*, pp. 85, 203.

[33] *The Argument with Dissenters About Subscriptions, and the Repeal of the Corporation and Test Acts, Briefly Stated* (London, 1735), p. 19.

[34] See also Francis Hare, *A Sermon Preached Before the House of Lords, in the Abbey-Church at Westminster, Upon Monday, January 31 1731* (London, 1732), pp. 8, 18.

For them, the civil restraints that best allowed individuals to submit to godly authority were those which bound the Established Church as closely as possible to the state and public office.

The threat that Dissent posed to the solidity of public religion further played out in partisan politics. Dissenters were, contemporaries supposed, a distinct electoral interest, seen as an important force in politics throughout the eighteenth century.[35] The natural coalescence of Dissent around Whig principles gave credence to the arguments of their opponents that Dissenters were acting from partisan self-interest rather than with the intent of aiding the welfare of the nation as a whole. The idea that Dissenters would use any additional freedoms to act merely in their own party's interests was consistently reinforced across the period with reference to the disruption and destruction of the mid-seventeenth century, the blame for which supporters of the Church interest laid squarely at the feet of Dissenters. Complaining against his alleged ill-treatment by Dissenters in 1707, the Exeter High Churchman John Agate asked what would happen if 'the Dissenting Mob of this City, [were] the Mob of the Nation', concluding that 'if we may be allow'd to make a Judgement from their late Actions, and their Manner of treating me … the Dissenters in 1707, would do the self-same Thing as their Forefathers actually did in 1641'.[36] Attempts by Dissenters and their supporters to shift the narrative away from a focus on the events of the Civil Wars were not entirely successful: in the 1740s sermons preached on the anniversary of the execution of Charles I still blamed Dissenters for sedition and rebellion.[37]

Disputes over religious differences in the first half of the eighteenth century were not generally centred on disagreement about the role of individual conscience, but on the nature of authority over public religion. Moments of political crisis, partisan conflict, and the still-resonant legacy of civil war allowed opponents of Dissent to suggest that a narrow definition of public religion confined to the Established Church was vital to the integrity of the political nation. The Toleration Act substantially improved

---

[35] James E. Bradley, 'Nonconformity and the Electorate in Eighteenth-Century England', *Parliamentary History*, 6, 2 (1987), pp. 237.

[36] John Agate, *A Reply to a Pamphlet, Intituled: A True and Impartial Account of What Occurr'd at the Late Conference in Exon* (Exeter, 1707), p. 80. A similar argument can be seen in Mary Astell, *Moderation Truly Stated: Or, a Review of a Late Pamphlet, Entitul'd, Moderation a Vertue* (London, 1704), p. 88.

[37] George Coade, *A Letter to a Clergyman, Relating to His Sermon on the 30th of January: Being a Compleat Answer to All the Sermons that Have Ever Been, or Ever Shall Be, Preached, in the Like Strain, on That Anniversary* (London, 1746), pp. 75–6.

the position of Dissenters by allowing them to practise their religion in public. However, the increased public position of Dissent was more of an unintended consequence than an intention of the Act, and this was reflected by the fact that Dissenters had to fight for their place in public religious life. Both toleration and resistance to it in this period can be understood in terms of a process by which contemporaries struggled to redefine the meaning of public religion. This was a subject for conflict that spilled out beyond high political discussion, with important implications for the management of religious difference on a local level.

Contesting Public Religion in the Parish

Nowhere was better ground to test and negotiate the inclusivity of public religion than the parish. Political participation through office-holding, as well as governance of local charitable foundations such as schools and almshouses, was an affirmation of citizenship and status; it was also a claim to represent the best interests of other parishioners.[38] Furthermore, the governance of a parish – both civil and ecclesiastical – was carried out largely through its vestry, with the result that local administration was inextricably associated with the building and institution of the Established Church. However, while the Test Act made it clear that Dissenters could not qualify for public office without taking communion, there was no such disqualification from the lower offices of the parish. Dissenters therefore had every right to participate, but this participation was not necessarily uncontested. As the following examples show, the potential inclusivity of parish governance could be a cause of religious tension, and the powers of parish administration could be used as a means to challenge the local status of Dissent. Religious difference, in these instances, was at the heart of the politics of the parish; parish politics provided a testing ground for the religious limits of inclusion in public life.

It should be noted that religiously inflected tension over parish governance was not necessarily the norm in all parishes; the examples of dispute given here are not intended to be a generalisation. Prior to 1689, members of the Established Church who held office differed considerably in the degree to which they were willing to report cases of Dissent, with the

---

[38] Mark Goldie, 'The Unacknowledged Republic: Officeholding in Early Modern England', in Tim Harris (ed.) *The Politics of the Excluded* (Basingstoke: Palgrave Macmillan, 2001), pp. 164, 168; Henry French, *The Middle Sort of People in Provincial England, 1600–1750* (Oxford and New York: Oxford University Press, 2007), pp. 126–7.

result that in some parishes there was a tacit toleration even before this date.[39] Furthermore, in many locations before and after the Toleration Act Dissenters held parish office, both with and without their position and authority being challenged.[40] Local politics and religious dynamics often shaped the degree to which Dissenters were considered acceptable by, and as, parish officers, and cases of conflict therefore have to be read as characteristic of a particular locality. What the examples given here do indicate, however, is the considerable capacity for tensions over the meaning of public religion to be played out through varied interpretation of the Toleration Act at a parish level. The implementation and determination of the meaning of national governance was highly dependent on the co-operation and competence of parish administration; as Mark Goldie has argued, central control 'was compromised and mediated by what was felt to be tolerable in local communities'.[41] There was thus significant latitude for local administrators to use the organs of parish governance to signal the inclusion or exclusion of Dissent, and this sent out strong messages about the degree to which Dissenters could be considered as contributors to the public religious – and civil – life of the parish.

In theory, the Toleration Act widened participation in parish governance for some Dissenters. Not only did it make it unequivocally clear that Dissenting office-holding was accepted, but it laid out the means by which it could be accessible to all. A key stipulation was that any Dissenter 'chosen or otherwise appointed to beare the Office of High Constable or Petty Constable Churchwarden Overseer of the Poore or any other Parochiall or Ward Office' who felt unable to take the necessary oaths could appoint a Deputy in their stead.[42] Deputising may have been a practice used by Dissenters in some locations before 1689, but this stipulation meant that those Dissenters – such as Quakers – who particularly objected to oaths and were still unable to take up office themselves, were now explicitly able to assert their influence through the choice of a Deputy.[43] In theory,

[39] Eric Carlson, 'The Origins, Function, and Status of the Office of Churchwarden, with Particular Reference to the Diocese of Ely', in Margaret Spufford (ed.), *The World of Rural Dissenters, 1520–1725* (Cambridge: Cambridge University Press, 1995), pp. 178–80.

[40] Adrian Davies, *The Quakers in English Society, c. 1660–1725* (Oxford: Oxford University Press, 2000), pp. 204–5; Mark Goldie and John Spurr, 'Politics and the Restoration Parish: Edward Fowler and the Struggle for St Giles Cripplegate', *English Historical Review*, 109, 432 (1994), p. 582.

[41] Goldie, 'The Unacknowledged Republic', p. 166.

[42] 'William and Mary, 1688: An Act for Exempting their Majestyes Protestant Subjects dissenting from the Church of England from the Penalties of certaine Lawes'.

[43] Many thanks to Jonah Miller for discussion on this issue.

therefore, Dissenters were recognised as equal citizens within the commonwealth of the parish.

However, this was evidently not something that all those who wielded local power were willing to accept. The capacity for flexible interpretation of the law at local level was made particularly apparent in one case concerning a potential Quaker churchwarden in Hertford in 1738. Usually, if an individual was reluctant to do their duty in public office, they would be compelled to do so anyway – office-holding was 'coextensive with being a citizen'.[44] However, in this instance John Andrew, Commissary and Official of the Archdeaconry of Huntingdon, thought it best that the Quaker was not made to take on the role. Writing to Benjamin Woodward, Registrar, he made it clear that he wished to limit Dissenting involvement in parish administration. He acknowledged that there was 'no Doubt but your Quaker may be compell'd to serve by Deputy according to the act of Toleration', but thought it 'very Improper for the members of the Church to put their Care of their Church & of its Service under those who Dissent from It, & without Distinguishing between the Quaker & any other Dissenter I doun't think my self In Justice oblidged … to Confirm Such Choice & Compel this person to Serve'.[45] Dissenters were not, in Andrew's opinion, fit to serve in the public life of the parish, or to have a say over who did so in their place, even if the Toleration Act allowed it. In spite of the terms of the Toleration Act, Andrew was framing the office of churchwarden as a public duty inseparable from loyalty to the Church. In suggesting that Dissenters were unsuitable for office, he was questioning their participation and citizenship within the parish.

The religious temperature of parish administration was not just determined by who was included in and excluded from parish office; it was also shaped by who was considered constitutive of parish opinion. In the vestry minute books of Yardley, Hertfordshire, in 1719 Dissenters were literally marginalised in the lists of the inhabitants. One list, showing the residences of twenty-seven families, was ruled off with a note underneath reading 'Peter Parker & family. Quakers. all the Rest coms to Church'.[46] A further list gave details of twenty-one families, before noting separately at the bottom 'Wid. Raisin a Quaker. / Jno Rayment a Dissenter of He

[44] Goldie, 'The Unacknowledged Republic', p. 170.
[45] John Andrew to Benjamin Woodward, 22 April 1738, AH/38/9/275/26, Huntingdonshire Archives, Huntingdon.
[46] Yardley (Ardley) Vestry minutes, October 1719, p. 109, DP/6/8/1, Hertfordshire Archives, Hertford.

knows not what sort / Jno Oliver & W. Quakers but very good natured
people / all the Rest com to Church'.[47] While the latter example acknowledged the good humour of Quakers John Oliver and his wife, the fact that
no Dissenters were included in the main list of inhabitants suggests that
their place in the parish was considered to be distinct from others'. The
sense that Dissenters were somehow different from other inhabitants was
also apparent following a parish election in St Botolph without Aldgate
in 1713, in which complaints were raised about the validity of Dissenters'
votes. The testimony of one witness suggested there was a strongly political rather than religious motivation to the complaints, pointing out that
if the complainant '"had happned to have had more votes or pollers for
him or on his side who were Dissenters from the Church of England then
the Ministrant had hee would not then have made objections ag[ains]t
Dissenters as haveing no right'".[48] Nevertheless, the fact that it was even
conceivable to raise Dissent as a possible (if not entirely plausible) reason
for disqualification from participation in the parish election suggests that
issues of religious difference still resonated through parish politics.

The potential for Dissenters to be considered on the borders of the public community of the parish is further suggested by the claims about the
exclusivity of parish opinion made by those in positions of power. An
example of this can be seen in the attempts of staunch supporters of the
Established Church in West Newton, Somerset, to wrest back control of
the local Charity School. In 1737 William Moore, local gentleman and
patron of the rectory of nearby Lyng, wrote to the future MP and High
Churchman Thomas Carew in an attempt to replace the Presbyterian
teacher at the Charity School with his favoured Church candidate.[49] He
noted that the current school mistress was 'a strict Presbyterian' who
'therefore might Intimate such notions into Youth as might do great prejudice', a situation which he blamed on 'the neglect of the successors of
the Trustees' of the charity. His basis for challenging her position was that

---

[47] Ibid., p. 112.

[48] Jonah Miller, 'Officeholding, Patriarchy and the State in England, 1660–1750' (Unpublished PhD
thesis, King's College London, 2020), p. 58.

[49] On William Moore see A. P. Baggs and M. C. Siraut, 'Lyng: Manor and Other Estates', in R. W.
Dunning and C. R. Elrington (eds.), *A History of the County of Somerset: Volume 6, Andersfield,
Cannington, and North Petherton Hundreds (Bridgwater and Neighbouring Parishes)* (London, 1992),
pp. 56–58, via *British History Online*, www.british-history.ac.uk/vch/som/vol6/pp56-58, accessed
18 December 2020. On Thomas Carew see Shirley Williams, 'CAREW, Thomas (1702–66), of
Crowcombe, nr. Minehead, Som.', in R Sedgwick (ed.), *The History of Parliament: The House of
Commons 1715–1754* (1970), via *History of Parliament Online*, www.historyofparliamentonline.org/vol-
ume/1715-1754/member/carew-thomas-1702-66, accessed 18 December 2020.

'The Parish in general and the Heirs and successors of the Trustees' were 'very desireous to appoint Hum: Culliford Schoolmaster'.[50]

In claiming to speak for parish opinion in general, Moore was implicitly suggesting that that the parish was a unit against Dissenting influence in the life of the community, thereby tacitly excluding local Dissenters. However, while he appears to have been successful in placing Humphry Culliford as schoolmaster, Dissenting influence was perhaps less easy to dismiss than he had thought: in September 1746 he was once again writing to Carew to discuss a suit against Culliford undertaken by the Derham family, who 'are Dissenters and supported at the expence of several of that perswasion'.[51] For those who saw community life as something that should be exclusively in the hands of those loyal to the Established Church, parish politics was a potential means of solidifying their interests. But it was not infallible; Dissenters were now unequivocally protected by the law, and were as able as anyone else to seek redress in the courts. In this instance, the local Established Church interest wanted to assert the essential religious exclusivity of parish life, but local Dissenters were also determined to secure their influence. More than fifty years after the Toleration Act had facilitated what some feared was a rival status for Dissenters in opposition to the Church, the role of religious affiliation in determining power and responsibility in this parish had still not been fully worked out.

West Newton was not alone in its tensions over control of local schooling. The Lancashire Presbyterian Richard Kay grumbled in his diary on 26 November 1747 that 'some of our High Church Men' had met at the school in Baldingstone 'and this not the first Meeting neither, in order to wrest the Power of the School out of the Hands of the Presbyterians'. He reported that they objected that the 'Schoolmaster does not go constantly to the Church, and that Children shou'd be educated in the Principles of the Church of England, tho' they cannot produce one Instance wherein we believe or act repugnant to the Principles of it.'[52] The control of an important parish institution such as a school was evidently a concern that related to determining the religious future of the parish. But, as Kay's phrase 'wrest the Power of the School' suggests, the ability to control the

---

[50] William Moore, at Bridgewater, to Thomas Carew Esq, 28 November 1737, DD\TB/24/11, Somerset Heritage Centre (SHC), Taunton.

[51] William Moore, at Bridgewater, to Thomas Carew Esq, 19 September 1746, DD\TB/24/11, SHC.

[52] W. Brockbank and F. Kenworthy (eds.), *The Diary of Richard Kay, 1716–51, of Baldingstone, Near Bury. A Lancashire Doctor* (Manchester: Manchester University Press for The Chetham Society, 1968), p. 124.

local school was also more broadly a question of who should have public influence in the parish, and in Baldingstone views about this were very clearly divided along religious lines.

The place of Dissenters within the public life of their community was also challenged through disputes about the distribution of parish relief. Social historians have noted the crucial importance of poor law administration in this period to the identity of parish communities and individuals within them. Steve Hindle has suggested that it was often parish officers that determined who 'belonged' within the community, and that analysing parish relief is crucial for identifying 'the processes of inclusion and exclusion through which local communities were constructed, sustained, and ultimately absorbed into a national political culture'.[53] Given this, it is perhaps unsurprising that poor law prosecutions were a further way in which some parish officers tried to illustrate the inferior place of Dissent within their communities.

In 1725, for example, a congregation of Dissenters in the parish of St Thomas, Southwark, appealed to the Justices of the Peace against a poor rate being assessed on their meeting house. The petitioners, James and Aaron Atkins, were 'greatly aggreived' at the building having been assessed at 'four pounds per Annum tho the said meeting house stands Empty at all other times and is not Inhabited or Occupied by any person or persons whensoever or made use off for any Purpose whatsoever save for the Performance of divine Service', and declared the charge 'Unjust and contrary to Law'.[54] Their petition was successful, but the levelling of the charge in first instance appears more than a clerical error, especially because notice had been given of the intention of the congregation to appeal against the poor rate, giving the assessors plenty of opportunity to drop the charge.[55] The attempt to make the meeting house chargeable was a tacit slight against the Meeting as a form of public worship. The treatment of the meeting house as if it were merely a residential building and not a place of worship appears as a diminishment of the status of Dissent in the public religious life of that community. No one would have thought to levy poor rates against the parish church.

---

[53] Steve Hindle, *On the Parish? The Micro-Politics of Poor Relief in Rural England, c. 1550–1750* (Oxford: Oxford University Press, 2004), pp. 7, 352.

[54] Petition of James Adams and Aaron Atkins, members of the congregation of Dissenting Protestants, Against the Poor Rate Assessed on Their Meeting House, 1725, QS2/6/1725/Mic/32, Surrey History Centre (SuHC), Woking.

[55] Notice by Nathaniel Sheffield, on Behalf of the Ministers and Congregation of Dissenters, of His Intention to Appear at the Next Sessions to Appeal Against a Roor Rate Assessment, 1725, QS2/6/1725/Mic/42, SuHC.

Cases brought against individual Dissenters also illustrate that the poor law was used as a tacit suggestion that the contribution that Dissent made to public life was inferior. The Derbyshire Presbyterian Minister James Clegg, for instance, was in 1735 given charge of a pauper child by the parish officer. Clegg believed his status as minister – regardless of his Dissent – excused him from taking care of the child, and he took it as 'a token of their [the officers'] enmity'.[56] This was an enmity possibly stoked by the attempt of fellow Dissenter 'Mr Tricket' to prosecute the parish curate for immorality; Clegg wrote in his diary in April 1734 that he wished Tricket 'had not begun it, it creates much ill will'.[57] For Clegg, the attempt to make him take on a pauper child sent the clear signal that the position of a Dissenting minister in the public religious life of the parish was inferior to that of the Established Church clergy.

In different ways, the actions taken in the cases above suggested that Dissenters were peripheral – or even dangerous – to the public life of the parish. They highlight the degree to which, after the 1689 Act, some local communities continued to play out religious tensions through the organs of local political power. It is notable that in none of these cases were the attempts of Established Church interests to diminish Dissenters' place within the community entirely successful. In the case of the Hertford Quaker, he did not in fact wish to become a churchwarden, so his deliberate exclusion can hardly be regarded as much of an inconvenience. In West Newton, although the Presbyterian schoolmistress was replaced with an Established Church schoolmaster, local Dissenters were able to challenge his position by bringing suits over land usage. The meeting house in Southwark was relieved of its liability for the poor rate, and, after an appeal to the Justices, James Clegg did not in the end have to take on a parish pauper.[58]

The position of Dissenters within their communities had therefore vastly improved from the period before the Toleration Act. Prior to 1689, if those in positions of power in the parish felt threatened by local Dissenters, they had recourse to a significant suite of laws through which Dissenters might be persecuted. After 1689, unless local Dissenters actually broke the terms of the Toleration Act, there were few clear-cut ways of excluding Dissenters from parish interests, and this is perhaps reflected in the poor

[56] Vanessa S. Doe (ed.), *The Diary of James Clegg of Chapel en le Frith, 1708–1755, Part I* (Derby: Derbyshire Record Society, 1978), p. 217.

[57] Ibid., p. 193.

[58] Doe (ed.), *The Diary of James Clegg of Chapel en le Frith, 1708–1755, Part I*, pp. 230, 231.

success rate of those who attempted to do so. However, while Dissenters were evidently in a stronger legal position, they were not immune from tacit or explicit attempts at exclusion on a local level. The importance of these cases lies therefore not so much in whether or not they succeeded, but in the fact that, decades after the Toleration Act, they were still happening. The parish was an arena in which the religious and the civic were, through the very structure of parish administration, inextricably associated. The Toleration Act raised fundamental questions about public religion; differences in opinion about who should be included within the public religious life of the nation were played out not just through pamphlet debates and clerical utterings, but also through the organisation and implementation of parish administration.

Contesting Public Religious Space

Unresolved tensions surrounding the public influence of Dissent on a local level were also reflected in differing views about the appropriate location for the physical expressions of religion. This was particularly evident in disputes over the registration, building, and public use of spaces for Dissenting worship. The requirement under the Toleration Act that Dissenters' meeting houses be registered essentially placed Dissent under the control of the bishop. While this was a restriction on Dissenters' religious freedom, successful registration nevertheless legitimated the registered space as an area for public worship. It is unsurprising, therefore, that meeting houses were spaces around which tension over the public influence of Dissent could build. This was demonstrated both in accounts of hostility towards and attacks upon Dissenting meeting houses, and in the caution that some Dissenters showed over where and when they erected their places for worship. Incidents surrounding meeting houses demonstrate the practical difficulties that Dissenters faced in a period when those hostile to Dissent sought to limit what they saw as damaging changes caused by the Toleration Act.

In the years following the Act, Dissenters did have considerable success in establishing new meeting houses. From 1689 to 1700 Presbyterians, Congregationalists, and Baptists registered 2,418 buildings for worship, many of them newly built, and Quakers also erected many meeting houses in this period.[59] Meeting houses continued to be built after this date, and

[59] Martin S. Briggs, *Puritan Architecture and Its Future* (London and Redhill: Lutterworth Press, 1946), p. 22.

Dissenters were able to establish meetings in increasingly public spaces throughout the eighteenth century. If meeting houses were seen by contemporaries as a threat to the established structures of authority, then their location and number were dependent on how confident Dissenters felt about their positions within local and national society.

Current scholars have emphasised, as did nineteenth-century antiquaries, that in the years immediately after the Toleration Act, Dissenters continued to be cautious about where they located their meeting houses, and how ostentatiously they built them. The nineteenth-century antiquary Edward Gray commented that in the early days of Dissent fear of attack 'induced them to withdraw their places of meeting, as much as possible, from public observation, and to seek for safety, in comparatively obscure and unobtrusive situations'.[60] The construction of new meeting houses more visible to passers-by has equally been seen as representing the confidence of contemporary Dissent in a particular location. Even as early as 1714 the Quaker diarist Edward Belson was donating money for a Quaker meeting house to be constructed 'near Church Lane in Reading', presumably close to the parish church.[61] The ability of Dissenters to build such structures has been interpreted as indicative of their strength of interest. The antiquary John Dunkin, for instance, wrote of the meeting house built in Bicester after 1739 that 'At the erection of the meeting-house the dissenters in this town were numerous and opulent; and this structure is a lasting monument of their zeal and liberality.'[62]

Cartographic evidence also suggests that Dissenters were better able to build meeting houses in prominent locations as the century went on. In Birmingham, for instance, the Presbyterian congregation took advantage of the expansion of the city to build a new meeting house in 1730 'fronting to Moor Street, from whence it is seen to advantage'.[63] The location of the new meeting house was considerably more prominent that the old one.[64] Given that land fronting a thoroughfare was in high demand, it seems reasonable to suggest that the much more prominent location of the new

---

[60] Edward William Gray, *The History and Antiquities of Newbury and Its Environs, Including Twenty-Eight Parishes Situate in the County of Berks* (Speenhamland: 1839), p. 121; Briggs, *Puritan Architecture*, pp. 24–6.

[61] Diary of Edward Belson, fol. 33r, D/EZ12/1, Berkshire Record Office, Reading.

[62] John Dunkin, *The History and Antiquities of Bicester, a Market Town in Oxfordshire* (London, 1816), p. 121.

[63] William Smith, *A New and Compendious History, of the County of Warwick* (Birmingham, 1830), p. 331.

[64] The location of both the old and the new meeting house is visible on Samuel Bradford, *A Plan of Birmingham: Surveyed in MDCCL* (London, 1750).

meeting house in relation to the previous one represented the Presbyterian congregation's growing confidence in their ability to maintain a visible position in the city. It would seem that the status of Dissent as a form of publicly acceptable religion, as embodied by the building of registered meeting houses, was improving.

However, the right to build new meeting houses, and the increased ability to do so in prominent places, could be just as much of a cause of tension as it was a marker of acceptance. This was seen in the anxiety of the Commissions for Building Fifty New Churches in London (established 1711) that, in a city left short of parish churches after the 1666 fire, Dissenters were erecting places of worship far faster than the Established Church.[65] Indeed, when individual parishes in London requested that new churches be built, they often made their case partly on the basis of the existence of Dissenting meeting houses there. In January 1714 the parishioners of St Mary Magdalene, Bermondsey, petitioned for the Commission for Building New Churches to expedite a planned church in the new area, complaining of

> the great inconvenience wee labor under for want of a Church Our Inhabit-ants being Very Numerous and many because they are not willing totally to omit the publick Worship of God on the Lords day are Under Necesity of Frequenting the Dissenting Meeting House at that End of the parish weare the Church is wanting tho. brought up in the Discipline of the Estab-lished Church of England, the consideration of which wee humbly hope will induce Your Honour Speedily to build us a New Church.[66]

Plans that were made for the new church in Bermondsey demonstrated a consciousness of the need to compete with the Dissenters' meeting house, particularly by ensuring that the church was the most visible building in the area. One drawing from 1711 shows measurements for a large area of ground on which the church and churchyard were to be built (Figure 2.1). At the top-centre of the plan a meeting house was labelled in very close proximity to the intended church, such that the new building would have literally overshadowed the Dissenters' place of worship. In 1714, as plans developed, those involved with informing the Commission emphasised the need to make the new church both prominent and easy to reach from all approaches. In one letter to the Commission it was stated that

[65] M. H. Port (ed.), *The Commissions for Building Fifty New Churches: The Minute Book 1711–27: A Calendar* (London: London Record Society, 1986), p. ix.

[66] Petition of Parishioners of St Mary Magdalen Bermondsey to the Commissioners Appointed for Building Fifty New Churches, 12 January 1714, MS 2717, fol. 23r, Lambeth Palace Library (Lambeth Lib.), London.

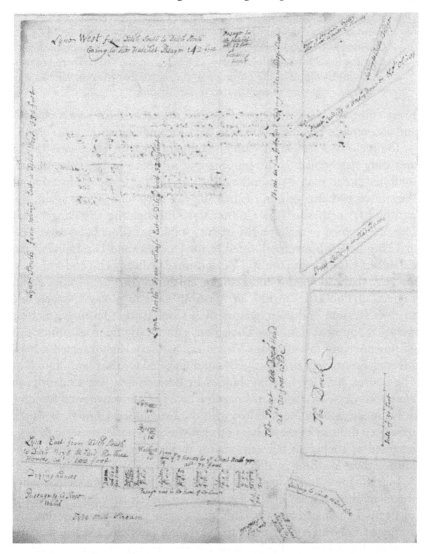

Figure 2.1   Plan of area for proposed church and churchyard in St Mary Magdalene, Bermondsey, 6 November 1711, MS 2717, fol. 6r, Lambeth Lib. The Dissenters' meeting house is shown top-centre.

a Small peece of ground now in the hands of Mr Stevens & a Shed & a boarded house Standing next the Bank, Must be Removed to Make an Opening 25 foot wide next the Thames, which will make that approach very Commodious for such Inhabitants as dwell next the river. There is also a watch-house that is in the possesion of the Parish that Must be taken a way to give a better view of the Church to the Thames.[67]

Every effort was being made to ensure that the new church was as obvious and accessible as possible to those in the surrounding parish.

The sense of Established Church competition with Dissenters in the area only heightened as the bureaucratic processes of the Commission inhibited progress in Bermondsey. By 1725 the plans for the location of the church had changed, but it had still not been built. Once again, the parishioners petitioned the Commission, highlighting the danger that Dissenters posed to the integrity of the Established Church, because 'several Hundreds who were educated in the Doctrine and Discipline of the Establisht Church, and are still Zealous for her Prosperity and Honour; are realy reduc'd to this unfortunate Dilemma; that they must either neglect all Publick Worship, or Worship God in a way Disagreeable to their Reason, and even against their Conscience'. To make matters worse, it appeared that 'The Dissenters gain greatly upon us under this Misfortune; and to encourage Proselites have very lately Erected a New Meeting house, very near to the Ground Devoted for the New Church.'[68] The construction of meeting houses in Bermondsey was evidently an enormous cause of tension in a parish where Dissent was viewed by some as being a dangerous competitor with the Established Church. It would have been difficult in the context of what contemporaries do seem to have regarded as a religious marketplace for them to 'learn to differ in opinions, without dividing in affection'.[69]

Indeed, some individuals saw Dissenters' meeting houses as such a threat to the primacy of the Established Church that they attempted to hamper their registration. This was a clear means of restricting the ability of Dissenters to express their religion publicly, a tactic that the Tory-inclined Deputy Registrar of Chester, Henry Prescott, employed

---

[67] Letter from Edmund Halley and John King to the Commissioner for Building Fifty New Churches, 15 July 1714, MS 2717, fol. 17v, Lambeth Lib.

[68] Petition of Parishioners of St Mary Magdalen Bermondsey to the Commissioners Appointed for Building Fifty New Churches, 8 October 1725, MS 2717, fol. 31r, Lambeth Lib.

[69] Penelope Corfield, '"An Age of Infidelity": Secularization in Eighteenth-Century England', *Social History*, 39, 2 (2014), p. 232; Turner, *A Compendium of Social Religion*, p. xviii.

on several occasions. Sometimes he noted in his diary outright refusal
to register meetings. On 29 February 1711, for instance, he wrote that
'One Mr. Rothwel of Holcomb, a Dissenter, offers mee a Certificate for
a Meeting place, and is earnest with mee to register, but I refuse it.'[70]
On other occasions he directed Dissenters' attempts to register meeting
houses away from the attentions of the Bishop: on 3 September 1717 he
reported 'Mr. Griffith of Rhual designing to offer a Certificate of his
house for a religious Meeting place to my Lord. I indevor to divert him
and hee generously desists on my Account.'[71] Prescott gave no explicit
indication of his motivation in doing so, or indeed whether he was ultimately successful, but he showed little sympathy for the expanding public
influence of Dissent in other contexts. In April 1704 he wrote glumly in
his diary that 'The News tells of Earl Nottingham laid down his office of
principal Secretary, and a prospect of other changes at Court, acceptable
to Dissenters, melancholy to others.'[72] It seems likely, therefore, that
Prescott's apparent desire to make the registration of meeting houses
difficult for Dissenters was motivated by his general animosity towards a
perceived spread of Dissenting influence.

Prescott may not have been the only individual trying to make it difficult to build or register new meeting houses. A fee farm grant including
a 'ruinous old building, called Saint Nicholas Hall' made in October
1738 to William Freeman, a Coventry baker, specified that if he 'causes a
meeting house or house of worship to be built there he shall not make a
doorway to the rear of the Hall … he shall not remove a public conduit
to the East'.[73] Although there may have been other reasons for restricting the ways in which Freeman could refurbish the hall, the fact that
these conditions applied explicitly to building a meeting house indicates
a possible attempt to make the location less desirable or less accessible
for a Dissenting meeting (nevertheless, by 1749 there was a Presbyterian
meeting house in this location).[74] Attempts to limit the building and
accessibility of Dissenting meeting houses were expressions of the desire

---

[70] John Addy and Peter McNiven (eds.), *The Diary of Henry Prescott, LL. B., Deputy Registrar of Chester Diocese*, vol. 2, *25 March 1711–24 May 1719*, Record Society of Lancashire and Cheshire, CXXXII (1994), p. 343.

[71] Ibid., p. 592.

[72] John Addy (ed.), *The Diary of Henry Prescott, LL. B., Deputy Registrar of Chester Diocese*, vol. 1, *28 March 1704–24 March 1711*, Record Society of Lancashire and Cheshire, CXXVII (1987), p. 4.

[73] Coventry Corporation to William Freeman of Coventry, Baker, Grant in Fee Farm for £55.5s; Fine and £6 Fee Farm Rent, 4 October 1738, PA 90/21, Coventry History Centre, Coventry.

[74] See Samuel Bradford, *A Plan of the City of Coventry Surveyed in 1748 and 1749* (London, 1750).

of some members of the Established Church to minimise the public influence of Dissent.

Furthermore, even if Dissenting churches were successful in building meeting houses, their very presence could act as an irritant to local Established Church interests. In Denton, Norfolk, for example, the construction of an Independent meeting house 'purposely in the midst of the Parish to call them together' appeared to be a cause of significant annoyance to the parish vicar, who reported exasperatedly 'that the Number of the Parishioners of both Sexes of 16 Years Age & upwards, who come at any time to the Church, is not more than 20 Persons', in comparison to at least 180 Dissenters.[75] The prominence of the meeting house in the parish was evidently held by the vicar to be part of the problem.

This was certainly the professed view of one author, writing in c.1750, who had become a Dissenter after a strict upbringing in the Established Church. In the preface to his justification for this conversion, he recalled his youthful prejudice, stating that

> Whenever we pass'd by the Dissenter's [sic] Place of Publick Worship, which stood very near to the Church, we could not regard the very Materials of which the Building was composed, with a charitable Eye. But on a *Sunday*, when we have seen the Dissenters passing and re-passing the Church-yard, through which lay the principal Way to the Meeting-House, how have our young Hearts been fired with Resentment of their being suffered to pass through our consecrated Ground to their unhallow'd Rendezvous? Nay, and what still aggravated the Enormity, that they should dare to brave us in our very Churches, by having their Meetings at the same Time that we went to our lawful established Church, so that we could not avail either their mingling with us in the Church-yard, or our seeing them through the Church Doors, and Windows.[76]

The author may have been exaggerating the extent of his youthful prejudice as a means of condemning the Church from which he had converted, but the focus of his description is nevertheless revealing. It was the proximity of the Dissenters' meeting house, and the visibility of Dissent to members of the Established Church that was, he claimed, the greatest cause of tension. In this instance it is clear that the visibility of the Dissenters' meeting house provided a focal point for prejudice rather than a marker of the acceptance of Dissent as part of the nation's Protestant interest.

---

[75] Answers from Denton Concerning Nonconformists and Church Bells, 1709, MSC2/19, Norfolk Record Office, Norwich.

[76] G. B., *The Convert: Or, an Apology for the Conduct of a Young Gentleman* (London, c.1750), pp. 9–10, emphasis original.

This was also the case in Lambeth in the first decade of the eighteenth century, where the Dissenting congregation, newly under the ministry of one William Clark, moved to a 'more suitable and commodious' meeting house than they had been in previously.[77] Shortly after this, Clarke found himself before the Midsummer Quarter Sessions of that year accused of spending time with his landlady, Widow Coleman, 'in a rude and disorderly manner'.[78] Five of his neighbours had gathered on several days at the end of May that year in the upper room of a house adjacent to Widow Coleman's with, they claimed, a clear view through the window into Clarke's lodgings. They gave evidence that they saw that 'the said Clarke came and sett himselfe down by her [Coleman] and Embraced and kissed her Severall times … and then he took her in his armes and laid her downe in the bed and went himself into bed after her' and that the tryst was repeated on at least one other occasion.[79] Witnesses testified that upon searches of Clarke's room they 'found the widdow Colemans shews and stockings lyeing by the bed side and her Apron in a cheare … and lookeing into the bed there was an Impression of two peoples heads uppon the two pilloews'.[80] The evidence appeared damning, but it seems Clarke was acquitted, not least on the grounds that the alleged scene would not have in fact been visible from the window his neighbours claimed to have gathered around.[81]

Critically, Clark perceived that it was his congregation's new meeting house that particularly provoked the High Church action against him. Writing a narrative of his opponents' conduct, he alleged that upon leading him to the Quarter Sessions, they had told him that 'if … you will part with your Meeting-place to Us, I will assure ye, you shall find nothing but Civility'.[82] Whether or not these words were actually spoken to Clark, they are telling: it is evident that he recognised the new meeting house, and the strength of local Dissent that it represented, as a focal point of conflict and the cause of a malicious attack on his reputation.

The fact that meeting houses were often targeted in attacks on Dissenters during moments of local and national crisis further suggests that their

[77] William Clark, *The Sheep in His Own Cloathing: Or, Mr William Clark's Narrative of the High-Church Treatment of Himself and the Dissenters in Lambeth* (London, 1708), p. 1.

[78] Affidavits of Jane and John Leaf, Anne Henderson and John Skinner, 1708, QS2/6/1708/Mid/7, fol. 1r, SuHC.

[79] Ibid., fols 1r, 1v.

[80] Affidavit of John Bagshaw of Lambeth, 1708, QS2/6/1708/Mid/5, SuHC; Affidavit of Edward Standard of Lambeth, 1708, QS2/6/1708/Mid/6, SuHC.

[81] Clark, *The Sheep in His Own Cloathing*, p. 3.

[82] Ibid., p. 4.

public presence could act as a daily affront to stalwarts of the Established Church. The Presbyterian minister Matthew Henry recorded in his diary for 8 March 1710 that 'we hear of great riots & disorders at London last Tuesd. & Wedn. on occasion of Sacheverels Trial the Jacobite mob rise and pulld down several Dissenters meeting places', and a few days later wrote that "tis whisper'd that there is a design to demolish our meeting place – but God will create a defence upon our glory'.[83] Matthew Henry's experience was one shared by Dissenters across the land; as James Clegg reported in November 1710, 'The cry was against the dissenters, and the heat run through the nation.'[84] Similar attacks were seen during Jacobite disturbances. Clegg recorded on 5 August 1715 that in response to the actions of the French King 'The mobs in all places vented their rage in demolishing the meeting places of the dissenters with any manner of Provocation, but the dissenters were known to be the firmest friends to Liberty and the succession in the Protestant line.'[85]

In towns across England where there was a strong High Church interest in 1714 and 1715, Presbyterian, Baptist, and Quaker meeting houses were seriously damaged by the mob, and in some instances individual Dissenters suffered physical attacks.[86] In Preston, around the time of George I's birth-day in May 1715, local tensions surrounding a verbal exchange between Presbyterians and an Established Church minister over the content of his sermon broke out into extended violent dispute which involved breaking the windows of the meeting house and setting it alight.[87] Support for the Jacobite cause was further manifested in attacks on Dissenters' meeting houses in the 1740s and early 1750s: in Walsall in 1751 a not-yet-finished Presbyterian chapel was destroyed in the night by a mob singing Jacobite songs.[88] While Dissenters saw themselves as contributors to a broad pub-lic interest, their opponents demonstrated through their actions during political crises that they maintained a narrow definition of public religion in which Church and State remained intimately intertwined. The meeting

---

[83] Diary of Matthew Henry, 1705–1713, fol. 81r, MS. Eng. misc. e. 330, Bod.

[84] Doe (ed.), *The Diary of James Clegg, Part 1*, p. 3.

[85] Ibid., p. 8.

[86] John Miller, *Cities Divided: Politics and Religion in English Provincial Towns, 1660–1722* (Oxford and New York: Oxford University Press, 2007), pp. 283–6.

[87] Draft Depositions Concerning a Rift Between Churchmen and Dissenters, n.d., DDKE/2/5/63, Lancashire Archives (LA), Preston.

[88] Paul Monod, 'A Voyage out of Staffordshire; or Samuel Johnson's Jacobite Journey', in Jonathan Clark and Howard Erskine-Hill (eds.), *Samuel Johnson in Historical Context* (Basingstoke: Palgrave Macmillan, 2002), p. 30

house, as the most public symbol of Dissent, was the principal target for the physical expression of these views.

Violence against meeting houses in the first half of the eighteenth century has been well documented, but challenges to Dissenters based around the meeting house could also occur without violence. In Winsham in Somerset in September 1718 Richard Scrinen, a carpenter, gave evidence that one Samuel Allen had attached a libellous letter to the door of the Independent meeting house. The fact that Scrinen had been lying in wait 'in his father's Garden ... to finde out any person who might offer to fix up any Papers or Libells to the meeting house ... and to observe night Walkers who had often by there acting and Writing disturbing the Neighbourhood' suggests that this was not the first time this had happened.[89] In this case it was probably the public prominence of the meeting house that made it a target. Allen was evidently turning the public nature of a Dissenting place of worship to his own advantage by using it to make sure that his libellous accusations were widely read. While the fact that Dissenters were able to build meeting houses in relatively prominent places gave their public position a degree of security through the legitimation of their worship under the 1689 Act, the repeated attacks that were launched upon them emphasise that their status was far from universally accepted.

Dissenters' apparent success in staking their claims to public space did not necessarily signify that members of the Established Church were resigned to Dissenters' public position. Instead, contests over meeting houses and places of worship highlight the extent to which the Toleration Act sparked a period of negotiation over how to adjust to the public presence of Protestant Dissent. While the increasing ability of Dissenters across the period to build meeting houses in prominent locations is a marker of the substantial change in Dissenters' status brought about in 1689, it should also be noted that these public emblems of Dissent were regarded by many supporters of the Established Church as extremely provocative. It is likely that over time contemporaries became used to the sight of more prominent Dissenting meeting houses, but these buildings do appear to have provided a focus for resentment well into the middle of the century. In attempts to prevent meeting houses being registered, and attacks on them at moments of tension, those who feared the public influence of

---

[89] Evidence of Richard Scrinen of Winsham, Carpenter, in a Case Concerning Samuel Allen of Winsham who Allegedly Attached a Libellous Letter to the Door of the Meeting House, 3 September 1718, Q/SR/284/2, SHC.

Dissent repeatedly aired their concerns in physical form. The competitive atmosphere that this reflected and perpetuated made the promotion of the broad Protestant interest suggested by the Toleration Act difficult to imagine in practice.

This has important implications for how we understand the dynamics of inter-confessional sociability after the Toleration Act. Explanations of peaceful inter-confessional relations in the early modern period have often been configured around divisions between public religion (as established by law) and private religion (as followed discreetly by individuals). This has been most demonstrable in studies of the Dutch Republic, such as that of Benjamin Kaplan, who has argued for the significance of a differentiation between public and private in establishing a degree of toleration.[90] Focusing on the way in which *schuilkerken*, or clandestine churches, were tolerated on the basis of a fictional 'privacy' that depended on their non-interference with public institutions and pretence to secrecy, Kaplan is not the only historian of this period to find the line between public and private a useful explanatory tool.[91] Several scholars have suggested that peaceful inter-confessional relations in the Dutch Republic were based on negotiating the difference between acceptable public and private behaviour in specifically religious matters.[92] In areas where it was theoretically illegal to deviate from the state religion, a framework of relative tolerance of religious difference could be constructed around the distinction between public and private.

This framework has been applied to some analyses of the nature of inter-confessional relations in England after the Toleration Act. John Miller has argued that increased diversity of opinion in matters of religion facilitated inter-confessional relations on a local level, with religious divisions sometimes proving less powerful than ties of neighbourliness 'as more people came to accept religious pluralism and treat belief as a personal matter'.[93] Bill Stevenson's study of post-Restoration Dissenters also supports this viewpoint, highlighting how involvement in the day-to-day life of the parish allowed Dissenters to integrate despite their closed and

[90] Benjamin Kaplan, *Divided by Faith. Religious Conflict and the Practice of Toleration in Early Modern Europe* (Cambridge, MA: Belknap Press, 2007), p. 171.
[91] See Benjamin Kaplan, 'Fictions of Privacy: House Chapels and the Spatial Accommodation of Religious Dissent in Early Modern Europe', *American Historical Review*, 107, 4 (2002), pp. 1031–64.
[92] Jesse Spohnholz, *The Tactics of Toleration. A Refugee Community in the Age of Religious Wars* (Newark, DE: University of Delaware Press, 2011), pp. 61, 68, 73; Willem Frijhoff, *Embodied Belief. Ten Essays on Religious Culture in Dutch History* (Hilversum: Uitgeverij Verbren, 2002), pp. 65.
[93] Miller, *Cities Divided*, p. 13.

tight-knit religious groupings.[94] However, as the case of meeting houses shows, the way in which we understand the construction of these neighbourly relations after 1689 cannot be premised on the idea that Dissenters were confining their religion to private practice. The building of meeting houses in prominent places was a clear physical reminder of the public presence of Dissent. The successful management of religious difference on a local level thus relied not upon keeping private religion out of view, but on contemporaries establishing a shared understanding of public religion that could accommodate the pluralism inadvertently instituted by the Toleration Act.

Contesting Public Religious Behaviour: Funerary Practices

As local examples of competition between the Established Church clergy and Dissenting ministers demonstrate, such an adjustment to a shared understanding of public religion was not necessarily forthcoming. The use of public space for worship became even more contentious when it intersected with differences in opinion over moments of community significance, such as rites of passage.

Nowhere were the practical challenges of religious difference more clearly demonstrated than in disputes over the conduct of funerals and burial practices. Funerals were public expressions of religion, social standing, and community cohesion. As such they were perhaps the most basic test of the success or failure of a broadly inclusive public Protestantism. As David Cressy has highlighted, the celebration or commemoration of life events through ritual in the early modern period represented the enactment of uniformity, incorporation into the community, and reinforcement of the local social order.[95] Funeral ritual was important for this, and as a result burial practices were often contested because they made a 'principled statement about social inclusion or exclusion in a community'.[96] For Dissenters and members of the Established Church alike, death marked the passage of an individual out of the community. It was important to recognise it properly.[97]

---

[94] Bill Stevenson, 'The Social Integration of Post-Restoration Dissenters, 1660–1725', in Margaret Spufford (ed.), *The World of Rural Dissenters, 1520–1725* (Cambridge: Cambridge University Press, 1995), p. 385.

[95] David Cressy, *Birth, Marriage and Death. Ritual, Religion, and the Life-Cycle in Tudor and Stuart England* (Oxford: Oxford University Press, 1997), pp. 2, 97, 164, 475–6, *passim*.

[96] R. A. Houston, *Punishing the Dead? Suicide, Lordship, and Community in Britain, 1500–1830* (Oxford: Oxford University Press, 2010), p. 223.

[97] Eryn White, 'Baptisms, Burials and Brawls: Church and Community in Mid-Eighteenth Century Wales', in Joan Allen and Richard C. Allen (eds.), *Faith of Our Fathers: Popular Culture and Belief in Post-Reformation England* (Newcastle-upon-Tyne: Cambridge Scholars Publishing, 2009), p. 42.

We should not assume that funerals were inevitably a cause of inter-confessional tension. As studies of the period before 1689 have shown, they were attended by Dissenters and members of the Established Church alike, and most Dissenters sought burial in parish churchyards.[98] The continuation of burial as a community occasion after 1689 is evident from Dissenters' accounts of funeral attendance. The fact that several Dissenting diarists made note of occasions when they were excluded from local funerals, for instance, indicates that they had expected to be present. The Presbyterian minister Matthew Henry recorded with some disgust in June 1706 that Benjamin Dod, who had fallen from his horse (the irony of the fact that Dod 'us'd to drink a health to Sorrel the horse that thres [threw] King William' did not escape him), had given instruction that no 'moderate low church men, or occasional conformists [were] to have any thing to do at his Funeral – This is a High Churchman'.[99] While Henry evidently did not agree with the political and religious stance of the deceased, he still took it as a particular mark of Dod's objectionable character that he explicitly excluded some members of the community from attendance at his funeral.

The Cheshire Dissenting minister Peter Walkden, writing on 23 March 1733, equally thought it notable that the local gentleman 'Ferrice of Bushal hall', whose burial was to occur that day, had ordered 'that none shod be bid to the burial but his tennants'.[100] It was Walkden's expectation that other members of the local community might be invited to pay their respects. Equally, even when they wanted to keep burials as quiet as possible, Dissenters might concede to the expectation that funerals should in some sense be public. Thus in an exchange of letters between two Independent ministers, William King and Samuel Say, in 1736, King recounted the death of his school assistant, Mr Guillam, adding that 'We have in as private manner as was consistent with Decency buried him this Evening in the Church Yard.'[101] This acknowledgement that a desire for privacy in burial had to be balanced with social expectations of some degree of publicity further indicates that Dissenters understood funerals to be relatively public and cross-denominational occasions.

---

[98] Cressy, *Birth, Marriage and Death*, p. 416; Ralph Houlbrooke, *Death, Religion, and the Family in England, 1480–1750* (Oxford: Clarendon Press, 1998), pp. 278, 334–6.

[99] Diary of Matthew Henry, 1705–1713, fol. 22v.

[100] Diary of Peter Walkden, 1684–1769, p. 53, ZCR 678, Cheshire Archives and Local Studies (CALS), Chester.

[101] William King to Samuel Say, 12 February 1736, 12.107(268), Dr Williams's Library, London.

The inter-denominational nature of funerals across this period indicates that there was some basic public acceptance of Dissenters of all varieties within the wider community as defined by participation in funerary practices. Even Quakers, who did not usually bury their dead in the parish churchyard, might still expect some individuals who were not Friends to attend their burial, and it was not unusual to find Quakers at the funerals of others. This much was evident from the instruction of the London Yearly Meeting in April 1745 that Friends were not to wear mourning apparel, and that those who were invited to funerals were 'Requested to Signify to the Persons concerned, the Uneasiness and Difficulty they are put under' by the custom of wearing mourning.[102] Strikingly, one argument that Quakers made against the Occasional Conformity Bill was that penalising individuals for having been at religious assemblies outside of the Established Church 'when the Occasion may be on the Acct of A Funerall ... will not only infringe the Tolleration, but Render Illegall the Common Offices of Love and Humanity betwixt friends and Relations, and not only to those, who do Occasionally Conform, but also to Constant Conformists'.[103] If the Occasional Conformity Bill was passed, the argument went, members of the Established Church who attended Dissenters' funerals might be unfairly prosecuted. It was evidently common practice for Dissenters and members of the Established Church to mix at funerals.

This is borne out by descriptions of individual funerals. Records of the Hardshaw Friends' Monthly Meeting noted the attendance of 'many friends and others' at the burials of their members in 1719 and 1723.[104] Denominational mixing was by no means confined to Quakers; neither was it simply a matter of social duty. Dissenters could find spiritual nourishment at the funerals of members of the Established Church. The Presbyterian Anne Dawson recorded in her diary for 14 April 1722 that 'This day I have been at the funeral of Mr Pigot our Vicar ... Oh that the spectels of mortality that is daly before my eyes may make me think of how frail I am.'[105] Dawson's use of the funeral of the parish minister as a reminder of the shared mortality of all humankind emphasised a common subjection to

---

[102] Letter from London Yearly Meeting to Lancashire Quarterly Meeting, 7 June 1745, FRL 21/1/5/25, LA.

[103] Felsted Monthly Meeting: 'Considerations on the Bill Depending for Preventing Occasional Conformity Humbly Offered by the People Called Quakers', n.d., A13685/Box51/BoxK (uncatalogued), Essex County Record Office (ERO), Chelmsford.

[104] Society of Friends, Hardshaw Monthly Meeting book, fols. 29r, 31v, 32v, M85/1/12/1, Manchester Archives (MA), Manchester.

[105] Diary of Anne (Dawson) Evans 1721–1722, fol. 20r, Add MS 71626, British Library, London.

God's power that overrode all denominational boundaries. Matthew Henry
also attended the funeral of his local vicar, who had 'order'd I should be
invited to his Funeral … and sent to desire I would pray for him'.[106] Henry
recorded the peaceable nature of the vicar, and his desire that his parishioners should 'love all good people'.[107] On this occasion both Henry and
the deceased vicar understood death and burial as a time for mutual love
and prayer between Christians of all sorts. On his own death in 1714 (he
too fell from his horse), Henry was interred in Trinity (Parish) Church,
Chester, 'attended by large numbers', indicating that his funeral was one
that crossed boundaries between Established Church and Dissent.[108] Peter
Walkden evidently saw it as part of his pastoral duty to attend the burials
of members of the parish in which he was a nonconformist minister, even
when they were not part of his congregation, and his diary includes numerous references to this, often also recording the text that the parish minister
preached on.[109] For these Presbyterians, funerals were public reminders of
the shared Christian experience of mortality. These were not occasions at
which 'public religion' was denominationally bound. Rather, they were
shared experiences of a common Christian community.

In one sense, this was a continuation of how these communal events
were treated before the Toleration Act. Dissenters had participated in some
shared means of publicly commemorating members of the community
before 1689.[110] However, accounts of local disputes over funerals suggest
that the legalisation of Dissent may in some circumstances have encouraged contention around these occasions. The public nature of funerals
made them a prime opportunity for those who opposed a generous interpretation of the 1689 Act to attempt to enforce religious exclusivity on a
local level. Disputes over where Dissenters should be buried reveal that
some members of the Established Church used funerals and burial to reinforce a narrow definition of their local religious community. This is evident
from the records of the Protestant Dissenting Deputies (Presbyterian,
Independent, and Baptist), who from the late 1730s began to act on behalf
of Dissenters across the country in cases of unfair treatment. The *Sketch*
of the work of the Deputies published in 1813 gives many examples of

---

[106] Diary of Matthew Henry, fol. 63r.
[107] Ibid.
[108] Matthew Henry's Chapel Church Book, 1687–1928, fol. 14v, D/MH/1, CALS.
[109] Diary of Peter Walkden, 1684–1769, see for example p. 33 (23 February 1733) and p. 35 (26 February 1733).
[110] Cressy, *Birth, Marriage and Death*, p. 416; Houlbrooke, *Death, Religion, and the Family*, pp. 278, 334–6.

their actions in this area, recording for instance that 'Very soon after the appointment of the Deputies, they received complaints from various quarters, of clergymen refusing the rites of burial to those who had not been baptized according to the forms of the established church.'[111]

Such cases were on the whole resisted successfully by the Deputies, because anyone who had been baptised in the name of the Trinity had the right to be buried in their parish churchyard. However, there were cases in which religious differences prevented the deceased from being buried where they or their family wished. In 1715 Nicholas Jekyll of Castle Hedingham, Essex, wrote in some concern to his antiquarian friend William Holman about the refusal of a minister to bury a child of Dissenting parents, despite it having been baptised. The father, Christopher Finch, instead 'buried it in his yeard', and Jekyll lamented that "'tis what few of our Clergy in London or Country refuse, I mean to bury a Corps of a Christian for so they are who themselves or Parents profess Christ Jesus'.[112] Jekyll evidently held to the notion that burial was a shared Protestant affair; Mr Cook, the local vicar, apparently disagreed. While some Dissenters found no opposition to their burial within the fold of the parish, this acceptance was clearly not universal.

Although tension over the burial of Dissenters in parish churchyards was a cause of dispute before the 1689 Act, the suspension of penalties against Dissent may have made the situation worse. Common burial grounds for nonconformists, such as Bunhill Fields in London, had existed since the Restoration, but the increasing establishment of separate burial grounds for Dissenting congregations near or alongside meeting houses after 1689 meant that there were more viable alternatives to churchyard burial. Established Church ministers had more reason to see refusal to bury Dissenters in the parish churchyard as a justifiable action now that more options were available to Dissenters. Thomas Laqueur has suggested that legal struggles between Dissenters and the Established Church clergy over burial contributed to the disintegration of the notion of a community of the dead in the space they were buried, and an increased use of denominationally bound cemeteries in place of churchyards.[113] But it may also have been that the greater ease with which Dissenters could now build alternative spaces

[111] *Sketch of the History and Proceedings of the Deputies: Appointed to Protect the Civil Rights of the Protestant Dissenters* (London, 1813), p. 13.

[112] Nicholas Jekyll to William Holman, 8 April 1715, D/Y 1/1/111/31, ERO.

[113] Thomas W. Laqueur, 'Cemeteries, Religion, and the Culture of Capitalism', in Jane Garnett and Colin Matthew (eds.), *Revival and Religion Since 1700. Essays for John Walsh* (London and Rio Grande, TX: The Hambledon Press, 1993), p. 194-5.

for burial facilitated arguments for the exclusion of Dissenters from the communal space of the parish churchyard.

Indeed, disputes over how funerals were conducted indicate an increased confidence among Dissenting ministers in asserting their role in the public commemoration of individuals, to the chagrin of their Established Church counterparts. This appears to have been the case in two instances in Somerset in the 1690s, noted in the Quarter Sessions records, concerning interrupted funerals and burials that were not conducted according to the rites of the Church of England. In the first, in Stowell in April 1691, Isaack Stone, a Baptist minister, and Lawrence Hooper, the son of the deceased, were accused of having obstructed the parish rector, Thomas Mogg, as he tried to carry out his duty at the burial service of Elizabeth Hooper. Stone and Hooper first prevented the corpse from being carried into the Church. Stone then declared that he would bury the dead; Hooper allegedly pulled Mogg away from the grave-side, grabbing him at the shoulder and telling him 'hee would take him thence or throw him in'.[114] Stone had encouraged Hooper to interrupt the proceedings on the grounds that 'it was not the will of the dead to have it soe'.[115] The local rector evidently saw it as his duty, and perhaps also his right, to carry out the service for the burial of the dead even when he was told that this was contrary to the intention of the deceased. Stone and Hooper wanted to use the communal space of the parish churchyard, but on their own terms. Had it not been for the fact that Stone was a legally practising Dissenting minister under the terms of the Toleration Act, it seems unlikely that he could have made such a confident assertion of the importance of the will of dead, and his own right to tend to the matter. Quite apart from the fact that before 1689 the risk of prosecution and severe penalties would have been much greater, the legal establishment of separate meetings for worship after the Toleration Act to some extent legitimated the roles of Dissenting ministers as leaders of religious life within their local communities. This increased public role may have been a key factor in Stone's remarkable confidence in interfering with this funeral.

A similar tension was seen in Brislington, nearly forty miles north of Stowell, in October of the same year. The Dissenting minister, Samuel

---

[114] Evidence of Thomas Mogg, Rector of Stowell, and Edward Longman of Stowell Against Lawrence Hooper Junior and Isaack Stone of Charlton Horethorne, Baptist Preacher, Concerning the Interruption of the Funeral of Elizabeth Hooper, 12 February 1691, Q/SR/184/9, SHC.

[115] Evidence of Robert Wadman of Charlton Horethorne Against Lawrence Hooper Junior and Isaack Stone of Charlton Horethorne, Baptist Preacher, Concerning the Interruption of the Funeral of Elizabeth Hooper, 15 April 1691, Q/SR/184/8, SHC.

Young, was accused of having come into the parish church while the curate, Samuel Paine, was conducting the funeral service of Josias Daniel. Allegedly, he then used 'very uncivil language ... on purpose to disturb the said Mr Paine in the duty of burying of a corpse'.[116] Furthermore, Young ordered the corpse to be removed from the church (which it was).[117] However, he clearly had no fundamental objection to the funeral being carried out in the church. According to the evidence of John Horton, a Bristol gentleman, 'the said Samuell Young did afterwards preach in the said parish church att Brisstleton and bury the said Corpse' despite being 'forbidden so to doe by the said Mr Paine Minister of the said Church'.[118] This was further affirmed by Richard Peasley of Brislington, clerk, who said that 'after Mr Paine was gone out of the Church, the Corps was brought into the Church again & putt in the usuall place, & then Mr Young went into the Reading desk & read some of the Burial service, & after that preached & then interred the said Corps but not according to the Liturgy of the Church of England'.[119] In this incident, as in the previous case, the Dissenting and Established Church ministers were in direct competition with each other in a dispute which showed little obvious regard for the peaceful dignity of the dead. The Toleration Act did not sanction such interference with the rites of the Established Church, but by legalising Dissent and acknowledging the pastoral status of Dissenting ministers within their local communities, it may have given them greater confidence to do so.

These particular instances of dispute occurred in the 1690s, not long after the passage of the Toleration Act. It seems unlikely that this level of outward and indeed violent dispute between the clergy in these communities could have been sustained for many years after this. Nevertheless, the fact that from the 1730s the Protestant Dissenting Deputies were still attempting to resolve numerous cases of Established Church clergy

---

[116] Evidence of John Horton of Bristol, Gentleman, Concerning the Burial of a Corpse in Brislington Parish Church which Burial was Not in Accordance with the Laws of the Church of England, 27 October 1691, Q/SR/187/10, SHC.

[117] Evidence of Charles Waller of Brislington, Concerning the Burial of a Corpse in Brislington Parish Church, 20 November 1691, Q/SR/187/9, SHC; Evidence of Samuel Paine of Bristol, Minister, Concerning the Burial of a Corpse in Brislington Parish Church Which Burial was Not in Accordance with the Laws of the Church of England, October 1691, Q/SR/187/11, SHC.

[118] Evidence of John Horton of Bristol, Gentleman, Concerning the Burial of a Corpse in Brislington Parish Church which Burial was not in Accordance with the Laws of the Church of England, 1691, Q/SR/187/14, SHC.

[119] Evidence of Richard Peasley of Brislington, Clark, Concerning the Burial of a Corpse in Brislington Parish Church Which Burial was Not in Accordance with the Laws of the Church of England, 30 October 1691, Q/SR/187/26, SHC.

refusing to bury Dissenters suggests that this rite of passage remained a possible cause of contention.[120]

In the case of funerary and burial practices, the more prominent role that the Toleration Act unintentionally gave Dissenters in public religious life changed the parameters of co-existence. Not only did the legislation result in a greater number of alternative spaces for burial, but it also gave legitimacy to alternative spiritual leaders to carry out Protestant burials. The result, as in disputes over meeting houses, appears to have been a sense of rivalry between Established Church and Dissent over who had authority over the public religious life of the community. This increased status of Dissenters threatened to wrest some of the power of the parish clergy from their hands. As Nicholas Jekyll's comments to the Independent Minister William Holman in November 1727 reveal, this could cause considerable frustration to some: he reported that 'The Reverend (but very drunken) Parson Edge at Lavenham has died of the epidemick fever ... he was always rayling against Protestant Dissenters', but claimed that 'had they said and done as he bid them', he would have 'used not a hard or ill word'.[121] The Toleration Act served to affirm the public status of Dissent in a way that enabled Dissenters to claim that they made an important contribution to public religion. The desire of opponents of the Act to limit these claims led to an intense rivalry over exactly what that public religion should look like.

Conclusion

The primary aim of the 1689 Toleration Act was not to facilitate individual conscience, but to unite 'their Majesties Protestant Subjects' by creating a definition of acceptable public worship that would best serve civil society.[122] Far from solidifying the boundary between public and private, the Toleration Act served to affirm the public status of Dissent in a way that enabled Dissenters to claim they made an important contribution to public religion. The management of religious difference in England after 1689 was not premised on Dissenters keeping their religion private; neither did Dissenters attempt to retreat from public life. Rather,

---

[120] *Sketch of the History and Proceedings of the Deputies*, p. 13.
[121] Nicholas Jekyll to William Holman, 15 November 1727, D/Y 1/1/111/145, ERO.
[122] 'William and Mary, 1688: An Act for Exempting their Majestyes Protestant Subjects Dissenting from the Church of England from the Penalties of Certaine Lawes'.

drawing on justifications of liberty of conscience relating to the role of civil government in facilitating individual obedience to God's authority, they pushed for a broad understanding of public religion in which religious difference could be accommodated. Within this framework, Dissent and the Established Church could remain distinct but under the umbrella of a shared Protestant national interest.

The attempts of supporters of the Established Church to defend their narrow view of public religion against this idea were crucial in shaping manifestations of tolerance and intolerance in this period. Failure to agree on the nature of public religion fed into national and local political and social disputes in which the parties attempted to carve out space for their differing religious beliefs and practices. The peaceful management of religious difference now relied on the recognition of sufficient common ground to create a sense of mutual interest. The fact that this common ground was in some instances hard to find on a local level shows the significant role that religious differences could play in the social and political life of the parish after 1689.

The acknowledgement of Dissenters' ongoing battle for a place within public religious life draws into question narratives of a retreat into quietism among Protestant Dissenters in the first half of the eighteenth century. The argument that the Toleration Act and the emergence of an emphasis on reason caused the zeal of Dissenters to wane in this period sits uneasily with the evidence provided in this chapter of Dissenters' resilience in arguing for their position and importance in public life.[123] Although, as the next chapter acknowledges, Dissenters were concerned about the apparent decline of their congregations in this period, the continuing attempts of Dissenters to contribute to public religious life after the 1689 Act mean that it is difficult to attribute any such decline to quietist retreat on their part. This is important, because emphasising the quietism of Dissenters may risk missing the significance of the continuing problem of religious difference in shaping key social and cultural developments in this period.

[123] Michael R. Watts, *The Dissenters. From the Reformation to the French Revolution* (Oxford: Clarendon Press, 1978), pp. 386, 391–2; John Coffey, 'Church and State, 1550–1750: The Emergence of Dissent', in Robert Pope (ed.), *T&T Clark Companion to Nonconformity* (London: Bloomsbury, 2013), p. 68; Robynne Rogers Healey, 'Quietist Quakerism, 1692-c.1805', in Stephen W. Angell and Ben Pink Dandelion (eds.), *The Oxford Handbook of Quaker Studies* (Oxford and New York: Oxford University Press, 2013), p. 49, *passim*.

Indeed, disputes about the nature of public religion after 1689 have wider implications for how we interpret some of the social and cultural changes of the eighteenth century. In recent work, historians have generally shown scepticism towards narratives of secularisation.[124] However, the argument that the period after the Toleration Act was one in which the influence of religion over public life was in retreat still holds significant sway.[125] This assumption that religion was increasingly a private matter in the eighteenth century continues to be reflected in the notable absence of religion in many social and cultural histories of the period. This emphasis on the 'secular' appears somewhat unjustified. Certainly, the sense that religion was a matter of debatable opinion rather than shared belief was important in facilitating disputes in this period.[126] Yet there was evidently little that was inevitable about this process, and by 1750 it was still the nature of public religion, rather than the intrinsic merits of it, that was being debated.

Such narratives of the privatisation of religion may well be rooted in the fact that there was an increasing acceptance that tender consciences ought to be at private liberty to choose their form of worship. However, as we have seen, this did not resolve the question of the place of religion in public life. If anything, by turning attention away from specific questions of private conscience, these changes in attitude created a particular focus on the nature of public religion. Opponents of Dissent sought alternative ways to maintain the prominence of the Established Church while avoiding accusations of immoderate and persecutory attitudes, and attempting to restrict public religion to the Established Church was one means of doing so.

It is, of course, the case that the influence of specific religious values over public life did eventually decline. British society is now (in practice

---

[124] J. C. D. Clark, 'Secularization and Modernization: The Failure of a "Grand Narrative"', *Historical Journal*, 55, 1 (2012), p. 163, *passim*; Tony Claydon, *William III and the Godly Revolution* (Cambridge: Cambridge University Press, 1996), pp. 5, 39–40, 44; Jeremy Gregory, 'Introduction: Transforming "the Age of Reason" into "an Age of Faiths": Or, Putting Religions and Beliefs (Back) Into the Eighteenth Century', *Journal for Eighteenth-Century Studies*, 32, 3 (2009), pp. 289–90. See also J. C. D Clark, *English Society, 1660–1832: Religion, Ideology and Politics During the Ancien Regime* (Cambridge: Cambridge University Press, 2nd edn 2002).

[125] Corfield, '"An Age of Infidelity"', p. 231; Brad S. Gregory, *The Unintended Reformation: How a Religious Revolution Secularized Society* (Cambridge, MA: Harvard University Press, 2012), pp. 368–9, 373–4, 376.

[126] Blair Worden, 'The Question of Secularization', in Alan Houston and Steve Pincus (eds.), *A Nation Transformed: England After the Restoration* (Cambridge: Cambridge University Press, 2001), pp. 24, 31; Bernard Capp, 'The Religious Marketplace: Public Disputations in Civil War and Interregnum England', *English Historical Review*, 129, 536 (2014), p. 78.

if not constitutionally) wholeheartedly secular. If the roots of this development cannot be straightforwardly traced back to the Toleration Act, then did the first half of the eighteenth century in fact have any part to play in this process? There is some merit to the argument that it did. Studies of changing attitudes to witchcraft and magic in the eighteenth century have suggested that although beliefs in these phenomena did not necessarily decline, people were increasingly unwilling to justify beliefs in witchcraft in public.[127] This was partly because of the repeated use of the supernatural in party politics, with the credibility of witchcraft accusations being undermined by their use as party tools.[128] Political dispute involving witchcraft did not necessarily eliminate belief in it, but it did undermine its effectiveness as a unifying discourse.

A similar framework might be cautiously posited for understanding the role of the process of adjustment to the Toleration Act in the eventual secularisation of England. The Toleration Act did not just allow freedom for private conscience; it set up Dissenting meetings as public institutions, creating a new opportunity for debate about where Dissent fitted within national life. In this sense, it certainly did not mark the beginning of a retreat of religion from public life, or a scepticism about the intrinsic importance of religion. However, as this chapter has shown, the ambiguous intention of the legislation of 1689 set off a process of contestation over the nature of public religion, an issue that was strongly intertwined with contemporary politics. It may have been that, in causing such a dispute, the Toleration Act inadvertently began to unravel the integrity of the principle that public religion in some form was indispensable to the functioning of civil society. The first half of the eighteenth century did not see a decline of the influence of religion in public life, but it may have set in motion the complex process by which this eventually happened.

Such hot dispute over the public place of Protestant Dissent in this period also had critical implications for emerging social and cultural discourses after the Toleration Act. Despite differences in opinion over definitions and chronology, historians exploring the developing culture of the 'public

---

[127] Jonathan Barry, 'Public Infidelity and Private Belief? The Discourse of Spirits in Enlightenment Bristol', in Owen Davies and Willem de Blécourt (eds.), *Beyond the Witch Trials. Witchcraft and Magic in Enlightenment Europe* (Manchester: Manchester University Press, 2004), p. 139; Michael Hunter, 'The Decline of Magic: Challenge and Response in Early Enlightenment England', *Historical Journal*, 55, 2 (2012), pp. 424–5.

[128] Alexandra Walsham, 'The Reformation and "the Disenchantment of the World" Reassessed', *Historical Journal*, 51, 2 (2008), pp. 521–2.

sphere' in the eighteenth century have generally agreed that it was pre-mised on ideas of politeness, civil conversation, and reasoned discussion.[129] Given that, as we have seen, much of the focus of dispute about the extent and nature of the Toleration Act was centred on the public position of Dissent, it was only logical that defenders of the Established Church inter-est sought to manage religious difference by excluding Dissenters through such discourses. In fact, as the next chapter demonstrates, emerging ideals of politeness and sociability became an essential tool for the attempted exclusion of Dissent from wider society after 1689.

[129] Lawrence E. Klein, 'Gender, Conversation, and the Public Sphere in Early Eighteenth-Century England', in Judith Still and Michael Worton (eds.), *Textuality and Sexuality: Reading Theories and Practices* (Manchester and New York: Manchester University Press, 1993), pp. 104–5, 108; Brian Cowan, 'The Rise of the Coffeehouse Reconsidered', *Historical Journal*, 47, 1 (2004), pp. 25–6; Ann C. Dean, *The Talk of the Town. Figurative Publics in Eighteenth-Century Britain* (Lewisburg, NJ: Bucknell University Press, 2007), pp. 11, 14–5; Paul Kelleher, 'Reason, Madness, and Sexuality in the British Public Sphere', *The Eighteenth Century*, 53, 3 (2012), pp. 292, 304–5.

CHAPTER 3

Politeness and Hypocrisy

'It is good to mark & observe those that are stirred up with passionate anger,' wrote William Coe, a conformist and anti-Quaker gentleman of Mildenhall, Suffolk, 'beholding their Countenance, how unseemly & disfigured it is; how rude their actions are; how absurd their words; how base & Contemptible all their behaviour is; And the sight of this in another will be some means to make him loath in it himselfe'.[1] Coe's comments might now be regarded as reasonable advice, but they were also a specific product of the age he was living in. The emphasis on the rejection of excessively 'enthusiastic' and passionate discourse that marked the decades after 1689 served to undermine the power of righteous anger: as printed discourse at the time of the Sacheverell crisis demonstrated, one man's righteous anger could easily be interpreted as another man's loss of reason.

This shift in expectations about the tone of discourse was a particular challenge when it came to religious tensions. At the moment that the Toleration Act became law in 1689, the aims of defenders of the Established Church remained much the same as they always had: to manage religious difference by eliminating it outright. However, the reality of England's religious settlement was that the law no longer aligned fully with this goal. The legislation of 1689 removed the hard instruments of persecution from the hands of those who sought to repress and exclude Protestant Dissenters into submission. The result was that (provided they met the terms of the Act) Dissenters were now free to worship as they pleased; there was very little concrete action that their opponents could take.

This did not, of course, stop them from trying. As we have already seen, those resistant to the terms of 1689 fought hard in the first few decades of

---

[1] Diary of William Coe, 1688–1729 [entry n.d.], fol. 110r, MS Add.6843, Cambridge University Library, Cambridge.

The following chapter draws on material from my previously published article 'Politeness, Hypocrisy, and Protestant Dissent in England after the Toleration Act, c.1689–c.1750', *Journal for Eighteenth-Century Studies*, 41, 1 (2018), pp. 61–80.

the eighteenth century to reverse toleration, or at the very least confine it
to its narrowest interpretation. For contemporaries on both sides of the
argument, there remained a real possibility that the 1689 Act would provide only a temporary suspension of penal legislation. However, as time
wore on, the chances that toleration would be swept away in its totality
looked slimmer. This coincided with the fact that the extreme and violent
language that had initially marked debates about toleration and occasional
conformity had begun to look outmoded and immoderate, and it represented a challenge. Supporters of the primacy of the Established Church
now needed other weapons, beyond legal recourse and vituperative argument, to challenge the position of Dissent. As all parties tried to work out
their shifting roles in the wake of legislative change, religious prejudice
began to find its expression in new forms. This chapter argues that politeness, in particular, became a mode of behaviour through which tacit religious exclusion could be reframed in new, more socially acceptable ways.
While the subtle social ostracism inherent in politeness lacked the sharp-
ness of the sword of state persecution, it was still a poison with significant
potential for harm.

Persecution by politeness might, at first glance, appear an unlikely phe-
nomenon. Proponents of this discourse in the first half of the eighteenth
century suggested that it was a mode of social interaction that facilitated
cohesion. As a result, the culture of politeness has generally been dis-
sociated from narratives of continuing religious division in this period,
with an historiographical emphasis on the importance of a 'more polite'
and socially affable religious culture that marked a departure from the
divisions of the previous century.[2] Furthermore, an increasing number
of contemporary commentators on trade looked to the example of the
Dutch Republic, and advocated religious toleration on the grounds that
it benefitted commercial relations. Given this, it would be expected that
the dominant social discourses of the eighteenth century would have been
geared towards tempering religious divisions.[3] However, this chapter demonstrates the contrary: the religiously inflected uses of the discourse of
politeness provide a striking demonstration of how an ostensibly neutral

[2] Jorge Arditi, 'Hegemony and Etiquette: An Exploration of the Transformation of Practice and
Power in Eighteenth-Century England', *British Journal of Sociology*, 45, 2 (1994), p. 178; Lawrence
Klein, 'Politeness and the Interpretation of the British Eighteenth Century', *Historical Journal*, 45, 4
(2002), p. 890.
[3] See for example Onslow Burrish, *Batavia Illustrata: Or, a View of the Policy and Commerce of the United
Provinces. Part I* (London, 1728), pp. 143–4; Josiah Child, *A New Discourse of Trade: Wherein Are
Recommended Several Weighty Points, Relating to Companies of Merchants* (London, 1745), pp. 6, 154.

social language could be used as a tool to delineate and embed religious differences in eighteenth-century England.

Politeness had an impact on portrayals of both Dissent and Dissenters' own attempts to navigate their place in eighteenth-century society. This was evident in characterisations of Dissenters in contemporary print and visual culture, which are discussed here in relation to the accusation of hypocrisy. While hypocrisy was but one of a number of charges laid against Dissenters from the seventeenth century onwards, it is particularly relevant here because the concept of politeness heightened concerns about the danger of hypocrisy in social interaction. The relationship between hypocrisy and politeness was emphasised by contemporaries in printed discussions of hypocrisy, which highlight how the label of impolite hypocrite became particularly potent against Dissenters in this context. As the life-writings of pious Dissenters and the printed advice of Dissenting preachers shows, this created significant difficulties for Dissenters who tried to balance polite social integration with the maintenance of their distinctive religious identities. Dissenters were acutely aware of the danger that polite behaviour might worsen the charges of hypocrisy already laid against them. The first sections of this chapter demonstrate these ideas in relation to Presbyterians, Independents, and Baptists, who, despite their clear differences, had sufficient collective identity as Dissenters to form a committee of 'Protestant Dissenting Deputies' in 1732.[4] The fourth and fifth sections discuss the contrasting experiences of Quakers and Catholics. By comparing the challenges faced by different groups after the Toleration Act, the degree to which religious differences shaped the cultural discourses of the eighteenth century becomes even more apparent.

Protestant Dissenters and Impolite Hypocrisy

Throughout the seventeenth century, 'Puritans' and nonconformists had been labelled as socially rigid, divisive, and hypocritical individuals.[5] These supposed attributes of the hotter sort of Protestant were consistently adapted to changing social and political purposes.[6] These labels therefore

---

[4] James E. Bradley, 'The Public, Parliament and the Protestant Dissenting Deputies, 1732–1740', *Parliamentary History*, 24, 1 (2005), p. 72.

[5] Patrick Collinson, 'Antipuritanism', in John Coffey and Paul C. H. Lim (eds.), *The Cambridge Companion to Puritanism* (Cambridge: Cambridge University Press, 2008), pp. 27–8.

[6] Peter Lake, 'Anti-Puritanism: The Structure of a Prejudice', in Kenneth Fincham and Peter Lake (eds.), *Religious Politics in Post-Reformation England. Essays in Honour of Nicholas Tyacke* (Woodbridge: The Boydell Press, 2006), pp. 81–2, 87.

indicate not just the nature of prejudices against Dissenters, but also the
relationship between religion and discourses about sociability. As contemporaries negotiated the new religious landscape created by the Toleration
Act, hackneyed characterisations of Dissenters became entangled with
emergent discourses about politeness. The resulting picture of Dissenters as
impolite hypocrites demonstrates the extent to which new and apparently
inclusive social discourses, such as politeness, could be used to reframe
religious divisions for the next chapter in England's religious history.

Historians have emphasised that as a discourse associated with socially
agreeable behaviour, politeness emerged in rejection of the excesses of the
previous century. As part of this, 'sociability and manners in religion were
urged as alternatives to enthusiasm and fanaticism'.[7] Yet at least one label
used against Dissenters – that of hypocrite – became more, rather than less,
potent when used in the context of the idealisation of politeness. Politeness
could itself be regarded as inherently hypocritical, because it prioritised
comely social behaviour over the expression of true feeling, and concern
about this featured in eighteenth-century discussions of polite education.[8]
However, proponents of politeness argued that as long as manners were
cultivated alongside good taste and natural theology, hypocrisy could be
avoided.[9] Indeed, for its advocates, politeness was a mode of conduct in
which 'social actors establish a trust that allows them then to tell the truth,
to criticise, and to urge reforms on others without offending them'.[10]

This view of politeness as a means to promote truth and virtue as well
as social ease could be used to interpret the supposed ill-manners of
Dissenters as symptomatic of hypocrisy. The arch-advocate of polite manners, Anthony Ashley-Cooper, Third Earl of Shaftesbury, made it clear
that the ill-humour of those who insisted on strictness and inflexibility
in discussing religious matters was not only impolite, but was in itself
a sign of hypocrisy. He argued that religious matters should be treated
with 'good humour' and religious principles examined with 'freedom and
familiarity … If it be spurious or mixed with any other imposture, it will
be detected and exposed.'[11] Excessive rigidity in religion was thus not a sign

---

Klein, 'Politeness and the Interpretation of the British Eighteenth Century', pp. 874, 875.
Jenny Davidson, *Hypocrisy and the Politics of Politeness: Manners and Morals from Locke to Austen* (Cambridge: Cambridge University Press, 2004), p. 46.
Nicholas Phillipson, 'Politeness and Politics in the Reigns of Anne and the Early Hanoverians', in J. G. A. Pocock, Gordon J. Schochet, and Lois Schwoerer (eds.), *The Varieties of British Political Thought, 1500–1800* (New York and Cambridge: Cambridge University Press, 1993), p. 225.
[10] Klein, 'Politeness and the Interpretation of the British Eighteenth Century', p. 890.
[11] Anthony Ashley Cooper, *A Letter Concerning Enthusiasm* (London, 1708), pp. 49–50.

of honesty, but an indication of unwillingness to subject it to free examination. Shaftesbury was by no means unsympathetic towards Dissent; his views expressed a general distaste for rigidity and fanaticism in social discourse, rather than a specific criticism of Dissenters. However, his position was symptomatic of a broader emphasis in this period on good manners in religion, and this could be used to attack the supposed position of Dissent. The view that, in a truly polite person, religion and manners were consonant with one another was also propounded by the author of *The Female Spectator*, Eliza Haywood, when she instructed that 'true Religion and *Good Manners*, which are built upon a solid and unshaken Foundation, are always uniform and constant'.[12] If Dissenters failed to subscribe to contemporary expectations of social behaviour, instead distinguishing themselves through a strict outward piety, they were demonstrating a hypocritical and self-interested zeal that would force others to 'suffer the Chagrin' of their 'ill-humour'.[13]

This was a view propagated with vehemence in contemporary 'character' literature, which frequently included descriptions of Dissenters. This genre, developed in the first half of the seventeenth century and popular well into the eighteenth, is useful for examining how the label of hypocrite was used and re-adapted in the light of new social discourses.[14] It should, nevertheless, be treated with care. In providing short snapshots of contemporary 'types', character literature tends to provide exaggerated generalisations, emphasising representations rather than relationships. Its significance therefore lies in the insights it provides into what authors thought their readers would identify as the commonly recognised characteristics of a type.

The idea of a Dissenter as an ill-humoured hypocrite is evident in Thomas Brown's 1705 *Legacy for the Ladies*, which contains a biting description of the 'pretended Godly woman', who uses religion as a cover for licentiousness, cuckolds her husband, and 'owns no other neighbour but those of her own profession'.[15] Similar themes appear in Ned Ward's character of 'The formal Precision; or, The devout Lady' in his 1708 *Modern World Disrob'd*. Not only was such a lady over-formal in her posture and appearance, but she was profane in private and unsuited to general society: she

---

[12] Eliza Haywood, *The Female Spectator* (London, 1745–6), vol. 4, p. 326, emphasis original.
[13] Jean Baptiste Morvan de Bellegarde, *Reflexions Upon the Politeness of Manners; With Maxims for Civil Society* (London, 1707), p. 146.
[14] Jim Daems, *Seventeenth-Century Literature and Culture* (London: Continuum, 2006), p. 74.
[15] Thomas Brown, *A Legacy for the Ladies, or Characters of the Women of the Age* (London, 1705), pp. 16–24.

was 'only a fit Companion for a formal Hypocrite … an agreeable Wife to a miserly Enthusiast'.[16] These themes were reproduced and adapted repeatedly elsewhere.[17] For these authors, the vice of those they described was twofold: Dissenters were socially exclusive and unable to conform to social expectation; they were also licentious in their private behaviour.

This notion drew on a long legacy of characterisation of Dissenters that had begun with John Earle's character of the 'She precise Hypocrite' in 1628. Earle described 'a Nonconformist' as a woman whose 'puritie consists much in her Linnen'.[18] He emphasised that she makes an outward show of religion, but has no real religious understanding whatsoever. Thus 'Her devotion at the Church is much in the turning up of her eye,' and she 'over flowes so with the Bible, that she spils it upon every occasion'.[19] Furthermore, her pretences to purity and unorthodox religious views made her a social nuisance, who 'rayles at other Women'.[20] She was an enemy to merriment, and 'is more fiery against the May-pole then her Husband'.[21] For Earle, the female religious nonconformist was both empty of religion and troublesome to society through behaviour that went against societal and gender norms.

Earle's text and ideas were recycled across the seventeenth century and into the eighteenth.[22] However, in eighteenth-century versions, the influence of concerns about fashion and politeness rose to the surface. The description of 'A female hypocrite, or devil in disguise' in *The True Characters* (1708), for instance, clearly drew on Earle, using phrases such as 'She never thinks a Sermon good, unless she ride five Mile to Hear it.'[23] However, the author substantially added to and changed Earle's text, drawing attention to both the lack of polite fashion and the ill-behaviour of those who pretended to piety. The result was that his 'female hypocrite' valued herself 'for being neither in, nor out of the Fashion. She wears the best of Silks and Linnen … but dress so *Odly*, that she spoils her Shape, and

---

[16] Ned Ward, *The Modern World Disrob'd: Or, Both Sexes Stript of their Pretended Vertue* (London, 1708), p. 8.

[17] See for instance William Pittis, *Aesop at Oxford: Or, a Few Select Fables in Verse* (London, 1708), pp. 19–23; *The World Display'd: Or Mankind Painted in Their Proper Colours* (London, 1742), pp. 69–71, 111–18.

[18] Peter Earle, *Micro-Cosmographie, or, a Peece of the World Discovered in Essayes and Characters* (London, 1628), sig. H5v.

[19] Ibid., sigs. H6r, H7r-v.

[20] Ibid., sigs. H7r, H7v.

[21] Ibid., sig. H8v.

[22] See for example *Mirth and Wisdom in a Miscellany of Different Characters, Relating to Different Persons and Perswasions* (London, 1703), p. 3.

[23] *The True Characters* (London, 1708), pp. 7, 9. See Earle, *Micro-Cosmographie*, p. 86.

the Make of her Face by screwing it into the Model of *Nonconformity*'.[24] Once again we see the hypocritical ill-humour of Dissenters represented as causing the double vice of, on the one hand, behaving hypocritically, and, on the other, failing to conform to social norms in public.

There was a gendered aspect to this particular theme of hypocrisy. Spiritual writers frequently suggested that women were more easily led astray because they tended towards wilfulness and carnal reasoning.[25] The view that women were more vulnerable in this way may have hardened in the eighteenth century as medical ideas about the distinctiveness of the female nervous system developed.[26] This was particularly important in the context of criticism of Dissent, because, as Ann Hughes has shown through the example of relations between the Restoration nonconformist Richard Baxter and his wife, some Dissenting women were encouraged to voice their religious views more freely than their conforming counterparts.[27] The choice made by authors of character literature to portray Dissent through a female figure may therefore have been both a criticism of the perceived freedom of expression of Dissenting women, and an attempt to reinforce the notion that Dissenters were particularly vulnerable to carnal hypocrisy.

However, the visual culture of the period perpetuated the view that all Dissenters were simultaneously impolite, unfashionable, and hypocritical. This was a striking theme of the illustrative print to the 1729 broadside *A Comical Sonnet on Ch------s Blue Bonnet*, which shows a nonconformist minister's cap as covering two faces at once, thus representing hypocrisy (Figure 3.1). As the ballad which accompanies the woodcut indicates, the hat is more than just a feeble garment with which to attempt to hide the hypocritical faces of Dissent.[28] It also embodies its sinful and low-born nature, hence how

---

[24] Ibid., p. 7, emphasis original.

[25] Patricia Crawford, 'Public Duty, Conscience, and Women in Early Modern England', in John Morrill, Paul Slack, and Daniel Woolf (eds.), *Public Duty and Private Conscience in Seventeenth-Century England: Essays Presented to G. E. Aylmer* (New York: Oxford University Press, 1993), p. 70; Anthony Fletcher, 'Beyond the Church: Women's Spiritual Experience at Home and in the Community, 1600–1900', in R. N. Swanson (ed.), *Gender and Christian Religion* (Woodbridge: The Boydell Press, 1998), p. 188.

[26] G. J. Barker-Benfield, *The Culture of Sensibility: Sex and Society in Eighteenth-Century Britain* (Chicago and London: Chicago University Press, 1992), pp. 27–8. See also Karen Harvey, 'The Substance of Sexual Difference: Change and Persistence in Representations of the Body in Eighteenth-Century England', *Gender and History*, 14, 2 (2002), pp. 202–23.

[27] Ann Hughes, 'Puritanism and Gender', in John Coffey and Paul C. H. Lim (eds.), *The Cambridge Companion to Puritanism* (Cambridge: Cambridge University Press, 2008), pp. 300, 302.

[28] *A Comical Sonnet on Ch----s Blue Bonnet* (London, 1729), fol. 1r.

Figure 3.1   Woodcut from *A Comical Sonnet on Ch------s Blue Bonnet* (Dublin, 1729).
Library of Trinity College Dublin: OLS Press A.7.5 no. 24. With kind permission
of The Board of Trinity College Dublin.

> This *Bonnet* will sanctify *Cobblers* and *Taylors*,
> And make even Saints of *Robbers* and *Jaylers;*
> This *Bonnet* enlightens *Black-smiths* and *Sow-gelders*,
> And qualifies *Weavers* and *Cutlers* for *Elders*.[29]

Indeed, it is suggested that as well as hiding two faces, the bonnet teaches
the wearer to act 'Just e'en as the present occasion may jump, / To move
with the *Head*, or to wag with the *Rump*'.[30] The bonnet thus allows even
the criminal in society to pretend to sanctity whilst simultaneously training them up in the supposed seditious and fickle practices of Dissent,
modelled by their Parliamentarian forefathers in the Civil Wars. In pre-
senting this image, the *Comical Sonnet* suggests a strong link between a
visually recognisable aspect of Dissent and seditious hypocrisy. At the

---

[29] Ibid., fol. 1v, emphasis original.
[30] Ibid., emphasis original.

Figure 3.2   Woodcut illustration of the cloak referred to in *A Merry New Joke, on Joseph's Old Cloak* (London, 1729). Cambridge University Library: Hib. 3. 730. 1, item no. 92.

same time, it emphasises that Dissent and the divisive behaviour associated with it is outdated. This is no new hat, conforming to the style of the age: 'The Fashion is Old.'[31] Dissenters were once again simultaneously criticised for both hypocrisy and a failure to conform to social and cultural norms.

This theme emerged in other visual depictions of Dissent. The *Comical Sonnet* was a sequel to another ballad published earlier that year, entitled *A Merry New Joke, on Joseph's Old Cloak* (Figure 3.2). The ballad tells the story of how the cloak 'cut in old Oliver's Days' had continued to be recut and used from the Interregnum to the time of writing and had so disintegrated as to be only fit to be made a bonnet. Throughout, the cloak is described as being used as a hypocritical cover for seditious acts:

[31] Ibid., fol. 1r.

This *Cloak* to no Party was yet ever true,
The Inside was *Black*, and the Outside was *Blue*:
'Twas smooth all without, and rough all within,
A Shew of *Religion*, a Mantle to Sin.[32]

The cloak's disintegration into scraps by the end of the ballad suggests that Dissent had lost all integrity. As with the bonnet, in this ballad the image of the cloak represents the sedition and hypocrisy of Dissenters. This three-way association between the appearance of Dissenters, the cloaking of truth through hypocritical behaviour, and apparent imperviousness to contemporary fashion is most clearly spelled out in the 1709 broadside *The Turncoats*, published in response to controversy over Dissenters' practice of occasional conformity (Figure 3.3). In the print, the figure on the left asks his tailor whether he could 'make this Gown into a Cloak upon Occasion'; the tailor in the middle tells his customer in the short (non-conformist) cloak 'let me take the length of your conscience', and receives the reply 'Let the Gown be lin'd with a Cloak to turn at pleasure.'[33] In this scene, the outer clothing of the clergyman becomes a tool to indicate the status of his allegiance to the Church at his own convenience. Although the charge of hypocrisy in *The Turncoats* does not apply exclusively to Dissenters, the implication is that allowing occasional conformity leads to moral vacuity, reducing religion to mere outward form.

The message given by each of these prints is not just that the cloak and the hat represent the seditious hypocrisy taken on by Dissenters, but that they are clinging to an old, outdated, unfashionable way of thinking. In each case the Dissenting viewpoint is presented not just as hypocritical, but also as entirely outmoded. By using these garments to represent the perceived hypocrisy of Dissent, the authors of these prints suggested not just that Dissenters were deceitful, but that they were unfashionably so.

In the context of the eighteenth century, the old charge of hypocrisy was sharpened by associations with impoliteness. However, this did not mean that if Dissenters conformed to polite, fashionable behaviour, they could escape criticism. Dissenters who subscribed to contemporary social norms might equally be regarded as hypocritical. Given that they claimed that their communion was more pious than that of the Church of England, if their behaviour was not discernibly different from others then their Dissent from the Established Church was hard to justify. The Cheshire Presbyterian and prolific diarist Sarah Savage was made aware of this in

---

[32] *A Merry New Joke, on Joseph's Old Cloak* (London, 1729), fol. 1r, emphasis original.
[33] *The Turncoats* (London, 1709–1710).

Figure 3.3 *The Turncoats* (London, 1709–10). Etching and engraving
on paper. 197 x 253mm. British Museum no. 1868,0808.3422,
© The Trustees of the British Museum.

June 1716, when her neighbour, Mr Wright, told her that he might be
more persuaded to go to a Dissenters' meeting with his wife "'if I could …
see you any better for going'".[34] It was on these grounds that the author
of a letter to *The Gentleman's Magazine* in December 1747 argued that 'a
change of our Church government for the Presbyterian, would be of no
advantage towards the amendment of the manners of our present age'.[35]

Expectations of polite behaviour presented Dissenters with a difficult problem. If they did not demonstrate difference from others in
their behaviour, they risked the accusation that their separation from the
Church of England was an unprincipled attempt to undermine stability

[34] Mrs Savage's Diary, 31 May 1714 to 25 December 1723 (eighteenth-century copy), p. 105, MS. Eng. misc. e. 331, Bodleian Library (Bod.), Oxford.

[35] *Miscellaneous Correspondence: Containing Essays, Dissertations, &c … Sent to the Author of the Gentleman's Magazine* (London, 1742–1748), p. 351.

and unity. As the writer and biographer Robert Sanders put it, 'no person can, with the least degree of reason, dissent from the Established Church, unless it be with a view of being a better man, or a sincerer Christian'.[36] If Dissenters did not show these attributes in their behaviour, their Dissent was pointless. While Dissenters who exhibited outward piety were, as we have seen, under suspicion of committing the dual vice of masking their impiety while behaving impolitely, a failure to demonstrate outwardly pious behaviour could equally leave Dissenters open to charges of hypocrisy. Whatever stance they took with regard to contemporary social expectations, Dissenters could be labelled as hypocritical outsiders.

Changing Meanings of Hypocrisy

Discourses of politeness and impoliteness could thus be used to transform the old charge of hypocrisy against Dissenters to fit the context of the eighteenth century. The impact of this was further enhanced by changes in perceptions of hypocrisy itself. While some late seventeenth- and eighteenth-century discussions of hypocrisy began to show willingness to tolerate it in some circumstances, in the context of an emphasis on politeness and social conformity, the impolite hypocrisy of Dissenters remained beyond the pale.

Studies of political and religious discourse in the later seventeenth and early eighteenth centuries have suggested that there was heightened concern about hypocrisy and the nature of truth.[37] The work of Mark Knights has been crucial in connecting this to the political and religious context of the time. Emphasising both the role of partisan dispute in creating ambiguity over the meaning of words and representations, and the extent to which religion became a tool of partisan polemic, he has demonstrated how religious and political diversity was a challenge for established ideas about sincerity.[38] Against this background, the threat that hypocrisy presented to social and political stability was a driving force in debates

---

[36] Robert Sanders, *Lucubrations of Gaffer Graybeard: Containing Many Curious Particulars Relating to the Manners of the People in England, During the Present Age* (London, 1774), p. 78.

[37] Kate Loveman, *Reading Fictions, 1660–1740: Deception in English Literary and Political Culture* (Farnham: Ashgate, 2008), pp. 3, 7–8; Jack Lynch, *Deception and Detection in Eighteenth-century Britain* (Farnham: Ashgate, 2008), pp. 1, 10.

[38] Mark Knights, *Representation and Misrepresentation in Later Stuart Britain: Partisanship and Political Culture* (Oxford and New York: Oxford University Press, 2005), pp. 22, 214–5; Mark Knights, *The Devil in Disguise: Deception, Delusion, and Fanaticism in the Early English Enlightenment* (Oxford and New York: Oxford University Press, 2011), p. 7.

about the practice of occasional conformity and the political position of Dissenters in the first decade of the eighteenth century. Having long been an element of the 'anti-Puritan' stereotype, the charge of hypocrisy was flung from all sides, reflecting 'a perception that interest rather than conscience prevailed'.[39]

Hypocrisy had numerous forms, some of which were regarded as more vicious than others. For many contemporaries, hypocrisy remained an unacceptable vice. The novelist and dramatist Henry Fielding was clear in his *Essay on the Knowledge and Characters of Men* (1743) that young people ought to be protected from 'the pernicious Designs of that detestable Fiend, Hypocrisy', and taught to identify it in all its various personifications, including such characters as 'A Flatterer', 'a Promiser', and 'a Saint'.[40] Fielding presumably would have approved of the mid-eighteenth-century commonplace book of John and Hannah Tylston and Hannah Lightbody, Unitarian children from Liverpool, which drew on a selection of texts to give a damning definition of hypocrisy. Quoting 'Brooks remedys', originally published in 1661, the entry for hypocrisy notes 'History speaks of a kind of witches that stirring a broad would put on their eyes, but returning home boxed them up again. So do Hypocrites.'[41] 'Hypocrisy' was generally regarded as a negative attribute; as Jenny Davidson highlights, even those who defended hypocrisy often did so under another name – manners, civility, decorum, politeness – because 'To defend hypocrisy under its own name means breaking a taboo.'[42]

Nevertheless, there were those who did just that. The justifications they gave, and the distinctions they made between different types of hypocrisy, are essential to understanding the changing nature and impact of the label as applied to Dissenters. The first form of hypocrisy actively promoted by some contemporaries was that associated with outward conformity to the law. The notion that abiding by the law contrary to private belief is an acceptable form of hypocrisy had been supported in the mid-seventeenth century by Thomas Hobbes. He proposed that for citizens the only certain

---

[39] Mark Knights, 'Occasional Conformity and the Representation of Dissent: Hypocrisy, Sincerity, Moderation, and Zeal', *Parliamentary History*, 24, 1 (2005), pp. 49, 51.

[40] Henry Fielding, 'An Essay on the Knowledge and Characters of Men', in Henry Knight Miller (ed.), *The Wesleyan Edition of the Works of Henry Fielding: Miscellanies by Henry Fielding, Esq* (Oxford: Oxford University Press and Wesleyan University Press, 1972), vol. 1, pp. 156, 164–7.

[41] Commonplace Book of John Tylston, with additions by Hannah Tylston and Hannah Lightbody, p. 45, MS. Eng. misc. d. 311, Bod. The original quotation can be found in Thomas Brooks, *Precious Remedies Against Satans Devices* (London, 1661), p. 105.

[42] Davidson, *Hypocrisy and the Politics of Politeness*, p. 6.

virtue was obedience to the law; disobedience to private conscience in aid
of this end was therefore justifiable for the sake of the peace and stability of
the state.[43] Some elements of his argument can be seen in the justification
of hypocrisy given by Jonathan Swift in his *Project for the Advancement of
Religion* (1709). Swift's view was that it was a ruler's duty to make virtuous
behaviour a qualification for public office in order to combat the spread
of profanity. Acknowledging that 'making Religion a necessary Step to
Interest and Favour, might encrease Hypocrisy among us', he advocated it
on the grounds that it 'is often with Religion as with Love; which by much
dissembling, at last grows real'.[44] Although Swift, unlike Hobbes, was concerned about personal morality, he too justified hypocrisy in moral matters
because even if it allowed for individual vice, it would benefit the nation as
a whole. Making virtue a qualification for office 'would quickly make Vice
so scandalous, that those who could not subdue, would at least endeavour
to disguise it'.[45] For both thinkers, rulers should encourage obedience and
virtue in society. Individual hypocrisy was justifiable for this end.

Swift was not alone in the early eighteenth century in promoting the
idea that hypocrisy, while ultimately undesirable, could be a force for good.
The Observator, a Whig periodical established by the political writer John
Tutchin, argued along very similar lines in April 1702 that 'If all *Prophane
and Vicious Persons* were ... not suffer'd to enjoy Places of *Profit* and *Trust*,
the powerful Argument of *Interest* would oblige Men to be Vertuous, or
at least to seem so ... the vile Hypocrite would only hurt himself, when
otherwise, his *open Prophaness* would be Contagious.'[46] Similarly, it was
concluded in the periodical the *British Apollo* in November 1708 that profanity was a greater sin than hypocrisy because 'The Profane Despises all
Religion, the Hypocrite thinks it Worth the *Counterfeit*' and 'The Profane
makes Prosylites to Profaneness; the Hypocrite wou'd not be want-
ing to make Prosylites to Hypocrisy.'[47] Hypocrisy was damaging for the
individual, but profanity spread its malicious influence among society. If
hypocrisy prevented profanity, it was therefore justifiable. In the words

[43] Thomas Hobbes, *De Corpore Politico, or, the Elements of Law, Moral and Politick* (London, 2nd edn 1652), pp. 130–1.
[44] Jonathan Swift, *A Project for the Advancement of Religion and the Reformation of Manners* (London, 1709), pp. 43–4.
[45] Ibid., p. 27.
[46] *The Observator*, issue 2, fol. 1r, London, 8 April 1702, emphasis original; J. A. Downie, 'Tutchin, John (1660–1707)', *Oxford Dictionary of National Biography* (Oxford University Press, 2004), www.oxforddnb.com/view/article/27899, accessed 30 May 2018.
[47] *British Apollo*, issue 79, fol. 1r, London, 10–12 November 1708.

of the *Spectator* in June 1712, 'Hypocrisie cannot indeed be too much detested, but at the same time is to be preferred to open Impiety. They are both equally destructive to the Person who is possessed of them; but in regard to others, Hypocrisie is not so pernicious as bare-faced Irreligion.'[48]

The principle that personal hypocrisy was acceptable if it benefitted wider society was a key part of justifications of hypocrisy in social conduct. The most famous of these, Bernard Mandeville's argument in *The Fable of the Bees* (1714) for 'Private vices publick benefits', suggested that it was socially useful to fake virtue, because while manners made for good personal relationships, vices promoted the commercial success of the kingdom.[49] Genuine virtue, Mandeville argued, could be damaging to a society that was stimulated by greed and pride.[50] Hypocrisy was thus in some respects in the public interest. Mandeville's view was a provocative one. He was widely condemned for promoting irreligion, and he should not be taken as representative of general attitudes to hypocrisy.[51] However, while other advocates of the social benefits of manners in covering up vice were less brazen in their arguments, they did come close to suggesting that hypocrisy was justifiable as a lesser evil if it was for the benefit of others. This was seen in a translation of the work of French conduct writer Jean Baptiste Morvan de Bellegarde, who, while condemning the 'Hypocrisy of … counterfeit *Politeness*', suggested that 'If you can't divest yourself of your bad Qualities … shrowd them from publick notice. Why will you have others suffer the Chagrin of your ill-humour?'[52] De Bellegarde's statements are somewhat contradictory, reflecting the contemporary difficulty in squaring ideas about politeness and good manners with ideals of sincerity and truth.[53] However, they resonate with other more explicit justifications of hypocrisy. Just as for Hobbes hypocrisy was permissible in the name of obedience to the law and the maintenance of the peace of society, and for Swift hypocritical pretence to morality could be accepted if it promoted virtue across wider society, for de Bellegarde some level of hypocrisy

---

[48] *Spectator*, issue CCCCLVIII, fol. 1v, London, 15 August 1712.
[49] Bernard Mandeville, *The Fable of the Bees, or, Private Vices Publick Benefits* (London, 1714), sig. A4r.
[50] David Runciman, *Political Hypocrisy. The Mask of Power from Hobbes to Orwell and Beyond* (Princeton and Oxford: Princeton University Press, 2008), p. 49.
[51] See for example John Dennis, *Vice and Luxury Publick Mischiefs: Or, Remarks on a Book Intituled, The Fable of the Bees; Or, Private Vices Publick Benefits* (London, 1724); George Blewitt, *An Enquiry Whether a General Practice of Virtue Tends to the Wealth or Poverty, Benefit or Disadvantage of a People?* (London, 1725).
[52] de Bellegarde, *Reflexions Upon the Politeness of Manners*, pp. 4, 146, emphasis original.
[53] Davidson, *Hypocrisy and the Politics of Politeness*, pp. 2, 8.

in social behaviour might be justifiable to protect wider company from an individual's morosity.

Given that in the seventeenth century hypocrisy had been regarded by many as 'the worst vice they could imagine', where had this apparent willingness (however patchy) to accept the benefits of some forms of hypocrisy come from?[54] Like the discourse of politeness, it was in part a response to the events of the previous century. Some churchmen feared that reactions to the rigid hypocrisy of Interregnum Puritans had led to open profanity, with the result that individuals no longer felt shame in declaring vice.[55] Against this, hypocrisy might be regarded as the lesser of two evils. However, this did not mean that the perceived hypocrisy of the hotter sort of Protestant could be regarded as tolerable. This was made clear in the narrative of the anti-Whig and anti-Dissenting nonjuror Charles Leslie, who wrote that since the 'Deluge of *Enthusiasm*' that characterised the Interregnum, '*Atheism* has appeared barefaced, and the *War* is carried on, with the Help of the Confederate *Sects*, against all *Religion* in General. And open *Blasphemy* has succeeded *Hypocrisy*.'[56] Hypocrisy was indeed the lesser evil, but for Leslie both hypocrisy and blasphemy were promoted by those who deviated from mainstream Protestantism.

Hypocrisy was therefore in part being rehabilitated as a tool in the battle against open profanity, but Dissenters continued to be labelled negatively as hypocritical. This was possible because there were some types of hypocrisy that everyone considered unacceptable. Thus in *An Enquiry Into the Origin of Honour* (1732), Mandeville distinguished between 'Fashionable hypocrites', who go to Church without real devotion, 'from no other Principle than an Aversion to singularity, and a Desire of being in the Fashion', and 'Malicious hypocrites', who 'pretend to a great Deal of Religion, when they know their Pretensions to be false; who take Pains to appear Pious and Devout ... in Hopes that they shall be trusted'.[57] Malicious hypocrites gave false appearances for their own ends; fashionable hypocrites were merely seeking to fit the norms of society. This was not so far from Hobbes's resolute condemnation of the hypocrisy of those

---

[54] Jacques Bos, 'The Hidden Self of the Hypocrite', in Toon van Houdt, Jan L. de Jong, Zoran Kwak, Marijke Pies, and Mare van Vaeck (eds.), *On the Edge of Truth and Honesty: Principles and Strategies of Fraud and Deceit in the Early Modern Period* (Leiden and Boston, MA: Brill, 2002), p. 67.

[55] John Kay, 'The Hypocrisy of Jonathan Swift: Swift's *Project* Reconsidered', *University of Toronto Quarterly*, 44, 3 (1975), p. 215.

[56] Charles Leslie, *View of the Times Their Principles and Practices* (London, 4 vols., 1708–9), vol.1, issue 250, 8 October 1707, emphasis original.

[57] Bernard Mandeville, *An Enquiry Into the Origin of Honour* (London, 1732), pp. 201–2.

who, during the Civil Wars, failed 'to perceive that the Laws of the Land were made by the King, to oblige his Subjects to Peace and Justice' and instead concealed the ultimate vice of disobedience to the state behind the language of godliness and piety.[58] Hypocrisy could only ever be considered acceptable if it conferred a benefit on wider society. If its ends were selfish, it was always condemned, and the impolite hypocrisy ascribed to Dissenters fitted into this latter category. It was self-serving behaviour that sought to conceal impiety in an unmannerly fashion, the sort of hypocrisy that even Mandeville would have regarded as 'malicious'.[59]

Social Integration and Pious Distinction

The labels being applied to Dissenters in eighteenth-century England were not conducive to the resolution of problems created by religious differences. Despite changes in understandings of it, hypocrisy was a charge that was repeatedly interpreted negatively in relation to Dissent. Furthermore, against the backdrop of new discourses about politeness and fashionable conduct, Dissenters faced the additional problem of their hypocrisy being associated with impolite, outdated, and socially unacceptable behaviour.

Dissenters were highly sensitive to these criticisms, and this played heavily into internal debates about how they should behave in relation to the rest of society after the Toleration Act. In 1730 the Dissenter and controversialist Strickland Gough wrote that Dissenters might benefit from employing a dancing master at their academies, 'to give them a gracefulness and gentility of address, and prune off all clumsiness and aukwardness that is disagreeable to people of fashion'.[60] Gough had by 1735 taken holy orders within the Established Church, but his *Enquiry Into the Causes of the Decay of the Dissenting Interest* sparked debate among his Dissenting contemporaries.[61] Arguing that Dissenting ministers had a poor understanding of their own principles and that they displayed a conduct that did little justice to their interests, he suggested that the primary objections to Dissent were based on 'the aukwardness and impoliteness

---

[58] Thomas Hobbes, *Behemoth, or, an Epitome of the Civil Wars of England, from 1640 to 1660* (London, 1679), p. 163; Runciman, *Political Hypocrisy*, p. 34.

[59] Mandeville, *Enquiry Into the Origin of Honour*, pp. 201–2.

[60] Strickland Gough, *An Enquiry Into the Causes of the Decay of the Dissenting Interest* (London, 1730), p. 43.

[61] Alexander Gordon, revised by Marilyn L. Brooks, 'Gough, Strickland (*d.* 1752)', *Oxford Dictionary of National Biography* (Oxford University Press, 2004), www.oxforddnb.com/view/article/11142, accessed 30 May 2018.

of our Preachers', and that their cause would be strengthened if preachers adjusted their manner of address accordingly.[62] The replies of leading Dissenting ministers to his suggestions were mixed. While they recognised the necessity of ensuring that Dissent was socially acceptable, writers such as Isaac Watts and Philip Doddridge were concerned that an emphasis on respectability and social conformity might endanger the distinctive identity of the Dissenting interest, leading to further decline of the cause and leaving it open to attacks from its opponents on the grounds of hypocrisy. Their arguments reveal Dissenters' consciousness of the degree to which religious prejudice was perpetuated in social terms after the Toleration Act.

Gough's suggestion that embracing politeness might be a way to counter the perceived decline of Dissent received some sympathy from those who replied to him in print. The Northamptonshire Independent minister Philip Doddridge acknowledged that 'some care should be taken ... to engage students to a genteel and complaisant behaviour' on the basis that 'the common people ... are peculiarly pleas'd with the visits and converse of those, who they know may be welcome to greater company'.[63] Doddridge was wary of neglecting the need for socially appealing and polite behaviour. However, he denied that impoliteness was the reason behind the decline of Dissent. Politeness would not win back consciences 'for those that are truly religious ... attend of publick worship, not that they may be amused with a form or a sound ... but that their hearts may be enlarged as in the presence of God'.[64] Those who had conformed, he argued, had done so on the grounds of political interest, marriage, and a dislike of piety, not because Dissenters were ill-mannered.[65]

Doddridge, alongside others, stressed instead that a pious manner of living was the only way of maintaining the reputation of Dissent.[66] The London Independent minister Abraham Taylor emphasised that 'that which recommends ... [ministers] to the greater part of our people, is the piety of their lives, and their plain, serious, and scriptural way of preaching'.[67] Although in disagreement with Taylor over other matters,

---

[62] Gough, *An Enquiry*, pp. 34, 37–8.

[63] Philip Doddridge, *Free Thoughts on the Most Probable Means of Reviving the Dissenting Interest* (London, 1730), p. 38.

[64] Ibid., p. 20.

[65] Ibid., p. 16.

[66] Ibid., p. 6.

[67] Abraham Taylor, *A Letter to the Author of an Enquiry Into the Causes of the Decay of the Dissenting Interest* (London, 1730), p. 4.

the Southampton minister Isaac Watts supported this idea, arguing that Dissenters ought to be ashamed if they were found inferior to members of the Established Church 'either in Virtue towards Men or Piety towards God'.[68] Watts's substantial work, attempting to revive 'practical religion' in the name of sustaining the Dissenting interest, sets out clearly that a key element of Dissenting identity had to be their superior piety, asking his readers 'What do all our Pretences to separation mean, if we ascend to no superior Degrees of Goodness?'[69] For Watts, Dissenters had to justify their continued Dissent by representing their religion in every aspect of their lives and behaviour: 'your Goodness toward Men [ought to] distinguish you if possible from your Neighbours, as much as you are distinguished by your protest and publick Separation from their Forms or Worship'.[70] Far from promoting politeness and integration by conformity to contemporary manners and fashions, Watts suggested that the survival and distinction of the Dissenting interest rested on rejecting them.

What is evident on both sides of the debate, however, is that all parties were preoccupied with how to act in a manner that would avoid playing into the hands of their critics. In particular, they were concerned that the mode of behaviour they promoted should not leave Dissenters vulnerable to charges of hypocrisy. This was spelled out clearly by Watts in his warning to Dissenters that keeping profane company and being taken along with the fashionable vices of the world would 'give too just an Occasion to charge you with Hypocrisy'.[71] Doddridge also opposed those who placed too great an emphasis on politeness, on the grounds that 'a cause may be ruin'd by learned and polite men, if, with their other furniture, they have not religion and prudence too'.[72] Yet in many ways, Gough, who argued the opposite, was preoccupied with the same concerns. His desire to make preachers less censorious in their sermons would ensure both that 'they would no longer terrify and frighten' individuals from the church and that no one had 'an opportunity of complaining that they do not act consistently with their principles'.[73] Gough, Watts, and Doddridge were all worried about how to maintain the Dissenting interest's distinctive identity while avoiding criticism on the grounds of hypocritical

---

[68] Isaac Watts, *An Humble Attempt Toward the Revival of Practical Religion Among Christians, and Particularly the Protestant Dissenters* (London, 1731), p. 171.
[69] Ibid., p. 169.
[70] Ibid., p. 236.
[71] Ibid., p. 228.
[72] Ibid., p. 10.
[73] Gough, *An Enquiry*, pp. 37–8.

behaviour. Doddridge and Watts proposed that the Dissenting cause was based on their claim to practical religion and piety, and that they thus had to observe a strictness in their conduct. By contrast, Gough argued that Dissenters should not claim greater piety than others, instead emphasising their adherence to the cause of liberty and the need to demonstrate graceful and agreeable religion. The Dissent envisaged by Watts and Doddridge was one that avoided hypocrisy by maintaining the strict standards of piety to which it made claim; in Gough's scheme Dissenters avoided hypocrisy by denying claims to higher piety in the first place.

This debate highlights how the label of hypocrisy as applied to Dissenters after 1689 had an important impact on their self-presentation. The desire to avoid hypocrisy was crucial in determining Dissenters' attempts to define their identity and maintain their cause after they had been granted a degree of legal toleration. Centring on the need for Dissenters to show simultaneously that they were grateful for the liberty of conscience that they had been granted, that they posed no threat to civil society, and that they still had a distinctive identity, this debate threw the old charge of hypocrisy into a new cultural context in which an emphasis on politeness created a greater need for social conformity. This heady mix of new social demands, old stereotypes, and changing ideology created a background against which it was particularly challenging for Dissenters to create a distinct or unified cause.

There may have been a temptation in published debates for Dissenting ministers to exaggerate the difficulties that Dissenters faced in order to reignite zeal for their cause in a period when Dissenters' religious affiliation no longer brought danger to life and liberty. However, this sensitivity to hypocrisy and the belief that it was more incumbent upon Dissenters than others to lead a demonstrably pious life is also evident in the accounts of some particularly anxious Dissenters. The young Presbyterian diarist Anne Dawson, for instance, recorded numerous occasions when she was ashamed of her conduct because she believed that she, as a Dissenter, should know better. She wrote on 9 October 1721 that although she was grateful that her education had kept her from cursing, swearing, and obscene discourse, she had often indulged in sinful jesting and lying, and had caused sin in others through her words, stating 'I who ought to have been an example of piety to others have instead of that incoraged to sin.'[74] Dawson placed great emphasis throughout her diary on pious conduct

---

[74] Diary of Anne (Dawson) Evans 1721–1722, fol. 4r, Add MS 71626, British Library, London.

and the difference between her behaviour and that of the rest of the world. Her determination to retain a Christian character free from hypocrisy is further evident in her entry for 9 May 1722, when she was contemplating breaking off her courtship with a man who she felt had been dishonest, writing that 'it is my earnest endeavour to cary well to him & if I do cast him of to do it like a Christian & not in anger and passion no I abhor such a carriage in others & will not do it my self'.[75] For Dawson, her aspiration to a truly Christian identity was defined against the danger of hypocrisy. At the other end of life, the prolific diarist Sarah Savage also demonstrated awareness of the danger that any sign of hypocrisy posed to Dissenters. Writing in 1743, she expressed concern at the behaviours of Methodists, some of whom had attended her Presbyterian meeting. She described how they 'Pretend to the Spirit, & its Motions', and felt that it "tis too True that Religion is Wounded by such as we thought its Friend'.[76] Savage was keen that what she saw as the hypocritical pretences of the Methodists be not mixed up with the religion of her congregation.

Savage's brother, the prominent Presbyterian minister Matthew Henry, was equally concerned that he avoid the label of hypocrisy, and his diary and letters to his father discuss numerous occasions on which he fought against it. He was highly censorious of drunkenness, to the extent that he showed little sympathy for those who died or were injured as a result of their inebriation.[77] His willingness to challenge 'obstinate Drunkeness' may have been the motivation behind false accusations that he himself had fallen into drink, brought against him in the 1690s.[78] Faced in court with the testimony of a number of witnesses to Henry's sobriety, his accusers 'solemnly profess'd … that there was not the least ground or footstep of truth in the Story'. Henry was anxious that his name be cleared, and noted that the outcome of the case had been recorded 'in the Book', sending a copy to his father. His relief was apparent in his comment that the verdict 'I trust may tend to the furtherance of the Gospel, especially to remove an objection commenly made against the Testimony I desire upon all occasions to bear against Drunkenness'.[79] Henry's attempts to enforce sobriety in his local area were clearly not popular, and the false charges against him appear in this context to have been a concerted attempt to label him a

---

[75] Ibid., fol. 28r.
[76] Sarah Savage's Journal, 1743–8, entry for 30 May 1743, Henry MSS 90.2, Dr Williams's Library, London.
[77] Diary of Matthew Henry, 1705–1713, fol. 5r, MS Eng. misc. e. 330, Bod.
[78] Ibid., fol. 10r.
[79] Matthew Henry to Philip Henry, 4 September, n.d. (c.1694), MS Eng. lett. e. 29/149, Bod.

hypocrite. Henry was acutely aware of the damage that this could do not only to his personal reputation, but also to the cause of Dissenters in general. Piety was a badge of distinction for these individuals, but it was also integral to the reputation of the Dissenting cause.

This was not to say that all, or even most, Dissenters shied away from praising polite behaviour. Indeed, the funeral sermons of ministers often mentioned their polite comportment. However, they were also careful to emphasise that this politeness came from inner goodness rather than the observance of social norms, and that it should not take precedence over godliness. Thus, in his account of the life of the Irish Presbyterian minister Michael Bruce, fellow Presbyterian James Kirkpatrick wrote that 'He was a gentleman of polite manners and address, and of a most generous spirit,' but also stressed that

> the imitation of God consists principally in goodness ... A careful observer must have seen in him, that if he had not been genteely educated, yet the goodness of his heart would have made him a well bred man; an ingenuous disposition to oblige every one, would have produced effects of the same kind in him, that politeness does in others.[80]

Bruce's polite education was incidental; his conduct was a product of his innately godly disposition.

However, even the most outwardly pious of Dissenters might find themselves capitulating to the need to be polite under social pressure. This caused considerable anxiety for some individuals who were concerned that in doing so they were both betraying their pious cause and exposing themselves to the accusation of hypocrisy. This is suggested by the words of Sarah Savage in January 1717, when she recorded that 'we dined at Wrenbury Hall with Mr Voice, a splendid entertainment – I envy not the great man state more inward satisfaction with a good Book in my own Closet that with all the Visits, modes, & forms, &c. yet think it duty to be friendly & respectful to those who are so to us'.[81] She was cautious about showing too much enthusiasm for this presumably lavish affair, emphasising that, despite her willingness to attend the occasion, she engaged with 'modes and forms' out of duty rather than preference.

---

[80] James Duchal and James Kirkpatrick, *A Sermon on Occasion of the Much Lamented Death of the Late Reverend Mr John Abernethy ... by James Duchal. With an Appendix Containing Some Brief Memoirs of the Lives and Characters of the Late Revd Messieurs Thomas Shaw, William Taylor, Michael Bruce, and Samuel Haliday... by James Kirkpatrick* (Dublin, 1741), pp. 30, 28.

[81] *Mrs Savage's Diary*, pp. 133–4.

This sense of internal conflict with regard to social conduct is also present in Anne Dawson's account. She lamented her frequent failures to exhibit suitably pious behaviour in the company of others: on 19 May 1722 she reflected that 'If I take a View of my carrage this Week I must be ashamed of it tho I have not spent mush of it in idleness yet I have spent it in trifling and visiting ... I am oft forced to look back on most of my visets with a sort of a regret,' wishing that 'serious or at least Profitable Discourse was more in fashion in this Gentel age'.[82] Dawson found social visits troubling; the implication is that she both found it difficult to act contrary to fashion while in company, and lamented that her social discomfort was not eased by more godly conversation. At the same time as such writers were eager to promote the piety of the Dissenting cause, social realities could prove difficult for some individuals to navigate.

Concerns about the socially divisive nature of Dissent were not, as we have seen, new to the eighteenth century. However, contemporary advice on Dissenters' conduct, particularly that given in printed sermons, suggests that Dissenters were now reading the dangers of the label of hypocrisy with the effects of the Toleration Act in mind. Such sermons reminded Dissenters not only that behaviour that could be interpreted as hypocritical was potentially damaging to the Dissenting interest, but also that relationships between Dissenters and members of the Established Church within smaller communities could be broken down by hypocritical action. Furthermore, it is clear that this advice was perceived to be particularly suitable in the wake of the Toleration Act.

In 1734 a Newcastle Dissenting minister, William Wilson, reminded his congregation that the 'mild and gentle' laws of the country which 'give every one of us Liberty to chuse our own Ministers' meant that his congregation had to be careful to respect that liberty in others, lest power fall into the hands of their opponents, who might 'justly ... say, what Reason have you to expect Liberty from us, when ye take it from one another'.[83] Advising his congregation on what might serve the maintenance of the Dissenting interest in this context, he claimed that 'serious Religion is its chief Support ... if these things fail among us; if our People grow loose and formal, or their Ministers become remiss and superficial in their Performances ... no lasting Establishment can be expected to our

---

[82] Diary of Anne (Dawson) Evans, fol. 28v.
[83] William Wilson, *Charity, as a Rule of Conduct in the Affairs of a Religious Society, Explain'd and Recommended. A Sermon Preach'd to a Congregation of Protestant Dissenters in Newcastle-Upon-Tyne, November the 22nd 1733* (London, 1734), pp. 25–6.

Cause. Without Piety, a Dissenter, any Dissenting Congregation, nay, the Interest itself, I humbly conceive, scarce deserves a Name.'[84] For Wilson, in the wake of the Toleration Act it was not viable to attempt to promote the Dissenting interest by suggesting that others were wrong, for that could only lead to accusations of hypocrisy. Instead, Dissenters had to mark out their distinctiveness through a demonstration of their sincere piety. Like Doddridge and Watts, Wilson believed that a dedicated and unblemished record of practical religiosity was the only way to demonstrate the validity of Dissent.

Wilson was not alone in reminding congregations of Protestant Dissenters to be grateful for liberty of conscience and avoid the hypocrisy of denying it to others. The sermon of a Lancashire Dissenting minister, Samuel Bourn, to a congregation in Dudley, Worcestershire, in 1738, celebrated that the Church of England had given up the 'terrible principles' of 'Calling conscientious Christians by ill Names, only for their upright Opinions, and teaching the way of Truth; and then doing to them ill Things to incapacitate and disqualify them for publick Service', by allowing liberty of conscience. He also warned Protestant Dissenters against getting left behind in this respect by continuing to rail against those of a different profession, reminding the congregation to 'Let not Protestant Dissenters be the last who open their Eyes, the last in throwing off this Remnant of Popery.'[85] Bourn recognised that the Toleration Act was an important moment for Dissenters in allowing them liberty, but he also saw that this swing in their fortunes created a new risk that Dissenters might demonstrate a hypocritical attitude towards those from whom they differed.

This view was equally evident in the sermon of another Dissenting minister, Benjamin Mills, given at Maidstone, Kent, in 1741, in which he encouraged his hearers and readers to 'carry [y]ourselves in so strictly, loyal, and peaceable a Manner, that we may hereby conciliate', rather than appearing sour about the remaining privileges that were barred to them under the law.[86] For these ministers, the change in the status of Dissent under the law made attention to the danger of hypocrisy particularly important, not just for the reputation of Dissent, but for maintaining their

[84] Ibid., p. 29.
[85] Samuel Bourn, *The True Christian Way of Striving for the Faith of the Gospel. A Sermon Preach'd to a Congregation of Protestant-Dissenters, Ministers, and Private Christians … in Dudley in Worcestershire, May 23 1738* (London, 1738), p. 26.
[86] Benjamin Mills, *A Sermon Preached to a Congregation of Protestant Dissenters, at Maidston, November 5, 1741* (London, 1741), pp. 33–4.

liberty.[87] The onus was on Dissenting congregations to ensure that the lives they lived were peaceable and pious, justifying both their separation from the Established Church and their 'toleration' under the law. The emphasis on conciliation suggests an awareness that their behaviour needed to be consonant with the supposedly inclusive polite discourse of the age.

Quakers, Hypocrisy, and Commercial Culture

Quakers were subject to many of the same accusations of hypocrisy as other Protestant Dissenters. However, Quakers had a slightly different relationship with emerging norms of politeness and fashion after the Toleration Act. The stress on differentiation from the world around them inherent in Quaker discipline meant that Friends' relationships to fashionable dress, behaviour, and material acquisition in the late seventeenth and early eighteenth century ostensibly set them at odds with contemporary society. This Quaker distinctiveness was derided by their opponents as a hypocritical cover for impiety. However, this was also a period in which Quakers were adapting successfully to engagement with the temporal world, expanding their influence in polite society, industry, and commerce.[88] The adaptations that Quakers made to their behaviour and conduct undoubtedly aided their assimilation in this period, and it might be expected that this would have taken the sting out of accusations of hypocrisy.[89] Yet Quaker attempts at politeness were themselves regarded as hypocritical, because conformity in social behaviour could be seen as contrary to Quaker claims to distinction. Many Quakers were highly successful in balancing temporal and spiritual impulses in the eighteenth century, but, whatever their behaviour, the label of 'hypocrite' was difficult to shake off.

From the 1650s, Quakers had been distinguishable by their deliberate social nonconformity. Although early Quakers did not always agree on what constituted 'plainness', the notion that Quakers should be visibly discernible from others through their dress and behaviour was rooted in

[87] Mark Goldie, 'The Theory of Religious Intolerance in Restoration England', in Ole Peter Grell, Jonathan Israel, and Nicholas Tyacke (eds.), *From Persecution to Toleration. The Glorious Revolution and Religion in England* (Oxford: Clarendon Press, 1991), p. 346.

[88] Robynne Rogers Healey, 'Quietist Quakerism, 1692-c.1805', in Stephen W. Angell and Ben Pink Dandelion (eds.), *The Oxford Handbook of Quaker Studies* (Oxford and New York: Oxford University Press, 2013), pp. 47, 55.

[89] Naomi Pullin, *Female Friends and the Making of Transatlantic Quakerism, 1650–c.1750* (Cambridge: Cambridge University Press, 2018), p. 251.

Quaker theology.[90] Quakers believed that all could discover the Inner
Light of Christ, and that once an individual had received the Light they
would be transformed from within to reject the ways of the world, including vanity in dress and lewdness in speech.[91] Furthermore, because the
Light could be received by all, they refused to recognise formal hierarchies in their modes of address. Although this did not mean that they
rejected social hierarchy altogether, it was expected that Quakers would be
appreciably different from others. The result of this was that to many non-
Quakers, Friends 'appeared to be shunning the conventions of politeness
and sociability'.[92]

Such deliberate forms of distinction from the rest of society not only provoked resentment at Quakers' failure to observe social norms and hierarchies, but also prompted accusations that their outward observance of strict
piety was a hypocritical mask for irreligious and socially deviant behaviour.
As with other forms of Protestant Dissent, this message was apparent in
character literature that, since the 1650s, had satirised Quakers. The mid-
seventeenth-century poet Samuel Austin suggested in his *Character of a
Quaker in His True and Proper Colours* that a Quaker's 'purity consists only
in his dress, and his Religion is, Not to speak like his Neighbour', concluding that 'a Quaker is a Canting thing that Cozens the world by the purity
of his Cloaths, a few Close-stool faces and whineing expressions, his Life is
only a real Lye, his Doctrine contrary to all sober Religion'.[93] This theme of
outward pretence to religion remained present in early eighteenth-century
characterisations of Quakers. In the anonymous *Character of a Quaker*,
published in 1704, a Quaker was 'a reproach to humane Nature; the reverse
of Reason and sound Argument; affects Singularity more than Sincerity,
and takes greater care of his Coat than his Conscience … His Religion must
needs be superficial, when 'tis no Deeper than his Cloaths.'[94] The message that Quakers were irrational and irreligious hypocrites whose outward
appearance belied their true nature was repeated in satire against Quakers
from their beginnings, and it was a message that stuck.

---

[90] Emma Jones Lapsansky, 'Past Plainness to Present Simplicity: A Search for Quaker Identity', in
Emma Jones Lapsansky and Anne A. Verplanck (eds.), *Quaker Aesthetics. Reflections on a Quaker
Ethic in American Design and Consumption* (Philadelphia, PA: Pennsylvania Press, 2003), p. 3.

[91] J. William Frost, 'From Plainness to Simplicity: Changing Quaker Ideals for Material Culture', in
Lapsansky and Verplanck, eds., *Quaker Aesthetics*, pp. 16–17.

[92] Pullin, *Female Friends*, p. 198.

[93] Samuel Austin, *The Character of a Quaker in His True and Proper Colours, or, the Clownish Hypocrite
Anatomized* (London, 1671), pp. 2, 17.

[94] *The Character of a Quaker* (London, 1704), p. 1.

This was evident from the fact that eighteenth-century playwrights made frequent use of the visually striking figure of a Quaker, often by implication suggesting that Quakers placed an undue stress on outward demonstration of their religion. This is seen clearly in Charles Shadwell's play *The Fair Quaker of Deal*, performed at the Theatre Royal, Drury Lane. In the play a prostitute dressed up as a Quaker betrothed to a ship's captain, declaring 'there, with Look demure, I'll pass for Saint; / No such fair Colour as Religious Paint', suggesting an emphasis on outward appearance among Quakers that did little to promote the piety of the inner self.[95] Elsewhere in the script, the Quaker's conforming sister dressed up as a Quaker man in an attempt to trick her sister out of her marriage.[96] In a similar manoeuvre in Richard Wilkinson's *The Quaker's Wedding*, 'Sir Feeble' successfully wooed the Quaker 'Widow Purelight' by adopting the dress and manner of a Quaker.[97] Quaker dress was further satirised on stage in Susanna Centlivre's play *A Bold Stroke for a Wife*, also performed at Drury Lane. In an argument with her Quaker guardian over her clothing, the eligible young lady at the centre of the plot is accused of inviting sin with her dress, to which she retorts 'Thou Blinder of the World, don't provoke me --- least I betray your Sanctity, and leave your Wife to judge of your Purity ... when you squeez'd Mary by the Hand last Night in the Pantry ... you had no Aversion to naked Bosoms, when you begg'd her to show you a little, little, little Bit of her delicious Bubby.'[98] Such allusions to sexual misdemeanour were a commonplace of both visual and verbal depictions of Quakers in this period, and represented a continuation of anti-Puritan stereotypes.[99] What is particularly crucial to note here, however, is the deliberate attention given to the physical attributes of Quakers not just in indicating but in actually shaping their immoral behaviour. The implication in all these instances is that the claims that Quakers made to piety through what they wore were a literal cloak for their sinful behaviour.

Quaker attitudes to distinction and social separation were, however, changing in the eighteenth century, and this might have been expected

[95] Charles Shadwell, *The Fair Quaker of Deal, or, the Humours of the Navy. A Comedy. As it is Acted at the Theatre-Royal in Drury-Lane* (London, 1761, first performed 1710), p. 34.
[96] Ibid., p. 58.
[97] Richard Wilkinson, *The Quaker's Wedding. A Comedy* (London: 1723), pp. 24–5.
[98] Susanna Centlivre, *A Bold Stroke for a Wife: A Comedy; as it is Acted at the Theatre in Little Lincoln's-Inn-Fields. By the Author of* The Busie-Body *and* The Gamester (London, 1718), pp. 16, 18.
[99] Knights, *The Devil in Disguise*, pp. 83–8.

to take the sting out of some of the charges against Quakers. As recent scholarship has stressed, Friends were less socially separate in this period than previously assumed, and both the Toleration Act and emergent cultures of consumption and luxury in the eighteenth century had a significant impact on their behaviour. After the extremity of behaviour of the early years of Quakerism, they sought 'strategies to negotiate the lines between the dichotomous worlds of the meeting and the outside world'.[100] Eighteenth-century Quakers became highly influential in trades such as drapery and clock making, as well as in mercantile activity and industrial development, and their success was supported by the heavy involvement of Friends' Meetings in the regulation of business.[101] Meetings surveyed members' business conduct closely, and required those who wanted to set up new trades to seek permission, thereby reducing the risk of debt or bad business practice, and ensuring that Friends were true to their faith in their business conduct.[102]

Alongside these expanding business interests, 'social and public forms of polite Quakerism' became more common, with leading 'polite Quakers' such as Mary Morris Knowles in the second half of the eighteenth century using engagement with polite society to overcome the legal and social difficulties that Quakers still faced.[103] Furthermore, as Naomi Pullin has highlighted in her important study of female Friends in the eighteenth century, one way in which Quakers were called to serve God was through the ordinary interactions of daily life, 'making complete isolation from wider society almost impossible'. Developing cultures of polite conversation and written exchange afforded opportunities for eighteenth-century Quaker women to proselytise in a less confrontational manner than in the seventeenth century.[104] Thus while the Quaker movement did not entertain the idea of polite conduct as a necessity after the Toleration Act, Quakers were clearly being influenced by cultures of politeness in this period, and this engagement undoubtedly aided the assimilation of Friends in the eighteenth century.

---

[100] Healey, 'Quietist Quakerism', p. 55.
[101] Richard C. Allen and Rosemary Moore, 'The Friends and Business in the Second Period', in Richard C. Allen and Rosemary Moore (eds.), *The Quakers, 1656–1723: The Evolution of an Alternative Community* (University Park, PA: Penn State University Press, 2018), pp. 247–8.
[102] Ann Prior and Maurice Kirby, 'The Society of Friends and Business Culture, 1700–1830', in David Jeremy (ed.), *Religion, Business, and Wealth in Modern Britain* (London: Routledge, 1998), pp. 118, 122.
[103] Judith Jennings, 'Mary Morris Knowles: Devout, Worldly, and "Gay"?', *Quaker Studies*, 14, 2 (2010), pp. 196, 202, 207.
[104] Pullin, *Female Friends*, pp. 247–8, 257.

However, even while this relationship with politeness and expanding commerce brought considerable financial and social success for many Quakers, it was far from unproblematic. The commercial activities of Quakers could create tension between their worldly and religious interests. This too was connected to the emergence of polite discourse as developed in the periodical press, which espoused the defence of trade as a 'legitimate basis of sociality' and a 'foundation of politeness and morality'.[105] Commercial success could be an aid to polite sociability; it was also in part dependent on it. Yet it remained that it was difficult to square the creation of wealth through commerce with the rejection of worldly goods and social customs.

In this context, plain clothing was one simple way for Friends to 'perform in the commercial sphere while maintaining distance from it', but this too illustrated some of the difficulties of balancing worldly and spiritual demands.[106] As fine materials and luxury goods became more readily available, many wealthier Quakers showed signs of adhering to the letter rather than the spirit of Quaker discipline by, for instance, wearing plain clothes made of luxury materials.[107] Such actions may have helped these Friends to participate in polite society, but they also played into the accusation that Quaker religion consisted solely in their outer clothing. Ironically, although the desire to maintain zeal, discipline, and Quaker identity after the Toleration Act led to more precise prescription of Quaker social conduct, it also allowed some Quakers to remain outwardly adherent to regulation, while failing to match the spiritual expectations of Quakerism.

Concerns about this trend were apparent in the actions and instructions of the London Yearly Meetings in the eighteenth century. The Epistle from the Meeting in 1691, for instance, instructed all Friends to 'avoid pride and immodesty in apparel, and extravagant wigs', and in 1717 the Meeting's minutes warned Quakers that they should not 'imitate the World in any distinction of habit Otherwise, as Marks or Token of Mourning for the dead'.[108] The Epistle from 1739 gave extensive space to

---

[105] Stephen Copley, 'Commerce, Conversation, and Politeness in the Early Eighteenth-century Periodical', *Journal for Eighteenth-Century Studies*, 18, 1 (1995), p. 67.

[106] Healey, 'Quietist Quakerism', pp. 57–9.

[107] Ross E. Martinie Eiler, 'Luxury, Capitalism, and the Quaker Reformation, 1737–1798', *Quaker History*, 97, 1 (2008), pp. 14–15.

[108] *A Collection of the Epistles from the Yearly Meeting of Friends in London to the Quarterly and Monthly Meetings in Great-Britain, Ireland and Elsewhere from 1675 to 1805* (Baltimore, 1806), p. 42; Felsted Monthly Meeting: Minutes of London Meeting, 1717, A13685 Box 51: Contents of Box K (uncatalogued), Essex Record Office, Chelmsford.

condemning jewellery and other rich adornments, quoting from Pauline injunctions against "'broidered hair, or pearls, or gold, or costly array'", and concluding that 'those, who of old were holy, and did trust in God, placed not their delight in such ornaments'.[109] Aware of the ways in which many Friends were adapting to fashionable consumer society, Meetings sought to steer their members away from such temptations, but evidently they were not wholly successful.

The result was that although as the century wore on, developments in Quaker culture made it less easy for critics of Quakers to accuse them of using social separation and eccentric behaviour as a hypocritical cover for immorality, eighteenth-century Quakers could continue to be charged with hypocrisy on the grounds that their pretences to politeness did not match their stated principles of differentiation from the ways of the world. This was reflected in Ned Ward's 1701 characterisation of a Quaker, which acknowledged the shifts that had occurred in the movement since the mid-seventeenth century. 'He has been often Metamorphos'd, like a Tadpole into a Frog, or a Silk-worm into a Butterfly', he wrote, 'and from a Crawling Insect, is become a Volatile Drone, who has soar'd upon the Wings of Tolleration, above the Church's Persecution: His chief Study is to Counterfeit Outward and Visible Signs of an Inward and Spiritual Grace.' Despite charging Quakers with undue attention to outer forms of piety, he noted that 'They have most of 'em shifted off their Preciseness, as a Troublesome Restraint they had put upon their own Natures; and are Conform'd, within half an Inch, to the accustom-ary Vices, as well as Habits and Manners of Mankind.'[110] The phrase 'Conform'd, within half an Inch' emphasised that Quakers more or less conformed to worldly norms and luxuries with only a nod to Quaker plainness. Ward's characterisation chimed with the way in which Quakers were mocked on stage for adhering rigidly to outward distinc-tions while behaving immorally, but he included the additional criticism that many Quakers had abandoned even these outward signs of piety. Whether adhering to contemporary social expectations or not, Quakers could be accused of hypocrisy.

Furthermore, some opponents of Quakerism argued that a tendency among some Quakers to conform more closely to worldly fashion was

---

[109] *A Collection of the Epistles from the Yearly Meeting of Friends*, p. 185.
[110] Ned Ward, *The Reformer: Or, the Vices of the Age Expos'd, In Several Characters* (London, 1701), pp. 11, 13.

made all the more unacceptable by the fact that it did not result in a reduction in their vocal opposition to the Established Church. Indeed, as the vehement anti-Quaker polemicist Francis Bugg suggested, their 'Libels, and bitter Invectives, against the Church of England, and the Ministers thereof' had increased 'especially since their Toleration, who instead thereby of growing more Mannerly, they grow more Insolent than ever'.[111] He thus observed that 'their Principles are the same from 1652 to 1706, without any Change or alteration, though of late a little smoother than formerly'.[112] Meanwhile, he complained, they continued 'To pretend to be plain, and desire to be known of Men, as they are known of God; and yet at the same time design nothing more than to hide their Principles under a mask of Religion'.[113] According to Bugg, Quakers had adopted smoother manners, but their opponents should not be fooled. They were still the divisive hypocrites they had always been, and their conduct was made all the more objectionable by their pretended conformity with the manners of the age.

Unsurprisingly, given the invective against them, the potential problems that an accommodation of Quaker behaviour to temporal concerns might present to the spiritual well-being of Friends were also acknowledged by prominent Quakers. The Pennsylvania minister John Woolman, influential on both sides of the Atlantic, wrote repeatedly against the excesses of riches, and gave up his successful retail merchandising business in order to pursue a simple life and the gainful occupation of tailoring.[114] After Woolman's death in 1772, the York Quarterly Meeting testified to his rejection of the worldly concerns that he feared were corrupting Quakerism, recording that 'Deeply sensible that the desire to gratify people's inclinations in luxury and superfluities is the principal ground of oppression, and the occasion of many unnecessary wants, he believed it to be his duty to be a pattern of great self-denial.'[115] Similarly, Samuel Bownas, a Quaker minister and merchant in Dorset at the time he was writing, warned his neighbours that 'Pomp and Luxury have ever been fatal Enemies to true Religion,' and in his later life became disillusioned

---

[111] Francis Bugg, *Goliah's Head Cut Off With His Own Sword, and the Quakers Routed by Their Own Weapons* (London, 1708), p. xl.

[112] Ibid., p. 264.

[113] Ibid., p. 270.

[114] David Sox, 'Woolman, John (1720–1772)', *Oxford Dictionary of National Biography* (Oxford University Press, 2004), www.oxforddnb.com/view/article/29960, accessed 30 May 2018.

[115] *A Journal of the Life, Gospel Labours, and Christian Experiences of that Faithful Minister of Jesus Christ, John Woolman, late of Mount-Holly, in Pennsylvania* (Dublin, 1776), p. vii.

with what he saw as a lack of true 'convincement' among Quakers.[116] The commercial developments of the eighteenth century presented both an important opportunity and a significant challenge for Friends, as Quaker distinctiveness came into tension with the growing availability of goods and the increased opportunity to improve quality of life. It is unsurprising, therefore, that by the mid-eighteenth century there were Quaker leaders on both sides of the Atlantic attempting to combat what they perceived to be a spiritual decline caused by an increase in luxury.[117]

Some Quakers also perceived that the passage of the Toleration Act itself had damaged the integrity of the movement. Although Friends continued to be concerned with serving God in the world, once they were legally tolerated Quakers became less focused on shaping the whole of society, and more centred on improving themselves.[118] Because the freedom of worship offered under the Toleration Act was conditional, 'Quakers wanted to appear as inoffensive as possible,' and tightened up their organisation and discipline over membership of the Society.[119] The apparent need for such strict discipline after 1689 was recognised by contemporaries. The Quaker preacher Richard Ashby wrote in 1715 that 'All they that remember how the Hand of the Lord was seen in the Day of Sufferings, can say, It was a good Time to the faithful ... as Afflictions abounded, Consolation did much more abound.' In contrast, he found that the zeal of Quakers had decreased 'in this Day of outward Ease and Liberty', and that 'There is an undue Liberty taken by too many, and that Plainness that was in the Beginning, is too much gone ... The undue Liberty that is taken in Attire, beyond a real Decency, to deck and adorn poor frail Bodies, that must die, and return to Dust, and neglect the inward Adorning of the never-dying Soul.'[120] Quakers were no longer brought together and marked out by their common suffering, and Ashby too was concerned that they were becoming prey to the temptations of fashionable society, and needed to restore their self-discipline.

[116] Samuel Bownas, *Considerations on a Pamphlet Entitul'd, the Duty of Consulting a Spiritual Guide, Considered* (London, 1724), n.p. (*Dedication*, p. 2); Gil Skidmore, 'Bownas, Samuel (1677–1753)', *Oxford Dictionary of National Biography* (Oxford University Press, 2004), www.oxforddnb.com/view/article/3083, accessed 30 May 2018.

[117] Eiler, 'Luxury, Capitalism, and the Quaker Reformation', pp. 16–18; Emma J. Lapsansky, 'Plainness and simplicity', in Angell and Pink Dandelion (eds.), *Oxford Handbook of Quaker Studies*, pp. 338–9.

[118] Frost, 'From Plainness to Simplicity', p. 25.

[119] Healey, 'Quietist Quakerism', pp. 49, 53.

[120] Richard Ashby, *An Epistle to the Called of God, Every-Where; In Order to Stir Up Their Minds, By Way of Remembrance, of the Great End for Which They are Called: With Exhortation to Keep Unity* (London, 1715), pp. 11, 23.

His references to 'outward Ease' and the neglect of the 'inward Adorning of the ... soul' demonstrate a concern from some – although certainly not all – within the Quaker movement that Friends were demonstrating a hypocritical laxity in their discipline.

Quaker concerns about politeness were not the same as other Protestant Dissenters' quandaries after the Toleration Act. Whereas other Protestant Dissenters were debating the extent to which they should be polite, Quaker theology and disciplinary messages from Meetings of the Society of Friends made it clear that Quakers should distance themselves from all 'vain fashions and Customs of this World', even as they engaged in business and commerce.[121] Adherence to polite principles was not given explicit consideration. Furthermore, it is undoubtedly the case that despite the pessimistic outlook of some prominent Quakers, and the criticisms of their opponents, many Quakers did continue to try to follow the spirit and not just the letter of Quaker testimony.

However, Quakers were unavoidably affected by both the changing commercial customs of the eighteenth century and the passage of the Toleration Act in a way that served to perpetuate and even heighten the charges of hypocrisy levelled against them. The limited liberty allowed to Quakers under the Toleration Act threatened to undermine their collective zeal and distinctive identity. This encouraged a new emphasis on organisation and discipline that created a more precise set of rules around clothing and behaviour, which in turn heightened the potency of the accusation that Friends placed too much emphasis on outer forms at the expense of the inner spirit. This more precise set of rules also appears to have enabled members to retain a sense of loyalty to their profession while still living in 'the world'. Furthermore, Quaker success in the commercial world brought them more closely than ever into contact with worldly vanities and luxuries. The tension between this and the spiritual separation inherent to Quakerism was a cause of considerable concern to some of the movement's leaders by the middle of the century.

Quaker testimony against fashion, vanity, and luxury therefore placed them in a particularly difficult situation in the context of the eighteenth century. Many Quakers derived a great deal of commercial and social success from conforming to behavioural norms and engaging with polite society, and indeed Quaker business was supported and monitored by

---

[121] Minutes of Nailsworth monthly meeting, 10th day 5th month 1718, D1340/B1/M1, Gloucestershire Archives, Gloucester.

Meetings. Some prominent Quakers saw such action as a betrayal of Quaker distinctiveness, which left them vulnerable to accusations of hypocrisy on the grounds of not living up to their principles. However, if Friends refused to conform to social norms, they ran the risk of continuing to be accused, as they had in the seventeenth century, of irrationality, social divisiveness, and using outward piety as a mask for hypocritical laxity.

Although Quaker attitudes to cultural expectations were in many ways quite distinct from those of other Protestant Dissenters, there were strong similarities in their situation. On the one hand, impulses towards commercial success and the need to prove themselves deserving of toleration after 1689 encouraged them towards behaviour more in line with wider social norms. On the other hand, the need to maintain a distinctive religious identity in the wake of that Act pulled both Quakers and other Dissenters towards a demonstration of distinctiveness in their outward social behaviour. Both options left them open to charges of hypocrisy. The supposedly inclusive social cultures of the eighteenth century presented a challenge to Quakers and other Protestant Dissenters alike.

Contrasting Experiences: Catholics, Hypocrisy, and Politeness

The social conundrums faced by all varieties of Protestant Dissenters are further emphasised by comparison with the experience of Catholics. Catholics can by no means be regarded as a 'control group' indicative of what the experience of Protestant Dissenters would have been without the limited liberty of 1689. Catholics and Protestant Dissenters were penalised for different reasons, and their social and political heritage and justifications for refusing to conform were at odds with one another. Nevertheless, comparison of the two is illuminating. While expectations of social behaviour among Catholics were inherently different from those of Protestant Dissenters, the contrasting ways in which they managed their social behaviour in defence of their religious positions are striking. For both Protestant Dissenters and Catholics, social conformity was a means of combatting intolerance by demonstrating integration. But whereas for Protestant Dissenters politeness endangered their distinctive identity, and left them open to charges of hypocrisy, for Catholics it was one of the principal means by which to defend their religious profession and assert their right to continue as worthy members of the nation. This difference can, at least partially, be attributed to their contrasting treatments under the terms of the Toleration Act.

The persecution and social ostracism experienced by Catholics was, unsurprisingly, based on different principles to that of Protestant Dissenters. Catholics, like Dissenters, were labelled as hypocritical. However, while Dissenters were accused on an individual level of hypocrisy in their personal conduct, the charge of hypocrisy against Catholics tended to be levelled at the institutions and authorities of the Church. Anti-Catholic polemic suggested that the rituals and forms of the Catholic Church induced hypocrisy by allowing individual worshippers to go through the motions of worship without real prayer in their hearts. The Leicestershire Presbyterian minister Benjamin Bennet made this case in 1714, when he stated that 'it's plain a Man may say his Prayers, hear Mass, and be a good Christian, at least a good Catholick, tho' there be no prevailing Love of the blessed God working in his Soul'. He went on to highlight the specific differences between Protestant and Catholic hypocrisy: 'Protestants … may be Hypocrites in their Worship, and too many of them alas are so; but they are taught better things,' 'Hypocrisie with them [Protestants] is against Principle. But here are a Company of Men [Catholics], that one might almost say are Hypocrites by Profession.'[122] Similarly, a later anonymous author, writing in the wake of the 1745 Jacobite Rebellion, suggested that the Catholic form of worship was used to trick potential converts into belief, because 'The glittering Gold in their Temples, and curious Images of Saints and Angels, the numerous and stately Altars, the mighty Silver Statues, the rich and glorious Vestments you see up and down their Churches, strike the Senses into a kind of Extacy.'[123] The Catholic adherent was thus seduced by the Church into a hypocritical worship, whereby they acted the part rather than expressed an inner belief. Unlike in critiques of Protestant Dissent, the root of hypocrisy was not necessarily found in the hearts of individual believers. Rather, it was institutionalised in the Church.

This was not to say that individual Catholics entirely escaped charges of hypocritical impiety. Since the dissolution of the monasteries, the wealthy, overindulgent, and sexually deviant priest, monk, or nun had been a trope of anti-Catholic polemic, and this remained the case in this period.[124] In his anti-Catholic *Discourses*, Bennet described monks as 'true and genuine Pharisees in this Respect: They have a sham Spirituality and heavenly

---

[122] Benjamin Bennet, *Several Discourses Against Popery* (London, 1714), pp. 355, 359.

[123] *The Artifices of the Romish Priests, in Making Converts to Popery: Or, an Account of the Various Methods, Practised by Popish Missionaries, to Deceive the Protestants of this Kingdom, and Deprive Them of Their Religion and Loyalty* (London, 1746).

[124] Colin Haydon, *Anti-Catholicism in Eighteenth-Century England: A Political and Social Study* (Manchester and New York: Manchester University Press, 1993), pp. 6, 27.

mindedness: Witness their withdrawing from the World, into religious Houses where they generally live in Luxury and Mirth'.[125] This luxury, the Church of England clergyman and controversialist Antonio Gavin alleged, was obtained by tricking good souls: 'If a modest, serious, religious Lady comes to confess', he wrote, 'he useth her in another way; for he knows that such Ladies never come to confess without giving up good Charity for Masses'. The result was that 'these ignorant, hypocritical Fryers are always follow'd by the ignorant People, who furnish them with Money and Presents for the Sake of their Prayers, and they live more comfortably than many rich People'.[126] Even more salaciously, monks and priests were accused of using the privacy of confession as an opportunity to break their vows of chastity. This was the clear message behind many visual satires of Catholic clerics in this period. The late-seventeenth-century print *A Lady at Confession* (Figure 3.4), for example, showed a heavily made-up lady sitting at the feet of a monk, supposedly confessing, while he takes the opportunity to gaze at her ankles. These were, however, very specific insinuations of hypocrisy aimed at figures of authority in the Catholic Church who had taken the vows of poverty, chastity, and obedience. They were not aimed at Catholics in general; lay Catholics, unlike Dissenters, made no particular claim to piety over others. The result was that they could not be charged with hypocrisy on these grounds.

Individual Catholics were, however, subject to the charge of political hypocrisy. Their opponents claimed that given Catholics' loyalty to the Pope, their protestations of allegiance to their monarch could only ever be hypocritical, because their faith demanded loyalty to a foreign prince. Thus, as the anonymous author of *The Desolations of a Popish Succession* put it in 1716, "tis the greatest Hypocrisy for these Men to talk of their Loyalty and Love to Kings, when the Consequences of their Principles must make their Kings but Tools and Vassals to Rome'.[127] As with accusations of hypocrisy that related to Catholic worship, it was argued that it was Catholics' loyalty to their religion that would make them hypocrites. It was impossible for them to live in a Protestant country and be truly loyal to the king. This was fundamentally different from how the charge of hypocrisy was applied to Dissenters: they were hypocrites because they failed to adhere to the proclaimed precepts of their faith, not because those precepts themselves induced hypocrisy.

---

[125] Bennet, *Several Discourses Against Popery*, p. 347.
[126] Antonio Gavin, *A Master-Key to Popery. In Five Parts* (London, 1725), pp. 46, 225.
[127] *The Desolations of a Popish Succession* (London, 1716), p. 12.

Figure 3.4 John Smith, *A Lady at Confession* (London, 1691). Mezzotint on paper. 253 x 200 mm. British Museum No. 1874,0808.2324, © The Trustees of the British Museum.

Crucially, however, the charges of hypocrisy levelled against lay Catholics in this period were far less relatable to principles of politeness than those pitched against Dissenters. This was largely because Catholicism did not place specific social expectations on its believers, as many Protestant Dissenting professions did. There was no particular requirement in Catholicism, for instance, for adherents to avoid excessive merriment. The young Catholic gentlewoman Mary Huddleston of Sawston, Cambridgeshire, for example, was expected to attend a ball at the horse races, where 'there is to be Cards for the Lady that doe not dance' – activities that, as we will see more extensively in the next chapter, were not encouraged frequently among her Dissenting counterparts.[128] As numerous studies have shown, the Catholic gentry in particular were often heavily involved in the sociability of their local gentry communities, attending horse races, hunts, dances, and other social activities.[129] Thus although Catholicism itself was not regarded as polite, Catholics themselves could be. The deceased Tudor cardinal, Reginald Pole, for example, was referred to in 1747 by the Established Church clergyman Daniel Lombard as 'that elegant, that polite, that humane man' despite his 'accursed Zeal for Popery'.[130] Lombard's contemporary Conyers Middleton was equally generous towards Catholic manners, writing to his readers that 'whatever be my Opinion of the general Scheme of their Religion, yet, out of justice to the particular Professors of it, I think my self obliged to declare, that I found much Candour, Humanity, and Politeness in all those I had the honour to converse with'.[131] Politeness does not seem to have stimulated contradictory impulses in Catholics in the way that it did Protestant Dissenters.

This difference in attitudes towards politeness, and the consequent differences in the way the charge of hypocrisy was applied to Dissenters and Catholics respectively, should not be attributed solely to their intrinsic differences. It was also a product of the fact that politeness served contrasting purposes for Catholics and Protestant Dissenters in the wake of the Toleration Act. As we have seen, for Dissenters, politeness was at once demanded of them as a means of showing integration and conformity in the wake of a limited and potentially unstable toleration, and also threatened the integrity of their religion by undermining their distinctive pious

---

[128] Elizabeth Marshe to Mary Huddleston, 1 August 1727, 488/C1/MH9, Cambridgeshire Archives, Cambridge.

[129] Leo Gooch, '"The Religion for a Gentleman": The Northern Catholic Gentry in the Eighteenth Century', *Recusant History*, 23, 4 (1997), pp. 547, 565; Carys Brown, 'Militant Catholicism, Interconfessional Relations, and the Rookwood Family of Stanningfield, Suffolk, c. 1689–1737', *Historical Journal*, 60, 1 (2017), p. 40.

[130] Daniel Lombard, *A Succinct History of Ancient and Modern Persecutions. Together With a Short Essay on Assassinations and Civil Wars* (London, 1747), p. 72.

[131] Conyers Middleton, *Letter from Rome, Shewing an Exact Conformity Between Popery and Paganism* (London, 1713), sig. A2v.

identity. Although they had gained a legal toleration, sociability remained both a means of distinction and a source of persecution.

Catholics did not have this problem. Their identity as religiously different was never in question: the law made that clear enough – the 1689 Act referred to the 'Dangers which may grow by Popish Recusants'.[132] Centuries of anti-Catholic legislation had labelled them as deeply untrustworthy, and the Toleration Act reinforced this.[133] Furthermore, in contrast to Dissenters, Catholics were attempting to circumvent the terms of the Toleration Act, not secure them. Social conformity was therefore unequivocally beneficial for Catholics in a way that it was not for Dissenters. Not only was participation in polite sociability a means of building up trust relationships with non-Catholics, but it could also prove essential for preventing the worst excesses of the law being implemented against Catholics. A clear example of this was seen in the East Riding of Yorkshire in 1733, when the Archbishop of York sought to bring prosecutions against some local Catholic gentlemen who appeared to have been sponsoring the evangelical efforts of Catholic priests. On learning of these prosecutions, the Protestant friends of the accused intervened until the Archbishop backed down, declaring that 'I am very glad The Gentlemen of Quality and Distinction among the Roman Catholics … are so good as to be satisfied in my true Intentions towards 'em.'[134] Protestant and Catholic gentlemen in the East Riding were involved in networks of sociability, centring on hunting, dining, and other gentlemanly activities, and it seems likely that this was essential in ensuring the Catholics' protection from prosecution.[135] Social conformity among Catholics thus formed part of a long legacy of employing 'spirited if silent defences of their social and religious position' against the persecutions of the Protestant state.[136] Polite sociability posed a threat to the reputation of Protestant Dissent, but it was essential for the survival of Catholicism.

---

[132] 'William and Mary, 1688: An Act for Exempting their Majestyes Protestant Subjects Dissenting from the Church of England from the Penalties of Certaine Lawes [Chapter XVIII. Rot. Parl. pt. 5. nu. 15.]' in John Raithby (ed.), *Statutes of the Realm* (n.p.., 1819), vol. VI, pp. 74–6. *British History Online*, www.british-history.ac.uk/statutes-realm/vol6/pp74-76.

[133] Carys Brown, 'Catholic Politics and Creating Trust in Eighteenth-Century England', *British Catholic History*, 33, 4 (2017), pp. 623–5.

[134] Sidney Leslie Ollard and Philip Charles Walker (eds.), *Archbishop Herring's Visitation Returns, 1743* (Cambridge: Cambridge University Press, 5 vols., 2013), vol. 4, p. 387.

[135] For examples of inter-confessional participation in hunting and racing in the region, see Lord Cardigan to Marmaduke Constable, 17 November 1728, UDDEV/60/84f, Hull History Centre, Hull; John Cherry, *An Historical List of All Horse-Matches Run, and of All Plates and Prizes Run for England and Wales* (London, 1729), pp. 16, 18, 21, 24, 128.

[136] Sandeep Kaushik, 'Resistance, Loyalty and Recusant Politics: Sir Thomas Tresham and the Elizabethan State', *Midland History*, 21, 1 (1996), p. 42.

In the Restoration period the religious beliefs and practices of both Catholics and Protestant Dissenters lay beyond the bounds of the law. Indeed, as demonstrated in the first chapter of this book, their opponents frequently equated the two. They were persecuted minorities that had no need to rely on social distinctions to mark out their profession; the law did that for them. After the passage of the Toleration Act, Catholics continued to be marked out as persecuted outsiders, and therefore relied on local social and political networks to ensure the survival of their religion and estates. By contrast, Dissenters were thrown into an uncertain position by the Act: they could no longer rely on their position as a beleaguered minority to mark out their identity; there was a greater onus on them to maintain their difference through their social behaviour. Hence while the Toleration Act represented for Catholics a continuation of their characterisation under the law as a seditious and dangerous threat to Church and State, for Protestant Dissenters it represented a shift from legal exclusion towards a focus on social conformity. As a result, Catholics showed resilience in defending their position, but Dissenters found themselves debating the extent to which they should compromise. Given this, it is unsurprising that while Catholics were styled by their opponents as politically disloyal and corrupt idol-worshippers, Dissenters were characterised as impolite hypocrites who failed to put principle into practice.

Conclusion

Many of the legal and social changes of the first half of the eighteenth century were highly favourable to the fortunes of Protestant Dissenters. The Toleration Act of 1689, albeit still limited in its provision, had tacitly acknowledged some degree of religious pluralism as inevitable. For the first time, the worship of Dissenters of all descriptions was protected by the law. Furthermore, modes of discussion and labels used to describe Dissent were subject to changing meanings and contexts. Hypocrisy, a charge long levelled against Puritans, nonconformists, and Quakers, and regarded as the ultimate vice for much of the seventeenth century, was beginning to be regarded by some as acceptable in certain contexts. In addition, the increasing dominance of discourses of 'politeness' and 'moderation', in reaction to 'the socially disruptive impact of religion in the seventeenth century', ostensibly discouraged the social marginalisation or abuse of Dissenters.[137]

---

[137] Klein, 'Politeness and the Interpretation of the British Eighteenth Century', p. 890.

However, the reality was not quite so straightforward. This chapter has emphasised the extent to which, while attempts to limit the legal and political benefits that Dissenters derived from toleration began to look increasingly futile as the century wore on, languages of social interaction evolved as powerful tools for exclusion. The label of hypocrisy was applied to Dissenters in this period with reference to ideals of politeness and social conformity, suggesting that far from promoting inclusivity and limiting religious divisions, politeness could be used to emphasise difference. This was evident in the double-edged criticism faced by Dissenters with regard to their social conduct. On the one hand, ostensibly pious behaviour was now being discussed not just in terms of its probable hypocrisy, but also as a symptom of Dissenters' impoliteness. On the other hand, Dissenters who failed to distinguish themselves significantly from others in their social behaviour could be regarded as hypocritical in their supposedly principled Dissent from the Established Church. Quakers likewise experienced competing impulses in how they framed their social behaviour. Quaker distinction was derided as impolite and divisive, as well as being a hypocritical disguise for impiety. However, increasing Quaker acceptance of luxury and involvement in commercial markets simultaneously presented a challenge to the distinct identity of Quakers and exposed them to further charges of hypocrisy in Quaker testimony. It appears that it was nearly impossible for Dissenters both to conform to emerging social expectations and to avoid the charge of hypocrisy.

The particular difficulty of managing this dual threat was reflected in the comments of pious Dissenters on their behaviour after 1689. The need to balance social integration with distinguishing the cause of Dissent through pious behaviour is apparent in the debates among leading ministers about the role that polite conduct should play in their ministry, and in the reactions of individual Dissenters to the awkward demands that social situations could place on them. The immense sensitivity of Dissenters to these concerns suggests that, contrary to pretences to inclusivity, when combined with the charge of selfish hypocrisy, the language of politeness could in fact be highly exclusive, acting to emphasise rather than brush over religious divides. For Quakers, emerging cultures of consumption and trade led to more prescriptive stipulations about Quaker behaviour, again emphasising impulses towards distinction rather than integration. In the face of continuing intolerant attitudes, social behaviour was at the heart of the tension between integration and distinction.

Politeness and associated trends in fashion and consumption were not, of course, the only frameworks of social interaction in the eighteenth century. We should be wary of creating dichotomies of polite–impolite behaviour, when the reality was that individuals adapted a much wider social register to a variety of contexts. It was in fact possible for 'multiple and often contradictory behaviours to co-exist'; politeness was but one of them.[138] In this sense, an analysis of attitudes towards Protestant Dissenters exclusively through the languages of hypocrisy and politeness paints a picture that is too black and white, emphasising inclusion and exclusion as opposites when the reality was much murkier, involving coterminous ideas about neighbourliness, civility, and trust. What it does highlight, however, is the extent to which even social languages that ostensibly promoted harmony could be manipulated to reinterpret the religious questions that had so catastrophically divided the country in the previous century. It suggests that, as much as proponents of politeness might have liked to pretend otherwise, it is difficult to understand the operation of the multiple social registers of the eighteenth century without keeping underlying religious divisions in mind.

---

[138] Kate Davison, 'Occasional Politeness and Gentlemen's Laughter in Eighteenth-Century England', *Historical Journal*, 57, 4 (2014), pp. 931, 945. See also Helen Berry, 'Rethinking Politeness in Eighteenth-Century England: Moll King's Coffee House and the Significance of "Flash Talk"', *Transactions of the Royal Historical Society*, 11 (2001), pp. 65–81.

CHAPTER 4

Drinking, Dancing, Talking

Whatever the challenges that faced them, Protestant Dissenters had to live as part of society: they traded and interacted with people not of their own religious professions; they engaged with contemporary social and cultural developments.[1] Commonplace as such observations might be, they raise some significant questions. Given that religious prejudices were prevalent in eighteenth-century society, it might be expected that this would affect social and professional interactions between Dissenters and others. But such interactions did occur – and regularly. Did both parties pragmatically suspend religious differences, or were religious differences simply not particularly relevant in this context? Dissenters appear to have been better integrated into contemporary social, cultural, and political life as the century wore on. What might this tell us about contemporary cultural life?[2] Did the presence of Dissenters at social occasions leave a discernible cultural mark, or were Dissenters simply being successfully assimilated into a cultural mainstream?

This chapter suggests both that religious differences were highly relevant to social interactions in key cultural contexts, and that the presence of Dissenters within these contexts was of wider cultural significance. It is evident from the preceding chapters that religious difference mattered

---

[1] See for example David L. Wykes, 'Religious Dissent and the Penal Laws: An Explanation of Business Success?' *History*, 75, 243 (1990), p. 44; Bill Stevenson, 'The Social Integration of Post-Restoration Dissenters, 1660–1725', in Margaret Spufford (ed.), *The World of Rural Dissenters, 1520–1725* (Cambridge: Cambridge University Press, 1995), pp. 361, 376–7, 385; Doreen Rosman, *The Evolution of the English Churches, 1500–2000* (Cambridge: Cambridge University Press, 2003), p. 129; Simon Dixon, 'Quakers and the London Parish 1670–1720', *The London Journal*, 32, 3 (2007), p. 231; Lindsay Houpt-Varner, 'Maintaining Moral Integrity: The Cultural and Economic Relationships of Quakers in North-East England, 1653–1700', in Adrian Green and Barbara Crosbie (eds.), *Economy and Culture in North-East England, 1500–1800* (Woodbridge: Boydell & Brewer, 2018), p. 154.

[2] Richard L. Greaves, 'Seditious Sectaries or "Sober and Useful Inhabitants"? Changing Conceptions of the Quakers in Early Modern Britain', *Albion*, 33, 1 (Spring 2001), p. 40; Ana M. Acosta, 'Spaces of Dissent and the Public Sphere in Hackney, Stoke Newington, and Newington Green', *Eighteenth-Century Life*, 27, 1 (2003), pp. 9, 15.

both to the negotiation of power on a local level, and to the development of ideals of social behaviour. In this chapter we see that religious difference also shaped the voluntary social interactions that formed the basis of the burgeoning culture of eighteenth-century England. It explores in detail the dynamics of Protestant Dissenters' sociability in different cultural venues and social situations, and the responses of members of the Established Church to their behaviour. In doing so, it not only encourages a more expansive understanding of the varieties of cultural interaction in eighteenth-century England, but also highlights some of the crucial ways in which awareness of religious differences shaped social and cultural behaviour.

The social and cultural history of the eighteenth century has frequently been underwritten by a focus on consumption, luxury, and pleasure, rather than piety or abstention. When historians have examined the lives of those who did not enjoy contemporary cultural trends, it has generally been through an emphasis on economic insecurity, which acted as a barrier to engagement.[3] However, scholars have now started to consider more seriously those who *chose* not to engage fully in emerging cultural modes. Helen Berry's work on 'the pleasures of austerity' has shown that if we focus on those who deliberately withdrew from aspects of contemporary culture, we are forced into expanding our range of definitions of contemporary sociability.[4] Doing so helps us to recognise the diversity of ways in which the common cultural modes and spaces of eighteenth-century England were interpreted. The contexts explored in this chapter suggest that the sociable piety of Dissenters – which might well be considered a form of 'pleasurable austerity' – was an important part of this picture. In the cases explored here, we see a symbiotic relationship between Dissenting expectations of piety and eighteenth-century cultural norms: Dissenters' behaviour was reactive to contemporary prejudice against Dissent, but Dissenters were also active in trying to mould the society they lived within. Members of the Established Church, perceiving differences between Dissenters and others, in turn sometimes shaped their social behaviour in reaction to Dissent. The result was that religious difference had an inevitable, although sometimes unintended, impact on contemporary interpretations of cultural life.

This argument is founded on a range of source material. Meeting books of Dissenting churches and ministerial records of congregational behaviour give

[3] Tawny Paul, *The Poverty of Disaster: Debt and Insecurity in Eighteenth-Century Britain* (Cambridge and New York: Cambridge University Press, 2019), pp. 4–7.
[4] Helen Berry, 'The Pleasures of Austerity', *Journal for Eighteenth-Century Studies*, 37, 2 (2014), p. 263.

some insight into ideals about social behaviour upheld by different churches. They also demonstrate that individual Dissenters frequently failed to live up to these ideals. However, these records tend to emphasise extremes, putting in the foreground an institutional emphasis on separation from worldly cultural norms, while also recording the exclusion of church members who experienced drastic lapses into drunken or debauched behaviour. In contrast, the diaries and letters of individuals, as well as court records, frequently highlight moments of social interaction between Dissenters and members of the Established Church. As is noted throughout this chapter, these social interactions were often themselves shaped by impulses to piety, but this did not mean Dissenters disengaged from the culture around them. Rather, they sought to use their piety to shape the behaviour of others through edification. It was this that makes their behaviour significant for expanding our understanding of contemporary culture.

Individual diaries cannot be taken as representative of the views and behaviours of all Dissenters. Those who kept spiritual diaries were, by their nature, particularly anxious and reflective about their social behaviour, and this probably resulted in them taking greater care in regulating their actions. As examples from court records and incidental mentions of the behaviour of Dissenters in life-writings of members of the Established Church demonstrate, there was a spectrum of social behaviour even within particular denominations and churches. In a sense, however, there is an advantage in looking at records that focus on the more consciously and conspicuously pious end of the Dissenting spectrum. Examining these individuals re-directs our attention away from an historiographical tendency to focus on luxury, generous consumption, and debauchery in characterisations of eighteenth-century cultural life. It was the behaviour of the most conspicuously pious Dissenters that members of the Established Church tended to pick up and comment on, and, against a backdrop of existing prejudice, these individuals had a disproportionate influence over the way religious difference was characterised in social terms in contemporary print. This fed back into the perceptions of members of the Established Church, with the result that an awareness of religious difference remained central to the operation of social interactions in eighteenth-century England.

Pious Sociability, or Sociable Piety?

In March 1717 the Bishop of London, John Robinson, sent a letter warning Richard Willis, the Bishop of Gloucester, about an errant Dissenting minister. Samuel Evans, who was seeking ordination in the Established

Church, had led a 'dissolute life', and had been 'turned out by his dissenting Congregation at Hammersmith, notwithstanding he had sollicited from house to house to be retained'. Strikingly, the Bishop reported that the Dissenters had 'declared in Conversation that tho he [Evans] was not fit to live among them, he might serve well enough for a Parson in the Church'. The Bishop of London was confident that Gloucester would 'know what to do with him', but the message from the Dissenting congregation was clear. While they wished to maintain their own pious integrity, they believed the bar for entering the Established Church was low.[5] In the contrasts they drew between the Established Church and their own, and in the ways Dissenters regulated the conduct of members of their congregations, it appears that they set themselves up as culturally different from the rest of society.

The relevance of religious differences to social interactions was, from the perspective of many Dissenters, undoubted. The desire to maintain the integrity and reputation of their communions meant that many Dissenting Meetings kept a close eye on the social behaviour of their brethren, condemning those who erred from the meetings' high standards, and maintaining a sense of distinction between the conduct of Dissenters and the behaviours of the world. This impulse to separation might be regarded as meaning that Dissenters' behaviour was of little cultural relevance beyond the confines of their own religious networks. However, as this section shows, Dissenters' attitudes to social activities beyond the community of the godly were far from simple. Aspects of sociability regarded as adiaphora – or things not explicitly endorsed or condemned by scripture – could sometimes demand engagement because they offered the chance for the edification of others. Dissenting involvement in contemporary culture did not necessarily demand a pragmatic suspension of a sense of religious difference, but rather could be actively informed by it.

Some Dissenters' records, like the Bishop of London's letter, suggest that Dissenters were cultural outliers, and indeed there were reasons for Dissenters to maintain a level of cultural distinction. In his work on early-seventeenth-century Puritans, Patrick Collinson stressed that whereas anti-separatist Puritans had to constantly maintain their godly singularity through 'social and cultural distinctiveness practised against neighbours with whom the godly were in daily face-to-face contact', separatists 'no longer need to affirm their singularity by continual and demonstrative

[5] Cautionary letter from the Bishop of London concerning Samuel Evans, late Dissenting teacher at Hammersmith, 3 March 1717, GDR/E3/4/1, Gloucestershire Archives (GA), Gloucester.

acts of abstention and disapprobation' – or at least not in prescriptive literature.[6] Dissenters after 1689 were in a different legal, political, and ecclesiological position, but the connection between religious and social separation might still be made. The failure by the 1690s of Presbyterian and some Independent hopes of comprehension within the Church meant that – against their will – they, along with Quakers and Baptists, were defined as clearly separate from the Established Church under the Toleration Act. As a result, it could be suggested according to Collinson's model that Dissenters of all denominations would have had no need to 'affirm their singularity' through social behaviour after 1689. However, the Toleration Act also defined Dissenters as part of a broader Protestant interest, thereby including them within a collective endeavour against the threat of popery, and removing the legal persecution that partially defined their singularity. As we saw in Chapter 1, the rhetoric of suffering had been important to the survival of Restoration Dissenters. Their successors now had to adapt, finding ways of maintaining group identities formed around senses of embattlement and difference, even when persecution was no longer reinforced by their legal status.

An apparent tendency towards social exclusivity and personal piety among Dissenters can be seen in the commitment of Presbyterians, Independents, Baptists, and Quakers to the maxim given in 2 Thessalonians 3:6: 'Now we command you, brethren, in the name of our Lord Jesus Christ, that ye withdraw yourselves from every brother that walketh disorderly, and not after the tradition which he received of us.'[7] This is not to say that 2 Thessalonians 3:6 was deemed irrelevant in the Established Church – it underpinned the principle of excommunication – but the frequency with which it was applied by Dissenters contrasts with contemporary and historical perceptions of a decline in the authority of Church courts in enforcing discipline in this period.[8] It was important for the identity of Dissenting Churches that the social conduct of their members reflected their principled dissention from an Established Church that

---

[6] Patrick Collinson, 'The Cohabitation of the Faithful with the Unfaithful', in Ole Peter Grell, Jonathan Irvine Israel, and Nicholas Tyacke (eds.), *From Persecution to Toleration: The Glorious Revolution and Religion in England* (Oxford: Clarendon Press, 1991), pp. 62. See also Alexandra Walsham, 'The Godly and Popular Culture', in John Coffey and Paul C. H. Lim (eds.), *The Cambridge Companion to Puritanism* (Cambridge: Cambridge University Press, 2008), p. 277.

[7] 2 Thessalonians 3:6 (King James Version).

[8] Martin Ingram, 'Church Courts in England', in Charles H. Parker and Gretchen D. Starr-LeBeau (eds.), *Judging Faith, Punishing Sin: Inquisitions and Consistories in the Early Modern World* (Cambridge: Cambridge University Press, 2017); Donald Spaeth, *The Church in an Age of Danger: Parsons and Parishioners, 1660–1740* (Cambridge: Cambridge University Press, 2000), pp. 59–60.

failed, in their opinion, to maintain the moral purity of its communion. As a result, the fact that Dissenters could more closely regulate the morality of their members was often used in justifications of their separation from the Established Church.[9]

References to 'disorderly walking', 'dishonour' to the profession, and the need to 'disown', 'withdraw from', and 'cut off' sinners are consequently seen repeatedly in the meeting books of Baptists, Quakers, and Independents, and in the personal records of Presbyterian ministers.[10] The meaning and application of these ideas varied between different types of Dissent, and even between different Churches or Meetings.[11] Systems of Church regulation and organisation also differed: the duty of disciplining the Presbyterian flock tended to fall on the minister, whereas Independents, Baptists, and Quakers usually shared responsibility for monitoring members' behaviour more evenly across congregations.[12] Quakers tended to place the clearest restrictions on social behaviour. They were at least theoretically required, as one Manchester Meeting made clear to its members, to avoid 'the vain and foolish customs, fashions, observances and fellowships of the world', and were advised to 'keep their children or those under their charge from the society of the worlds children, lest thereby they learn corrupt evil words and manners'.[13] Other denominations were less unequivocally restrictive. Kimbolton Independent Church, for example, debated in 1721 whether the 'wearing of fashionable hoops' by ladies 'be lawful or not'. Although 'The majoryty of the brethren ... answered in the negative that it was not lawfull,' the fact that they were even considering the question suggests

---

[9] See for example Jeremiah Hunt, *Dissenters No Schismaticks: Or, Dissenting Churches Orthodox* (London, 1714), pp. 24, 31–2; John Norman, *Lay-Nonconformity Justified, in a Dialogue Between a Gentleman of the Town in Communion with the Church of England, and His Dissenting Friend in the Country* (London, 1716), pp. 18–19.

[10] Examples are numerous in addition to those given below. See Stoke Orchard and Gloucester Meeting Minutes, esp. fols. 307r, 400v, 403v, 406-r–v, D1340/B2/M1, GA; Wooton-under-Edge Baptist Church, Church Book, 1717–1826, esp. fols. 6r–v, D2844/2/1, GA; Society of Friends, Hardshaw Monthly Meeting: Personal Condemnations and Testimonies of Denial, 1667–1797, esp. fols. 35r–v, 36v, M85/1/11, Manchester Archives (MA), Manchester; Meetings in East Devon, Chiefly at Loughwood Baptist Chapel in Dalwood Parish: Proceedings Book, 1653–1795, esp. pp. 17–18, 3700D/M/1, Devonshire Archives and Local Studies (DALS), Exeter; St Neots United Reformed Church: Church Book, 1691–1802, esp. pp. 234–6, FR16/1/1/1, Huntingdonshire Archives (HA), Huntingdon.

[11] Michael R. Watts, *The Dissenters. From the Reformation to the French Revolution* (Oxford: Clarendon Press, 1978), p. 321.

[12] Ibid., pp. 317, 322–4.

[13] Society of Friends, Hardshaw Monthly Meeting: Book for Recording Papers and Epistles &c, fols. 1r, 4r, M85/1/12/1, MA.

that the congregation's separation from worldly customs was not quite so clear-cut as the Quakers'.[14]

Nevertheless, most Meetings retained a strong message of pious exclusivity. By regulating members according to a framework which split behaviour into that belonging to the world, and that belonging to the true Church, Meetings implicitly created a sense of pious separation from wider society. In November 1752, for instance, Thomas Matthews of Loughwood Baptist Chapel, Devon, was 'rejected by the Church for a long unsavoury Conversation in the world'.[15] Even Presbyterians, who did not have the same separatist ecclesiology, made ample use of this language: James Clegg, the Presbyterian minister of Chapel-en-le-Frith, Derbyshire, for example, wrote in May 1737 that at a Meeting of Cheshire ministers Mr David Herbert 'was by them disownd and rejected and a letter orderd to be written to his hearers to withdraw from him as one that walkd very disorderly'.[16] It is clear that Dissenting leaders took seriously the injunction to keep their professions clear from moral lapses.

While separation from the world was far more extreme in some cases than in others, there was a consistent expectation that Dissenters would lead a particularly holy life, avoiding drunkenness, debauchery, and ill conversation. Records of Dissenting Church regulation thus give a strong impression that the pious sociability they expected of their members would to some extent divorce them from the cultural mainstream. After all, as Isaac Watts emphasised in his *Practical Religion*, it was incumbent upon Dissenters to reflect on the question 'What is there of Duty to God or Man wherein you Separatists from the publick Establishment exceed the rest of the Nation?'[17] If Dissenters could not argue that their aims were discernibly more pious than those of their counterparts in the Established Church, what was the point of Dissenting?

However, there were numerous ideological and practical considerations that pushed back against any straightforward emphasis on cultural separation. First, while generalisations about a straightforward shift from 'sect' to 'denomination' across all Dissenting groups should be avoided, Dissent did, broadly speaking, become more outward-facing in this period.

---

[14] Typed transcript of the Kimbolton Independent Church Book, pp. 10, 41, PGMD/3500/15, HA.

[15] Meetings in East Devon, Chiefly at Loughwood Baptist Chapel in Dalwood Parish: Proceedings Book, 1653–1795, p. 18, 3700D/M/1, DALS.

[16] Vanessa S. Doe (ed.), *The Diary of James Clegg of Chapel en le Frith, 1708–1755, Part 2* (Derby: Derbyshire Record Society, 1979), p. 314.

[17] Isaac Watts, *An Humble Attempt Toward the Revival of Practical Religion Among Christians, and Particularly the Protestant Dissenters* (London, 1731), p. 172.

Dissenters were, for instance, disproportionately involved in trade and mercantile activities. This did not necessarily give them cultural power, or result in a total conformity to social norms, but it certainly required regular engagement with 'worldly' matters.[18] Dissenters were no longer illegal oppositional groups; they had to find a way of living in a reluctantly pluralist society.

The relationship between 'worldly' interaction and pious identity was therefore complex. As Naomi Pullin has highlighted in relation to Quakers, increased co-operation with individuals outside of the faith did not necessarily lead to a decline in the importance of distinctive behaviour – in fact, it could make the need to distinguish oneself all the more urgent.[19] Maintaining strict standards of social behaviour was important for many individual Dissenters, and this may have meant detaching themselves from some aspects of contemporary culture. Yet there were also other reasons why it was important for even the most piously anxious Dissenters to mingle with religiously mixed company in the decades after 1689. Sociability, if undertaken piously, could be seen as highly productive, not just for maintaining the distinctive identity of the godly, but also for inspiring improvement in others. Alongside the need to guard their own behaviour, Dissenters aspired to be culturally and socially active in a way that contributed to their own, and others', edification; it was this that made Dissenters' behaviours important for the culture of the venues and spaces they socialised in.

Cultural engagement did not, then, as it might first appear, run completely contrary to the standards that Dissenting Meetings set their members. Injunctions to withdraw from or cut off sinners did not necessarily mean that Dissenters had to absent themselves from the company of anyone behaving sinfully. The condemnation of 'disorderly walkers' seen in Dissenters' meeting books related to those who had behaved immorally while claiming to be members of a godly society.[20] When it came to social interaction with those outside of their own communion, abstention or moderation in the company of others might be a more effective means of fulfilling religious duty than complete withdrawal. This socially oriented form of piety had been justified in Puritan interpretations of the Pauline concept of 'edification' since the late sixteenth century. Puritans saw edification not

---

[18] Acosta, 'Spaces of Dissent and the Public Sphere', pp. 3–4, 7.
[19] Naomi Pullin, *Female Friends and the Making of Transatlantic Quakerism, 1650–1750* (Cambridge: Cambridge University Press, 2018), pp. 254–5.
[20] Hunt, *Dissenters No Schismaticks*, p. 31.

as something that occurred subsequent to the establishment of a Church, but rather as the means by which a Church could come into being. It was regular interaction between individuals that allowed the Church to emerge 'in the midst of society'.[21] The result was that sociable piety was central to the ecclesiology of many Dissenting Churches: they viewed the right exercise of conscience and edification through charity to others as an essential means of constructing the Church through society. Sociability was, within this framework, an indispensable part and result of fostering mutual piety; spiritually speaking, Dissenters could not afford to isolate themselves.

Furthermore, social behaviour was counted among 'things indifferent', which had been central to sixteenth- and seventeenth-century Puritan discourse on moral behaviour. In his *Cases of Conscience*, the Puritan minister William Perkins identified things indifferent as actions 'which in themselves being neither good nor evil, may be done or not done without sin'. However, he also reminded readers that 'actions indifferent in the case of offence, or edification, cease to be indifferent', because 'it serveth to incourage every man … in the diligent performance of the duties of his calling'.[22] This attitude was more plainly laid out by the Restoration nonconformist Richard Baxter, who instructed believers to 'not take the course that pleaseth our selves; but that which by pleasing him may edifie our weak brother'. Baxter made a direct connection between the injunction towards edification given in Romans 15:2 and the duty of Christians not to tempt others into cards, dice, and other sports, highlighting that although they were 'bound to bear a thing indifferent' practised by their fellow creatures, they should also 'avoid the scandalizing or tempting of another' by encouraging them into it.[23] Attempts to model pious behaviour were themselves social acts, and this was an important aspect of the social and religious life of many Dissenters. The social nature of their piety was not just important for personal faith and integrity. Rather, it was a part of a religious duty to care for others.[24] Although most Dissenters (excepting some Quakers) rarely proselytised, they had no desire to keep their religion hidden from sight; they needed to enact it in society.

---

[21] John S. Coolidge, *The Pauline Renaissance in England. Puritanism and the Bible* (Oxford: Clarendon Press, 1970), pp. 49, 50.

[22] William Perkins, *The Whole Treatise of the Cases of Conscience Distinguished into Three Bookes* (Cambridge, 1608), pp. 8–9, 69–70.

[23] Richard Baxter, *A Christian Directory, or, A Summ of Practical Theologie and Cases of Conscience Directing Christians How to Use Their Knowledge and Faith* (London, 1673), pp. 218, 263–4.

[24] See for example Matthew Henry, *An Exposition of All the Books of the Old and New Testament*, (London, 3rd edn 1721–1725), vol. 6, p. 207.

This concept of edification fitted well communities of Dissenters that were increasingly active in trade and public life.[25] The Presbyterian minister Benjamin Andrewes Atkinson argued for a society based on speaking 'the Truth in Love [Ephesians 4:15]', providing 'a sufficient Foundation for a firm and lasting Union, leaving every one Liberty to differ, as they see Reason in lesser Matters ... without breaking Communion with them, or censuring them on account of their differing Sentiments'.[26] With this in mind, he pleaded for 'Peace and Love ... with mutual Forbearance in doubtful Matters', quoting Romans 15:2: 'let every one of us please his Neighbour, for his Good to Edification for even Christ pleased not himself'. On this basis he suggested that 'it will be better for us if our Lord at his Coming finds us cultivating such a Spirit and Temper, than judging or beating our Fellow Servants, because they don't think and speak in Religion just as we would have them'.[27] In this interpretation, stimulating piety and a godly community through society with others was of greater benefit to both personal and general religiosity than the proud separation of the godly.

This view was also supported by a continued Dissenting emphasis on the role of providence in daily life. After 1689, providential thinking formed an important justification for the involvement of Dissenters and others in moral reform. Many of those involved in attempts to reform morality in the decade following the Toleration Act interpreted England's struggles in war against France, as well as natural events such as the earthquakes of 1692, as a sign of God's wrath at the failure of the country to reform Church and State.[28] Indeed, in the face of concern about declining public morality in the 1690s, Societies for the Reformation of Manners worked to ensure the enforcement of England's moral legislation by the magistrate. Responding to the fact that the events of 1688–9 had challenged theocentric conceptions of the magistrate's role, these Societies shaped their case for moral reform in secular terms.[29] Many of the Societies were

---

[25] Acosta, 'Spaces of Dissent and the Public Sphere', pp. 3–4.

[26] Benjamin Andrewes Atkinson, *Catholick Principles, or St. Paul's Worship Faith, Hope and Practice Recommended to Christians of All Persuasions* (London, 1730), p. 3.

[27] Ibid., pp. 27–8.

[28] Craig Rose, 'Providence, Protestant Union and Godly Reformation in the 1690s', *Transactions of the Royal Historical Society*, 3 (1993), p. 155.

[29] Tina Isaacs, 'The Anglican Hierarchy and the Reformation of Manners, 1688–1738', *Journal of Ecclesiastical History*, 33, 3 (1982), p. 391; Shelley Burtt, 'The Societies for the Reformation of Manners: Between John Locke and the Devil in Augustan England', in Roger D. Lund (ed.), *The Margins of Orthodoxy. Heterodox Writing and Cultural Response, 1660–1750* (Cambridge and New York: Cambridge University Press, 1995), pp. 154, 158–9.

surprisingly ecumenical, incorporating both Anglicans and Dissenters in a Protestant union; they did not argue that Dissent itself encouraged immorality.[30] Nevertheless, the formation of such societies is indicative of wider concern that after 1689 neither Church nor State was taking sufficient action to protect the moral welfare of the nation.

Providence also had a broader role to play in Dissenting piety.[31] While some forms of providential belief – such as the interpretation of monstrous birth as a divine sign – appear to have decreased as the eighteenth century wore on, Dissenters continued to interpret natural phenomena as a sign of divine displeasure at contemporary morality.[32] A fire in Blandford Forum in Dorset, for instance, was in 1735 interpreted by Congregationalist Malachi Blake through a providential and moralistic lens. In a printed account of the fire, with an attached sermon, he described the 'Sad Providence', hoping that his sermon would be 'serviceable to this Town … to consider calmly and sedately of God's Dealings with us'.[33] Describing how the public buildings of the town had been burned down, including the town hall and places of worship, he suggested that 'both Magistrates and Ministers may take Occasion to inquire, whether by their Authority, Examples, Instructions, and Reproofs, they duly endeavoured the Suppression of Immorality, and the Promoting pure Religion and undefiled?'[34] Careful regulation of moral behaviour was essential not just for the reputations of Dissenters, but for their sense of shared responsibility for the broader well-being of the nation.

It was against this backdrop that pious Dissenters entered the social world of their contemporaries. Pauline expectations of the edification of others underpinned a basic need for Dissenters to enact their piety socially as well as in the safety of the closet. Continued providential beliefs gave urgency to the cause of moral reform, and ensured that it was particularly important for ministers and congregations to model piety. The advice to

---

[30] Rose, 'Providence, Protestant Union, and Godly Reformation in the 1690s', pp. 165–6; Brent Sirota, *Christian Monitors: The Church of England and the Age of Benevolence, 1680–1730* (New Haven: Yale University Press, 2014), pp. 89, 92–4.

[31] Michael P. Winship, *Seers of God. Puritan Providentialism in the Restoration and Early Enlightenment* (Baltimore, MD: Johns Hopkins University Press, 1996), p. 1; Naomi Pullin, 'Providence, Punishment, and Identity Formation in the Late-Stuart Quaker Community, c. 1650–1700', *Seventeenth Century*, 31, 4 (2016), pp. 471–94.

[32] William E. Burns, *An Age of Wonders. Prodigies, Politics, and Providence in England, 1657–1727* (Manchester and New York: Manchester University Press, 2002), pp. 138–9, 174.

[33] Malachi Blake, *A Brief Account of the Dreadful Fire at Blandford-Forum in the County of Dorset* (London, 1735), title page, p. vi.

[34] Ibid., p. 63.

Dissenters was to participate in society, but not to embrace it wholly; to tolerate others' sinfulness, but also to attempt to assuage it.

Dissenters, then, were not cultural outsiders, at least not in a simple sense. In fact, there were specific ecclesiological imperatives that made their engagement with society essential. As the rest of this chapter shows, Dissenters were part of religiously mixed company in key cultural venues, and it is important to recognise that such social interactions were not always pragmatic transgressions of pious expectation, but rather were theologically and ecclesiologically justified. The combination of Dissenters' specific modes of cultural engagement with the continuation and evolution of established stereotypes of Dissent had consequences not just for how Dissenters engaged with social forms and venues, but also for how these important aspects of contemporary culture were framed by understandings of religious difference.

Alehouses, Taverns, and Intoxication

The role of religious differences in shaping social interactions was not, as we have seen, simple for Dissenters. It was also far from straightforward for conforming Protestants. Within the context of drinking spaces, interactions between Protestants of different affiliations could vary from violent, to tense, to amicable, with everything in between. Such variety might be viewed as reflecting the general colour of social interaction in such venues. However, as this section shows, there is considerable evidence that even when such interactions were amicable, senses of religious difference could play an important part in how both Church and Dissent interpreted the social dynamics that underpinned their experiences of socialising in alehouses and taverns.

In the past two decades, historical explanations of the role of alcohol in the social and political landscape of the seventeenth and eighteenth centuries have expanded significantly. Far from being the refuge of the poor, destitute, and marginalised, intoxication and sociability are now recognised to have been 'deeply intertwined' across all social strata.[35] The alehouse has been rehabilitated as a central institution of the parish in seventeenth- and

---

[35] Vicki Hsueh, 'Intoxicated Reasons, Rational Feelings: Rethinking the Early Modern English Public Sphere', *Review of Politics*, 78, 1 (2016), p. 42. See also Phil Withington, 'Intoxicants and Society in Early Modern England', *Historical Journal*, 54, 3 (2011), pp. 631–57. For a discussion of the role of the alehouse for the poor, see Peter Clark, 'The Alehouse and Alternative Society', in Donald Pennington and Keith Thomas (eds.), *Puritans and Revolutionaries. Essays in Seventeenth-Century History Presented to Christopher Hill* (Oxford: Clarendon Press, 1978), pp. 53–6.

early eighteenth-century England, with recreational drinking, governed by the idea of 'good fellowship', acting as 'an important socio-cultural activity that was integral to the formation of positive identities'.[36] Furthermore, the practice of giving toasts and singing political drinking songs was common among drinking companies in a variety of venues, reinforcing the consumption of alcohol as a marker of inclusion and exclusion.[37] In an age when 'hard drinking was endemic among both sexes and all ranks of society', participation in social drinking was an important means of expressing political loyalties and demonstrating clubbability.[38]

For Protestant Dissenters, the role that intoxicated merriment played in social and political bonding might be expected to represent something of a problem. Nonconformists never explicitly advocated total abstention from alcohol, recognising its function as a form of refreshment, but the 'Puritan' impulse to restraint was a significant factor in attempts to regulate and control drink throughout the seventeenth and eighteenth centuries.[39] However, Dissenters were perhaps more engaged in sociable drinking than we might expect. Their participation in drinking practices – and their interactions with other denominations in this context – exemplify the possibility of ostensible conviviality between denominations when it came to drink. However, they also reveal that even convivial inter-denominational sociability could be inflected with an underlying awareness of, and anxiety about, religious difference.

Involvement in communal drinking was not without its risks for Dissenters. The combination of a wide variety of company with the presence of intoxicating substances in drinking spaces meant that they were far from free of the potential for religious argument. There is substantial

---

[36] Mark Hailwood, *Alehouses and Good Fellowship in Early Modern England* (Woodbridge: The Boydell Press, 2014), p. 169.

[37] Angela McShane, 'Material Culture and "Political Drinking" in Seventeenth-Century England', in Phil Withington and Angela McShane (eds.), *Cultures of Intoxication* (Oxford: Oxford University Press, Past and Present Supplementary Series, 2014), pp. 259, 272; Angela McShane, 'Drink, Song, and Politics in Early Modern England', *Popular Music*, 35, 2 (2016), p. 168.

[38] Roy Porter, 'The Drinking Man's Disease: The "Pre-History" of Alcoholism in Georgian Britain', *British Journal of Addiction*, 80, 4 (1985), p. 386; Hailwood, *Alehouses and Good Fellowship*, p. 9; Hsueh, 'Intoxicated Reasons', p. 44.

[39] James Nicholls, 'Vinum Britannicum: The "Drink Question" in Early Modern England', *Social History of Alcohol and Drugs*, 22, 2 (2008), pp. 194, 198, 204; Alexandra Shepard, '"Swil-bols and Tos-pots": Drink Culture and Male Bonding in England, c. 1560–1640', in Laura Gowing, Michael Hunter, and Miri Rubin (eds.), *Love, Friendship, and Faith in Europe, 1300–1800* (Basingstoke: Palgrave Macmillan, 2005), p. 116; Keith Wrightson, 'Alehouses, Order, and Reformation in Rural England, 1590–1660', in Eileen Yeo and Stephen Yeo (eds.), *Popular Culture and Class Conflict 1590–1914: Explorations in the History of Labour and Leisure* (Brighton: The Harvester Press, 1981), pp. 21–2.

evidence that the alehouse and the tavern were places where religion might be discussed, and this could easily become a point of tension. In a case heard in Chester Consistory Court in 1693–4, for example, a witness, Edmund Matthews, testified that in November 1693 'several persons or members of the company of shoemakers ... were in the evening together at John Nichols his house ... drinking a glass of ale together when there happened some discourse about matters of religion'. The discussion 'grew warm', leading to references to books written by Alderman Wilcock (Church of England) and Matthew Henry (Presbyterian). One Hugh Rhodes then declared loyalty to the Church, and John Sutton allegedly responded by (mis)quoting Presbyterian minister Matthew Henry as having said 'that all who went to Church [of England] were damned'.[40]

This incident provides a clear example of religiously mixed drinking. Presumably it was not uncommon for this company of shoemakers to drink together, so this was unlikely to have been a one-off occurrence. From this we can infer that the religious differences of the company were not always a barrier to peaceful social interaction; court records show us single instances of transgression, not samples of everyday life. Nevertheless, it also illustrates the potential for religious differences to sour social relations. Matthews's witness statement that 'there happened some discourse about matters of religion' suggests that discussion about religious matters was initially part of the natural flow of alehouse conversation, but the discussion quickly grew heated – this was an inflammatory topic, one grounded in controversy circulating in local print. The case occurred in the years immediately after the passage of the Toleration Act, when there were particular tensions between Church and Dissent among the laity in Chester, including an attempt to burn the Dissenting meeting house down in 1692.[41] Religious differences were perhaps particularly likely to lead to outward conflict in this context; in later, less fraught, times they might not have done.

Nevertheless, it seems that tense controversy over religious difference was sustained over a number of years in Chester, and that this was

[40] Harrison c Sutton, 1694, EDC 5/1693/21 (unfol.), Cheshire Archives and Local Studies (CALS), Chester. Transcribed by *Intoxicants in Early Modernity*, www.dhi.ac.uk/intoxicants/record.jsp?searc htype=browse&&source=courtpaper&courtpaper_ID=707, accessed 15 December 2020. This case is discussed in detail in Peter Bamford, "'For the Church or the Stable": A Chester Consistory Court Case of 1693–94', in Paul Middleton and Matthew Collins (eds.), *Matthew Henry: The Bible, Prayer, and Piety. A Tercentenary Celebration* (New York: T&T Clark, 2019), pp. 69–80.

[41] Matthew Henry to Phillip Henry, 21 October 1692, MS Eng. lett. e. 29/103, Bodleian Lib. (Bod.), Oxford.

expressed in the alehouses and taverns as much as it was in printed disputation. In February 1707, Matthew Henry reported in his diary that his fellow Dissenting minister 'Mr Kenr[ick] told us that some time ago being in company at a Tavern with Alderm. Peter Bennet, he raild bitterly at me, and swore by his maker three times if the Queen would give him leave he would cut my throat, & the throats of my Congregation.'[42] These snapshots of tension over religious differences in drinking spaces in Chester in this period are particularly interesting because there appears to have been a good relationship between Matthew Henry and the clergy in the town, suggesting that these differences were being perpetuated among the local laity, rather than emanating principally from the pulpit.[43]

In fact, additional evidence of religious tensions emerging in drinking spaces highlights the degree to which the religious differences expressed in these contexts could be products of other grievances. The lapsed Hackney Dissenter Dudley Ryder recorded in his diary in July 1715 that when he went to the Crown tavern in Ironmonger Lane near St Paul's 'One Mr Wadsworth who was there and is a Whig too was complaining of the dissenters and railing at them very vehemently. It seems he has been cheated by one of them and his prejudice seems to proceed from thence.' Ryder complained that 'Even the Whigs themselves that are churchmen have not all got over their prejudices. They look upon themselves as persons in a higher rank, of a superior degree and therefore grudge them all the privileges that they have.' Ryder felt he had dealt with the issue satisfactorily – he wrote that 'Mr Wadsworth was sufficiently answered both by myself and Mr Crisp who spoke very warmly upon this occasion' – but the incident provides a clear demonstration of how wider grievances could easily become attached to religious differences.[44] Drinking spaces, as places where individuals participated in sociable drinking that was crucial to identity-formation, were well-suited for airing frustrations and expressing ideas that identified an individual with a particular social group or viewpoint.[45] Once the presence of religiously mixed company had been added to this situation, there was significant potential for tensions over religious difference to surface.

---

[42] Diary of Matthew Henry, 1705–1713 (entry for 7 February 1707), MS. Eng. misc. e. 330, fol. 33r, Bod.
[43] Ibid., fol. 63r; William Tong, *An Account of the Life and Death of Mr. Matthew Henry, Minister of the Gospel at Hackney, Who Dy'd June 22. 1714. In the 52d Year of His Age. Chiefly Collected Out of His Own Papers* (London, 1716), pp. 59–60, 76–7, 201.
[44] William Matthews (ed.), *The Diary of Dudley Ryder, 1715–1716* (London: Methuen, 1939), p. 65.
[45] Hailwood, *Alehouses and Good Fellowship*, p. 169.

This is not to suggest that Protestant Dissenters were unable to enjoy a sociable drink. Alongside these instances of religious tension there are numerous examples of Dissenters drinking without apparent incident. The nonconformist minister Peter Walkden, for instance, recorded in his diary many occasions on which he drank sociably – albeit moderately – with others. On 7 March 1733 he found himself so wet and windswept on his journey home from a baptism that he 'put in my Nag at George Boltons of Hudder Bridge, and Laid off my wet coat, and set above an hour, dureing which Time, George and I drunk 3 pintes of ale'.[46] He then continued home, picking up some letters for a neighbour on the way, and conducted family prayers. On another occasion in April of that year he 'walked to Newton and was told by john cawson that oliver wood wanted to speak to me at Willy cawsons: I went to him at wills and he told me that he had a child to baptize, and made me drink of a pinte of Ale'.[47] On both these occasions there was an instrumental purpose to Walkden's visit to the alehouse, but the act of drinking was also sociable – in the first case he had an extended visit during which he drank more than can be regarded as strictly necessary for the purposes of refreshment, and in the second case his (perhaps slightly reluctant) drinking was a celebratory marker of the birth and baptism of a new child. Evidently, social drinking had its place for Dissenters such as Walkden.

There is further evidence beyond Dissenters' own records of sociable drinking among religiously mixed company. In a case heard at a Norfolk Church court in 1717–1718, for instance, John and Mary Thurston of Bradfield, who were not Dissenters, were charged with immorality – specifically of allowing people to drink and smoke tobacco in their house during divine service. Some witnesses testified to the Thurstons' regular church attendance, but one, Robert Overton, who had been drinking at their house, stated that he 'goes to the Presbyterian Meeting and he cannot tell whether they [the Thurstons] constantly keep the church'.[48] Because he had revealed his religious affiliation, Overton's account of the proceedings at the Thurstons' house that day gives an insight into an instance of interdenominational drinking. He recalled that

<hr/>

[46] Diary of Peter Walkden, 1733–5 (entry for 7 March 1733), ZCR 678, p. 43, CALS.
[47] Ibid., p. 58.
[48] Office c Thurston, December 1717–April 1718, DN/DEP 59/63 (unfol.), Norfolk Record Office, Norfolk. Transcribed by *Intoxicants in Early Modernity*, www.dhi.ac.uk/intoxicants/record.jsp?searchtype=browse&&source=courtpaper&courtpaper_ID=657, accessed 15 November 2019.

he with John Thurston and another person of the same town ... went to the
dwelling house of John Thurston in Bradfield, where being asked by one of
his companions to spend his penny, they called for some strong waters ...
Mary the wife of John Thurston brought them half a pint of strong waters
which was commonly called clove-waters, after that they had drunk the
same, he had a quarter of a pint more ... [he] and one of his companions
paid their halfpenny each for the same ... they stayed about three-quarters
of an hour at Thurston's house.[49]

Overton's drinking was moderate – he stayed for less than an hour and he
spent only about one and a half pennies on the consumption of drink –
but this was evidently a sociable activity. Overton was asked by a companion to drink with him, and he acquiesced, drinking not thirst-quenching
ale but 'strong waters'.

Incidental examples of Dissenters engaging in sociable inter-denominational drinking can also be found in the diary of Henry Prescott, the Deputy
Registrar of Cheshire Diocese, and staunch Established Church Tory. On
28 January 1708 he noted 'After Dinner, one Lee, a Sailer and Quaker calls
on Tom Birchal. I entertain him with my strong Ale.'[50] While the social
purpose of this episode is unclear, on other occasions Prescott was evidently
drinking socially alongside Quakers. On 24 September he recorded in his
diary that having received a summons from Lord Anglesey, he had joined
him and Mr Nutley, a judge. He went on to note 'the Collector and Capt.
Lawson are added presently to the Company. Mr. Rook, a Quaker, after,
makes it 8. The Table set and surrounded, my Lord calls freely, a cheerfull
Ayr rises and improves, as the wine circulates ... His Lordship, with excellent temper, true ingenuity and good language, delights the company and
concludes the Time past 12.'[51] No more is said about Mr Rook the Quaker's
participation in the company's drinking, but there can be no doubt that
he was part of this group, whose conviviality increased as the wine flowed.
Prescott's apparent willingness to drink with both Presbyterians and
Quakers is somewhat surprising, given the general distaste for Dissent that
he expressed throughout his diary. Certain forms of communal drinking
clearly had the potential to cross denominational boundaries.

---

[49] Ibid.
[50] John Addy (ed.), *The Diary of Henry Prescott, LL. B., Deputy Registrar of Chester Diocese, vol. 1, 28 March 1704–24 March 1711* (Manchester: Record Society of Lancashire and Cheshire, 1987), p. 218 (entry for 28 January 1708).
[51] John Addy and Peter McNiven (eds.), *The Diary of Henry Prescott, LL. B., Deputy Registrar of Chester Diocese, vol. 2, 25 March 1711–24 May 1719* (Manchester: Record Society of Lancashire and Cheshire, 1994), pp. 655–6 (entry for 24 September 1718).

From such contrasting examples of, on the one hand, religious conflict and, on the other, inter-denominational conviviality, it is difficult to
draw general conclusions about the role that religious differences played
in shaping sociability in drinking spaces. Each of these examples provides
a snapshot of a particular time and place created by the chance of archival
survival; without consistent evidence from a wide range of venues across
time, it is impossible to discern whether conflict, conviviality, or a mixture
between the two was the norm. There is, however, evidence that religious
differences could remain a factor in social interactions over drink, even
when those interactions were entirely peaceable. We should not, therefore,
assume from the mere fact of their occurrence that situations of apparent inter-denominational conviviality were unfettered by the dynamics of
religious difference.

Take, for example, Prescott's inter-denominational drinking. He clearly
considered that the Dissenting affiliation of his drinking company was
noteworthy enough to write it down, which suggests that even while
drinking with Dissenters he remained aware of their religious differences.
This is even more evident in comments he made about drinking with
Presbyterian company. On 27 June 1706, after prayers of national thanksgiving at the parish church, he headed to The Fountain, where he drank
with 'Mr. Hoghton, Heir to Sir Charles, Mrs. Charles Bunbury, Minshall,
Hoghton, the Glass passes full and freely even to distinction of humors',
and Prescott noted that, 'the yong Heir seems to inherit the opinions of his
Family'.[52] The Hoghtons were locally influential Presbyterians; evidently
this did not prevent them from drinking on a day of national thanksgiving
with those of similar social status, despite their different religious views.
Nevertheless, Prescott's comment that the drink was passed around 'even
to distinction of humors' suggests that while sharing alcohol among mixed
company had a powerful unifying symbolism, he was conscious of their
differences, and even expected that these might be in some way socially
problematic.

The potential for a 'distinction of humors' to become socially difficult
was perhaps created as much by the ambivalent attitude of some Dissenters
to drinking as it was by the prejudices of members of the Established
Church. In line with the picture of Dissenting cultural engagement outlined in the first section of this chapter, Dissenting Meetings tended to
condemn heavy drinking, but at the same time members did not – as we

---

[52] Addy (ed.), *The Diary of Henry Prescott, LL. B.*, vol. *1*, p. 105 (entry for 27 June 1706).

have seen – withdraw themselves from communal intoxication. Rebukes of those who did, in the eyes of other Dissenters, drink too much focused on excessive consumption among suspect company, rather than the act of sociable drinking in itself. When Benjamin Wallin, the minister of Maze Pond Baptist Church, London, rebuked one of his congregation, Edward Barnes, because 'when a certain Person has been charged even with intemperance your name has been mentioned as a companion which is very scandalous', his concern was that Barnes had been 'too frequent & too long at a certain Publick house in your Neighbourhood'.[53] Barnes's social visits to a public house were not in themselves problematic; the length and frequency of his stay there was. When Kimbolton Independent Meeting rebuked 'brother Sheperd' in August 1724 for his disorderly behaviour, he was accused of 'being among company drinking inordinately and staying late'.[54] The expectation was not of a total withdrawal from communal sociability, but rather that they would act to the credit of their religious profession by not drinking too much. There was an assumption that Dissenters who engaged in sociable drinking would reject cultures of heavy consumption.

Dissenters' accounts of their own drinking practices show that, as a result of this, even when they engaged in convivial inter-denominational drinking, the dynamics of religious difference continued to be a significant underlying element in their perception of social relations. For pious individuals, balancing social drinking with their own sense of religiosity was fraught with difficulty, and could create a sense of conflict at even the most genial of occasions.

The extensive diaries of James Clegg, a Presbyterian minister and physician living in Chapel-en-le-Frith, Derbyshire, covering the period 1708–55, yield a number of examples of this complex attitude towards drinking and how it shaped social interactions. Like many of his contemporaries, Clegg disapproved of what he regarded as excessive drinking. He was particularly concerned about his servant, whose drunken behaviour he recorded a number of times in the 1740s, including on 11 April 1742 when he was 'much disturb'd by my servant mans staying out late at the Alehouse after the Funeral of Alice Robinson'.[55] It is worth noting that a disapproval of drunkenness was by no means confined to Dissenters. Records

---

[53] Diary and Letters of Benjamin Wallin, draft letter to Edward Barnes, 20 February 1748, D/WAB, Angus Library and Archive, Oxford.
[54] Kimbolton Independent Church Book, p. 50.
[55] Doe (ed.), *The Diary of James Clegg of Chapel en le Frith, 1708–1755*, Part 2, p. 456.

of conformists equally show disapproval at, and remorse for, drinking. In the diary of a Manchester wigmaker, Edmund Harrold, for instance, we see a recognition that his bouts of excessive drinking 'hurt my body, offend against God, set bad example, torment my mind and break my rules, make my self a laughing stock to men, greive the holy spirit'.[56] The staunch conformist William Coe, who came from a Suffolk gentry family, similarly lamented instances of heavy drinking, writing in October 1708 that following an evening with company that included Sir Thomas Hanmer and Sir Henry Bunbury, he was 'very ill for a little time & almost fudled worse than I had been for many yeares before but I repent oh my God I repent'.[57] The connection between sin and excess in drink was made by individuals regardless of religious denomination.

Where the difference appears to have lain, however, was in what was regarded as excessive. Clegg had a more cautious attitude to drink than those around him. This was demonstrated in his censoriousness when wider company became merry: in June 1743, following a baptism, he recorded that 'There was a great deal of company and I fear of excess. I wish we might have no more of such Christenings or Meetings. I think proper endeavours should be used that such customs should be broken and laid aside.'[58] Clegg was clearly not entirely comfortable with the common – and indeed customary – drinking cultures of his locality. A moderate attitude to drink is also evident in his reflections on his own drinking. As years began or ended, he resolved in his diary to improve his conduct, including his drinking habits. In December 1708 he made resolutions 'against unsuitable company ... against unseasonable staying out of my house ... against excess and intemperance as to which my conscience reproves me'. In January 1712 he similarly resolved to 'avoid all unsuitable company and excess more carefully'.[59] In contrast to Coe and, in particular, Harrold, Clegg does not appear to have actually engaged in regular heavy drinking; his repentance was triggered by lower levels of consumption.

Clegg's diaries should be read somewhat against the grain. They served as a form of spiritual and moral reflection; he was more likely to record instances of sinful lapse in his own and others' conduct than he was to

---

[56] Craig Horner (ed.), *The Diary of Edmund Harrold, Wigmaker of Manchester, 1712–15* (Aldershot: Ashgate, 2008), p. 17, entry for 9 July 1712.

[57] Diary of William Coe, 1688–1729 (entry for 27 October 1708), MS Add 6843, p. 73, Cambridge University Library (CUL), Cambridge.

[58] Ibid., p. 490.

[59] Vanessa Doe (ed.), *The Diary of James Clegg of Chapel en le Frith, 1708–1755, Part 1* (Derby: Derbyshire Record Society, 1978), pp. 1, 6.

note ordinary, acceptable behaviour. Implicit in Clegg's reports of having drunk too much is the suggestion that he did in fact sometimes enjoy moderate drinking. Having paid his rents to the Receiver of the Land Tax in October 1751, for instance, he went for a drink, 'but by drinking several sorts of liquors, in several companies, my head was disordered. May the merciful God pardon my intemperance and make me more careful for the future.'[60] His statement, although lamenting this episode of drinking, indicates not only a partiality to numerous different sorts of drink, but also that he had multiple sets of companions with whom he could imbibe, making it unlikely that this was a singular instance of social drinking. Indeed, this was not the only occasion. On 1 April 1752 he 'staid too late' in Ford, and 'found the rum and water I drank disordered my head when I came out into the cold air … I must be more careful to avoid excess for the future, but I came safe home, blessed be God.'[61] There was no suggestion here that he saw sociable drinking itself as sinful, but rather was concerned at having drunk too much. The apparently negative attitude towards alcohol exhibited in Clegg's diary may be skewed by a tendency not to record the moderate consumption that was an ordinary part of life.

It is apparent then, that, like the High Churchman Henry Prescott, and like the other Dissenters mentioned here, Clegg engaged with mixed drinking companies, but this far from overrode his awareness of religious differences. Unlike Prescott, Clegg was averse to drinking if it made him feel mentally inhibited, and he disapproved of staying out late. From his comments on his own and others' consumption, it appears that he placed a lower bound on what he regarded as excessive drinking than some of his contemporaries. His religious beliefs and profession of piety required him to reflect carefully on his actions, and he appealed to God for forgiveness when he felt he had overindulged. However, he was certainly not entirely excluded from valuable social rituals surrounding alcohol, and he was included within companies of people drinking. In this sense, Clegg's drinking habits exemplify the ambiguous and sometimes strained engagement of Dissenters with contemporary culture. Dissenters' behaviour in relation to 'things indifferent' was an important means through which to maintain a sense of pious distinction after the Toleration Act of 1689, and this affected their cultural practice.

---

[60] Ibid., p. 781.
[61] Vanessa Doe (ed.), *The Diary of James Clegg of Chapel en le Frith, 1708–1755, Part 3* (Derby: Derbyshire Record Society, 1981), p. 794.

This variety of responses to drinking occasions complicates our understanding of everyday relations between Dissenters and members of the Established Church in this period. While social histories of tolerance have helpfully used evidence of social interactions between denominations to suggest peaceful relations between groups, this tells us little about the degree to which senses of religious difference remained an important part of their social dynamics. Members of the Established Church enjoyed drinking with Dissenters on occasion, but this did not prevent them from recognising religious differences which they expected might shape social behaviour. Amidst examples of seemingly straightforward inter-denominational sociability, we see that stereotypes of Dissenters, and expectations about their social behaviour, were carried into social interactions, shaping them in subtle – and sometimes not so subtle – ways. Equally, Dissenters' own sense of their religious difference evidently played a role in regulating their drinking practices; their behaviour indicated a carefully balanced participation shaped by pious sociability. On the whole, both Dissenters and members of the Established Church managed their sense of difference sufficiently that they could socialise. But, crucially, they did not have to suspend or challenge their prejudices and senses of difference in order to do so. Individuals continued to read their own and others' interactions around drink through the lens of religious difference, even when those interactions were convivial.

Looking at drinking practices through the lens of religion also has a broader utility. The behaviours of Dissenters highlight the functions of moderate social drinking cultures that sat beside more raucous and intoxicated practices. Existing studies of drink already acknowledge that different forms of alcohol, and the toasts and practices associated with heavy drinking, had political associations that often related to religious affiliation.[62] The work of James Nicholls has suggested that in the late seventeenth century convivial drinking became associated with definitions of Englishness grounded in individual liberty, in reaction to 'the Puritan attempt to define Englishness in terms of religious perfectionism'.[63] Looking at drinking from Dissenting perspectives both adds to and complicates this picture. Sociable inter-denominational drinking evidently did occur, but Dissenters such as Clegg sought appropriate moderation rather than complete abstinence.

---

[62] Angela McShane, 'Roaring Royalists and Ranting Brewers: The Politicisation of Drunkenness in Political Broadside Ballads from 1640 to 1689', in Adam Smyth (ed.), *A Pleasing Sinne. Drink and Conviviality in Seventeenth-Century England* (Cambridge: D. S. Brewer, 2004), pp. 69–87.

[63] Nicholls, 'Vinum Britannicum', p. 199.

With such pious individuals in mind, it is worth broadening historical approaches to drinking cultures. Historians of drink have tended to
study heavy drinking, emphasising that in this period it was 'prized ...
as a manly and sociable custom', and that 'nondrinkers – and especially
nonparticipants in toasting and drinking healths – were labelled traitors'.[64]
This was undoubtedly true, but a focus on heavy consumption perhaps dis-
tracts from the significance of less extreme behaviours. Bringing religious
affiliation into the investigation of drinking practices emphasises that there
were a variety of contemporary frameworks through which ideas about
consumption could be filtered. It thus provides further demonstration of
the significance of cultures of austerity and restraint, acting alongside those
of consumption and pleasure, in shaping eighteenth-century culture.[65] The
place and practices of apparently marginalised groups such as Protestant
Dissenters are essential to this picture.

Dances and Dancing

Instances of religiously mixed drinking highlight to some degree the way
in which cultural expectations and behaviours might be shaped by a combination of, on the one hand, Dissenters' particular attitudes to sociability,
and, on the other, the prevalent stereotypes of the time. This is made even
more apparent by looking at dances and dancing from the perspective
of religious difference. As with drinking, Dissenters were faced with the
challenge of maintaining the right balance between participation in and
reform of society. And, as with drinking, contemporaries applied dominant stereotypes to how they interpreted Dissenters' behaviour. Motivated
by a desire to edify themselves and others, Dissenters were cautious in their
engagement with dancing, but their attitudes became a frequent subject of
contemporary satire, and commentaries on Dissenters' behaviour encouraged – albeit tacitly – the association of dances with religious conformity.
Dissenters' behaviour, and contemporary reactions to it, inflected eighteenth-century dances with an awareness of religious difference.

Dancing was one of the prerequisites of social advancement in this
period.[66] Social dances took place in various fashionable locations,

---

[64] Porter, 'The Drinking Man's Disease', p. 385; Hsueh, 'Intoxicated Reasons', p. 51.
[65] Berry, 'The Pleasures of Austerity', p. 263.
[66] Anne Bloomfield and Ruth Watts, 'Pedagogue of the Dance: The Dancing Master as Educator in the Long Eighteenth Century', *History of Education*, 37, 4 (2008), p. 606; Mark Girouard, *The English Town: A History of Urban Life* (New Haven and London: Yale University Press, 1990), p. 132.

including assemblies, which were a crucial feature of the urban scene across England from the first decades of the century onwards.[67] The character of the assembly was not ostensibly defined by political or religious affiliation, but it formed an important 'arena for overt personal display', involving not only dancing but also conversation, tea-drinking, and card-playing.[68] Equally, privately organised dances were places where social acquaintances were solidified and potential spouses identified, and social status was affirmed.[69] Masquerades were a further occasion for dancing, and were distinguished by the requirement that guests wear character disguise. These gatherings involved the reinforcement of social hierarchy and expectation through both costume and dance; participants were expected to behave in a fashion recognisably appropriate for the character disguise they had chosen.[70] The nature and behaviour of the company at dances was crucial in reinforcing social expectations and determining the shape of polite society.

Learning to dance was in itself regarded by many well-off contemporaries as of value in teaching grace and social confidence, and maintaining physical strength.[71] John Locke advocated dancing for both boys and girls as a means of giving 'a freedom and easiness to all the motions of the body'.[72] For Philip Stanhope, Fourth Earl of Chesterfield, dancing was important in teaching his son 'decency', and to 'sit, stand, and walk genteelly'.[73] Such graceful movement was particularly important for involvement in social dancing, which, according to Scottish writer William McLain, 'Rejoices the Spirit, brings good Company together, rubs off all Harshness from

[67] Helen Berry, 'Creating Polite Space: The Organisation and Social Function of the Newcastle Assembly Rooms', in Helen Berry and Jeremy Gregory (eds.), *Creating and Consuming Culture in North-East England, 1660–1830* (Aldershot: Ashgate, 2004), p. 121.

[68] Peter Borsay, *The English Urban Renaissance. Culture and Society in the Provincial Town 1660–1770* (Oxford: Clarendon Press, 1989), p. 162; Gillian Russell, '"The Place Is Not Free to You": The Georgian Assembly Room and the Ends of Sociability', in Kevin Gilmartin (ed.), *Sociable Places: Locating Culture in Romantic-Period Britain* (Cambridge and New York: Cambridge University Press, 2017), pp. 145–6.

[69] Jane Rendell, 'Almack's Assembly Rooms: A Site of Sexual Pleasure', *Journal of Architectural Education*, 55, 3 (2002), p. 136.

[70] Meghan Kobza, 'Dazzling or Fantastically Dull? Re-Examining the Eighteenth-Century London Masquerade', *Journal for Eighteenth-Century Studies*, 43, 2 (2020), pp. 176–7.

[71] Bloomfield and Watts, 'Pedagogue of the Dance', pp. 613–4; Trevor Fawcett, 'Dance and Teachers of Dance in Eighteenth-Century Bath', *Bath History*, 2 (1988), pp. 27–8.

[72] John Locke, *Some Thoughts Concerning Education* (London, 1693), p. 296.

[73] 'Philip Dormer Stanhope, 4th Earl of Chesterfield to Philip Stanhope, Tuesday, 8 October 1748', and 'Philip Dormer Stanhope, 4th Earl of Chesterfield to Philip Stanhope, Tuesday, 4 August 1739', in Robert McNamee et al. (eds.), *Electronic Enlightenment Scholarly Edition of Correspondence*, Vers. 3.0 (University of Oxford: 2018), https://doi.org/10.13051/ee:doc/stanphOU0010094a1c.

Mens Humours and gives a great deal of Activity to their Bodies and Souls'.[74] Dances were a central part of eighteenth-century social life.

Unfortunately for piously anxious Dissenters, engagement in this aspect of sociability was not a straightforward matter. Debates over whether dancing would corrupt or benefit an individual had a long legacy, and writers of a Puritan persuasion from the sixteenth century onwards condemned dancing as encouraging fornication and causing physical incapacity.[75] In his *Dialogue Against Light, Lewde, and Lacivious Dancing*, for example, the Puritan minister Christopher Fetherstone wrote not only that many people 'have beene lamed with dauncing', or suffered 'incurable diseases ... through the extreme heat they have cast themselves in', but also that dancing was 'a vice ... opposite to the virtue sobrietie', and that it should therefore be forbidden, particularly on the Sabbath.[76]

In the eighteenth century, some Dissenting groups continued to maintain that dancing was unequivocally corrupting. A 1701 reprint of Robert Barclay's instructive guide for Quakers stressed that 'The Apostle *Peter* desires us, *To pass the Time of our Sojourning here in Fear ...* But will any say That such as use Dancing and Comedies, Carding and Dicing, do so much as mind this Precept in the Use of these Things?'[77] However, the views of ministers of other denominations were not so clear cut: dancing, after all, came under the category of 'things indifferent', acts not explicitly forbidden by scripture. The Independent Minister Philip Doddridge warned that the soul might be neglected when individuals went 'to the Dance', but he did not condemn those who learned to dance.[78] Isaac Watts, quoting Ecclesiastes 3:4, acknowledged that 'some persons may have Times for Dancing', while also warning readers to 'confine our Mirth within the Limits of Virtue, and take heed lest when we give a Loose to the sprightly Powers of animal Nature, we should transgress the Rules of

---

[74] William McLain, *An Essay Upon Dancing* (Edinburgh, 1711), p. 4.

[75] Skiles Howard, 'Rival Discourses of Dancing in Early Modern England', *Studies in English Literature, 1500–1900*, 36, 1 (1996), pp. 37–8; Darren Royston, '"Filthie Groping and Uncleane Handlings": An Examination of Touching Moments in Dance of Court and Courtship', in Jackie Watson and Amy Kenny (eds.), *The Senses in Early Modern England, 1558–1660* (Manchester: Manchester University Press, 2015), pp. 56–7.

[76] Christopher Fetherstone, *A Dialogue Agaynst Light, Lewde, and Lascivious Dauncing Wherin are Refuted All those Reasons, Which the Common People Use to Bring in Defence Thereof* (London, 1582), sigs. B1r–v, C4r.

[77] Robert Barclay, *An Apology for the True Christian Divinity, as the Same is Held Forth, and Preached, by the People, Called in Scorn, Quakers: Being a Full Explanation and Vindication of Their Principles and Doctrines* (London, 1701), pp. 537–8, emphasis original.

[78] Philip Doddridge, *The Care of the Soul Urged as One Thing Needful. A Sermon Preached at Maidwell in Northamptonshire, June 22, 1735* (London, 1735), p. 21.

Piety'.[79] For these authors, dancing might be acceptable in some circumstances, but only if the dancer could be sure that their actions did not distract from their piety. Instructive guidance for Dissenters of all denominations therefore often erred on the cautious side by suggesting that it was better not to attend dances. *The Practical Works of the Late Reverend and Pious Mr. Richard Baxter* (1707) showed a particular distaste for dancing, praising in the preface how in Baxter's youth 'while the rest were Dancing he [Baxter] was employ'd in Religious Exercises'.[80] Here dancing was portrayed as a potentially distracting and corrupting activity, against which Baxter's much-lauded religiosity was framed.

In the face of guidance that stressed that dancing might be ill-advised but did not actually forbid it, some Dissenters chose to take a cautious approach, balancing restraint and dissociation from disorderly conduct with a need to engage with society. Self-denial when surrounded by worldly temptation could have spiritual benefits, and this was a principle that Chewning and Abigail Blackmore were instilling in their fifteen-year-old daughter, Sarah, in 1725–6. She was expected to integrate herself into polite society: like many other girls of her age, she had been sent away to London to experience society beyond her native Worcester. However, her parents also demanded that she refuse to dance or play cards, and thereby act with greater restraint than her peers. In November 1725 Abigail Blackmore wrote to Sarah to remind her that 'your father has often spoke against Cards and Dacthes [Dances] I hope you will not put on the on[e] or Playe with the other if you are asked you may Refuse'.[81] The following year her father wrote 'Do not learn to play at Cards. If we will be good christians We must learn to Deny our selves, And not Do as the most Do.'[82]

Card-playing was not just a pastime; it was a crucial part of hospitality at a variety of occasions, including at dances, where it could serve to solidify social and commercial bonds among the middling sorts and the elite.[83]

[79] Isaac Watts, *Sermons on Various Subjects, Divine and Moral: With a Sacred Hymn Suited to Each Subject. In Two Volumes* (London, 1734), vol. 2, p. 8.

[80] Richard Baxter, *The Practical Works of the Late Reverend and Pious Mr. Richard Baxter, in Four Volumes* (London, 1707), p. iv.

[81] Abigail Blackmore to Sarah Blackmore, 20 November 1725, 12.40/62, Dr Williams's Library (DWL), London.

[82] Rev. Chewning Blackmore to Sarah Blackmore, 19 November 1726, 12.40/65, DWL.

[83] Janet E. Mullin, '"We Had Carding": Hospitable Card Play and Polite Domestic Sociability Among the Middling Sort in Eighteenth-Century England', *Journal of Social History*, 42, 4 (2009), pp. 993, 994–7, 1001.

Failure to participate in such activities might at best have put Dissenters at a social disadvantage, and at worst have been taken to represent a failure to play the role of a good guest. Yet abstention was also clearly regarded as of great benefit to young Dissenters, a way of teaching them to manage their piety in the face of others. The Independent Minister Samuel Say wrote to his daughter that 'It has pleas'd me to observe that You can deny Your Self without Pain ... that it is hardly an Act of Self denial in You to decline the Scenes of various Pleasure which others of Your Age & Sex pursue with such Eagerness. May You have Better Pleasures!'[84] For these young ladies, the emphasis was not on total separation from society, but on difference in behaviour from those who surrounded them. This was piety in a social context, unavoidably noticeable to others, and edifying for the individual by the very action of self-denial.

The problematic relationship between the desire to participate in polite dancing and the need to commit to a pious and edifying life also plagued some young men. James Clegg noted in his diary on 11 December 1736 that he had 'settled accounts with the dancing master' (probably for his son), so he evidently did not regard abstention from dancing as fundamental to the maintenance of piety. Yet, at the same time, he also noted that he 'payd that money with a grumbling conscience and am resolvd never to pay more on that account'.[85] He was evidently not completely comfortable with participation in dances. Another Presbyterian, Richard Kay, was also willing to engage in dancing to some degree, but it was not part of his ordinary social practice. He reported in his diary in October 1746 that he had 'spent the Evening at a Ball in the [Manchester] Exchange for the Benefit of Mr. Delamain the Dancing Master, who it seems has been Loyall these troublesome Times to the Prejudice of his School, there was a numerous Assembly of Loyalists, the Evening was spent with Musick and Dancing and Singing the Song of, God Save great George our King'.[86] Kay evidently did not feel that his merriment on this occasion went against his conscience, but this was something of an exception. Despite his repeated mentions of other social activities, this was the only time in Kay's extensive diary that he mentioned dancing; it is possible that he attended this ball specifically to support an individual with whom his own political

[84] Samuel Say to Sarah Say, n.d., c. 1738–1743, 12.108/14, DWL.
[85] Doe (ed.), *The Diary of James Clegg, Part 1*, p. 269.
[86] Brockbank, W., and Kenworthy, F. (eds.), *The Diary of Richard Kay, 1716–51, of Baldingstone, Near Bury. A Lancashire Doctor* (Manchester: Manchester University Press for the Chetham Society, 1968), p. 114.

sympathies chimed in the particularly tense aftermath of the Jacobite Rebellion of 1745.

These Dissenters' differing but not entirely straightforward relationships with social dances highlight one of the many ways in which the tension between charity towards their Christian brethren in matters indifferent, and the need to avoid corruption by disorderly behaviour and company, made it difficult for them to navigate contemporary sociability. While young Dissenters such as Sarah Blackmore were expected to engage with polite society to a degree, they were also expected to foster piety by abstaining from some activities. This, we might imagine, would have created significant social difficulty for some individuals, because the way that others interpreted Dissenters' behaviour affected their level of social integration. As the following examples show, rather than acknowledging the complex negotiation of piety that shaped pious Dissenters' engagement with dancing, contemporary stereotypes of Dissenters' behaviour simply portrayed dances as places where Dissenters unequivocally did not belong. This, when combined with the restrained behaviour of some Dissenters, tacitly encouraged a perception that dances were a form of sociability associated with polite conformity.

Exaggerations of Dissenters' lack of grace and ability when it came to dancing were common currency in satire. The second dialogue of Bernard Mandeville's *Treatise of the Hypochondriack and Hysterick Diseases* included an anecdote about a Presbyterian parson who, to his own immense embarrassment, was discovered to be taking dancing lessons. Desiring not to be seen as an 'egregious Coxcomb', he sought to explain that he had hitherto 'had a great Contempt for Compliments, Ceremonies and Cringes of all sorts', but had recently reached the conclusion that 'where graceful Motion and a genteel Behaviour pass for Virtues, an aukward Mien and uncouth Postures will ever be look'd upon as Vices', hence his desire to learn to dance.[87] The suggestion that Dissenters' dancing was an act of hypocrisy was clearly apparent in this fictional anecdote; it furthermore stressed that their usual abstention from such activity resulted in a lack of social grace.

It was also something of a trope of satires of Quakers to show a Friend being tempted into dancing. The anonymously published *Quakers Art of Courtship*, for instance, included an anecdote in which a Quaker, having got drunk with some 'Persons of Quality', was persuaded to go to a ball with them. Once at the ball, he initially remained a seated observer of

[87] Bernard Mandeville, *A Treatise of the Hypochondriack and Hysterick Diseases. In Three Dialogues* (London, 1730), pp. 176–7.

the dancing, but eventually 'a certain Lady (having on a Mask) came and took Friend by the hand'. Although he declared 'That he never understood what a Dance was … the Lady would by no means excuse him, and Friend was held fast by the hand, and managed by the Lady, sometimes following her leading up, sometimes falling back, till the Room was filled with Laughter'.[88] The anecdote relied on the reader sharing a number of common expectations about the social behaviour of Quakers when it came to dancing. First, there was an implicit assumption that Friends would not ordinarily attend balls. Secondly, it was a given that if they did attend such occasions, they would not dance. Lastly, there was a mockery of the Quaker expectation of sobriety, with the Quaker subject of this satire having easily fallen into alcohol-filled hypocrisy. As we saw in the last chapter, the accusation of hypocrisy against Dissenters was a crucial rhetorical tool for exclusion; when Dissenters decided whether or not to dance, concerns about hypocrisy can never have been far from the surface. In satire, dances and assemblies were portrayed as places where Dissenters would have been distinctly out of place. These works were comical exaggerations that failed to reflect the nuances of Dissenters' engagement with dancing. Nevertheless, the success of the polarities of exclusion set up by such satire rested on a grain of truth: some pious Dissenters were genuinely cautious about dancing, and this fed into cultural interpretations of dances.

Even outside of printed satire, contemporary reactions to dances and dancing were inflected with social characterisations of religious nonconformity. The perception that dancing and Dissent did not go together was reflected in the fact that when Dissenters did dance, their actions could be read highly critically. In the 1690s the Quaker serge weaver Peter Partington of Sutton, Lancashire, for instance, 'unhappily' found himself with 'a concourse of people met together, where they had Musick and other Vanities to Spoil away the time' and 'did neither bear testimony against their sports nor yet withdraw my self so soon from their Company as I ought to have done'. He evidently enjoyed himself enough to linger, but he paid for it, later finding that 'by carriage not answering my profession', he had given 'Occasion to some to speak evill of the people I have assembled with'.[89] In a polemical culture that stressed both the supposed allergy of Dissenters to dancing, and the hypocrisy of those who fell into

[88] Author of Teague-land Jests, *The Quakers Art of Courtship: Or, the Yea-and-Nay Academy of Compliments* (London, 1710), pp. 143–4.
[89] Society of Friends, Hardshaw Monthly Meeting, Personal Condemnations and Testimonies of Denial, fol. 36v.

temptation, the actions of Dissenters when it came to this social activity were watched carefully.

Partington's incident happened only two years after the Toleration Act, and the negative interpretation of his behaviour through a religiously inflected lens may have been in part a product of the heightened religious tension that was characteristic of this decade. It might be expected that by the 1720s, when the heat had somewhat gone out of disputes over England's religious settlement, such an incident would have attracted less comment. However, the notion that dancing and Dissent did not go together appears to have remained culturally resonant enough to affect the way members of the Established Church thought about dancing. A letter from Elizabeth Buxton (of the wealthy conforming East Anglian family of that name) to her eleven-year-old grandson, Robert, in January 1722, for instance, made it clear that an awareness of the fraught relationship between Dissent and dancing had seeped into the activities of her social circle. Seeking to provide her grandson with some entertaining news, Elizabeth told him of 'a masquerade we had here from Sir Robt Kemps family on wednesday night', and that 'we all wished you there to dance'. The occasion involved 'one couple dresed like a foreign prince & princes one like shepherds the other in quakers habit'.[90]

The choice of a Quaker's outfit as one of the costumes at first seems a strange one. However, in the context of contemporary observations about Dissenters', and particularly Quakers', sociability, the Quaker costume makes perfect sense. Such an outfit could easily be construed as an amusing joke precisely because a dance was the last place you would expect to see a Quaker. Evidently, the absence of Quakers from the dance floor was ordinarily sufficiently conspicuous that it occurred to Kemp's family to make a point of it, one that they presumably would have expected the other guests to find entertaining. As recent research on masquerades has demonstrated, participants were expected to behave in character, thereby reinforcing existing social hierarchies and expectations.[91] The costume in this particular instance would have both reflected and reinforced expectations about Dissenters' behaviour, further stressing that Dissenters were perceived as outsiders at these events.

In fact, so embedded was the idea that dancing was an activity largely confined to conformists that it appeared in advice given in John Dunton's *Athenian Oracle* to a 19-year-old reader who was concerned that learning

[90] Elizabeth Buxton, Laxfield, to Robert Buxton, 8 January 1722, MS Buxton 35/2, CUL.
[91] Kobza, 'Dazzling or Fantastically Dull?', pp. 176–7.

to dance would distract from 'Exercises of Piety and Devotion'. Dunton used Biblical quotations in favour of dancing to reassure his readers that it was spiritually commendable, including the verse in Psalm 149, 'Let them praise his name in the dance'; he also reminded his correspondent that there is 'a Time for Recreation as well as severer study and business'. Most strikingly, however, Dunton stated that although some people abstained from '*Publick Dancing*' for fear of 'occasioning ill thoughts', there was no reason they should avoid learning to dance in private, pointing out that 'Dissenters even Ministers themselves, have their children learnt to dance.'[92] Dunton's use of Dissenters as an example was not critical or satirical, but did suggest that Dissenters were commonly viewed as the benchmark for conservative attitudes: neither he nor his readers would have expected them to be seen dancing in public.

The attitudes towards dancing held by the Dissenters studied here were, like their engagement with drinking cultures, shaped by the difficulty of managing social behaviour that came under the category of 'things indifferent'. While dancing was not comprehensively forbidden for eighteenth-century Dissenters, its capacity to distract the soul from more pious thoughts was considered to be spiritually dangerous. At the same time, both Dissenting ecclesiology and the peculiar circumstances caused by the ambiguous Toleration Act meant that it was incumbent on Dissenters to engage with contemporary society. However, the subtleties of Dissenters' engagement with dancing received little attention in contemporary satire, which instead focused on their lack of social grace. These stereotypes built upon and reinforced the idea that dances were venues where Dissenters were out of place, tacitly suggesting that dancing was a primarily Anglican facet of polite society. As long as at least some Dissenters maintained a degree of difference, their behaviour was read by contemporaries, familiar with long-standing stereotypes, as a total failure to meet social norms. The result was that certain cultural venues and forms could be conceived of as antithetical to religious nonconformity.

Conversation and Coffeehouses

In other venues, the potential for social conventions and discourses to accentuate senses of religious difference was more obvious. Coffeehouses – with their associated conversational cultures – were one such location.

---

[92] *The Athenian Oracle. Being an Entire Collection of all the Valuable Questions and Answers in the Old Athenian Mercuries*, vol. 2 (London, 1728), pp. 67–8, emphasis original.

It is well known that coffeehouses often had political, professional, and even regional associations. Particularly in the metropolis, patrons 'could pick the place whose social or political tenor they found most agreeable'. In that sense, coffeehouses were key in helping to form and reinforce distinct communities within urban society.[93] However, the degree to which these cultural venues perpetuated religious difference has been given less consideration than their role in cementing party political loyalties, despite the intimate connection between the two.[94] Evidence of the association of particular coffeehouses with certain religious standpoints not only highlights some of the mechanisms by which religious differences could be sustained, but also adds to recent understanding of the ideal of polite conversation as only one of a number of different registers of sociability that could be drawn upon in venues such as these.[95]

Even more than dancing, conversation had a central role in eighteenth-century ideas about education, social refinement, and the promotion of a stable society.[96] The first half of the eighteenth century saw an explosion in the publication of guides to conversation, promoting the value of discourse as a means of drawing people together in harmony and mutual improvement.[97] According to contemporary writers, ideal conversation was open to all, and was structured around moderate language, allowing interlocutors to gain 'some Good, some Pleasure or Advantage from each

[93] Brian Cowan, *The Social Life of Coffee. The Emergence of the British Coffeehouse* (New Haven and London: Yale University Press, 2005), p. 169.

[94] Linda Colley, 'The Loyal Brotherhood and the Cocoa Tree: The London Organization of the Tory Party, 1727–1760', *Historical Journal*, 20, 1 (1977), p. 79–80; Geoffrey Holmes, *British Politics in the Age of Anne* (London and Ronceverte: The Hambledon Press, 1987), pp. 22–3; John Brewer, *Party Ideology and Popular Politics at the Accession of George III* (Cambridge: Cambridge University Press, 1976), pp. 150–1; Steve Pincus, '"Coffee Politicians Does Create": Coffeehouses and Restoration Political Culture', *Journal of Modern History*, 67, 4 (December, 1995), pp. 816–7.

[95] Kate Davison, 'Occasional Politeness and Gentleman's Laughter in Eighteenth-Century England', *Historical Journal*, 57, 4 (2014), p. 924; Helen Berry, 'Rethinking Politeness in Eighteenth-Century England: Moll King's Coffee House and the Significance of "Flash Talk"', *Transactions of the Royal Historical Society*, 11 (2001), pp. 74–5.

[96] Katie Halsey and Jane Slinn, 'Introduction', in Halsey and Slinn (eds.), *The Concept and Practice of Conversation in the Long Eighteenth Century, 1688–1848* (Newcastle upon Tyne: Cambridge Scholars Publishing, 2008), pp. ix, xxiv; Valérie Capdeville, 'Noise and Sound Reconciled: How London Clubs Shaped Conversation into a Social Art', *Etudes Epistémè*, 29 (2016), para. 16; Katherine Gleadle, '"Opinions Deliver'd in Conversation": Conversation, Politics, and gender in the late Eighteenth Century', in Jose Harris (ed.), *Civil Society in British History. Ideas, Identities, Institutions* (Oxford and New York: Oxford University Press, 2003), p. 62.

[97] Stephen Miller, *Conversation: A History of a Declining Art* (New Haven, CT: Yale University Press, 2008), p. 108; Leland E. Warren, 'Turning Reality Round Together: Guides to Conversation in Eighteenth-Century England', *Eighteenth-Century Life*, 8 (1983), pp. 66, 69.

other' through amicable discourse.[98] There were, however, contradictions in ideals about conversation. As the work of Jon Mee has emphasised, Enlightenment conversation rested both on the idea of mutual improvement through reciprocal dialogue, and on 'participation in the everyday world of coffee shop and tea table'. There was an inherent tension between these two aims. Reciprocity was difficult to establish in venues that were free and open to all, where a common voice or aim was not guaranteed.[99] If contemporaries were seeking amity and mutual improvement, it was better for them to seek company whose discourse they might expect to find agreeable. Yet if they conversed only with like-minded people, their mutual improvement might be limited by their opinions being insufficiently challenged. Conversational ideals thus placed the tricky demand on all contemporaries to balance the need to be subjected to a wide range of opinions with the establishment of reciprocal conversational relationships with like-minded people.

The difficulty of balancing these two conversational aims may have been heightened for Protestant Dissenters, who, as we have seen, had particular expectations about the need both to edify others and to maintain suitably pious sociability. This is apparent from the spiritual reflections of pious Dissenters. The Presbyterian Anne Dawson, for instance, was plagued in her mid-twenties by the challenge of watching against the 'tongue sins' characterised by 'foolish jesting' and 'loose expressions'.[100] She often recorded in her diary instances when she had failed to live up to her own expectations of piety, including when she was too 'Chearful & Mery' among others who were 'very back ward in communicating what is good', despite there being 'persons that I think realy pious' among them.[101] Peter Partington similarly confessed that he had 'in a light manner at times conversed with such company as drew me to lightness and Airyness'.[102] James Clegg regretted in March 1720 'that I have for some time past been very careless of my heart and in my conversation very loose and carnall'.[103]

---

[98] Henry Fielding, 'An Essay on Conversation' in Henry Miller (ed.), *Miscellanies by Henry Fielding, Esq. vol. 1* (Oxford: Oxford University Press and Wesleyan University Press, 1972), pp. 122–3; Halsey and Slinn, 'Introduction', p. ix.

[99] Jon Mee, 'Turning Things Around Together: Enlightenment and Conversation', in Alexander Cook, Ned Curthoys and Shino Konishi (eds.), *Representing Humanity in the Age of Enlightenment* (London: Pickering and Chatto, 2013), p. 63.

[100] Diary of Anne (Dawson) Evans, 1721–22, fols. 3v–4r, Add MS 71626, BL.

[101] Ibid., fol. 28v.

[102] Society of Friends, Hardshaw Monthly Meeting, Personal Condemnations and Testimonies of Denial, fol. 36v.

[103] Doe (ed.), *The Diary of James Clegg, Part 1*, p.13.

In contrast to these lamentations of unsuitable conversation, the obituary of the Independent minister Chewning Blackmore highlighted the ideal conversational balance for Dissenters. He was evidently – at least to the mind of his obituarist – masterful in his management of piety and sociability:

> His Conversation was most agreeable & Entertaining; altho' he was in himself decently grave, yet he wod be facetious & innocently pleasant & merry But that was always weltim'd His common Discourse was very correct, he cod not tell how to speak otherwise … His Manner was polite & his Address easy & he was … fitted to Converse with people of Character as he sometimes did, for he was as much a Gentleman, as he was a Christian or Divine.[104]

Blackmore gave appropriate due to his religion while adhering to norms of politeness. Gravity was essential, and pleasantries were dangerous if they went beyond the realms of innocence, but right conversation could be as much a way of expressing piety as private prayer. The implicit opposition of 'Gentleman' with 'Christian or Divine' here is telling: the author implied that the two were in tension with one another, making it notable that Blackmore was able to combine them. For all contemporaries there was a tension between allowing free conversation and securing company that would serve the purposes of mutual improvement, but for many Dissenters the balance between the demands of edification and pious behaviour when it came to conversation was especially delicate.

This may have been particularly the case in an urban context. Restoration nonconformists had emphasised the importance of pious conversation as a means of maintaining religious integrity in the face of increasing diversity, while avoiding outright religious conflict.[105] This need may have been made more urgent in towns, and particularly in London, where Anglican church-building failed to keep up with Dissenters' in meeting the needs of rapidly growing populations. The result was that some parishes complained that people were 'driven … to the separate Congregations' not out of conscientious objection to Established Church doctrine, but because they lacked a convenient alternative place of worship.[106] As Collinson's

---

[104] An account of the Rev. Chewning Blackmore by George Bewson, copied by Rev. Fr. Blackmore, 12.40/61, fol. 7r, DWL.
[105] Alison Hurley, 'Peculiar Christians, Circumstantial Courtiers, and the Making of Conversation in Seventeenth-Century England', *Representations*, III, 1 (2010), pp. 38–9.
[106] M. H. Port (ed.), *The Commissions for Building Fifty New Churches: The Minute Book, 1711–27: A Calendar* (London: London Record Society, 1986), p. ix (fn. 4).

work on separatists and non-separatists in the late sixteenth century suggested, the need to demonstrate difference through social behaviour may have been greater when the godly were not clearly identifiable by their differences in worship.[107] If attending places of worship with conformists heightened the need for religious nonconformists to maintain social difference, it may have been particularly important for Dissenters to demonstrate pious sociability in urban areas after 1689.

This is significant because the urban environment was central to the development of conversational cultures; coffeehouses in particular were viewed as a place in which civil society was fostered through conversation. Because they were places associated with relative openness to all patrons, promotors of conversational forms idealised them as spaces for polite and productive discourse, where religious extremity was submitted to 'social and civil discipline'.[108] Joseph Addison and Richard Steele's periodical *The Spectator* particularly focused on bringing philosophical discussion out of libraries and personal studies and into coffeehouses and clubs.[109] For such writers, the conversation that developed in coffeehouses was a 'medium for the circulation of news and the exchange of knowledge'.[110]

Coffeehouses were, of course, frequented by individuals of all religious stripes for quotidian purposes. The Reading distiller and Quaker diarist Edward Belson, for instance, regularly noted visits to the coffeehouse for news, such as on 7 July 1708, when he was 'at Coffee House to read the news of the Great Victory obtain by the Duke of Marlborough In the Netherlands'.[111] Like many others, the Wiltshire Presbyterian Nathaniel Fancourt made use of coffeehouses for business purposes, proposing in 1711 that an associate of his could be met 'on the Exchange or in the Coffee house in Cornhill'.[112] There is no reason to think that Belson's quiet reading of the news or Fancourt's suggested business meeting was of particular note or trouble to anyone else.

---

[107] Collinson, 'The Cohabitation of the Faithful with the Unfaithful', pp. 61–3.
[108] Lawrence E. Klein, 'Coffeehouse Civility, 1660–1714: An Aspect of Post-Courtly Culture in England', *Huntingdon Library Quarterly*, 59, 1 (1996), p. 44; Brian Cowan, 'The Rise of the Coffeehouse Reconsidered', *Historical Journal*, 47, 1 (2004), p. 29, 34; Cowan, *The Social Life of Coffee*, pp. 185, 227–9.
[109] Mee, 'Turning Things Around Together', pp. 54–5.
[110] Capdeville, 'Noise and Sound Reconciled', para. 5.
[111] Diary of Edward Belson, 1707–22 (entry for 7 July 1708), D/EZ12/1, Berkshire Record Office, Reading.
[112] Nathaniel Fancourt to John Butler, 9 January *c.*1711, 727/1/6, Wiltshire and Swindon History Centre, Chippenham.

Yet despite contemporary ideals about coffeehouse discourse, these locations contained the inherent potential for inflammatory discussion and the perpetuation of difference, particularly when the news was controversial. This is apparent from a defamation case brought to a Church court in Chester in July 1718, in which, according to Margaret Miller (a servant in the coffeehouse in Watergate Street, Chester), James Sylvester not only called Thomas Parry 'a scoundrel dog, a lousy dog, and a gross arse', but also 'a fanatic'. John Brandwood, a patron of the coffeehouse, also recorded hearing 'a mixed and confused discourse in the said company about the dissenters and fanatics'. There was a further allegation that Sylvester called 'the said Mr Parry a fanatical dog, the Bishop of Bangor a sorry dog, or the Duke of Marlborough a saucy Jack'.[113]

It does not seem likely that Parry was actually a Dissenter – one of the witnesses quoted Parry as having said that 'he was no more a fanatic than he the defendant was a papist' – but the role of the label of 'fanatic' and 'dissenter', used synonymously in witness testimony, is revealing.[114] Several of the witnesses stated that the dispute occurred when the two men – regulars at the coffeehouse – sat down together over the news; the insults exchanged between them had clear roots in contemporary affairs. From the mention of the Bishop of Bangor, it appears that the particular issue was the so-called 'Bangorian controversy' over whether there was any Biblical basis for Church government. High Church and Tory opposition to the Bishop of Bangor's view that there was no such basis associated Bangor's ideas with the perceived threat of Dissent: in Brecon in June 1718, for instance, rioters attacked the house of a Dissenter, James Jones, calling him '"Ben Hoadly's [the Bishop of Bangor] Secretary"'.[115]

However, it is unlikely that the tension between Parry and Sylvester was solely based on this single issue. In his testimony, Brandwood described the heated exchange between Parry and Sylvester as beginning with 'Mr Parry speaking to the said Mr Sylvester say[ing] were thou art a pitiful sorry fellow and a knave, and then rides about to cheat the country', to which Sylvester answered, 'art thou a lawyer, thou art a liar, I do not cheat the country'.[116] These statements suggest that there may have been a

[113] Parry c Sylvester, 1718, EDC 5/1718/2 (unfol.), CALS. Transcribed by *Intoxicants in Early Modernity*, www.dhi.ac.uk/intoxicants/record.jsp?&source=courtpaper&courtpaper_ID=708, accessed 15 December 2020.

[114] Ibid.

[115] *Flying-Post*, 26–8 June 1718, quoted in Andrew Starkie, *The Church of England and the Bangorian Controversy, 1716–1721* (Woodbridge: The Boydell Press, 2007), p. 67.

[116] Parry c Sylvester, 1718.

wider dispute between the two men. The coffeehouse, with its facility for spreading news, in this instance seems to have served as a space in which a broader dispute could be focused down to an issue of religious and political difference, and in which labels connected with controversial news, such as 'dissenter' and 'fanatic', could be combined in a derogatory fashion with more generic insults, such as 'lousy dog'. Far from submitting religious extremity to social discipline, the space of the coffeehouse in this case witnessed the use of religious slurs in wider dispute.

Given the potential for social intercourse to mix badly with the news in coffeehouses, it should come as no surprise that the Dissenting use of such venues was not always necessarily regarded as a socially neutral action. Set against the backdrop of existing religious disputes, the patronage of certain coffeehouses by Dissenters could in fact serve to perpetuate tensions. This is strikingly apparent from a pamphlet exchange between John Agate, the Rector of Stawley, Somerset, and John Withers, an Exeter Presbyterian minister, between 1707 and 1715. A dispute between the men had begun when Agate insulted another Presbyterian minister, George Trosse, calling him 'an Insincere Practitioner in Religion'.[117] Agate and Withers agreed to meet to debate the matter, but were unable to settle on the terms of the conference, with the result that the dispute continued in print. In this pamphlet debate each party, alongside extensive discussions of the nature of the communion of the Church, the relationship between Church and State, the role of religion in the Civil Wars of the previous century, and the expression of loyalty to the crown, accused the other of having deliberately spread rumours and false allegations around the city of Exeter.[118]

Most significantly for the present discussion, denominationally inflected attendance at certain Exeter coffeehouses appears to have played a central role in perpetuating the disagreement. Both authors accused the other of causing public division through insulting behaviour in coffeehouses. Agate, for instance, claimed that if anyone should mistakenly believe that the Dissenters had grown moderate, and no longer represented a national danger, they should 'go to Couse's Coffee-House in particular ... There

---

[117] John Withers, *A Defence of the True and Impartial Account of What Occurr'd at the Late Conference in Exon, and the Dissenters Vindicated from Mr. Agate's False Accusations* (Exon, 1707), p. 14; John Agate, *A Reply to a Pamphlet, Intituled. A True and Impartial Account of What Occurr'd at the Late Conference in Exon* (Exon, 1707), pp. 10–11.

[118] John Withers, *A True and Impartial Account of What Occurred at the Late Conference in Exon. Publish'd to Prevent Misrepresentations* (Exon, 1707), pp. 7, 10; Agate, *A Reply to a Pamphlet, Intituled. A True and Impartial Account*, pp. 3–4, 12–13, 39; Withers, *A Defence of the True and Impartial Account*, p. 3.

the Party, the Moderate Dissenters, Regale themselves with these poisonous Papers.'[119] Meanwhile, Withers suggested that Agate had 'challeng'd
and insulted (as we are credibly informed)' him in 'Coffee-Houses, and
other publick places'.[120] The identification of specific coffeehouses, such
as Couse's, with Dissent is striking. In this case, Dissenters were discernibly present in a particular coffeehouse, and, because of a background of
religious tension in the city, their engagement in coffeehouse sociability
served to perpetuate dispute.

The preoccupation of both authors with the public nature of their disagreement was symptomatic of wider concerns about the impact of an
increasingly influential press. Agate's perception that words set in print
were being spread through conversation in coffeehouses reflected 'an
awareness of replication and circulation as general social phenomena' in
this period, which perpetuated the idea that discussions in print were part
of a wider circulation of talk.[121] Part of the popularity of coffeehouses was
their role in news circulation; when mentioning these venues in print, it is
likely that both authors were also imagining that their texts might themselves be circulated and discussed in these contexts.[122] This much is evident
from Agate's reference to the reading of 'poisonous Papers' in Couse's coffeehouse.[123] The coffeehouse can therefore be seen as central in this dispute
between Church and Dissent, a place where partisan divisions and religious differences were perpetuated through both word of mouth and print
in a period when High Churchmen in particular were concerned about
the State's failure to control the press.[124] Coffeehouses were places where
people could engage in polite discourse and debate, illustrate and cultivate
their wit, and mull over the political issues of the day, but they were also
venues where religious controversy could be fostered.

There are numerous other indications in print that some coffeehouses
were, despite their ostensible openness to all, identifiable by religious
allegiances. Blackwell's Coffeehouse, near Queen's Street, London,
for instance, was the meeting place of Calvinist (or Particular) Baptist

---

[119] Agate, *A Reply to a Pamphlet, Intituled. A True and Impartial Account*, p. 64.
[120] Withers, *A True and Impartial Account*, p. 7. See also Withers, *A Defence of the True and Impartial Account*, p. 15.
[121] Ann C. Dean, *The Talk of the Town. Figurative Publics in Eighteenth-Century Britain*, (Lewisburg, NJ: Bucknell University Press, 2007), pp. 14–15.
[122] Pincus, '"Coffee Politicians Does Create"', p. 834.
[123] Agate, *A Reply to a Pamphlet, Intituled. A True and Impartial Account*, p. 64.
[124] Alex W. Barber, 'Censorship, Salvation and the Preaching of Francis Higgins: A Reconsideration of High Church Politics and Theology in the Early 18th Century', *Parliamentary History*, 33, 1 (2014), p. 118.

ministers.[125] While the fact that the ministers met there does not suggest that all the clientele were necessarily of a Baptist persuasion, it is nevertheless some indication of that coffeehouse's culture. The converse of this was that other coffeehouses were associated with High Church opinion. One pamphlet discussing the impeachment of Sacheverell in 1710, for example, took the form of a discussion between a 'High-Church Captain, a Stanch'd Whig, and a Coffee-man'. The pamphlet opens with the Captain reading aloud from the trial of King Charles I, followed by a comment that 'Here's Trayterous Villains ... Ah Presbyterian Dogs, they deserv'd to be cut as small as Herbs to the Pot.' Significantly, the coffee-man replied 'Captain you dare not say so much at *Dick's* Coffee-house at *Temple-Bar*,' thereby identifying the different religious and political tenor of that coffeehouse.[126] Here, the author clearly delineated High Church and Dissenting venues, expecting the reader to recognise the limited freedom of conversation in coffeehouses that were effectively exclusive along both political and religious lines.

It might reasonably be suggested that this pamphlet, as well as the Agate–Withers dispute, was a product of the particularly heated religious politics of the first decade of the eighteenth century, and that as the temperature of debate cooled, so might the tendency of contemporaries to group at particular venues according to religious affiliation. Yet as the century wore on, pamphleteers and playwriters continued to associate certain coffeehouses with particular religious as well as political standpoints. *The Inquisition: A Farce* – a series of mock dialogues concerning the Bangorian controversy – opened with a scene in Child's Coffeehouse near St Paul's Cathedral in London, in which a group of High Church and nonjuring divines lamented that Hoadly was 'a little too calm always against the Dissenters'.[127] Because of its location near St Paul's, Child's Coffeehouse was a common place for clerics to gather; presumably this sort of comment against Dissent was perceived to be more likely to be heard there than elsewhere.[128] This was not the only publication to link Child's Coffeehouse

[125] Sayer Rudd, *A Letter to the Reverend the Ministers of the Calvinistical Baptist Persuasion, Meeting at Blackwell's Coffee-House, near Queen's-Street, London* (London, 1735).
[126] *A Full Reply to the Substantial Impeachment of Dr. Sacheverell, in A Dialogue between An High-Church Captain, a Stanch'd Whigg, and a Coffee-man; As the Matter of Fact was really transacted on Friday last in B--s Coffee-House in Westminster Hall* (London, 1710), p. 2, emphasis original.
[127] J. Philips, *The Inquisition. A Farce. As it was Acted at Child's Coffee-House, and the King's-Arms Tavern, In St Paul's Church-Yard* (London, 1717), p. 3.
[128] Child's Coffeehouse had also been earlier associated with a pro-Sacheverell position. See *The Manager's Pro and Con: Or, An Account of what is said at Child's and Tom's Coffee-House For and Against Dr. Sacheverell* (London, 1710).

with High Church discussion. An anonymous verse entitled *Coffee: A Tale*, published in 1727, characterised the attitude of 'A corpulent Vicar' towards coffeehouses, stating his belief that 'The Law should suppress it [coffee], / Nor grant Toleration.' In the verse, the evidently High Church vicar condemns these 'Nests, / Of curs'd Coffee and News' as harmful to society, but in a clear reference to Child's and St Paul's coffeehouses admits that 'Some indeed, about St Paul's, / Are such as become her.'[129] The poem assumed that these were identifiably High Church locations.

The varying religious 'temperature' of different London coffeehouses was perhaps most clearly outlined in a collected edition of Richard Steele's periodical *Tatler*, entitled *The Lucubrations of Isaac Bickerstaff, Esq*. In one issue, 'Bickerstaff' has a thermometer that measures religious temperature on a scale that reads 'Ignorance, Persecution, Wrath, Zeal, CHURCH, Moderation, Lukewarmness, Infidelity, and Ignorance'.[130] Taking it into several of London's coffeehouses, he reports that 'At St *James*'s Coffee-house the Liquor stood at *Moderation*; but at *Will*'s, to my great Surprize, it subsided to the very lowest Mark on the Glass [Ignorance]. At the *Grecian* it mounted but just one Point higher [Infidelity]; at the *Rainbow* it still ascended two Degrees [Moderation]. *Child*'s fetched it up to *Zeal*, and other adjacent Coffee-houses to *Wrath*.'[131] Although this was clearly a satirical exaggeration, intended both to mock the vituperative nature of religious politics, and to represent moderate Established Church allegiance as the golden mean of religious behaviour, it is notable that the success of this humour relied on contemporaries' shared association of particular coffeehouses with certain religious characteristics.

Printed works naturally tend to focus on the larger, better-known coffeehouses, which may have gained notoriety precisely because they had a distinctive professional, political, or religious culture. It should be noted that there were also many smaller coffeehouses, especially in London, that primarily served neighbourhood residents.[132] It is unlikely that these would have been such highly charged centres of opinion. Nevertheless, the association of coffeehouses with particular religious affiliations may have also been common elsewhere. In his diary, the High Churchman Henry Prescott frequently mentioned going to the coffeehouse with his co-religionists in Chester immediately after church. On 1 October 1707,

[129] *Coffee: A Tale* (London, 1727), pp. 2–3, 5.
[130] *The Lucubrations of Isaac Bickerstaff, Esq* (London, 1749), vol. 4, p. 117.
[131] Ibid., p. 118, emphasis original.
[132] Cowan, *The Social Life of Coffee*, p. 157.

for example, he went 'To early prayers after which a concourse to the Coffee house'.[133] If coffeehouse sociability followed on immediately from prayers, the company there would be expected to have been fairly religiously homogeneous. Indeed, Prescott thought it notable on 10 June 1705 that when he attended the coffeehouse as usual after evening prayers, there was a 'mixt room of protestants and papists' on account of the visit of the Catholic Lord Frederic Howard, implying that he did not usually encounter religiously mixed company there.[134] Religious affiliation, while not the sole determinant of coffeehouse culture, was one of a number of key factors that shaped the dynamics of coffeehouse conversation.

The influence of religious affiliation over the culture of some coffeehouses has implications for our understanding of conversational cultures. Historians such as Kate Davison have drawn attention to the existence of multiple different conversational modes beyond that of politeness; as other work has shown, in the context of the coffeehouse, polite discourse could also be replaced with much more bawdy behaviour.[135] Evidence that the norms of conversation in certain coffeehouses were shaped by their religious temperature adds to our understanding of the diversity of conversational registers in coffeehouses that were in tension with, or coexisted alongside, politeness. Looking at coffeehouse conversation from the perspective of religious difference helps to expand our understanding of the layers of religious, social, and political preference that shaped contemporary cultural engagement.

Conclusion

The individual cases studied here show the multiple ways in which religious differences shaped the social dynamics of some of the central cultural institutions of this period. Dissenters' engagement with drinking cultures reveals the ways in which a deep awareness of religious difference could inflect what ostensibly appears as convivial co-existence. In the case of dances, the caution of many Dissenters about public dancing was picked up and commented on by members of the Established Church, thereby creating a cultural association between dances and religious conformity. The example of coffeehouses makes it evident that some cultural venues

---

[133] Addy (ed.), *The Diary of Henry Prescott*, p. 169.
[134] Ibid., p. 53.
[135] Davison, 'Occasional Politeness and Gentleman's Laughter', p. 924; Berry, 'Rethinking Politeness in Eighteenth-Century England', pp. 74–5.

could actually serve as vehicles for the perpetuation of religious difference, particularly when combined with an inflammatory press.

Investigating the nature of Dissenting engagement with cultural norms also highlights how focusing on the pious can throw light on hitherto understudied aspects of eighteenth-century culture. The examples given in this chapter support Helen Berry's proposal that a different picture of Georgian England might appear if we paid attention to those who abstained from cultures of consumption and pleasure.[136] In particular, we have seen the utility of looking at Dissenters' drinking behaviours in order to examine the range of different drinking cultures beyond heavy intoxication. This is furthermore the case when considering the varieties of conversational culture seen in coffeehouses. Looking at the ways in which those who were suspicious of contemporary cultural norms navigated contemporary social life highlights the diversity of eighteenth-century culture beyond the much-studied tropes of consumption, luxury, and politeness. Although limited to specific venues, the examples given here are indicative of the potential analytical power of religious difference as an aspect of eighteenth-century culture.

These examples are too much of a patchwork to straightforwardly chart change, but the social consequences of religious difference were, in all likelihood, expressed differently across the period. In the immediate decades after the Toleration Act, tensions over religious difference manifested themselves more obviously in outward conflict. As the years rolled on, and the productivity of rancorously contesting England's religious settlement became more questionable, it is probable that outright dispute became less likely. Despite its significant shortcomings, one important consequence of the Toleration Act was that legal exclusion and violent action ceased (albeit slowly) to appear viable options for those who sought to maintain the supremacy of the Established Church. But the High Church interest did not simply cease to believe that loyalty to the Church mattered. Instead, as new social modes and cultural venues developed, assumptions about religious difference were embedded into norms of social interaction in a way that sustained distinctions without necessarily spilling over into outright conflict. Thus, across the range of venues and cultural forms described here, we see religious differences being associated with social failure, with suspicion of disreputability, and expectation of social misunderstanding. What many of the examples here show is that religious

---

[136] Berry, 'The Pleasures of Austerity', p. 274.

differences did not have to be expressed violently to be a structuring element of social encounters. Rather, through Dissenters' theological and ecclesiological approaches to sociability, and through the projection of stereotypes onto daily cultural life, perceptions of religious difference could be woven into assumptions, expectations, and actions which continued to shape the cultural and social experiences of both Church and Dissent well into the middle of the century.

CHAPTER 5

Neighbours, Friends, Company

In 1735, at twenty-three years old, the Quaker Mary Weston was on her first ministerial tour of the British Isles. In early June she was in Dover, where, after holding a meeting, she was pleased to find that 'Divers who were not called by our Name came & invited us to their Houses, for which we acknowledged their Kindness, and left them with many good Wishes bestowed upon us.' Delighted at the gesture, she was 'ready to conclude there was some nearer to the Kingdom than others who had made long Profession with us'.[1] Providing for the needs of others was one way in which contemporaries of all religious persuasions could fulfil their Christian obligation to show love towards others, whether friends, neighbours, or those they regarded as sinners. As Weston's comment shows, the realisation of this duty could serve to oil the wheels of inter-confessional relations, creating an amity that transcended the boundaries of religious difference.

However, while the idea of neighbourliness – this most basic of Christian precepts – was evidently central to managing religious difference in this period, it tells us little about whether underlying religious tensions were being resolved, ignored, or perpetuated within local communities. Indeed, as this chapter shows, the concept of neighbourliness gives us little indication of the ways that religious difference interacted with a local sociability that was multi-faceted, involving many different degrees of warmth and co-operation between individuals and groups. We have observed already the close interaction of religious expectation with social norms in this period, and the degree to which we need to examine religious difference within its social framework. It is with this in mind that the social dynamics of inter-confessional relations after 1689 appear particularly important. As is evident in the following discussion, Dissenters acted to maintain both

---

[1] Journal of Mary Weston 1735–1752, p. 4, MS Vol 312, Library of the Society of Friends (Friends' Lib.), London.

religious integrity and social conformity within their local communities after the Toleration Act. The resulting social dynamic, in which they used different frameworks of social interaction depending on religious affiliation, ensured that issues of religious difference continued to shape community formation and local social interaction in the eighteenth century.

The social basis of inter-confessional relations has, for the past thirty years, been at the heart of the work of historians of religious co-existence across Europe, and this is the starting point of this chapter. However, taking up the recent work of historians of sociability, it goes on to question whether the emphasis on neighbourliness common to many studies of inter-confessional relations is the most productive approach. Instead, it examines the different ways in which Dissenters described their 'neighbours', 'friends', and 'company' in relation to one another, using this as a means to understand the extent to which all types of Protestant Dissenters excluded themselves from society. It demonstrates that looking at other ways of describing sociability, in addition to the language of neighbourliness, provides a much broader view of the different levels and boundaries of inter-confessional social interaction.

Neighbourliness and Inter-Confessional Relations

The concept of neighbourliness is crucial to understanding how early modern communities functioned. Since Keith Wrightson's proposition in the 1980s that neighbourliness was a key structure in this period, characterised by 'a recognition of reciprocal obligations … and a degree of normative consensus as to the nature of proper behaviour between neighbours', much debate about the early modern community has centred around this concept.[2] Neighbourliness has been understood as a way of interpreting the horizontal relationships of community that are inadequately described through the lens of patriarchal structures. As a result, it has fed into discussions of community regulation, the negotiation of authority, the development of the Poor Law and charity, challenges to community relations, and analysis of the 'intangible boundaries of social cohesion'.[3]

---

[2] Keith Wrightson, *English Society: 1580–1680* (London: Hutchinson, 1982), pp. 51–4.

[3] Sara Mendelson, 'Neighbourhood as Female Community in the Life of Anne Dormer', in Stephanie Tarbin and Susan Broomhall (eds.), *Women, Identities and Communities in Early Modern Europe* (Aldershot: Ashgate, 2008), p. 157. See also Steve Hindle, 'The Keeping of the Public Peace', in Paul Griffiths, Adam Fox, and Steve Hindle (eds.), *The Experience of Authority in Early Modern England* (Basingstoke: Palgrave Macmillan 1996), pp. 213–48; Michael Braddick, 'Administrative Performance: The Representation of Political Authority in Early Modern England', in Michael

The concept of neighbourliness remained important in the eighteenth century. Much of the scholarship on this subject has debated whether it was in decline by this period. Wrightson initially presented neighbourliness as an 'enduring structure' of English society.[4] However, subsequent challenges to the stability of the concept and its ability to facilitate agreement between neighbours led him to suggest that due to the changing nature of English communities in the context of urban expansion and religious difference, neighbourliness may in fact have been in decline by the end of the early modern period.[5] This supposed decline has been useful in explaining changes in related behaviour, such as attitudes to witchcraft accusations and the organisation of poor relief.[6] Yet this decline is far from certain. The principle of neighbourliness was still reinforced through translations of the Bible in this period, and, even when it was challenged, contemporaries used the language of neighbourliness to moderate dispute.[7] Indeed, for the late sixteenth and early seventeenth centuries, Andy Wood has found that the notion that neighbourliness was constantly contested is more useful than that of decline.[8] Furthermore, ideas of neighbourliness and parish community continued to be central to individuals' social, economic, and political lives well into the nineteenth century.[9] More formalised methods of community support, such as the Poor Law, did not necessarily prevent neighbourly charity from remaining important throughout the eighteenth century and beyond.[10] Aspects of community structure may have changed, but obligations to

---

Braddick and John Walter (eds.), *Negotiating Power in Early Modern Society: Order, Hierarchy and Subordination in Britain and Ireland* (Cambridge and New York: Cambridge University Press, 2001), p. 171; Andy Wood, *Faith, Hope, and Charity: English Neighbourhoods, 1500–1640* (Cambridge: Cambridge University Press, 2020), p. 16, *passim*.

[4] Wrightson, *English Society*, pp. 59–65.

[5] Hindle, 'The Keeping of the Public Peace', p. 213; Keith Wrightson, 'The "Decline of Neighbourliness" Revisited', in Norman L. Jones and Daniel Woolf (eds.), *Local Identities in Late Medieval and Early Modern England* (Basingstoke: Palgrave Macmillan, 2007), pp. 39–40.

[6] Malcolm Gaskill, 'Witchcraft and Neighbourliness in Early Modern England', in Steve Hindle, Alexandra Shepard, and John Walter (eds.), *Remaking English Society: Social Relations and Social Change in Early Modern England* (Woodbridge: The Boydell Press, 2013), p. 230; Steve Hindle, *On the Parish? The Micro-Politics of Poor Relief in Rural England, c. 1550–1750* (Oxford: Oxford University Press, 2004), p. 454.

[7] Naomi Tadmor, 'Friends and Neighbours in Early Modern England: Biblical Translations and Social Norms', in Laura Gowing, Michael Hunter, and Miri Rubin (eds.), *Love, Friendship and Faith in Europe, 1300–1800* (Basingstoke: Plagrave Macmillan, 2005), pp. 158, 161–3, 167.

[8] Wood, *Faith, Hope, and Charity*, p. ix.

[9] K. D. M. Snell, *Parish and Belonging. Community, Identity and Welfare in England and Wales, 1700–1950* (Cambridge: Cambridge University Press, 2006), pp. 499, 502–3.

[10] Jonathan Healey, '"By the Charitie of Good People": Poverty and Neighbourly Support in Seventeenth Century Lancashire', *Family and Community History*, 19, 2 (2016), p. 93.

those living in proximity were still important. Neighbourliness remains of analytical value for the eighteenth century.

Given the enduring importance of neighbourliness in discussions of early modern community and social relations, it is hardly surprising that it has been highly influential in debates about inter-confessional relations in this period. The concept has proved particularly illuminating in understanding the 'tolerance of practical rationality': the everyday ways in which individuals and groups with differing religious beliefs navigated their way to maintaining communal harmony.[11] With this in mind, the influential work of Bill Sheils proposed that the language of neighbourliness was the best way of understanding co-existence at a local level.[12] Subsequent studies of inter-confessional relations in the seventeenth and eighteenth centuries have tended to follow in this vein, viewing local structures of neighbourliness as crucial to mitigating religious differences.[13]

There can be little doubt that adherence to the precepts of neighbourliness was essential for peaceful co-existence between Protestant Dissenters and members of the Established Church in the first half of the eighteenth century. This was perhaps most starkly demonstrated when inter-confessional relations broke down. More often than not, the actions of individuals involved in such disputes were described through the language of neighbourliness, and attempts to restore peace were often based upon appeals to neighbourly action. This was made clear when Dissenting ministers preached in favour of liberty of conscience. Responding to the failure of attempts by Dissenters of all varieties to achieve the repeal of the Test and Corporation Acts in the early 1730s, one minister reminded his hearers and readers not to 'bring sufferings on themselves' by acting in an unneighbourly fashion, warning that 'if instead of minding your own business, and studying to be quiet, you will needlessly step out of your way, to inspect and censure the conduct of your neighbours, you may at last end in

[11] Alexandra Walsham, *Charitable Hatred. Tolerance and Intolerance in England, 1500–1700* (Manchester: Manchester University Press, 2006), pp. 231, 269–80.
[12] William Sheils, '"Getting On" and "Getting Along" in Parish and Town: English Catholics and Their Neighbours', in Benjamin J. Kaplan, Bob Moore, Henk van Nierop, and Judith Pollmann (eds.), *Catholic Communities in Protestant States: Britain and the Netherlands 1580–1720* (Manchester: Manchester University Press, 2009), pp. 67–83.
[13] Nadine Lewycky and Adam Morton, 'Introduction', in Nadine Lewycky and Adam Morton (eds.), *Getting along? Religious Identities and Confessional Relations in Early Modern England – Essays in Honour of Professor W. J. Sheils* (Farnham: Ashgate, 2012), pp. 7–9; Carys Brown, 'Militant Catholicism, Interconfessional Relations, and the Rookwood Family of Stanningfield, Suffolk, c. 1689–1737', *Historical Journal*, 60, 1 (2017), pp. 40, 43–5.

rapine and blood-shed'.[14] If Dissenters acted in an unneighbourly fashion, they could not expect toleration.

The converse of this was that if Dissenters did conform to the principles of good neighbourliness, they should, Dissenting ministers argued, be treated with amity and respect. This was the view put forward by the Dissenting minister John Norman, whose arrival in Petersfield in 1722 occasioned a vehemently anti-Dissenting sermon from the rector of the parish, William Louth.[15] Writing in reply to Louth, Norman argued that 'all Mankind have a *Right* to serve God in such a Way as their Consciences pronounce to be the best'. There was no reason to be angry with parishioners who followed their conscience outside of the Established Church, given that 'they continue as good Neighbours, and live as quietly, and as much like Christians, as when they attended on the Worship of God in your Church'.[16] Norman sought to remind his Established Church counterpart that so long as the foundations of good neighbourliness remained in place, then he really had no grounds for complaint. Neighbourliness was, at least in the view of these ministers, the common denominator: if they did not adhere to it, Dissenters could expect to be persecuted and reviled; if they remained good neighbours, they ought justly to expect peaceful co-existence. This argument was hardly surprising given the Biblical precedent for advocating neighbourliness, which was especially apparent in Jesus's teaching that after love for God, the commandment 'Thou shalt love thy neighbour as thyself' was the most important in Mosaic law.[17]

The centrality of neighbourly principles to determining the limits of inclusion in a community was demonstrated in practice in instances where individual Dissenters faced exclusion or ostracism in their localities. Criticisms of the behaviour of local Dissenters were often framed in the language of neighbourliness. In Kirkham, Lancashire, in 1691, for example, the vicar complained to the Justices that the Quaker preacher Margaret Colbron 'doth Conventickle from house to house & disquiet

---

[14] *Christian Sufferers: Or, Seasonable Advice to Protestant Dissenters, Relating to Their Behaviour Under Their Present Disappointment. A Sermon Preached in the Country, January 28 1732–3* (London, 1733), p. 16.
[15] William Gibson, '"A Happy Fertile Soil Which Bringeth Forth Abundantly": The Diocese of Winchester, 1689–1800', in Jeremy Gregory and Jeffrey S. Chamberlain (eds.), *The National Church in Local Perspective: The Church of England and the Regions, 1660–1800* (Woodbridge: The Boydell Press, 2003), p. 108.
[16] John Norman, *Remarks on a Sermon Preached at Petersfield, June the 7th, 1722, by the Reverend Mr William Louth, Rector of that Parish, and Prebendary of Winchester. In a Letter to Himself* (London, 1723), pp. 43–4, emphasis original.
[17] Mark 12:31 (King James Version).

her better neighbours in their owne houses'. The fact that the vicar chose to mention the social disruption that she was causing, before he complained more specifically that she was attempting to convert her neighbours (by telling them that 'they must be Quakers or perish'), suggests that he realised the power of accusations of unneighbourly behaviour against Dissenters.[18] Equally, in 1693, when John and Mary Cooper of Warrington, Cheshire, were rebuked by their Meeting after they did 'in an Unruly and unbridled passion fall into words raising discord' between themselves, it was primarily because they 'became to our great shame and the dishonour of our profession exposed to the Notice and observation of our Neighbours'. They were anxious to reassure the Meeting that 'These things we were willing to let our Neighbours know were done by us in our haste and passion … that none may reflect upon the way of truth we have professed.'[19] The Coopers were clearly acutely aware that the discord they created through their individual actions in their neighbourhood might easily be attributed to their religious profession in general. When opponents of the Dissenting interest wished to challenge the position of Dissenters on a local level, it was often on the grounds of unneighbourliness that they chose to do so, and Dissenters sought to defend themselves against this. Neighbourliness was central to the negotiation of peaceful co-existence in this period; both Protestant Dissenters and members of the Established Church were aware that lapses in neighbourliness could signal or stimulate conflict.

Given this, it is unsurprising that Dissenters themselves defended their cause through the language of neighbourliness. When justifying the righteousness of their cause and making the case for their acceptance within communities, Dissenters made reference to their good neighbourly behaviour. In her diaries the Cheshire Presbyterian Sarah Savage reassured herself that her neighbourly attitude towards those who acted with discrimination towards her justified the righteousness of her position. In October 1687 she wrote that 'we dayly hear of the scoffs & scorns of our Neighbors but if wee can do our duty so that the Master say well done tis no great matter what the fellow servants say'.[20] Some thirty years later,

---

[18] Kellamergh and Freckleton: Mock-Marriage at Christopher Lealands by Mr Parr, and Ill-Behaviour of Margaret Colbron, *c.*1691, QSP/705/11, Lancashire Archives, Preston.

[19] Society of Friends, Hardshaw Monthly Meeting, Personal Condemnations and Testimonies of Denial, 1667–1791, fol. 38v, M85/1/11, Manchester Archives (MA), Manchester.

[20] Sarah Savage Diary, 1686–88, fol. 22v, ZDBasten/8, Cheshire Archives and Local Studies (CALS), Chester.

in May 1716, she was 'concern'd to see neighbours look shy, & cold, on us (as we are Dissenters) alass I am a stranger & a Pilgrim', but her solution was that 'I should walk circumspectly giving no offence to the natives.'[21] When faced with local exclusion, Savage tried to act in ways inoffensive to her community, conducting her duty such that she was innocent of any potential charges of unneighbourly behaviour. The fact that both opponents of Dissent and Dissenters themselves expressed local religiously related conflict and discord in terms of neighbourliness suggests that adherence to neighbourly principles was indeed essential for maintaining peaceful co-existence.

This connection between neighbourliness and co-existence is reinforced by the fact that many successful interactions between Dissenters and members of the Established Church in local communities were expressed through the language of good neighbourhood. There are numerous references in Dissenters' diaries and journals to having cared for neighbours in times of sickness: Mary Churchman of Cambridgeshire was reportedly converted from zealous Anglicanism to participation in a Congregational Meeting by 'the persuasion of a Neighbour that had been usefull to me in my Illness'; in October 1686 Sarah Savage reported having attended to her neighbour in labour, and in March 1687 helped a young neighbour dying of consumption, in whom she sadly 'could perceive little sense shee has of what is before her'.[22] There are also other records of neighbours of different religious professions doing favours for each other, or joining together for the good of the wider community: Richard Kay, a Presbyterian physician from Baldingstone, Lancashire, recorded how in the aftermath of the disruption of the 1745 Jacobite Rebellion he met 'with some of our Neighbours … on Account of our Township's Affairs'.[23] A letter from the Presbyterian minister Matthew Henry to his mother in 1699 also suggests neighbourly intermingling at events of community significance. Henry wrote that he was sending his children to stay with his mother while he attended the local fair, but that he expected 'to see Joseph Ridgeway at the Fair, and by him or some other of your neighbours shal hear how you

[21] Mrs Savage's Diary, 31 May 1714 to 25 December 1723 (eighteenth-century copy), pp. 97–8, MS Eng. misc. e. 331, Bodleian (Bod.), Oxford.

[22] Commonplace Book: 'John Churchman His Book': Account of Mary Churchman's Life, Given by Her Daughter Mary, 1732–4, D/DQs 22, Essex Record Office, Chelmsford; Sarah Savage Diary, 1686–88, fols. 3r, 9v.

[23] W. Brockbank and F. Kenworthy (eds.), *The Diary of Richard Kay, 1716–51, of Baldingstone, Near Bury. A Lancashire Doctor* (Manchester: Manchester University Press for the Chetham Society, 1968), p. 116.

do'.[24] Clearly the fair was a local occasion at which neighbours would mix and exchange news, regardless of religious profession.

It is undoubtedly the case that the concept of neighbourliness was at the heart of how contemporaries understood their relationships with those they lived alongside. This applied as much to inter-confessional relationships as it did to others. As is apparent from accounts of inter-confessional tension, and from instances of more successful interaction, neighbourliness was a basic condition for peaceful co-existence in this period. When Dissenters were perceived to be unneighbourly, their behaviour could quickly be used to fuel slights against their religion. Furthermore, if opponents of Dissent wished to damage Dissenters' positions within their local community, they often suggested that their behaviour was unneighbourly. Equally, Dissenters trying to defend their local position and right to liberty of conscience made appeals to their good neighbourly behaviour as a justification of their position. It is evident that any discussion of inter-confessional relations in this period must take account of the basic importance of neighbourliness in shaping co-existence on a local level.

The Limitations of Neighbourliness

Evidently, neighbourliness, as an analytical concept, can tell us a lot about the negotiation of religious difference in this period. It tells us that appeals to neighbourliness could be used as a tool against intolerant attitudes; equally, accusations of unneighbourliness could be used to argue against tolerance. The concept of neighbourliness is essential for understanding early modern inter-confessional relations, and it was indeed significant in relationships between Protestant Dissenters and members of the Established Church in the first half of the eighteenth century.

However, neighbourliness can only take us so far. Love for one's neighbour was a basic precept of Christianity, so the ability to live peaceably with neighbours was a minimum requirement of all.[25] While it was a basic necessity for tolerance, neighbourliness was not necessarily indicative of a genuine *bon amis*. It therefore tells us little about the social texture of inter-confessional relations; it has limited capacity for revealing the varieties of social relationships between Dissenters and members of the Established

---

[24] Matthew Henry to His Mother, 25 September *c*.1699, Add MS 42849, fol. 69r, British Library, London.

[25] Tadmor, 'Friends and Neighbours in Early Modern England', pp. 150–1.

Church in this period. Neighbourliness helps to reveal that, on an every-day basis, people of differing beliefs were able to 'get along' for the sake of everyday community functioning in this period.[26] However, as we have already observed, Dissenters' relationships with those outside their faith went beyond mere co-existence to a liminal and sometimes uncomfort-able space between co-existence and assimilation. To understand the extent to which this led to social integration and amity between different groups, and the nature of those relationships, we need to look to alterna-tive descriptions of sociability.

This is important, because it has significant consequences for under-standing the social dynamics of Protestantism after 1689. Historians of religious tolerance and co-existence in this period have suggested that a tacit acceptance of religious pluralism emerged from the Toleration Act, encouraging 'sectarian and separatist impulses' as Dissenting groups were no longer so clearly differentiated by the law and prejudice became more focused on 'social exclusiveness and foreignness'.[27] However, the focus on neighbourliness in most studies of Dissenters' relationships to the com-munities they lived in makes it difficult to account for the impact of any such change. Instead, the emphasis is on continued neighbourly charity and participation in a common civic community.[28] This has meant that the social reality and consequences of attempts by Dissenters to differenti-ate themselves from their peers beyond the necessary functions of neigh-bourliness has been largely unexplored. By looking for new ways in which to examine Dissenters' social relationships, we may be able to create a clearer picture of the social manifestations of religious identity after the Toleration Act.

Social historians of the sixteenth, seventeenth, and eighteenth centuries have recognised the limitations of neighbourliness for understanding the multi-faceted nature of social relations within communities. The work of Phil Withington has emphasised that not all incidents and social occa-sions in the early modern period are described adequately by structures

---

[26] Sheils, '"Getting On" and "Getting Along" in Parish and Town', p. 68, 73.
[27] Walsham, Charitable Hatred, p. 319.
[28] John Miller, Cities Divided: Politics and Religion in English Provincial Towns, 1660–1722 (Oxford: Oxford University Press, 2007), p. 310; Richard C. Allen, Quaker Communities in Early Modern Wales: From Resistance to Respectability (Cardiff: University of Wales Press, 2007), p. 120; Simon Dixon, 'Quakers and the London Parish, 1670–1720', The London Journal, 32, 3 (2007), pp. 231, 244; Bill Stevenson, 'The Social Integration of Post-Restoration Dissenters, 1660–1725', in M. Spufford (ed.), The World of Rural Dissenters, 1520–1725 (Cambridge: Cambridge University Press, 1995), pp. 369, 378.

of neighbourliness or paternalism. Pointing out that early modern people 'had a very clear sense of sociability as a distinct social practice', he suggested that in order to analyse contemporary social behaviour, we should pay greater attention to how they 'described and discussed their own sociability'.[29] In particular, he highlighted that the term 'company' was a highly useful lens through which to understand how contemporaries chose to draw and negotiate the boundaries of their sociability within the existing structures of society.[30] This idea has proved illuminating in other studies. Definitions of 'company' among seventeenth-century labourers reveal a sense of occupational identity among tradesmen in the alehouse.[31] In an eighteenth-century context, examinations of 'how company intersected with polite manners' can help us to move beyond the polite–impolite dichotomy prevalent in many discussions of eighteenth-century culture, recognising instead the multiple different forms of sociability that were shaped by context.[32] Attention to how contemporaries described their social circles is thus proving an important route into understanding how social relationships and boundaries were formed.

Historians of inter-confessional relations are yet to incorporate this development into interpretations of this period. This is surprising given that recent scholarship has demonstrated the value of examining social boundaries between groups in order to unpick the dynamics of inter-confessional conflict. Keith Luria's study of Protestant–Catholic relations in France, for instance, found a focus on the construction of different types of boundary between these groups helpful to understanding the conditions for inter-confessional conflict and concord.[33] Despite the apparent productivity of this approach, its application elsewhere has been limited, and the utility of contemporary social descriptors as a means of understanding how confessional group identity moulded social relations remains largely untested.

If we follow the lead of social historians in examining contemporary descriptions of social relations, the limitations of a focus on neighbourliness

[29] Phil Withington, 'Company and Sociability in Early Modern England', *Social History*, 32, 3 (2007), pp. 296, 297.

[30] Ibid., pp. 299, 302–7.

[31] Mark Hailwood, 'Sociability, Work and Labouring Identity in Seventeenth-Century England', *Cultural and Social History*, 8, 1 (2011), pp. 17, 25.

[32] Kate Davison, 'Occasional Politeness and Gentlemen's Laughter in Eighteenth-Century England', *Historical Journal*, 57, 4 (2014), pp. 923–4.

[33] Keith P. Luria, *Sacred Boundaries. Religious Coexistence and Conflict in Early Modern France* (Washington, DC: The Catholic University of America Press, 2005), pp. xxiii, xxvii, 316.

become more apparent. Dissenters did make reference to their neighbours, but an initial survey of the language they used to discuss their social lives reveals that they primarily used the terms 'friends' and 'company'. An examination of the ways in which Dissenters used these different terms allows a more detailed picture of how social and religious boundaries were intertwined with one another in this period. It emphasises how different levels of social interaction were connected to religious affiliation in a way that is obscured by a focus on neighbourliness alone.

The following discussion uses a wide selection of Dissenters' personal papers to draw out a general picture of how contemporaries used these terms. These include the diaries and journals of Presbyterians: James Clegg, a Derbyshire minister; Richard Kay, a Lancashire physician; Matthew Henry, a Cheshire minister; Sarah Savage, Cheshire; Peter Walkden, a Lancashire minister; Anne Dawson, Lancashire. It also includes the correspondence of the Henry family of Cheshire and Flintshire (Presbyterian), the Say family of Norfolk (Independent), the Blackmore family of Worcestershire (Independent), the Fancourts of Wiltshire (Independent and Presbyterian), Benjamin Davies of Pembrokeshire (Baptist), Robert Stevenson of Devon (Quaker), and meeting records of Quakers from Exeter, Lancashire, Manchester, and Essex, Baptists from Gloucestershire, and Independents from Cambridgeshire. Caution is taken in using these types of sources in parallel. Diaries and journals were personal reflections, generally intended for the benefit of the author, their families, and their close associates. It is worth noting that those who kept diaries as a form of spiritual monitoring were perhaps especially conscious of the connection between their religious profession and their behaviour. Nevertheless, the social labels an individual applied to their contacts in these contexts would have little implication for anyone but the author, and do not necessarily imply a conscious attempt to foster an impression of piety. In contrast, meeting records were authored collectively, intended as a group record, and often heavily morally loaded in order to regulate members' behaviour. Social labels used in this context must therefore be approached with this intent in mind.

This is a qualitative rather than quantitative analysis of word usage, limited to instances where contemporaries used the precise terms 'friends', 'company', or 'neighbour', rather than any of their cognates. Attention is given both to whom these social labels were applied, and the context in which they were used. By examining usage across a wide range of sources, a general picture of how Dissenters were using each of these terms emerges. This approach may over-generalise, with the effect of obscuring variation between different types of Dissent, as well as differences relating to region, gender, and social status. To mitigate the effects of this, this general discussion is followed by a series of more detailed case studies of individual Dissenters from different groups, which draw out some of these distinctions.

Before turning to 'friends' and 'company', it is necessary to explore the full range of contexts in which the individuals in these sources referred to their 'neighbours'. Regardless of their type of Dissent, they used the term 'neighbour' in several key ways. First, they used it to refer to interactions brought about simply as a result of living in close proximity. When James Clegg travelled to Derby in May 1734 for the election, he went on his journey 'with many neighbours'. They were all going to the same place for the same purpose; it was natural that they would travel together.[34] More alarmingly for everyone concerned, in October 1692, Matthew Henry found himself side by side with 'Rich. Lee our neighbor tho' an enemy to the Chapel' when they both sought to put out a fire in the Dissenters' meeting house; Lee had an interest in quenching the flames 'because his own Hey-loft joyns up to it'.[35] Lee and Henry clearly did not see eye to eye on religious matters, but their physical proximity as neighbours forced them into common interest. Those who lived alongside one another regarded themselves as neighbours even when they vehemently disagreed over religion. The Cheshire Presbyterian Sarah Savage, for example, had a landlord, Mr Starky, who was 'a great enemy to us as Dissenters', but Savage still referred to him repeatedly as 'our neighbour'.[36] In 1687, Edward Tyrer and William Jenkinson complained to Hardshaw Friends' Meeting that they were unable to protect their grain from being taken for tithes 'because severall of my Neighbours had a way through my Land'.[37] Despite the unwelcome removal of their grain, Tyrer and Jenkinson still regarded those who passed through their land as their neighbours because they were physically proximate. Unlike other forms of social interaction, many encounters with neighbours were unavoidable. Neighbours were not chosen acquaintances, but a simple fact of life.

Dissenters did, however, sometimes use the term 'neighbour' when referring to social interactions they had chosen to undertake. One of the

---

[34] Vanessa S. Doe (ed.), *The Diary of James Clegg of Chapel en le Frith, 1708–1755, Part 1* (Derby: Derbyshire Record Society, 1978), p. 195.

[35] Matthew Henry to Phillip Henry, 21 October 1692, MS Eng. lett. e. 29/103, Bod.

[36] Mrs Savage's Diary, pp. 35, 36.

[37] Society of Friends, Hardshaw Monthly Meeting, Accounts of Sufferings and Distraints, 1654–1816, p. 20, M85/1/4, MA.

most common contexts in which female Dissenters in particular recorded contact with neighbours was, as we saw above, in times of sickness or at funerals of members of the community. They might also choose to extend hospitality to one another on festive occasions: Richard Kay, a Presbyterian physician from Lancashire, invited his neighbouring tenants to sup with his household every Christmas Day.[38] Furthermore, they clearly allowed themselves to be involved in economic relationships with their neighbours. In Cullompton, Devon, for instance, Thomas Jarman (a member of the Established Church) complained to the local Quaker Meeting that one of their members, Alexander Richards, had caused him financial ruin after he had been arrested, and 'sent for me being a Neighbour desireing I would becom one of his Sureties' only to allow his bail to be 'Levyed on me … to the utter ruin of my temporall well being'.[39] While Richards had clearly let his neighbour down, the fact that he called on Jarman in the first place suggests that the expectation of neighbourly duty in such matters of financial well-being was not overridden by religious difference. Similarly, Joseph Tipping, a Gloucestershire Baptist, was rebuked by his Church after 'he lyed to his neighbour in that he said he had money Due to him enow to pay what he owd him when it was utterly falce'.[40] Again, this was clearly a moment when a neighbourly economic relationship broke down; such everyday interactions are more likely to have been recorded when they went wrong. Nevertheless, these glimpses into neighbourly economic relationships highlight that economic need, in addition to physical proximity, was one of the primary ways in which Dissenters' interaction with their neighbours was shaped.

The final key context in which Dissenters referred to their neighbours in their diaries, letters, and meeting books was when they attempted to regulate or attack one another's behaviour in a community context. This was a particularly important duty in the light of Paul's injunction in his letter to the Ephesians to 'walk worthy of the vocation wherewith ye are called' as part of 'the whole body' which 'fitly joined together and compacted by that which every joint supplieth, according to the effectual working in the measure of every part, maketh increase of the body unto the edifying of itself in love'.[41] The consequent concern to keep a check on the behaviour of

[38] Brockbank and Kenworthy (eds.), *The Diary of Richard Kay*, p. 40.

[39] Miscellaneous Papers of Cullompton Monthly Meeting, 1692–1777: Letter of Thomas Jarman, 874D/o/M/112-155, Devon Archives and Local Studies (DALS), Exeter.

[40] Wooton-under-Edge Baptist Church, Church Book 1717–1826, fol. 6v, D2844/2/1, Gloucestershire Archives, Gloucestershire.

[41] Ephesians 4:1, 16 (King James Version).

Church members is seen most obviously in records of discipline in Church meeting books, which often gave the danger of neighbourly admonishment as a particular reason to avoid lewd and disorderly behaviour. At Kimbolton Independent Church on 16 May 1726, for instance, 'brother Jackson' was 'admonished for abusing of his wife in beating of her, the fact being known in the neighbourhood'.[42] Dissenters appear to have been highly conscious of the fact that if any of their congregation showed themselves to be acting in an unneighbourly fashion, they could expect it to be used as a slight against their profession in general.

In line with general understandings of the role of neighbours in early modern England, Dissenters' relationships with their neighbours were shaped by physical proximity, economic necessity, and matters of community regulation. While accusations of unneighbourly behaviour could, as we have seen, be used as a tool to facilitate religious prejudice, neighbours were not chosen social acquaintances. It is unsurprising, therefore, that Dissenters rarely seem to have been discriminatory in who they regarded as their neighbour. It is also unsurprising that their Established Church neighbours interacted with them. They were 'getting along' in order to 'get on'.[43] However, this ability of Dissenting neighbours to get along with their Established Church neighbours on a practical everyday level, while crucial, is indicative of little more than the barest level of tolerance needed for life to continue in a more religiously pluralistic landscape.

In contrast, Dissenters' references to being in 'company' with others were far more discriminating. The company an individual kept was much more a matter of personal choice. Crucially, for Dissenters of all varieties, religious affiliation appears to have been an important determining factor in the constitution of their sociable company. Mentions of company in the records studied here can largely be divided into 'good' and 'bad' company. 'Good' company consisted of those with whom Dissenters conversed, went riding, ate, travelled to sermons, and entertained themselves. The benefits of good company could be merely social – as when Abigail Blackmore, an Independent from Worcester, wrote to her daughter that she 'wanted yor help a Little in Pers:macking and your Company', or when James Clegg went into Chapel-en-le-Frith with some friends for

---

[42] Typed transcript of the Kimbolton Independent Church Book, 1692–1809, p. 54, PGMD/3500/15, Huntingdonshire Archives, Huntingdon.
[43] Sheils, '"Getting On" and "Getting Along" in Parish and Town'.

the evening 'and the company diverted themselves an hour or two and we returnd home'.[44] However, 'company' could also denote a group of individuals gathered for more serious spiritual or intellectual purposes. In November 1732, for instance, Clegg 'met an emissary of the church of Rome [in] Sheffield' to debate with him in order to persuade the daughter of a member of his congregation of the ills of the Catholic faith. He reported that 'about 20 were present, most of the company were fully satisfied'.[45] In this context the 'company' were those who had chosen to gather together for spiritual edification, rather than entertainment. The term was used in a similar fashion by the Quaker Robert Barrows in his account of the death and burial of George Fox, who in his final moments 'spoke many living powerful sentences, to the tendering of the company present'.[46] The Lancashire Presbyterian Anne Dawson was determined that spiritual and social benefit should be combined in the company she kept, recording in June 1722 'we have had company all week from Chobent their company are very agreable because of their parts and piety'.[47] Good company consisted of those who had chosen to gather together for spiritual or social benefit.

Significantly, it is rare in the manuscript materials examined here to find instances in which the good company being referred to did not consist of co-religionists. Matthew Henry does record in his diary that his friend Mr Kenrick had given a report of ill words spoken against him in 1707, which he heard while he was 'in company at a Tavern with Alderman Peter Bennet', presumably in a social capacity.[48] In general, however, among a sea of references to Dissenting 'company' in these sources there is a notable absence of discussion of 'company' of mixed religious affiliation. This does not, of course, mean that Dissenters did not socialise with members of the Established Church, or indeed Dissenters of different varieties. As the preceding chapters demonstrate, they certainly did. But it does suggest that the way that the individuals studied here drew boundaries around and understood their social relationships was strongly determined by their religious outlook.

---

[44] Abigail Blackmore to Sarah Blackmore, 13 December, n.d. (c.1725), 12.40/33, Dr Williams's Library (DWL), London.
[45] Doe (ed.), *The Diary of James Clegg, Part 1*, p. 157.
[46] File of Miscellaneous Papers, Probably Records of the Cullompton or Spiceland Monthly Meeting, 1666–1772: Robert Barrows, London, to Henry Coward, Thomas Green, Thomas Dockery, Richard, Burrow, William Hugginson and Thomas Widers, 1690, 874D/o/M/51-111, DALS.
[47] Diary of Anne (Dawson) Evans 1721–22, fol. 31r, Add MS 71626, BL.
[48] Diary of Matthew Henry, 1705–1713, MS Eng. misc. e. 330, Bod.

This becomes further apparent when we examine what Dissenters appear to have perceived to be 'bad' company. These were groups of people who were regarded as endangering an individual's piety: the Quaker John Croker, for example, had to suffer a non-Quaker master who was 'Provd to be an Ill Company Keeper and a Night playing Man, that Caused me often to walk the streets in the Night to Search the Taverns'.[49] James Strettle, a Quaker from Manchester, wrote a warning to young people before he died, telling of how in his youth 'I let my mind out to keep bad company, which was given to much drinking, gameing & running after Young-women,' but that after he had found his faith, he 'then disliked the company of those young men, my former Companions'.[50] With faith, he suggested, came a more scrupulous attitude to sociability. It was not only Quakers who feared that the company of those not of their spiritual bent might lead them astray. From the 1650s it had been determined by the Presbyterian Exeter Assembly that when a 'Scandalous offender' had been admonished by ministers but failed to reform, it was 'a Good Expedient ... for the Reformation of our Congragations' that 'others may have no Company with him'.[51] The importance of the principle that bad company could corrupt the spiritual life of an individual is further highlighted by the entry for 'company' in the commonplace book of the Liverpool Unitarian children John and Hannah Tylston, from the mid-eighteenth century. The book contains headings in alphabetical order, under which the children copied out relevant quotations and Bible verses. None of the quotations entered under 'company' are positive. Instead, they warn against the effects of ill company: quotations given from Thomas Brook's *Precious Remedies Against Satan's Devices* (1661) included 'O Lord let me not go to Hell where the wicked are, for Lord thou Knowest I never lov'd their company here,' and 'guilt or grief is all the good gracious souls get by conversing with wicked men'.[52] The presumed connection between bad company in this world and punishment in the next was thereby made abundantly clear.

---

[49] *Something by Way of a Journal or Part of the Life of John Croker*, c.1720, p. 28, MS BOX D3/5, Friends' Lib.

[50] Society of Friends, Hardshaw Monthy Meeting – Book for Recording Papers and Epistles &c, fol. 8v: 'A Warning to Young People by James Strettle Deceased', c.1708, M85/1/12/1, MA.

[51] The Exeter Assembly, Presbyterian, Minute Books, 1652–1794, entry for 5 May 1659, 3542D/M/1/1, DALS.

[52] Commonplace Book of John Tylston, with Additions by Hannah Tylston and Hannah Lightbody, p. 136, MS Eng. misc. d. 311, Bod.

In comparison with the circumstances in which Dissenters recorded interacting with neighbours, their uses of the term 'company' were, as might be expected, far more value-laden. Whereas neighbourly interactions were determined by the obligation to support one another within a community, and the necessity of interaction that physical proximity entailed, to enter into company was regarded far more as a matter of choice. As descriptions of both 'good' and 'bad' company emphasise, most Dissenters believed that selection of company had profound implications for an individual's spiritual life, and therefore had to be made with that in mind. At the level of neighbourly social obligation, Dissenters' sociability appears religiously inclusive. When they had a choice of company, however, the social boundaries that Dissenters constructed around themselves appear to have been far more exclusive.

This was even more the case when it came to friendship. As Naomi Tadmor's important study of friendship in eighteenth-century England has shown, the term 'friend' could refer to multiple types of relationship, including kinship, sentimental ties, economic bonds, intellectual and spiritual connections, and political alliances.[53] However, as her case study of a Sussex shopkeeper, Thomas Turner, demonstrates, individual use of the term was often quite precise, confining it to a select set of people who met certain criteria.[54] This was the case for the individuals studied here. Across all groups of Dissenters, the 'friends' that they referred to in their personal papers were almost always developed in a spiritual context. Unlike good 'company', friendship did not have to be maintained in the physical presence of one another. Far more important appears to have been a mutual spiritual outlook and a willingness to provide spiritual and temporal support in times of difficulty. Thus when Michael Fletcher, of the Platt Dissenters' chapel in Rusholme, Manchester, wrote to his fellow Dissenting minister Rev. Hesketh to vouch for the spiritual integrity of one of his congregation who was moving to Hesketh's area, he signed off as his 'assur'd friend & unworthy Brother'; their shared spiritual interest was sufficient for him to be regarded as a friend, despite their physical distance.[55]

Unlike descriptions of 'company', which usually referred to those present at specific events and activities, references to friends were often

[53] Naomi Tadmor, *Family and Friends in Eighteenth-Century England* (Cambridge: Cambridge University Press, 2001), p. 167.
[54] Ibid., pp. 173–4.
[55] Michael Fletcher to Revd Mr Hesketh, 15 June 1706, M35/6/3/21, MA.

made in discussions of situations where an individual had acted, or was expected to act, in the interests of another. Friends were temporal and spiritual well-wishers: upon the marriage of her granddaughter in April 1744 Sarah Savage was comforted that 'she has her Friends advice & Prayers'; when Peter Walkden's 'hearty friend' and fellow Presbyterian Robert Earnishaw died, Walkden went to another friend's house, where 'we found several friends came together, to prayers'.[56] The Wiltshire Presbyterian minister Nathaniel Fancourt regarded an individual 'ready to press what I have moved' in a business transaction as a friend, but this was not simply because he favoured his business interests; he was also a fellow Dissenter, in contrast to another person with whom Fancourt was doing business, who 'be no Friend to one of my Character'.[57] Fancourt's temporal friends were his spiritual ones, and vice versa. This was also clearly the sense in which the minister John Evans was using the term 'friends' when he wrote to Matthew Henry concerning measures to prevent occasional conformity in January 1705, enclosing with his letter 'a paper agreed upon by all the denominations of Dissenters, Presbyterians, Independents, Anabaptists & Quakers to be sent to their friends in the Countrey as their Agreed sense about the next Election'.[58] In this context, the 'friends' of each of these groups were regarded as those of their co-religionists who were expected to act in the shared interest of the wider group. It is notable that whether the matter concerned was temporal or spiritual, Dissenters appear to have looked primarily to those of their own religion for support.

This is to some extent unsurprising, given that this social language of friendship was ascribed spiritual significance in scripture. In the Gospel of John, shortly before his arrest and crucifixion, Jesus tells his disciples 'Ye are my friends, if ye do whatsoever I command you. / Henceforth I call you not servants; for the servant knoweth not what his lord doeth: but I have called you friends; for all things that I have heard of my Father I have made known unto you.'[59] In this passage, those who were friends were those with shared spiritual knowledge. Quakers' use of the term 'Friend' to describe fellow believers from the 1650s onwards may therefore have had

---

[56] Sarah Savage's Journal, 1743–8, Entry for 1 April 1744, Henry MSS 90.2, DWL; Peter Walkden, Nonconformist Minister, Diary, 1733–5, p. 48, ZCR 678, CALS.

[57] Nathaniel Fancourt to John Butler, 9 January c.1711, 727/1/6, Wiltshire and Swindon History Centre, Chippenham.

[58] John Evans, London, to Matthew Henry, Chester, 23 January 1705, MS Eng. lett. e. 29/220, Bod.

[59] John 15:14–15 (King James Version).

roots in this part of the Gospel, indicating those who were sharing in the knowledge of God, although the precise origin of this term is unknown.[60] In any case, the scriptural implications of the term 'friend' appear particularly significant given that Dissenters in general tended to use this term only to refer to their co-religionists.

These distinctions between how Dissenters regarded neighbours, company, and friends are further demonstrated in sermons by Dissenting ministers on these topics. Discussions of neighbourliness were strongly associated with Christian charity, which 'lives in the Heart, where Persons love their Neighbours as themselves'. It was, for William Wilson, a Dissenting preacher and schoolmaster in Newcastle, a means to heal 'all the Disorders in Society'.[61] Neighbourly behaviour was therefore about maintaining social order, and was to be applied generally 'to our Fellow-Creatures, as Partakers with us of the same common Nature'.[62] In the context of long-running accusations that Dissent was disruptive to state and society, it was in the interests of Dissenting ministers to demonstrate publicly in their sermons that they encouraged neighbourly behaviour among their congregations. Nevertheless, Wilson was still willing to differentiate between how he expected his flock to treat those who shared their beliefs and how he expected them to treat those those who did not: a 'special Regard' was owed to 'our Fellow-christians, who are a Community or Society united under the same Head, and have one common Interest, and sacred Bond of Friendship with one another'.[63] Those who were in Christian society with one another were regarded as friends because they had the same interest at heart, and they therefore had to give each other particular care and attention.

On the other hand, the London Presbyterian minister and writer Samuel Chandler complained that

> even good Men of different Denominations, are apt to entertain the most *unfriendly* Suspicions of each other, merely because of the different Denominations they belong to, and are sometimes almost afraid to *converse* together, through an Apprehension of some *bad Design* upon one

[60] Many thanks to Kate Peters for discussion of this issue.
[61] William Wilson, *Charity, as a Rule of Conduct in the Affairs of a Religious Society, Explain'd and Recommended: A Sermon Preach'd to a Congregation of Protestant Dissenters in Newcastle upon Tyne, on November the 22nd, 1733* (London, 1734), pp. 10, 16.
[62] John Barker, *Charity Recommended Upon the Motives and Incouragements of Christianity: A Sermon Preach'd at the Old Jewry, Mark 5, 1739 to the Society for Relief of the Widows and Orphans of Dissenting Ministers* (London, 1740), p. 12.
[63] Ibid., pp. 21–2.

another ... imagining themselves in a kind of Danger, whilst in the Society of any but those of their own *Inclosure*.[64]

Chandler may have been exaggerating, but it is clear that there was a tendency among some Dissenters to regard only their co-religionists as reliably likely to act in their best interests.

The religious inclusivity that appears present in Dissenters' interactions with their neighbours was thus not mirrored in the social choices that Dissenters made with regards to friendship and company. Like those who lived alongside Thomas Turner, the subject of Tadmor's study, many of those who came into regular contact with Dissenters were not identified by them as friends.[65] As in Turner's case, the relationships of Dissenters with friends were 'special and different' from those that they had with neighbours; friendship was a 'moral and reciprocal relationship' in which friends would serve the interests of each other as best they could.[66] Yet in contrast to Turner, whose friendships were sometimes based on intellectual and spiritual interests but were equally a product of business and political connections, Dissenters appear to have given strong priority to spiritual affinity.

Given that friendships 'were often the most significant relationships in an individual's life', and that they were important in shaping the social order through networks of interest and support, the religious exclusivity of these Dissenters' friendships, while not entirely unsurprising, is significant.[67] If the ways in which religious groups constructed their social boundaries had a substantial impact on the nature and permanence of peaceful inter-confessional relations, then the exclusive nature of Dissenters' relationships is worth greater attention.[68] Whereas neighbours were those with whom Dissenters interacted due to circumstance, and company were those with whom they passed time, it was only friends who were expected to actively serve each other's interests. The fact that Dissenters almost exclusively drew those whom they regarded as 'friends' from their own religious grouping thus indicates where the limits of inter-confessional trust lay. It highlights that frameworks of friendship and company allow for a fuller exploration of the changing social dynamics of religious difference than a

---

[64] Samuel Chandler, *St Paul's Rules of Charity, and His Manner of Recommending It, Considered: In a Sermon Preached to the Society for Relieving the Widows and Orphans of Protestant Dissenting Ministers, at the Old Jury, March 1st 1748* (London, 1749), p. 25, emphasis original.

[65] Tadmor, *Family and Friends*, p. 212.

[66] Ibid., pp. 174, 213.

[67] Ibid., pp. 273, 277.

[68] Luria, *Sacred Boundaries*, p. 316.

focus on neighbourliness alone. The next section therefore offers, by way of a series of case studies, an indication of how this might be done.

Friendship, Company, and the Social Lives of Dissenters

As Tadmor's study of Turner's friendships shows, the way individuals categorised their social relationships was highly individual, and often revealed their social and personal priorities.[69] The following short case studies are a means of examining what these priorities may have been for individual Dissenters, selected here to demonstrate perspectives from a variety of religious standpoints, geographical locations, and circumstances. Their accounts are taken as personal; they are not understood to be representative of all others of the same religious standpoint but merely emblematic of some of the ways in which the languages of sociability were used by Dissenters in this period. Nevertheless, it is possible to draw out parallels and comparisons between them that provide some indication of how the construction of social boundaries by pious Dissenters of differing religious professions may have shaped their interactions with wider society in the eighteenth century.

Richard Kay and Sociability in Town and Country

Richard Kay was a Presbyterian physician and diarist from Baldingstone, near Bury, Lancashire. His diary, beginning 11 April 1737 and ending 19 July 1750, is a record of his medical practice and spiritual and social life.[70] He usually wrote three or four sentences for each entry, but even these short summaries of his day provide a wealth of detail about his daily activities, travels, and social contacts. Each entry ends with a short prayer, usually in some way relating to the activities of the day, providing an interesting insight into his state of mind regarding his daily activities. On 19 October 1743, for instance, after he had been particularly struck by the death and affliction in the London hospitals he was visiting, and had drunk part of a bottle of wine with a friend, he wrote 'Lord, let no Affliction or Heaviness whatever damp the Vigour and Improvement of my Mind,' indicating perhaps both a regret at the suffering he saw and an acknowledgement of the effects of drink.[71] This was during the year he spent in medical training

---

[69] Tadmor, *Family and Friends*, p. 174.

[70] See also Anne Pimlott Baker, 'Kay, Richard (1716–1751)', *Oxford Dictionary of National Biography* (Oxford University Press, 2004), www.oxforddnb.com/view/article/68345, accessed 4 June 2018.

[71] Brockbank and Kenworthy (eds.), *The Diary of Richard Kay*, p. 73.

at Guy's Hospital in London. The records that Kay gives of his time in the city are useful as a means to compare his social interactions there with those in his small rural community at home in Lancashire. These contrasting situations provide the opportunity to reflect on the key criteria that Kay's acquaintances had to meet in order to be regarded as friends or company, and also highlight some of the similarities and differences between urban and rural contexts. The overall picture of a sociability that was largely determined by Kay's religious outlook presents a very different image from that which a focus on neighbourliness alone allows.

As discussed previously, Kay appears to have been a good neighbour and member of his community. He distributed bread and cloth to the poor at Christmas; he joined in with his neighbours in celebrating the defeat of Jacobite rebels; he met with them to discuss local affairs.[72] He was not immune from involvement in local factional dispute between High and Low Church, particularly over the management of the school, but in general he adhered to expectations of neighbourliness.[73] On the whole, he appears to have lived according to the principle of Christian charity towards his neighbours, praying that 'Lord, as thou hast loved us in sending thine only begotten Son Jesus Christ into the World, that we might live through him; so may we also love one another.'[74] When it came to neighbourly interaction, Kay showed no obvious signs of discrimination according to religious profession, expressing an equal duty to all those living in proximity to him.

However, Kay did not frame the majority of his social interactions in his diary in terms of neighbourliness. He much more commonly referred to 'friends' and 'company'. Analysing who was included in the interactions when he used these labels, and where they took place, reveals a far more exclusive sociability than is suggested by his neighbourly interactions. There were four key contexts in which Kay tended to mention friends or company: meetings for spiritual interactions, family visits, recreational activities, and business interactions. Within this there are some notable variations in Kay's uses of the terms according to situation. As has been noted by historians of friendship in this period, the term 'friend' was often used to refer to blood relations, and such was the case for Kay.[75]

[72] Ibid., pp. 40, 109, 116.
[73] Ibid., pp. 116, 124.
[74] Ibid., p. 40.
[75] Tadmor, *Family and Friends*, pp. 175–91; Keith Thomas, *The Ends of Life: Roads to Fulfilment in Early Modern England* (Oxford and New York: Oxford University Press, 2009), p. 190.

However, when it came to meetings for spiritual purposes, Kay appears to have regarded anyone present who shared his religious beliefs as a 'friend'. Thus on 9 September 1737 he recorded that 'This Day hath been a Day of Prayer here, which is monthly observ'd by me dear Father and some of our christian Friends.'[76] This was further demonstrated in his grief at his brother-in-law Joseph Baron's death in June 1750, when he wrote

> I got up having had no Sleep to Night Friends at Bury being so much in my thoughts ... we have generally met at his [Joseph Baron's] House on Sabbath Day Morning before Service, yea his House has been a kind of general Rendevous for Friends, for near twenty Years past; he was seldom absent, and I believe never failed to behave to his Friends like a Friend and a Brother.[77]

His religious community had both a spiritual and a social purpose. They were a tight-knit group who gathered, prayed, worshipped, and ate together regularly. Those who participated in this could be regarded as Kay's 'friends'.

In contrast, Kay very rarely used the term 'friend' when discussing business interactions, even when those involved were in other situations described as such. Instead, meetings, visits, and journeys undertaken in the name of business and medical practice were done 'in Company' with others. On 7 May 1744 Kay 'enter'd upon a Course of Midwifry with Mr Smelley the Man Midwife ... in Company with Mr Stead, Mr Ellington an Apothecary in the Burrough and a young Physician belonging to St Thos'.[78] Similarly, when he recorded journeys undertaken for recreational purposes or to visit family, those who were with him were regarded as his company; in May 1743 he went on a recreational visit to Harrogate 'in Company with Mr James Baron of Redivals, Mr James Hardman of Rochdale and his Brother Mr Jno Hardman of Liverpool, the Revnds Mr Owen of Rochdale Mr Mills from Bolton, and some other Company'.[79] These were all individuals who shared his religious outlook and who, in other circumstances, Kay regarded as his friends. In all these situations it appears that it was the shared activity being undertaken that rendered those present 'in company' with one another; it was only in cases where the company had a clear shared interest and purpose that Kay wrote of friendship.

[76] Brockbank and Kenworthy (eds.), *The Diary of Richard Kay*, p. 13.
[77] Ibid., p. 158.
[78] Ibid., p. 83.
[79] Ibid., p. 62.

What is most striking, however, is that despite Kay's frequent interaction with local individuals who did not share his religious outlook, those who he mentioned as friends and company were almost all his co-religionists. The only exceptions to this were during his year in London, when he was largely away from his usual social circle, and was engaged in medical training alongside a variety of men of a similar age. During this period, he did mention going to see landmarks and attending lectures 'in company' with a number of individuals who appear not to have been Dissenters.[80] It thus might be suggested that Kay's apparent religious exclusivity in his social relationships in Lancashire was merely a product of his situation. In Baldingstone and Bury he was surrounded by his family and a tight-knit congregation of Presbyterians, and it was therefore only natural that he would socialise with them, whereas in London the social-religious community he had been born into was absent and the urban environment lent itself to a greater range of activities and acquaintances; his social connections were more religiously plural as a result. However, even when he was in London, Kay showed a distinct religious bias in the way he constructed his social circle. Those whom he regarded as his 'friends' while in London were all fellow Dissenters, and he sought out their company. In fact, his religious affiliation appears to have been helpful to him in settling into the unfamiliar city. Notably, the 'most agreeable and the most intimate Acquaintance' he had in London was that of Rev. John Jolly, with whom he lodged from August to September 1744 and who, as his 'very agreable friend', was 'in Company' with Kay for part of his journey home to Lancashire.[81] Although Kay clearly spent time with those who did not share his religious outlook while he was in London, the majority of his 'company', and all of his 'friends' were drawn from his co-religionists. Even without the religiously based social community he was born into in Lancashire, the social boundaries that Kay drew around himself were largely religious in nature.

The multiple layers of Richard Kay's social world reveal the extent and limits of inter-confessional sociability among those with whom he interacted on an everyday basis. On the whole, the offices of neighbourliness in Baldingstone and the surrounding area appear to have been immune to confessional difference: neighbours oiled the wheels of community function by helping one another in poverty and sickness. Yet the tenor of this social contact was very different from that which Kay had with friends and

---

[80] Ibid., pp. 75, 78, 80, 83.
[81] Ibid., pp. 119, 87, 89.

among company, as was the selectivity of the personnel involved. Kay's friends were those who shared his Christian interests and purposes, his company were those with whom he chose to travel and eat. They were his family members, ministers, school friends, peers, and members of the same congregation, but crucially they were all Dissenters.

Anne Dawson and Godly Society

Unlike Richard Kay, whose twenty-three-year record offers an insight into his social life across almost the entirety of his adult life, Anne Dawson's diary only covers the years 1721–1722, when she was in her mid-twenties. The daughter of a Presbyterian minister, Joseph Dawson, Anne was born into a Rochdale Dissenting family in a period when there were around 200 Dissenters in that town, and a substantial number in the surrounding area.[82] Her diary acts as both a spiritual record and a place for reflection on her social actions, with entries that range from detailed discussions of sermons, to self-critical accounts of her behaviour among company, to pained reports of her dispute with her mother over her much-maligned suitor, John Roper. It therefore provides a rich snapshot of the social life of a young pious Presbyterian woman of middling social standing living in a small town in the north-west of England.

In her discussion of this period, Patricia Crawford highlighted that after 1689 'Nonconformist women experienced social ostracism' and that, due to the fact that women in communities depended on the support of each other for daily domestic tasks, 'the loss of neighbourliness was a handicap'.[83] This does not appear to have been Anne Dawson's experience. In her diary she records no animosity between herself and her neighbours, and she was clearly part of a functioning community, undertaking the neighbourly offices that might be expected of a woman of her position. On 7 June 1722 she and her sisters 'went from one house to another through the town to inquire how many had had the small pox since last December & what numbers died & recovered', and she was not remiss in her duty to visit the sick.[84] She was also clearly on amicable enough terms with members of the Established Church to attend the funeral of the local

---

[82] Henry Fishwick, *A History of the Parish of Rochdale in the County of Lancaster* (Rochdale: J. Clegg, 1889), p. 251.

[83] Patricia Crawford, *Women and Religion in England, 1500–1720* (London and New York: Routledge, 1993), p. 191.

[84] Diary of Anne (Dawson) Evans 1721–22, fols. 31v, 39v.

vicar, Mr Pigot, who it is reasonable to suspect was, at ninety-four years of age, a significant figure in the local community.[85] In terms of her neighbourly relationships, Dawson's, like Kay's, appear to have crossed confessional boundaries.

However, the way in which she understood her social world was quite different. Unlike Kay, who appears to have enjoyed society with his co-religionists, and made only brief mention of social situations in which he felt he had deviated from the behaviour suitable to his profession, Dawson gives the impression of being constantly under siege from social danger. This is apparent in the very different, and rather more sparing, way in which she uses the terms 'friends' and 'company'. The two contexts in which she referred to 'friends' were in reflection on a sermon she heard about walking righteously in order to please friends and disappoint enemies, and in discussion of 'friends ... droping into eternity'.[86] On both of these occasions she portrayed the world in binary terms, divided between her Christian friends, bound for 'that happe society where all fears shall be wiped away', and the sinners who might encourage her to deviate from this path.[87] A similar view of her prospective social acquaintances is apparent in Dawson's use of the term 'company'. Her favoured 'company' were her co-religionists, who visited on occasions such as in June 1722, when she recorded that 'we have had company all week from Chobent their company are very agreeable because of their parts and piety'.[88] However, even among pious company, she feared that they would distract her from 'conversing with herself' or leave her too inclined to be 'Chearful and Mery'.[89] Dawson's 'friends' and 'company' were her family and other co-religionists, but she viewed her sociability as fraught with the danger of distraction from a godly life.

Dawson's uses of 'friends' and 'company' are therefore notable by their infrequency in the light of her regular references to social activities. Instead, she frequently expressed her fear of being dragged into unspiritual practice through social contact by drawing contrasts between things and people belonging to 'the world', and those associated with godly life. On 4 September 1721 she wrote 'I am sensable that I am now Launching into a world of sin & temptation ... lord teach me to watch & pray that I may

[85] Ibid., fol. 32v.
[86] Ibid., fols. 2v, 37v.
[87] Ibid., fols. 37v.
[88] Ibid., fol. 31r.
[89] Ibid., fol. 31r, 28v.

not be overcome by the solicitations of the Divel or the world or my own heart.'[90] She continued to be watchful that social interaction did not corrupt her path and divert her into worldly ways; after a particularly unsatisfactory social visit in February 1722 she wished 'that for my own part I may in all places behave my self like one that is traviling to a better Country', and in March 1722 she wrote that 'tho I profess to be bound for a better Country yet I act & cary as if I thought to take up my rest here ... if the rightious scarcely be saved where shall such as I that love the World & the things of it so much appear'.[91] In May 1722 she was marginally more positive about her own engagement with the world, writing in relation to discussions over her marriage 'I wish I may cary as I ought to do as becomes a Christian ... & let the mad World banter such proceedings ... I hope by gods help never to fall into their measures.'[92] But in all these situations, she understood sociability to be tightly bound up with worldly temptation. Given that 'company' was to some extent to be feared, it is unsurprising that Dawson used the term sparingly.

Dawson's religion appears to have shaped her sociability in almost the opposite way to that identified by Crawford for nonconformist women in general.[93] She was willing to engage in neighbourly interactions with members of her community, apparently without discrimination on religious grounds, and neither seemed to feel threatened by this social contact, nor complained of a loss of neighbourliness as a result of her religious profession. Yet when it came to her chosen social interactions – those that went beyond the necessities of neighbourliness – she drew strict boundaries around acceptable company. For Dawson, sociability was acceptable only if it was disconnected from the things of the world and compatible with 'traviling to a better country'. From her neighbourly deeds alone, Anne Dawson appears a figure embedded in the fabric of her community. Her highly exclusive and in some senses isolating social outlook presents a very different picture.

Benjamin Wallin: Demarcating Baptist Sociability

The diary and draft letters of the London Particular Baptist minister Benjamin Wallin differ from the accounts of Richard Kay and Anne

---

[90] Ibid., fol. 2v.
[91] Ibid., fols. 18r, 19v.
[92] Ibid., fol. 27r.
[93] Crawford, *Women and Religion in England*, p. 191.

Dawson in that they focus heavily on his ministerial duties. His situation was also different: he was a minister of a Baptist Meeting in the heart of London, and almost all of his social interactions took place in an urban context. His diary begins in 1741, at the start of his career as pastor of Maze Pond Church.[94] In it, he recorded preaching, church meetings, illnesses, and the death of family members and friends, as well as some social occasions and journeys undertaken for recreation. His draft letters, found at the back of his diary, are largely concerned with his pastoral duties and the difficulties of his life as a minister. Despite the little that he says about his own sociability, the expectations he placed on others under his pastoral care reveal the social framework within which he hoped his flock would operate.

Wallin's personal papers are also valuable in providing the perspective of an individual with an explicit belief in exclusive redemption. As a Particular Baptist, Wallin subscribed to the Calvinist doctrine that only the elect would be saved. Particular Baptists therefore met in gathered congregations, voluntary associations of the faithful, separate from other individuals in the parish. In contrast, Presbyterian congregations, although they still generally believed in predestination, were less exclusive, and their meetings more generally open to all, with ministers often regarding themselves as serving everyone within the geographical boundary of the parish. It might therefore be expected that Wallin's perspectives on neighbourliness would be more exclusive than Richard Kay's or Anne Dawson's. However, on examining his papers, it appears that the way in which he differentiated between neighbours, friends, and company had strong similarities with the individuals already explored.

The overall impression given by Wallin's diary was that he socialised entirely within the circles of Particular Baptists. The occasions on which he dined or had tea socially were usually on account of those present having travelled to give a sermon or attend worship together. On 15 July 1741, for instance, his church held a prayer meeting, after which 'Brethren dined with me at Kings Arms'; on 28 June 1749 'Mr Heath with me set forth to Waltham Abbey we dined at Mrs Rights I preached in the afternoon from Romans 16. 20.'[95] Such occasions were typical of the way his ministerial activities were interspersed with social activities among his flock. He did

[94] Michael A. G. Haykin, 'Wallin, Benjamin (1711–1782)', *Oxford Dictionary of National Biography* (Oxford University Press, 2004), www.oxforddnb.com/view/article/71075, accessed 4 June 2018.

[95] Diary and Letters of Benjamin Wallin, Diary Entries for 15 July 1741 and 28 June 1749, D/WAB, Regent's Park College, Angus Library and Archive, Oxford.

occasionally record purely recreational activities, such as on 19 July 1748, when he went 'with Mr Slade & Miss Burnhill & Wife to Mr Powell at Pimlico walked before dinner to Physick Gardens saw several Plants that excited reflections Cedars of Lebanon Tall Majestic spreading under which many may shelter'.[96] Even here, however, those present were his co-religionists. Wallin's sociability appears highly denominationally exclusive.

However, the simple fact that Wallin's consistent social contact was with his co-religionists tells us very little of how he understood these social relationships to operate. It therefore gives limited insight into how he drew social boundaries between his co-religionists and the rest of the community within which he lives. It is in attempting to access this that analysing his relative use of 'neighbours', 'friends', and 'company' becomes most helpful.

At first glance, Wallin makes scant reference to his 'neighbours' in his diary or letters. There is, however, some indication that he coexisted reasonably peacefully alongside them. In his account of the earthquake that shook London in February 1750, for instance, he recounted how

> I felt the Desk move the floor shake and the Front of the house seemed to incline forwards the strut … In this manner the whole Row of Nieghbours [*sic*] Houses were surprized and immediately enquiry what had happened at each others Habitations but we soon percived it was one great shock common to us all – Blessed be God the Ground did not open to make one Common Grave for us and our houses.[97]

While it is hardly surprising that on the occasion of such an alarming occurrence he consulted those around him, the fact that he and his neighbours immediately communicated with one another, and that he saw it as a 'common' experience, suggests that he had a working neighbourly relationship with those living in physical proximity to him.

However, Wallin appears to have had very different expectations of his relationships with those he regarded as his neighbours than of those he saw as his Christian brethren and friends. This is evident from an appeal he made to the Deacons in July 1749 regarding what he felt was neglect of his spiritual and material welfare. Highlighting the material losses he had undergone as a result of taking up pastoral office, he expressed the view that he had been neglected by his brethren in the church: 'I must say it is somewhat extraordinary that among such a number of People that I serve I

---

[96] Ibid., entry for 19 July 1748.
[97] Ibid., entry for 11 February 1749/50.

should scarce find an Instance of respect except from a Nieghbouring [*sic*] family throughout the year to help towards more comfortable subsistance of my Family.'[98] In the context of a letter that otherwise presents him as utterly neglected by those of his profession, the fact that Wallin chose to mention that the one family who helped him in his distress were neighbours suggests that he was highlighting his isolation from all but those who were tied to him through neighbourly obligation.

Wallin saw this sort of support as the duty of his friends, rather than his neighbours, and this was further emphasised in a letter he sent to a fellow Particular Baptist, Thomas Cox, on 21 May 1751. Finding that he had 'an immediate call for about £50 to pay off one who is no longer able or willing to trust me' he believed that 'To apply to the World or Strangers in this emergency would be very imprudent if not fruitless My Proposal is to borrow it of 2 or 3 of our Friends and return it out of what Providence may afford me within 3 years or (God willing) sooner.'[99] It was clearly a conceivable possibility that Wallin might ask 'the World' – i.e. those who he knew (he differentiates them from 'Strangers') but who did not share his Particular Baptist faith – to lend him the money. However, he evidently did not see this as a sensible choice. Far more prudent was to ask his 'Friends' among his own congregation for a loan. This suggests not only that he confined his friends to his co-religionists, but also that he had specific expectations of them that were greater than those he had of his worldly neighbours.

Indeed, Wallin appears to have subscribed to the view that Christian brethren owed a particular duty of friendship to one another. In December 1750 he wrote a letter to a gentleman who had attended a lecture Wallin had given in the City of London, rebuking him for spreading misleading notions of the intentions of his discourse. The gentleman had apparently 'in the Company' of Deacon John Manypenny and 'some other Christian Friends' insinuated 'that at a Lecture in the City I impertinently handled a Subject which seemed to carry some Reflection' on Manypenny's conduct.[100] Wallin complained to the man concerned, Mr G. Baskerville, that his words were 'were very unkind and I think not becoming the character of a Friend or a Gentleman'.[101] Wallin's use of the term 'friend' is interesting here. Despite not being familiar with, or even fully aware of, the

[98] Ibid., letter to the Deacons, July 1750.
[99] Ibid., letter to Thomas Cox, 21 May 1751.
[100] Ibid., letter to John Manypenny, 22 December 1750.
[101] Ibid., letter to Mr G. Baskerville, 22 December 1750.

individuals involved in the reported conversation, Wallin regarded them
as 'Friends' because of their common faith. Furthermore, his response to
Baskerville denotes that with such Christian friendship came an expectation of certain characteristics of behaviour. He thought Baskerville's treatment of him 'ungenrous' and was concerned that it might create an 'ill
Impression on the Minds of Christian Friends whose welfare and Comfort
I should rejoice'.[102] Through this exchange, Wallin makes it clear that to
qualify as a 'friend' familiarity was not the principal criterion, but rather
a shared Christian outlook and desire to support each other's welfare and
interests through kindly support. It is unsurprising therefore that he felt
that to apply to Christian friends for financial aid might be more fruitful
than to ask worldly neighbours, despite the support that these neighbours
had given in the past.

   Wallin expected his co-religionists to act in a friendly manner towards
one another; he also had a clear idea of what constituted appropriate company. Like Anne Dawson, he clearly feared the infectious influence of bad
company. Writing to Edward Barnes, a young member of his flock, in
February 1748, he was worried that Barnes's 'chosen companions' were
young men 'who walk disorderly [sic] without any Temptation but what
arises from the instability & lusts of their own minds'.[103] As we saw in
the previous chapter, Wallin was particularly alarmed that Barnes's character was 'in some degree already affected with others for being too frequent & too long at a certain Publick house in your Nieghbourhood [sic],
so that when a certain Person has been charged even with intemperance
your name has been mentioned as a companion which is very scandalous'. He warned Barnes against 'the least appearance of evil', and rebuked
him for sparking the report which he was sure was 'disgracefull to the
name of Christ'.[104] It is unsurprising that Wallin would rebuke a member
of his flock for implication in intemperate behaviour, but it is notable
that he describes the errant young men as Barnes's 'chosen companions',
thereby highlighting that an individual's 'company' was something they
should take care in selecting for themselves. Wallin was even clearer in his
emphasis that company should be taken from among the godly when he
wrote to a friend following his friend's marriage, hurt that he had not been
informed of the proceedings, and concerned that he may have married
out of the Church, a practice that he regarded as 'the bane of Churches,

[102] Ibid., letter to John Manypenny, 22 December 1750.
[103] Ibid., letter to Edward Barnes, 20 February 1748.
[104] Ibid.

being an inlet to disorder & confusion destructive of every thing that is valuable in social Religion'.[105] Clearly he regarded the social function of the gathered church as highly important, and companionship beyond the congregation as liable to undermine this.

Wallin evidently did interact with his 'wordly' neighbours, even if he made rare mention of this in his diary entries. However, perhaps even more so than Richard Kay or Anne Dawson, it was not from his neighbours that he primarily sought support. This could be seen as a product of his urban situation. As the number of voluntary associations, charities, and societies increased in towns, some of the functions of neighbourliness were fulfilled by alternative forms of organisation.[106] However, neighbourly support, including financial aid, remained common in urban neighbourhoods in the eighteenth century, and it seems likely that it was Wallin's religious profession, rather his urban residence, that shaped his behaviour.[107] His expectations of Christian care lay primarily among 'friends' of the same Baptist faith, and not in the wider community. Equally, it was from among these Christian friends that Wallin expected his flock to draw their companions. This clear line between neighbourly sociability in 'the world' and friendship within the Church may have been all the more acute because of the exclusivity of Particular Baptist ecclesiology. Glimpses of Wallin's relationship with his neighbours, albeit scant, leave no suggestion of animosity, and indeed there was at least one instance of neighbourly support. But this cannot be read as a sign of Wallin's integration into the social life of the community. From his religiously exclusive definitions of friendship and company, it appears that Wallin and his flock may have socialised in the presence of, but not with, those who did not share their religious standpoint.

John Croker and Quaker Integration

It might be expected that of all Dissenters, Quakers would be the most exclusive in their sociability. As highlighted in earlier chapters, the instructions

---

[105] Ibid., letter to Brother D____s, n.d., *c.*1748–9.
[106] Sylvia Pinches, 'Women as Objects and Agents of Charity in Eighteenth-Century Birmingham', in Rosemary Sweet and Penelope Lane (ed.), *Women and Urban Life in Eighteenth-Century England* (London and New York: Routledge, 2016), p. 65. See also Owen Davies, 'Urbanization and the Decline of Witchcraft: An Examination of London', *Journal of Social History*, 30, 3 (1997), p. 607.
[107] Carl Estabrook, *Urbane and Rustic England: Cultural Ties and Social Spheres in the Provinces 1660–1780* (Manchester: Manchester University Press, 1998), p. 74; Jon Stobart, 'Social and Geographical Contexts of Property Transmission in the Eighteenth Century', in Jon Stobart and Alastair Owens (eds.), *Urban Fortunes: Property and Inheritance in the Town, 1700–1900* (London and New York: Routledge, 2016), pp. 118–9.

of the London Yearly Meetings made it clear that Friends should avoid involvement in the 'worldly' activity of non-Quakers wherever possible. However, as has been shown in numerous studies, this did not necessarily exclude Quakers from participation in the neighbourly offices of the parish.[108] As Simon Dixon has suggested in his detailed analysis of the diary of the London Quaker Peter Briggins, by focusing heavily on Quaker meeting accounts we may be in danger of placing 'too much emphasis on those aspects of popular culture of which Friends strongly disapproved'. The daily life of Peter Briggins demonstrates that he was well embedded in the neighbourly networks of the parish, and seemed to move 'effortlessly, and without any apparent sense of contradiction, between trade and commerce and religion'.[109] Yet as discussed above, indications of neighbourliness may give a misleading impression of the extent of inter-confessional social interaction. Expectations of neighbourliness were the bare minimum that those within a community had of one another. Relationships of friendship and of company often tell a different story.

The life account of John Croker makes for an interesting Quaker comparison with the cases discussed above. Born in Devon in 1678, he decided to go into trade as a fuller and later went into the tobacco business with his father. His account of his life is retrospective: written in about 1720, it begins with his move to Exeter in about 1695.[110] It therefore stretches across a substantial period of his life, demonstrating a variety of business, family, and social relationships. Most interestingly for the issues discussed here is that, while he experienced some social ostracism on account of his faith, his social relationships appear to have been less denominationally exclusive than those of the individuals discussed above.

Croker's account of his first years in trade gives the impression of a man at odds with society, and alienated from those who did not share his religious outlook. Like Richard Kay, Anne Dawson, and Benjamin Wallin, he was wary of the corrupting effects of ill company. When he was apprenticed at the age of 17 or 18 to a man who was not a Quaker, he found himself walking the streets at night searching alehouses and taverns for his master and his 'ill company', suffering repeated attempts to tempt him into playing cards.[111] He suffered for this poor choice of master, who

---

[108] Adrian Davies, *The Quakers in English Society, 1655–1725* (Oxford and New York: Oxford University Press, 2000), pp. 218–9, 223; Dixon, 'Quakers and the London Parish', pp. 229–49.

[109] Simon Dixon, 'The Life and Times of Peter Briggins', *Quaker Studies*, 10, 2 (2006), pp. 193, 198.

[110] *Something by Way of a Journal or Part of the Life of John Croker*, c.1720, p. 27.

[111] Ibid., p. 28.

went bankrupt. At this point Croker found himself in search of another master, but this was difficult on account of his Quakerism: he was reportedly 'willing to Attain to my Business if it could be, But being a Quaker few would be concerned with me'.[112] From this account, it appears that few had neighbourly sympathy towards Croker except his co-religionists – he was forced to lodge 'at a Friends house, boarding myself' while working as a journeyman.[113] He was suspicious of company who were not his co-religionists; others in turn did not concern themselves with him because of his Quakerism.

This rather bleak tale is, however, in sharp contrast with the tenor of the account he gives of his sociability in later life. Analysis of the use of the term 'friend' in the context of Quaker sociability is complicated by the fact that Quakers, as the Society of Friends, referred to all their co-religionists as 'Friends'. This is in itself significant, but in this context is not helpful in unpicking the variegated nature of an individual's social relationships. However, what is striking in Croker's account is the way he differentiates between Friends (i.e. Quakers) and other people he spent time with. Later in his life he found himself in Plymouth, having set up shop there after his remarriage. However, unable to make sufficient profit, he and his wife decided to move to her birthplace of Horsham. Before they left, they 'spent a little time together with Friends and other sober Neighbours with many Embraces and hearty good wishes', and were accompanied on the first part of their journey 'by Friends and Others to a place where we Eat and Drank together'.[114] Croker's description of those who wished his family well on their way is very telling. On the one hand, he clearly regarded his Quaker Friends as in some way socially distinct from others: he chose to identify them separately from his 'other sober Neighbours' and from 'Others'. In that sense his sociability might be regarded as religiously exclusive; his Quaker social contacts formed a specific group, the primary qualification for which was religion. Yet Croker in fact appears far less exclusive in his sociability than, for instance, Benjamin Wallin. He was evidently happy to mix socially with neighbours he regarded as 'sober' and, at least according to his account, they appear to have had a warm regard for him that went beyond the simple call of neighbourly duty. Croker differentiated between Quaker and non-Quaker social contacts, but he did keep company with those who were not Quakers. Sobriety, rather

[112] Ibid., p. 29.
[113] Ibid.
[114] Ibid., p. 55.

than specific religious affiliation, appears to have been the qualification for inclusion within Croker's social circle.

Croker seems, at least in his early years, to have suffered from a lack of neighbourly support on account of his religion, and was forced to fall back on the support of his co-religionists. Yet the social boundaries that he constructed around himself were not as religiously exclusive as might be expected. As with Wallin, this may have been partly a product of the ecclesiology of his religious profession. While Quakers sought to differentiate those who had found the Light from those who had not, unlike Particular Baptists they believed that salvation was potentially attainable by all. There was therefore a greater onus on Quakers to lead others towards salvation. While Croker made a clear distinction between Quakers and other social contacts, he did keep sociable company with 'sober Neighbours' who were not of his profession. He does not give any indication of what qualified as sobriety, and it may have been that his sociability was still reasonably exclusive according to broader criteria of religiosity. Nevertheless, from comparing the terms he used to describe his social contacts, it is possible to gain a picture of Croker's sociability that occurred on at least two levels: an inner circle of Quaker Friends, and a wider circle of sober 'Others' whose general conduct and good wishes towards him meant that they were an important part of his social life.

Conclusion

Richard Kay, Anne Dawson, Benjamin Wallin, and John Croker evidently led differing social lives and had varying levels of social interaction with their neighbours. However, there are some important parallels in their experiences from which wider conclusions may be drawn. In agreement with the findings of other studies of Dissenters' interactions with neighbours in this period, none of the four individuals studied here can be considered to have been excluded from their neighbourly community on account of their religion.[115] Indeed, in the cases of Kay and Dawson, there is clear evidence of their significant involvement in the neighbourly duties of their locality. Neighbourliness does not appear to have been bound by religious affiliation.

[115] See Dixon, 'The Life and Times of Peter Briggins', *passim*; Miller, *Cities Divided*, p. 310; Stevenson, 'The Social Integration of Post-Restoration Dissenters, 1660–1725', pp. 369, 378; Carys Brown, 'Women and Religious Coexistence in England, c. 1689–c.1750', in Naomi Pullin and Kathryn Woods (eds.), *Negotiating Exclusion in the Early Modern England, 1550–1750* (London and New York: Routledge, 2021), pp. 68–87.

Yet beyond this most basic level of sociability, all four of these individuals to varying degrees erected a religiously exclusive boundary around their social interactions that meant that their 'friends' and 'company' were almost without exception drawn from their co-religionists. A focus on the different ways in which individuals labelled their social contacts thus reveals the multi-textured nature of their sociability, in which religious affiliation appears to have been an important determining factor. As Withington pointed out in his essay on company and sociability in early modern England, not all social interactions 'can easily be explained by the converging pressures of neighbourliness and paternalism' that are often applied in descriptions of social relations in this period.[116] When this principle is applied to inter-confessional interaction, moving beyond a framework in which neighbourly and unneighbourly interactions are considered the primary measure of how society dealt with religious difference, we are able to gain a much clearer idea of the way inter-confessional social relations operated.

In both the overview of Dissenters' uses of 'neighbours', 'friends', and 'company', and in the case studies examined above, a multi-layered picture of social interaction appears, in which social boundaries were drawn according to religious criteria. At the widest level of social interaction, the broad Christian duty of neighbourliness was in operation. It was when this broke down that tension between religious groups was most in evidence, and it was on the grounds of unneighbourliness that Dissenters most easily came under attack from their opponents. Neighbourliness was a duty commonly agreed upon, and to fail in this was to set oneself outside the bounds of a community broadly conceived. Yet interactions with neighbours, however amicable, were regarded as having a different quality to the social relationships that Dissenters had with their friends, who were almost exclusively their co-religionists. These were the individuals who could be relied upon to act in their best interests, and who would provide support and spiritual succour. It is in examining these types of relationships that the complexity of negotiating religious differences through social expectation and behaviour becomes most apparent.

This distinction in types of social interaction is important, because it may help us to explain how Dissenters dealt with the contradictory impulses to integration and distinction created by the Toleration Act. The religious boundaries that they drew around their sociability may have been

---

[116] Withington, 'Company and Sociability', p. 294.

a way of maintaining their piety while remaining engaged with wider society. On the one hand, the Christian injunction to neighbourliness meant that they were both bound to and justified in interacting with those not of their faith. On the other, the religiously exclusive definitions of friendship and company that appear to have been common to all Dissenters could enable them to maintain a sense, at least mentally, of social distinction and pious difference.

Such graduated layers of religious exclusivity in Dissenters' sociability were crucial for sustaining senses of religious difference in this period. Throughout this book we have seen how after 1689 Dissenters and supporters of the Established Church were engaged in messy processes of negotiation on national, local, and individual levels. As all parties sought ways to manage religious difference in the wake of substantive legal change, they developed social strategies by which they could carve their route through society. Faced with the need to demonstrate solidarity with a shared Protestant cause, fight accusations of sedition and division, and emphasise pious conduct without encouraging social ostracism, Dissenters needed to shape their sociability in a way that was at once in harmony with their local communities and at odds with the corrupt ways of the world. The religiously inflected definitional boundaries they drew around their social circles may have been one important way of doing this.

Conclusion

By 1744, at the age of seventy-nine, the Cheshire Presbyterian Sarah Savage had lived through an extraordinary shift in England's religious landscape. Born into a family of reluctant nonconformists, she had experienced persecution by law and mob violence, state indulgence and partial conformity, neighbourly accommodation and local hostility. Despite this, she had survived in relative comfort into her old age, surrounded by friends and family. The temperature of dispute between Church and Dissent had by the 1740s undoubtedly cooled, and she and her brother no longer needed to fear, as they had in 1710 and 1715, that their homes or local meeting house might be pulled down by the mob.[1]

Nevertheless, Savage remained a witness to religious violence in the final decade of her life. On 29 January 1744 she wrote in her diary 'This week much Hurry'd & astonisht with a Mob who consist of many Hundreds, go into many Houses, rifle and Break their goods – all that imbrace the Weslys & their Cause many Neighbours Bring some Goods in hither to secure 'em.'[2] This violence was a product of the fact that the 1740s saw the growth of a new apparent threat to the religious – and therefore social – stability of England: Methodism.

Despite having provided assistance to those fearing anti-Methodist violence in her local area, Savage herself was highly suspicious of Methodism. In the previous year she had been alarmed by disturbances at her meeting house created 'by some of these Wesslys People that Pretend to the Spirit, & its Motions ... [it] can be no good End To hear em make a noise & disturb the Hearers ... We Know not what to think of such

---

[1] Diary of Matthew Henry, 1705–1713, fols. 81r, 82v, MS. Eng. misc. e. 330, Bodleian (Bod.), Oxford; Mrs Savage's Diary, 31 May 1714 to 25 Dec. 1723 (eighteenth-century copy), pp. 55–7, MS. Eng. misc. e. 331, Bod.

[2] Sarah Savage's Journal, 1743–8, entry for 29 January 1744, Henry MSS, 90.2, Dr Williams's Library, London.

things – suspect that Popery is at the Bottom.'[3] Her reaction was typical of many of her contemporaries, both Dissenters and members of the Established Church. The noisy, emotional nature of preaching by those known as Methodists, who frequently held outdoor meetings, caused particular alarm. Their emphasis on an unusually experiential piety, outward holiness, and the need for a new birth out of mankind's state of total depravity, as well as the intense and vocal spiritual expression of their followers, and the itinerate habits of their preachers, made them into objects of considerable suspicion.

The contemporary response to Methodism is important, because it simultaneously illustrates shifts in the nature of debate about religion over the first half of the eighteenth century, and the degree to which the problem of religious difference continued to shape English society. In the 1740s and 1750s many Methodist preachers and followers, who still regarded themselves as operating within the Established Church, were subject to serious violence and abuse. The Yorkshire Methodist preacher John Nelson described how when he first preached in Leeds in the 1740s he stood up in the street only to be 'struck on the head with an egg and two potatoes', but the ammunition of his enemies in that town was soft compared to that in Manchester, where he was hit on the head with a stone, and preached with blood running down his face.[4] The summer of 1748 saw serious anti-Methodist riots, particularly in Lancashire, with mobs of lower social status being supported and even encouraged by their social superiors, including Anglican clergy.[5]

Why did Methodism cause such a reaction, at a time when the temperature of debate over England's religious differences had ostensibly cooled significantly in comparison with the time of the anti-Dissenting riots in 1710 and 1714–15?[6] In contrast to attempts to limit the influence of Dissent in the decades immediately after 1689, criticisms of Methodism made no explicit attempt to place restrictions on liberty of conscience, or to suggest that Methodists' consciences were fundamentally in error. In fact, some arguments against Methodism suggested that the passions

---

[3] Ibid., entry for 30 May 1743.
[4] John Nelson, *The Journal of Mr John Nelson, Preacher of the Gospel ... Written by Himself* (London: J. Mason, n.d.), pp. 75, 81.
[5] David Hempton, *Methodism: Empire of the Spirit* (New Haven and London: Yale University Press, 2005), pp. 90–1.
[6] Jeremy Gregory, '"In the Church I Will Live and Die"': John Wesley, the Church of England, and Methodism', in William Gibson and Robert G. Ingram (eds.), *Religious Identities in Britain, 1660–1832* (London and New York: Routledge, 2016 (1st edn 2005)), p. 175.

engendered by Methodist preaching and worship represented a threat to the right and reasoned expression of conscience.[7] Although defenders of the Established Church continued to argue that ties between Church and State were important for the civil and spiritual welfare of the nation, as far as the question of liberty of conscience was concerned, the parameters of debate had shifted significantly by the 1740s.[8]

There were other aspects of Methodism that made it alarming to contemporaries. For one, Methodism placed a significant emphasis on personal piety, and allowed lay preachers from humble backgrounds to travel around the country preaching the Word. This was seen by many as a threat to social order and community life. This was certainly the view of John Hailstone, a clergyman in York, who wrote to his son in July 1751 remarking on the negative influence of Methodists in the town. In particular, he was concerned that 'though Christ hath Indulged to the meanest & weakest Christian a Liberty to read & Judge of the Scriptures for himself yet he hath neither thereby nor there-with granted him a liberty publickly to Expound & preach the word to others thats quite another thing'. He objected to 'so many Raw Novices & Illiterate Tradesmen' being sent to preach, fearing that not only would it cause people to turn away from their church ministers, but also that it would draw away working people 'to the Neglect of there families, and Straitning there Circumstances in the world'.[9] For Hailstone, Methodism was not only ecclesiologically unsound, but also highly damaging to the social order.

Hailstone was not alone in this view. The Derbyshire Presbyterian minister James Clegg had been very concerned at the arrival of a Methodist preacher in his area in 1742, not only because the doctrines he preached were 'Antinomian to the highest degree', but also because of the social disruption he caused. According to Clegg, the preacher went 'to houses where he is never invited and tells the more serious and pious women, they are whores, fornicators, Adulterers and murderers etc.' So shocking was this discourse to one woman, Sarah Carrington, who was 'of good sence and

---

[7] See for example William Bowman, *The Imposture of Methodism Display'd: In a Letter to the Inhabitants of the Parish of Dewsbury. Occasion'd by the Rise of Certain Modern Sect of Enthusiasts, (Among Them) Call'd Methodists* (London, 1740), pp. 48, 49.

[8] Martin Hugh Fitzpatrick, 'From Natural Law to Natural Rights? Protestant Dissent and Toleration in the Late Eighteenth Century', *History of European Ideas*, 42, 2 (2016), pp. 202–3; Stephen Taylor, 'William Warburton and the Alliance of Church and State', *Journal of Ecclesiastical History*, 43, 2 (1992), pp. 279–80, 283.

[9] John Hailstone, York, to His Son 'Johny', 8 July 1751, Add 9450/A/10, Cambridge University Library, Cambridge.

of an unblemished character', that 'the fright it put her into went near to cause a miscarriage which would have endangered her life'.[10] Clegg's fear that Methodism was a threat to this pregnant woman was perhaps reflective of wider concerns about the fact that Methodism seemed to attract a disproportionate number of women.[11] By the 1740s, Anglican writers had particularly linked together the safety of the Anglican religion with a female piety that promoted domestic order and wider social stability; the active involvement of women in Methodist preaching and evangelism went against these ideals.[12] As a result, the Methodists' appeal to women potentially struck at the very heart of family life.

Evidently, there were specific aspects of Methodism that made it a particular concern to contemporaries. However, reactions to early Methodism also highlight that, despite contemporaries having used an armoury of strategies to navigate around religious distinctions in the first half of the eighteenth century, many tensions surrounding issues of religious difference remained unresolved. Amidst concerns that were associated with specific aspects of Methodism, the varied manifestations of anti-Methodism appeared to be fundamentally underpinned by the same concerns about religious differences that Dissenters and supporters of the Established Church had wrestled with throughout the first half of the eighteenth century. In both anti-Methodist and anti-Dissenting print, for example, women were portrayed as particularly susceptible to the emotional intensity of religion, and in some cases were seen as having been seduced by preachers into erotic relationships.[13] In one satirical tale of an actor, published in 1770, the protagonist met a Methodist preacher who had been having sexual liaisons with a farmer's wife in a chapel of ease, alongside numerous other unchaste relationships with women in the farmer's household, but nevertheless continued to preach on the value of chastity.[14] The creation of satire around such themes of hypocrisy and illicit sexual relations clearly drew from the long pedigree of anti-Puritan and

---

[10] Vanessa Doe (ed.), *The Diary of James Clegg of Chapel en le Frith, 1708–1755, Part 2* (Derby: Derbyshire Record Society, 1979), pp. 447–8.

[11] Brian Curtis Clark and Joanna Cruickshank, 'Converting Mrs Crouch: Women, Wonders, and the Formation of English Methodism, 1738–1741', *Journal of Ecclesiastical History*, 65, 1 (2014), p. 67.

[12] Cynthia J. Cupples, 'Pious Ladies and Methodist Madams: Sex and Gender in Anti-Methodist Writings of Eighteenth-Century England', *Critical Matrix*, 5, 2 (1990), pp. 41, 52–3.

[13] Emma Major, *Madam Britannia: Women, Church, and Nation, 1712–1812* (Oxford and New York: Oxford University Press, 2011), pp. 136–7, 143.

[14] *The Adventures of an Actor, in the Characters of a Merry-Andrew, a Methodist-Preacher, and a Fortune-Teller. Founded on Facts* (London, 1770), pp. 128, 137–8.

anti-Dissenting writings that, since the seventeenth and early eighteenth centuries, had suggested that women of such persuasions would 'ride five Miles' to hear a preacher 'because it covers an Assignation upon the Way', and that their preachers 'preach up Chastity, as a Cardinal Vertue, and yet shall be the first that will Debauch your Wife'.[15] The strong resemblance that criticisms of Methodism bore to the accusations of hypocrisy and of disruption to social and gender norms that had long been associated with anti-Dissenting satire suggests the resonance of the same fundamental concerns about the socially disruptive nature of religious difference.

Furthermore, anti-Methodism in this period was also based on continuing fears about the threat posed by Catholicism. Methodism, like Dissent, apparently risked letting popery in through the back door. As Sarah Savage's comment that she suspected that 'Popery is at the Bottom' of Methodist activity demonstrates, this was a view not only held by staunch supporters of the Established Church, but also by some Dissenters.[16] Numerous anti-Methodist publications drew parallels between Methodism and Catholicism, making suggestions that although Methodists pretended to oppose popery, 'they are doing the Papists work for them, and agree with them in some of their Principles'.[17] Contemporary reactions to Methodism demonstrate that a widespread acceptance of the principle of liberty of conscience, and the reality of religious pluralism, did not remove alarm at the 'popish' threat, or the sense that religious difference could undermine the stability of society.

As with attacks on Dissent, at the centre of concerns about Methodism was the familiar fear of religious 'enthusiasm', a spectre still regarded as a danger in a society that had not forgotten the tribulations of the 1640s and 1650s.[18] Aside from questioning the reasonableness of Methodists, William Bowman highlighted how 'The Confusion and Disorder, the Irregularity and Indecency in the publick Worship

---

[15] *The True Characters* (London, 1708), p. 8; Ned Ward, *The Reformer: Or, the Vices of the Age Expos'd, I. In Several Characters* (London, 1701), pp. 6–7. See also John Earle, *Micro-Cosmographie, or, a Peece of the World Discouered in Essayes and Characters* (London, 1628), sig. H6v.

[16] Ibid., entry for 30 May 1743.

[17] George Lavington, *The Enthusiasm of Methodists and Papists Compared, Part I* (London, 1749), p. 10. See also the preface to John Tottie, *Two Charges Delivered to the Clergy of the Diocese of Worcester in the Years 1763 and 1766, Being Designed as Preservatives Against the Sophistical Arts of the Papists and the Delusions of the Methodists* (Oxford, 1766).

[18] Michael Francis Snape, 'Anti-Methodism in Eighteenth-Century England: The Pendle Forest Riots of 1748', *Journal of Ecclesiastical History*, 49, 2 (1998), p. 258; David W. Bebbington, *Evangelicalism in Modern Britain: A History from the 1730s to the 1980s* (London: Taylor and Francis, 1989), p. 51.

of Almighty God' brought about by Methodism would be accompanied by 'violent Hatreds, and cruel Persecutions, which are generally the Consequences of such a religious Separation'. The ultimate result would be, he argued, 'nothing but a wretched State of Anarchy and Dissention, an utter Subversion of all Rule and Government, and an eternal Destruction of every thing else, which can any way contribute to the Support or Preservation of Society'.[19] The links between Methodists and the 'enthusiasts' of the Civil Wars were made even more explicitly by Scottish physician James Makittrick Adair in his anonymously published *The Methodist and Mimick: A tale, in Hudibrastick verse*. This 'Hudibrastick' form referenced Samuel Butler's *Hudibras*, a narrative poem first published in the 1660s and 1670s in mockery of Puritans and Presbyterians, as well as other Civil War factions, thereby suggesting a clear parallel between the disruption of the Civil Wars and Methodism.[20] The rupture of the Civil Wars of the seventeenth century informed contemporary perceptions of religious difference well into the middle of the eighteenth.

Concerns about the social threat that Methodism represented were heightened by the way in which politeness as a mode of social behaviour had become tied up with the duties of the Anglican clergy. As was illustrated in Chapter 3, the growth of the mode of politeness was in part a response to the perceived danger of religious enthusiasm, and despite its pretensions to inclusivity it was an inherently exclusive discourse. In response to the reaction against enthusiasm in the first decades after the Toleration Act, many Anglican clergy had become distinctly polite in aspiration.[21] Although not all clergy agreed that polite preaching styles were wholly beneficial, Methodism represented a considerable challenge to many Anglican clergy.[22] It was considered particularly alarming because while its modes of preaching were seen as representative of 'madness and depravity ... the effectiveness of its agents could not be denied'.[23] The emotive preaching of Methodists was worrying for the Anglican clergy: it

---

[19] Bowman, *The Imposture of Methodism Display'd*, p. 18.
[20] Peter Paragraph [James Makittrick Adair], *The Methodist and Mimick. A Tale, in Hudibrastick Verse* (London, 1766).
[21] Colin Haydon, 'Rural Religion and the Politeness of Parsons: The Church of England in South Warwickshire, c. 1689-c.1820', *Studies in Church History*, 42 (2006), p. 286.
[22] Paul Goring, 'Anglicanism, Enthusiasm, and Quixotism: Preaching and Politeness in Mid-Eighteenth-Century Literature', *Literature and Theology*, 15, 4 (2001), p. 326.
[23] Ibid., p. 328.

demonstrated that the 'enthusiasm' that they had for so long been working to counter was in fact highly effective in gaining the attention and devotion of followers.

By the 1740s, more than eighty years had passed since the Restoration, and the prospects of those who did not conform to the practices of the mainstream Established Church were completely different: they did not face the spectre of state persecution; they did not face the denial of the validity of their conscience; they lived in a culture that actively sought to dissipate religious tensions, rather than coerce those of a differing stance into conformity. However, in spite of all this, fears about popish corruption and social disruption still led contemporaries, when sufficiently provoked, to put poisonous pen to paper and raise their weapons in anger against their neighbours.

Such intense hostility towards Methodism did not last forever. Methodist preachers proved effective at defending their cause in public contexts, countering some of the ridicule that anti-Methodist stereotypes encouraged.[24] More broadly speaking, by the later eighteenth century the hope of some Anglican ministers that the enforcement of religious uniformity would ever be possible had been thoroughly eroded, resulting in a clear change in the 'balance of power between the producers and consumers of Anglicanism'.[25] It does appear that, particularly in urban areas, individuals and families more frequently shopped around for places of worship.[26] Furthermore, collective efforts to improve the lot of the poor resulted in the establishment of inter-denominational Sunday Schools (although some of these efforts at collaboration later collapsed).[27] As recent research has emphasised, the social changes that came about with industrialisation were not necessarily detrimental to religiosity, but did bring about shifts in the way that religious ideas were spread. Evangelicals were particularly adept at exploiting the technologies and commerce of the urban environment, and adapting to increased migration in other areas, using travelling preachers and printed tracts to spread ideas within a variety of religious

[24] Mary Thale, 'Deists, Papists, and Methodists at London Debating Societies, 1749–1799', *History*, 86, 283 (2001), pp. 340–1.

[25] David Hempton, 'Enlightenment and Faith', in Paul Langford (ed.), *The Eighteenth Century, 1688–1815* (Oxford and New York: Oxford University Press, 2002), p. 83.

[26] Rosemary Sweet, 'Introduction', in Rosemary Sweet and Penelope Lane (eds.), *Women and Urban Life in Eighteenth-Century England: "On the Town"* (London: Routledge, 2016), p. 18.

[27] A. P. Wadsworth, 'The First Manchester Sunday Schools', *Bulletin of the John Rylands Library*, 33, 2 (1951), pp. 300, 315–17.

denominations.[28] These developments are suggestive of a society that had become much better adapted to religious pluralism.

However, the dynamics of religious difference also left their scars. Particularly at times of economic, social, or political tension, religious deviance was an obvious target for grievances. The largest riots of this period – the Gordon Riots of 1780 and the Birmingham Riots of 1791 – were characterised by a contemporary association of political or economic problems with the influence of religious minorities, in these instances Catholics and Unitarians, respectively. On a smaller scale, the arrival in England of news of the British victory at the Battle of Fort Washington in New York in November 1776 sparked attacks on Dissenters' property, based on suspicions of Dissenting support for the revolutionary cause.[29] This reflected the fact that, despite apparent general acceptance of religious pluralism, many individuals retained an inherent suspicion of religious difference that remained manifest in everyday life even by the early nineteenth century. This included people such as George Strafford, a house, sign, and furniture painter from Wakefield, who in 1815 was outraged that Dissenters, rather than he, a loyal Anglican, had been employed to decorate the local grammar school. Writing to the local vicar, he maintained the view that where 'in their [Dissenters'] power they would over-throw our venerable establishment in favour of their own disentant and dogmatical forms of worship'.[30] Strafford evidently expected that economic advantage would be given to members of the Established Church; his words reflected attitudes towards Dissent that had been recognisable throughout the previous century.

It is beyond the remit of this book to consider the ways in which religious difference shaped – or indeed ceased to shape – the social and cultural changes of the later eighteenth and early nineteenth centuries. Nevertheless, the fact that religious prejudices continued to resonate in this period, combined with the evidence presented here of the enduring influence of religious difference over the first half of the century, suggests

[28] Joseph Stubenrach, *The Evangelical Age of Ingenuity in Industrial Britain* (Oxford and New York: Oxford University Press, 2016), pp. 11, 13, 148–9.

[29] Manuscript Notebook Containing Copies of Letters from William Turner to His Son, p. 55, 59–60, letters from November 1776, UCC/3/1/5, University of Manchester Special Collections, Manchester. I examined this archival material, and that used in the next reference, as part of work for 'Faith in the Town: Lay Religion, Urbanisation and Industrialisation in England, 1740–1830', an Arts and Humanities Research Council-funded project, University of Manchester (2018–2021).

[30] George Strafford, Wakefield, to Samuel Sharp, Wakefield, 12 May 1815, C281/4/1/8, West Yorkshire Archive Service, Wakefield.

that it is unlikely that religious difference ceased to have a broader impact after 1750. Indeed, the repeal of the Test and Corporation Acts in 1828, and debates about Tractarianism in the middle of the nineteenth century, revealed underlying insecurities about the status of the Church that reinvigorated debates about and interpretations of the Reformation.[31] As current research is already beginning to underline, we can gain a much greater understanding of industrialising society if we consider the ways in which religion remained intertwined with, and complementary to, developments often associated with 'modernity'.[32]

****

What was it about the relationship between religious change and social and cultural developments in the first half of the century that allowed underlying concerns about religious difference to be repeatedly transmuted into new contexts? Over the first half of the eighteenth century, English society had been engaged in a process: an exercise in managing, but never quite resolving, religious difference. The legislation of 1689 represented an unprecedented acceptance that state efforts to enforce conformity might do more harm than good. However, it lacked clarity on many issues and allowed room for multiple interpretations of its ultimate implications; it was a politically expedient measure imposed on a society that was by no means wholly reconciled to the existence of different religious professions within public life. This meant that individuals and groups tried to sustain divergent views of what the 1689 Act meant, and how it should shape English society.

In the immediate aftermath of the Act stalwarts of the Established Church sought to cling on to an older exclusionary legal framework, against the vehement opposition of both Whigs and Dissenters. By the 1720s the temperature of debate was cooling considerably in the context of changing political alignments and a greater realisation of the unproductivity of rancorous debate. However, this tacit recognition that the 'toleration' of

---

[31] Richard Rex, 'Introduction: The Morning Star or the Sunset of the Reformation?' *Bulletin of the John Rylands Library*, 90, 1 (2014), pp. 10–11; Alison Shell, 'Sacrilege, Tractarian Fiction and the Very Long Reformation', *Reformation*, 24, 2 (2019), pp. 195–209.

[32] Stubenrach, *The Evangelical Age of Ingenuity*, pp. 21, 251–4; Lucy Cory Allen, 'Enchanting the Field: Where Should the History of Victorian and Edwardian Religion and Belief Go from Here?', *Cultural and Social History*, 18, 4 (2021), p. 482. See also the work of Hannah Barker, Jeremy Gregory, Kate Gibson, and Carys Brown on 'Faith in the Town: Lay Religion, Urbanisation and Industrialisation in England, 1740–1830', Arts and Humanities Research Council-funded project, University of Manchester (2018–2021), https://faithinthetown.wordpress.com/.

1689 was here to stay did not mean that religious difference was no longer an issue. Instead, in a period when prejudices remained ingrained but were no longer fully facilitated by the law, contemporaries sought ways to live with religious diversity. We have seen throughout this book that religious differences were managed through social means, with individuals and communities setting the boundaries of inclusion and exclusion in terms of social behaviours and preferences. While in many ways this helped to mitigate the disruption caused by religious tensions, it also embedded the importance of religious difference for contemporary culture. The result of all of this was a society in which social norms and behaviour were highly dependent on, and reactive to, religious difference. The nature of public religion continued to be hotly debated as supporters of the Established Church periodically faced their worst fears of Dissenting dominance on a local level. The language with which contemporaries described themselves and others continued to be deeply affected by their religious stance. Dissenters and members of the Established Church alike continued to define themselves and others by linking their social behaviour with religious affiliation.

By showing the significance of religious difference in shaping both everyday interactions and the nature of some of the key cultural modes of the century, this book prompts social historians to consider religious difference as a key explanatory factor in other areas of eighteenth-century social life. As we have seen, there was wide variety in the tenor of quotidian exchanges between people of different religious standpoints, from the outright hostile to the genuinely caring. But an awareness of religious difference could also be part of the social dynamic even when it was not clearly mentioned, and this is apparent in the language with which they recalled or described social interactions. Looking at the different language that contemporaries used to describe their social relationships can highlight how they retained varying degrees of social distance depending on religious affiliation. This allows us to look beyond mere neighbourliness to the many shades of grey between wholehearted assimilation and pragmatic co-existence. This approach – looking for patterns in the social languages different groups used to describe themselves and one another – may be applied usefully to understanding the diverse nature of inter-confessional relationships at other times and in other places in early modern Europe. Crucially, unpicking the varied quality of social relations in this way may help us to understand latent dynamics of tension that caused seemingly strong inter-confessional relationships to break down sporadically in post-Reformation Europe.

At the same time, this approach also has a broader use for understanding the social history of England in this period. Highlighting these different layers of social interaction depending on religious difference can give an insight into how underlying tensions might be suppressed or bubble over within a given community. Acknowledging that different languages of social interaction had a function in structuring social relationships according to religious difference points us towards the limitations and strengths of, as well as changes in, concepts such as 'neighbourliness' as a crucial part of the social organisation of late-seventeenth- and eighteenth-century communities. While the criteria for neighbourliness might be broad, and achievable by a wide range of individuals, relationships based on company and friendship were often more selective, and religious affiliation could be a key factor in that selection. Recognising the subtle role that religious difference played in shaping the nature of social relationships therefore adds a further layer of understanding to the complex nexus of ideas about community, social behaviour, and conformity that shaped perceptions of creditworthiness, reputation, and belonging in this period.

Community belonging was often constructed within and around the boundaries of the parish, and we have also seen how religious difference could affect perceptions and uses of space and power within that forum. The physical presence of alternative places of worship within a parish could act for some as a daily reminder of difference, and as a focal point for conflict. A community's buildings could represent sites of contested power, where hierarchies and social norms could be maintained or challenged. It is widely acknowledged that buildings such as country houses, merchant town-houses, and churches conveyed power, status, and community identity through their presence and architecture.[33] But the extent to which the meeting house was a target of communal grievance highlights the destabilising effect of religious pluralism on the 'topographies of power' within local communities.[34] Changes in religious practice and the emergence of religious diversity had been an often tense experience for communities

---

[33] Peter Borsay, *The English Urban Renaissance: Culture and Society in the Provincial Town, 1660–1770* (Oxford: Clarendon, 1989), pp. 111–12; Sukanya Dasgupta, '"Of Polish'd Pillars or a Roofe of Gold": Authority and Affluence in the English Country-House Poem', in Matthew P. Romaniello and Charles Lipp (eds.), *Contested Spaces of Nobility in Early Modern Europe* (Farnham: Ashgate, 2011), pp. 189–212; W. M Jacob, '"… This Congregation Here Present …": Seating in Parish Churches During the Long Eighteenth Century', *Studies in Church History*, 42 (2006), p. 295.

[34] Peter Borsay, 'The Topography of Power: Elites and the Political Landscape of the English Town, 1660–1760', in Stewart J. Brown, Frances Knight, and John Morgan-Guy (eds.), *Religion, Identity, and Conflict in Britain: From the Restoration to the Twentieth Century* (Farnham: Ashgate, 2013), p. 50; Jonathan Barry, 'Bristol Pride: Civic Identity in Bristol, c. 1640–1775', in Madge Dresser and Philip Ollerenshaw (eds.), *The Making of Modern Bristol* (Tiverton: Redcliffe Press, 1996), pp. 32–3.

throughout the sixteenth and seventeenth centuries, but never before had the buildings of the Church had a direct public competitor.

With hindsight, it appears that meeting houses, with their lack of state sponsorship, their divergent denominations, and – in some cases – extra-parochial structure, could never have represented a fatal threat to the Established Church. Nevertheless, as we have seen, for many contemporaries this was far from obvious. With the passage of the Toleration Act, Dissenters' Meetings could be presented as direct competitors to public worship. This sense of competition between Established Church and Dissent over parish power was seen in disputes about parish office, attacks on the reputations of Dissenting ministers, and disputes over funerals and burial practices. These were to varying degrees all matters of religious propriety, but they also affected the establishment of local hierarchy and status. And while it can by no means be said that these disputes happened everywhere, evidence of such instances appears with enough frequency and across a wide enough geography that it should be taken seriously. Given that the social history of the parish in the sixteenth and seventeenth centuries has stressed the significance of the parish church and its associated functions as a locus of power and community identity, the social impact of the emergence of an 'alternative' in the eighteenth century is worthy of greater consideration.

The emerging modes, discourses, and venues of eighteenth-century culture also developed in conversation with issues of religious diversity. In this book, using the lens of religious difference to look at emerging discourses around social behaviour in the first part of the eighteenth century has opened up a different perspective on the discourse of politeness, one that places an emphasis on its previously unacknowledged ability to cement religious exclusion: social language could trumpet the rejection of past divisions while simultaneously perpetuating them in new ways. If religious difference played a role – albeit backstage – in the performance of politeness, it is reasonable to suggest that it also had a part in other forms of social discourse. Indeed, a focus on the impact of religious difference does help us to expand understandings of the types of social interaction that took place in tandem with specific eighteenth-century cultural activities. As we have seen, religious difference shaped social interactions in some of the central venues for eighteenth-century sociability. Not every interaction in the alehouse, the assembly room, or the coffeehouse was dependent on the religious professions of those concerned. However, religious difference was undeniably one of a number of intersecting factors – including social status, gender, and age – at play in shaping the social dynamics of interactions when contemporaries drank, danced, and conversed.

In these, and in other examples throughout this book, we see that English society was deeply affected by religious difference. Questions about religious difference should, therefore, be integral to the social history of this period. Giving religious difference serious consideration in explorations of the social worlds of the eighteenth century may help us to uncover to a greater extent the diversity of English social and cultural life. From the individual exchanges that shaped daily life, to the relational construction of parish politics, and the new cultural discourses and forms that have been regarded as emblematic of eighteenth-century life, distinctions along religious lines were a means of defining identity, distinguishing status, and drawing the boundaries of community. This was a society shaped less by its rejection of a persecutory past than by the precarious process of negotiating the implications of its unprecedented – but nevertheless limited – toleration.

Bibliography

Primary Manuscripts

Angus Library and Archive, Oxford

D/WAB – Diary and Letters of Benjamin Wallin, 1740–*c*.1782.

Berkshire Record Office, Reading

D/EZ12/1 – Diary of Edward Belson, 1707–22.

Bodleian Library, Oxford

MS Eng. lett. e. 29 – Correspondence of the Henry Family, 1652–1713:
  MS Eng. lett. e. 29/89 – Phillip Henry to Matthew Henry, 1 June 1689.
  MS Eng. lett. e. 29/103 – Matthew Henry to Phillip Henry, 21 October 1692.
  MS Eng. lett. e. 29/149 – Matthew Henry to Phillip Henry, 4 September, n.d.
    (*c*.1694).
  MS Eng. lett. e. 29/220 – John Evans to Matthew Henry, 23 January 1705.
MS. Eng. misc. d. 311 – Commonplace Book of John Tylston, with Additions by
    Hannah Tylston and Hannah Lightbody, n.d. (mid-eighteenth century).
MS. Eng. misc. e. 330 – Diary of Matthew Henry, 1705–13.
MS. Eng. misc. e. 331 – Mrs Savage's Diary, 31 May 1714 to 25 December 1723
    (eighteenth-century copy).

The British Library, London

Henry Papers:
  Add MS 42849, fol. 34r – Matthew Henry to Katherine Henry, 8 January 1701.
  Add MS 42849, fol. 69r – Matthew Henry to His Mother, 25 September
    c.1699.
Add MS 71626 – Diary of Anne (Dawson) Evans 1721–2.
Stowe MS 747, Vol. V., fol. 16 – John Hampden, Jun., to Rev. [Francis] Tallents,
    London, 27 May 1693.

Cambridgeshire Archives, Cambridge

488/C1/MH9 – Elizabeth Marshe to Mary Huddleston, 1 August 1727.

Cambridge University Library, Cambridge

MS Add 9450/A/10 – John Hailstone, York, to His Son 'Johny', 8 July 1751.
MS Add.106 – The Sum and Substance of a Dispute Between William Couch an Elder of the Baptist Congregation, and Thomas Upsher, One of Those in Scorn Called Quakers at Burnham in Denge Hundred, 1699.
MS Add.6843 – Diary of William Coe, 1688–1729.
MS Buxton 35/2 – Elizabeth Buxton, Laxfield, to Robert Buxton, 8 January 1722.

Cheshire Archives and Local Studies, Chester

D/MH/1 – Matthew Henry's Chapel Church Book, 1687–1928.
ZCR 678 – Diary of Peter Walkden, 1684–1769.
ZDBasten/8 – Sarah Savage Diary, 1686–88.

Coventry History Centre, Coventry

PA 90/21 – Coventry Corporation to William Freeman of Coventry, Baker: Grant in Fee Farm for £55.5s; Fine and £6 Fee Farm Rent, 4 October 1738.

Devonshire Archives and Local Studies, Exeter

3542D/M/1/1 – The Exeter Assembly, Presbyterian, Minute Books, 1652–1794.
3700D/M/1 – Meetings in East Devon, Chiefly at Loughwood Baptist Chapel in Dalwood Parish: Proceedings Book, 1653–1795.
874D/o/M/51-111 – File of Miscellaneous Papers, Probably Records of the Cullompton or Spiceland Monthly Meeting, 1666–1772: Robert Barrows, London, to Henry Coward, Thomas Green, Thomas Dockery, Richard Burrow, William Hugginson, and Thomas Widers, 1690.
874D/o/M/112-155 – File of Miscellaneous Papers of Cullompton Monthly Meeting, 1692–1777.
Z19/40/8a-b/1/6b – Richard Coffin to John Coffin, n.d.

Dr Williams's Library, London

Blackmore Family Papers:
   12.40/33 – Abigail Blackmore to Sarah Blackmore, 13 December, n.d (*c.*1725).
   12.40/61 – An Account of the Rev. Chewning Blackmore by George Bewson, copied by Rev. Fr. Blackmore.

12.40/62 – Abigail Blackmore to Sarah Blackmore, 20 November 1725.
12.40/65 – Rev. Chewning Blackmore to Sarah Blackmore, 19 November 1726.
Henry MSS:
90.2 – Sarah Savage's Journal, 1743–8.
Say Family Papers:
12.107(63) – Samuel Say, Lowestoft, to John Paris, London, 21 December 1709.
12.107(268) – William King to Samuel Say, 12 February 1736.
12.108(14) – Samuel Say to Sarah Say, n.d., c.1738–43.

Essex Record Office, Chelmsford

A13685 Box 51/Contents of Box K – Felsted Monthly Meeting (Uncatalogued):
Letter from London Yearly Meeting Regarding the Affirmation of Loyalty,
30th 3/mo 1713; Minutes of London Meeting, 1717; 'Considerations on the
Bill Depending for Preventing Occasional Conformity Humbly Offered by
the People Called Quakers' (n.d.).
D/DQs 22 – Commonplace Book: 'John Churchman His Book', 1749.
D/Y 1/1/111/31 – Nicholas Jekyll to William Holman, 8 April 1715.
D/Y 1/1/111/145 – Nicholas Jekyll to William Holman, 15 November 1727.

Gloucestershire Archives, Gloucester

D1340/B1/M1 – Minutes of Nailsworth Monthly Meeting, 1668–1743.
D1340/B1/M2 – Minutes of Nailsworth Monthly Meeting, 1744–86.
D1340/B2/M1 – Stoke Orchard and Gloucester Meeting Minutes, 1671–1783.
D2844/2/1 – Wotton-under-Edge Baptist Church, Church Book, 1717–1826.
D3549/2/4/29, Part 1 – Notes, Memoranda, Printed Items and Other Material
Gathered by Bishop Lloyd ... Including Particulars of a Dissenting Sect at
Rothwell and Elsewhere in Northants Organised by Richard Davies in 1692.
D3549/6/1/B5 – Letter of Robert Banks to Archbishop of York Regarding
'Nonconformist' Marriages Being Preferred to Marriage by License, 6 March
1692.
D6026/6/6 – Gloucester Southgate Church Meeting Minutes, 1716–1832.
GDR/E3/4/1 – Cautionary Letter from the Bishop of London Concerning Samuel
Evans, Late Dissenting Teacher at Hammersmith, 3 March 1717.

Hertfordshire Archives, Hertford

DP/6/8/1 – Yardley (Ardley) Vestry Minutes, October 1719.

Hull History Centre, Hull

UDDEV/60/84f – Lord Cardigan to Marmaduke Constable, 17 November 1728.

Huntingdonshire Archives, Huntingdon

AH/38/9/275/26 – John Andrew to Benjamin Woodward, 22 April 1738.

FR6/1/1 – Great Gransden Baptist Church: Church Book, 1694–1777.

FR16/1/1/1 – St Neots United Reformed Church: Church Book, 1691–1802.

PGMD/3500/15 – Typed Transcript of the Kimbolton Independent Church Book, 1692–1809.

Lambeth Palace Library, London

MS 2717, fol. 6r – Plan of Area for Proposed Church and Church Yard in St Mary Magdalene, Bermondsey, 6 November 1711.

MS 2717, fols 17–18 – Letter from Edmund Halley and John King to the Commissioner for Building Fifty New Churches, 15 July 1714.

MS 2717, fol. 23r – Petition of Parishioners of St Mary Magdalen Bermondsey to the Commissioners Appointed for Building Fifty New Churches, 12 January 1714.

MS 2717, fol. 31r – Petition of Parishioners of St Mary Magdalen Bermondsey to the Commissioners Appointed for Building Fifty New Churches, 8 October 1725.

Lancashire Archives, Preston

DDKE/2/5/63 – Draft Depositions Concerning a Rift Between Churchmen and Dissenters, n.d.

FRL 21/1/5/22 – Letter Relating to Ministers and Their Auditors, and on Friends' Restrained Behaviour in Public, 11 June 1731.

FRL 21/1/5/25 – Letter from London Yearly Meeting to Lancashire Quarterly Meeting, 7 June 1745.

QSP/705/11 – Kellamergh and Freckleton: Mock-Marriage at Christopher Lealands by Mr Parr, and Ill-Behaviour of Margaret Colbron, c.1691 [microfilm].

Library of the Society of Friends, London

MS BOX D3/5 – Something by Way of a Journal or Part of the Life of John Croker, c.1720.

MS Vol 312 – Journal of Mary Weston, 1735–52.

Manchester Archives, Manchester

M35/6/3/21 – Michael Fletcher to Revd Mr Hesketh, 15 June 1706.

M85/1/12/1 – Society of Friends, Hardshaw Monthly Meeting Book: Book for Recording Papers and Epistles &c, 1699–1794.

M85/1/4 – Society of Friends, Hardshaw Monthly Meeting, Accounts of Sufferings and Distraints, 1654–1816.

M85/1/11 – Society of Friends, Hardshaw Monthly Meeting: Personal Condemnations and Testimonies of Denial, 1667–1797.

Norfolk Record Office, Norwich

MC 2577/4/1/ – Notebook Containing a Compilation of Free Church [Congregationalist] Material, Eighteenth Century.
MSC2/19 – Answers from Denton Concerning Nonconformists and Church Bells, 1706.

Somerset Heritage Centre, Taunton

DD\TB/24/11, William Moore, at Bridgewater, to Thomas Carew Esq, 28 November 1737; William Moore, at Bridgewater, to Thomas Carew Esq, 19 September 1746.
Q/SR/184/8 – Evidence of Robert Wadman of Charlton Horethorne against Lawrence Hooper Junior and Isaack Stone of Charlton Horethorne, Baptist Preacher, Concerning the Interruption of the Funeral of Elizabeth Hooper, 15 April 1691.
Q/SR/184/9 – Evidence of Thomas Mogg, Rector of Stowell, and Edward Longman of Stowell against Lawrence Hooper Junior and Isaack Stone of Charlton Horethorne, Baptist Preacher, Concerning the Interruption of the Funeral of Elizabeth Hooper, 12 February 1691.
Q/SR/187/9 – Evidence of Charles Waller of Brislington, Concerning the Burial of a Corpse in Brislington Parish Church, 20 November 1691.
Q/SR/187/10 – Evidence of John Horton of Bristol, Gentleman, Concerning the Burial of a Corpse in Brislington Parish Church which Burial was Not in Accordance with the Laws of the Church of England, 27 October 1691.
Q/SR/187/11 – Evidence of Samuel Paine of Bristol, Minister, Concerning the Burial of a Corpse in Brislington Parish Church which Burial was Not in Accordance with the Laws of the Church of England, October 1691.
Q/SR/187/14 – Evidence of John Horton of Bristol, Gentleman, Concerning the Burial of a Corpse in Brislington Parish Church which Burial was Not in Accordance with the Laws of the Church of England, 27 October 1691.
Q/SR/187/26 – Evidence of Richard Peasley of Brislington, Clark, Concerning the Burial of a Corpse in Brislington Parish Church which Burial was Not in Accordance with the Laws of the Church of England, 30 October 1691.
Q/SR/284/2 – Evidence of Richard Scrinen of Winsham, Carpenter, in a Case Concerning Samuel Allen of Winsham who Allegedly Attached a Libellous Letter to the Door of the Meeting House, 3 September 1718.

Surrey History Centre, Woking

QS2/6/1708/Mid/5 – Affidavit of John Bugshaw of Lambeth, 1708.
QS2/6/1708/Mid/6 – Affidavit of Edward Standard of Lambeth, 1708.

QS2/6/1708/Mid/7 – Affidavits of Jane and John Leaf, Anne Henderson, and John Skinner, eighbours of Widow Coleman, 1708.

QS2/6/1725/Mic/32 – Petition of James Adams and Aaron Atkins, Members of the Congregation of Dissenting Protestants, Against the Poor Rate Assessed on Their Meeting House, 1725 [microfilm].

QS2/6/1725/Mic/42 – Notice by Nathaniel Sheffield, on Behalf of the Ministers and Congregation of Dissenters, of His Intention to Appear at the Next Sessions to Appeal Against a Poor Rate Assessment, 1725 [microfilm].

University of Manchester Special Collections, Manchester

UCC/3/1/5 – Manuscript Notebook Containing Copies of Letters from William Turner to His Son.

West Yorkshire Archive Service, Wakefield

C281/4/1/8 – George Strafford, Wakefield, to Samuel Sharp, Wakefield, 12 May 1815.

Wiltshire and Swindon History Centre, Chippenham

161/170 – Journal of Thomas Smith of Shaw House, 1715–16, 1717–21, 1721–2.

727/1/6 – Nathaniel Fancourt to John Butler, 9 January c.1711.

Digitised Manuscripts

'Intoxicants and Early Modernity Project': www.intoxicantsproject.org/

Transcription of Harrison c Sutton, 1694, EDC 5/1693/21 (unfol.), Cheshire Archives and Local Studies (CALS), Chester, accessed 15 December 2020.

Transcription of Office c Thurston, December 1717–April 1718, DN/DEP 59/63 (unfol.), Norfolk Record Office, Norfolk, accessed 26 June 2018.

Parry c Sylvester, 1718, EDC 5/1718/2 (unfol.), CALS, accessed 15 December 2020.

Primary Printed Materials (Place of Publication London, unless Otherwise Stated)

The Absolute Necessity of Standing by the Present Government, or, a View of What Both Church Men and Dissenters Must Expect if by Their Unhappy Divisions Popery and Tyranny Should Return Again (1689).

Addy, John (ed.), *The Diary of Henry Prescott, LL. B., Deputy Registrar of Chester Diocese, vol. 1, 28 March 1704–24 March 1711* (Manchester: Record Society of Lancashire and Cheshire, 1987).

Addy, John and McNiven, Peter (eds.), *The Diary of Henry Prescott, LL. B., Deputy Registrar of Chester Diocese, vol. 2, 25 March 1711–24 May 1719* (Manchester: Record Society of Lancashire and Cheshire, 1994).

The Adventures of an Actor, in the Characters of a Merry-Andrew, a Methodist-Preacher, and a Fortune-Teller. Founded on Facts (1770).

Agate, John, *A Reply to a Pamphlet, Intituled. A True and Impartial Account of What Occurr'd at the Late Conference in Exon* (Exeter, 1707).

Anglia Rediviva: A Poem on His Majesties Most Joyfull Reception into Enland [sic] (1660).

The Argument with Dissenters about Subscriptions, and the Repeal of the Corporation and Test Acts, Briefly Stated (1735).

The Artifices of the Romish Priests, in Making Converts to Popery: Or, an Account of the Various Methods, practised by Popish Missionaries, to deceive the Protestants of this Kingdom, and deprive them of their Religion and Loyalty (1746).

Ashby, Richard, *An Epistle to the Called of God, Every-Where; In Order to stir up their Minds, by way of Remembrance, of the Great End for which they are Called: With Exhortation to keep Unity* (1715).

Astell, Mary, *Moderation Truly Stated: Or, a Review of a Late Pamphlet, Entitul'd, Moderation a Vertue* (1704).

The Athenian Oracle. Being an Entire Collection of all the Valuable Questions and Answers in the Old Athenian Mercuries, vol. 2 (1728).

Atkinson, Benjamin Andrewes, *Catholick Principles, or St. Paul's Worship Faith, Hope and Practice Recommended to Christians of All Persuasions* (1730).

Austin, Samuel, *The Character of a Quaker in His True and Proper Colours, or, the Clownish Hypocrite Anatomized* (1671).

Author of Teague-land Jests, *The Quakers Art of Courtship: Or, the Yea-and-Nay Academy of Compliments* (1710).

B., A., *A Church of England Man's Serious Thoughts Upon the Bill Against Dissenting School-Masters* (1714).

B., G., *The Convert: Or, an Apology for the Conduct of a Young Gentleman* (c.1750).

Ball, Nathaniel, *Sermons on Several Important Subjects* (1745).

Barclay, Robert, *An Apology for the True Christian Divinity, as the same is Held Forth, and Preached, by the People, called in Scorn, Quakers: Being A Full Explanation and Vindication of their Principles and Doctrines* (1701).

Barker, John, *Charity Recommended Upon the Motives and Incouragements of Christianity: A Sermon Preach'd at the Old Jewry, Mark 5, 1739 to the Society for Relief of the Widows and Orphans of Dissenting Ministers* (1740).

Barrington, John Shute, *The Rights of Protestant Dissenters: In Two Parts* (1704–5).

Baxter, Richard, *A Christian Directory, or, A Summ of Practical Theologie and Cases of Conscience Directing Christians How to Use Their Knowledge and Faith* (1673).

Baxter, Richard, *The Practical Works of the Late Reverend and Pious Mr. Richard Baxter, in Four Volumes* (1707).

de Bellegarde, Jean Baptiste Morvan, *Reflexions Upon the Politeness of Manners; With Maxims for Civil Society* (1707).

Bennet, Benjamin, *Several Discourses Against Popery* (1714).

Blake, Malachi, *A Brief Account of the Dreadful Fire at Blandford-Forum in the County of Dorset* (1735).

Blewitt, George, *An Enquiry Whether a General Practice of Virtue Tends to the Wealth or Poverty, Benefit or Disadvantage of a People?* (1725).

Bourn, Samuel, *The True Christian Way of Striving for the Faith of the Gospel. A Sermon Preach'd to a Congregation of Protestant-Dissenters, Ministers, and Private Christians … in Dudley in Worcestershire, May 23 1738* (1738).

Bowman, William, *The Imposture of Methodism Display'd: In a Letter to the Inhabitants of the Parish of Dewsbury. Occasion'd by the Rise of Certain Modern Sect of Enthusiasts, (Among Them) Call'd Methodists* (1740).

Bownas, Samuel, *Considerations on a Pamphlet Entitul'd, the Duty of Consulting a Spiritual Guide, Considered* (1724).

Boyer, Abel, *An Impartial History of the Occasional Conformity and Schism Bills* (1717).

Bradford, Samuel, *A Plan of Birmingham: Surveyed in MDCCL* (1750).

Bradford, Samuel, *A Plan of the City of Coventry Surveyed in 1748 and 1749* (1750).

A Brief Account of the Methods Used to Propagate Popery, in Great Britain and Ireland; Ever Since the Reformation, to the Present Rebellion (1745).

A Brief Description or Character of the Religion and Manners of the Phanatiques in Generall (1660).

British Apollo, Issue 79, 10–12 November 1708.

Brockbank, W., and Kenworthy, F. (eds.), *The Diary of Richard Kay, 1716–51, of Baldingstone, Near Bury. A Lancashire Doctor* (Manchester: Manchester University Press for the Chetham Society, 1968).

Brooks, Thomas, *Precious Remedies Against Satans Devices* (1661).

Brown, Thomas, *A Legacy for the Ladies, or Characters of the Women of the Age* (1705).

Bugg, Francis, *Goliah's Head Cut Off with His Own Sword, and the Quakers Routed By Their Own Weapons* (1708).

Burrish, Onslow, *Batavia Illustrata: Or, a View of the Policy and Commerce of the United Provinces. Part I* (1728).

Calamy, Edmund, *Comfort and Counsel to Protestant Dissenters* (1712).

Centlivre, Susanna, *A Bold Stroke for a Wife: A Comedy; As It Is Acted at the Theatre in Little Lincoln's-Inn-Fields. By the Author of The Busie-Body and The Gamester* (1718).

Chandler, Samuel, *St Paul's Rules of Charity, and His Manner of Recommending It, Considered: In a Sermon Preached to the Society for Relieving the Widows and Orphans of Protestant Dissenting Ministers, at the Old Jury, March 1st 1748* (1749).

The Character of a Phanatique (1660).

The Character of a Quaker (London, 1704).

Cherry, John, *An Historical List of All Horse-Matches Run, and of All Plates and Prizes Run for England and Wales* (1729).

Child, Josiah, *A New Discourse of Trade: Wherein Are Recommended Several Weighty Points, Relating to Companies of Merchants* (1745).

Christian Sufferers: Or, Seasonable Advice to Protestant Dissenters, Relating to Their Behaviour, Under Their Present Disappointment. A Sermon Preach'd in the Country, January 28 1732–3 (1732–3).

Civil Security, Not Conscience, Concern'd in the Bill Concerning Occasional Conformity (1702).

Clark, William, *The Sheep in His Own Cloathing: Or, Mr William Clark's Narrative of the High-Church Treatment of Himself and the Dissenters in Lambeth* (London, 1708).

Coade, George, *A Letter to a Clergyman, Relating to His Sermon on the 30th of January: Being a Compleat Answer to All the Sermons That Have Ever Been, or Ever Shall Be, Preached, in the Like Strain, on That Anniversary* (1746).

Coffee: A Tale (1727).

A Collection of the Epistles from the Yearly Meeting of Friends in London to the Quarterly and Monthly Meetings in Great-Britain, Ireland and Elsewhere from 1675 to 1805 (Baltimore, MD, 1806).

A Collection of Several Letters and Declarations, Sent by General Monck Unto the Lord Lambert, the Lord Fleetwood, and the Rest of the General Council of Officers in the Army (1660).

Collier, Phillip, *The Duty and Advantages of Promoting the Peace and Prosperity, Both of Church and State. A Sermon* (Exeter, 1712).

A Comical Sonnet on Ch----s Blue Bonnet (1729).

The Committee, or Popery in Masquerade (1680).

Cooper, Anthony Ashley, *A Letter Concerning Enthusiasm* (1708).

Crosby, Thomas, *The History of the English Baptists, From the Reformation to the Beginning of the Reign of King George I* (1738), vol. 4.

D., M., *Friendly Advice to Protestants, or, An Essay Towards Comprehending and Uniting of All Protestant Dissenters to the Church of England* (1680).

'Declaration of Indulgence of James II, 4 April 1687', in Andrew Browning (ed.), *English Historical Documents, 1660–1714*, (Eyre & Spottiswoode, 1953), pp. 399–400.

Defoe, Daniel, *An Essay on the History of Parties, and Persecution in Britain* (1711).

Defoe, Daniel, *Wise as Serpents: Being an Enquiry into the Present Circumstances of the Dissenters, and What Measures They Ought to Take in Order to Disappoint the Designs of Their Enemies* (1712).

Defoe, Daniel, *The Weakest Go to the Wall, or the Dissenters Sacrific'd By All Parties: Being a True State of the Dissenters Case* (1714).

Dennis, John, *Vice and Luxury Publick Mischiefs: Or, Remarks on a Book Intituled, The Fable of the Bees; Or, Private Vices Publick Benefits* (1724).

The Desolations of a Popish Succession (1716).

The Dissenter Truely Described (1681).

Doe, Vanessa S. (ed.), *The Diary of James Clegg of Chapel en le Frith, 1708–1755* (Derby: Derbyshire Record Society, 3 vols. 1978–81).

Doddridge, Philip, *Free Thoughts on the Most Probable Means of Reviving the Dissenting Interest* (1730).

Doddridge, Philip, *The Care of the Soul Urged as One Thing Needful. A Sermon Preached at Maidwell in Northamptonshire, June 22, 1735* (1735).

Doddridge, Philip, *The Necessity of a General Reformation in Order to a Well-Grounded Hope of Success in War: Represented in a Sermon Preached at Northampton, January 9 1739–40* (1740).

Downes, John, *A Defence of Set or Prescribed Forms of Prayer; Being an Answer to Mr Phelps's Remarks Upon a Sermon Preached on that Subject* (1746).

Drew, Patrick, *The Church and England's Late Conflict With, and Triumph Over the Spirit of Fanaticism* (1710).

Duchal, James and Kirkpatrick, James, *A Sermon on Occasion of the Much Lamented Death of the Late Reverend Mr John Abernethy ... by James Duchal. With an Appendix Containing Some Brief Memoirs of the Lives and Characters of the Late Revd Messieurs Thomas Shaw, William Taylor, Michael Bruce, and Samuel Haliday ... by James Kirkpatrick* (Dublin, 1741).

Dudley, John, *A Charge to the Clergy Within the Archdeaconry of Bedford: In Which are Some Remarks Concerning the Late Application of the Dissenters for a Repeal of the Test Act. Delivered at a Visitation Held at Ampthill, April 30th, 1736* (1736).

Earle, Peter, *Micro-Cosmographie, Or, a Peece of the World Discovered in Essayes and Characters* (1628).

An Epistle to O------r H----nl--y; Containing, Some Remarks on the Discourses Set Forth at the Conventicle the Corner of Lincoln's-Inn-Fields (1746).

The Fanatick Feast. A Pleasant Comedy. As It Was Acted at a Wedding-Dinner in Gr------ (1710).

The Fetter Lane Loyalist or a Description of a True Sonne of Rome (1681).

Fetherstone, Christopher, *A Dialogue Agaynst Light, Lewde, and Lascivious Dauncing Wherin are Refuted All Those Reasons, Which the Common People Use to Bring in Defence Thereof* (1582).

Fielding, Henry, 'An Essay on the Knowledge and Characters of Men', and 'An Essay on Conversation', in Henry Knight Miller (ed.), *The Wesleyan Edition of the Works of Henry Fielding: Miscellanies by Henry Fielding, Esq* (Oxford: Oxford University Press and Wesleyan University Press, 1972), vol. 1, pp. 153–78.

A Full Reply to the Substantial Impeachment of Dr. Sacheverell, in A Dialogue between An High-Church Captain, a Stanch'd Whigg, and a Coffee-man; As the Matter of Fact was really transacted on Friday last in B--s Coffee-House in Westminster Hall (1710).

Gavin, Antonio, *A Master-Key to Popery. In Five Parts* (1725).

Gilling, Isaac, *A Sermon Preach'd at Lyme Regis in the County of Dorset, at a Quarterly Lecture, Appointed for the Promoting the Reformation of Manners* (Exeter, 1705).

Gough, Strickland, *An Enquiry Into the Causes of the Decay of the Dissenting Interest, and the Case of Those Who Have Lately Deserted It* (1731).

The Grand Designs of the Dissenting Teachers Discover'd and Exposed to Publick View (1710).

Grascome, Samuel, *The Mask of Moderation Pull'd Off the Foul Face of Occasional Conformity* (1704).

Hare, Francis, *A Sermon Preached Before the House of Lords, in the Abbey-Church at Westminster, Upon Monday, January 31, 1731* (1732).

Haywood, Eliza, *The Female Spectator* (1745–6), vol. 4.

Henry, Matthew, *An Exposition of All the Books of the Old and New Testament* (1721–1725), vols. 4, 6.

An Historical Emblematical Fan in Honour of the Church of England (1711).

Hobbes, Thomas, *De Corpore Politico, Or, the Elements of Law, Moral and Politick* (2nd edn, 1652).

Hobbes, Thomas, *Behemoth, or, an Epitome of the Civil Wars of England, from 1640 to 1660* (1679).

Horner, Craig (ed.), *The Diary of Edmund Harrold, Wigmaker of Manchester, 1712–15* (Aldershot: Ashgate, 2008).

Hunt, Jeremiah, *Dissenters No Schismaticks: Or, Dissenting Churches Orthodox* (1714).

Impartial Pen, *What the Dissenters Would Have. Or, the Case of the Dissenters Briefly Yet Plainly Stated* (1717).

An Inquiry into the Miracle Said to Have Been Wrought in the Fifth Century Upon Some Orthodox Christians (1730).

A Journal of the Life, Gospel Labours, and Christian Experiences of That Faithful Minister of Jesus Christ, John Woolman, Late of Mount-Holly, in Pennysylvania (Dublin, 1776).

Lavington, George, *The Enthusiasm of Methodists and Papists Compared, Part I* (1749).

Leslie, Charles, *View of the Times: Their Principles and Practices* (4 vols., 1708–9), vol.1.

Locke, John, 'A Letter Concerning Toleration [2nd edn, 1690]', in Mark Goldie (ed.), *John Locke: A Letter Concerning Toleration and Other Writings* (Indianapolis, IN: Liberty Fund, 2010), pp. 1–68.

Locke, John, *Some Thoughts Concerning Education* (1693).

Lombard, Daniel, *A Succinct History of Ancient and Modern Persecutions. Together with a Short Essay on Assassinations and Civil Wars* (1747).

Long, Thomas, *The Case of Persecution, Charg'd on the Church of England, Consider'd and Discharg'd, in Order to Her Justification, and a Desired Union of Protestant Dissenters* (1689).

A Looking-Glass for Fanaticks (1730).

The Lucubrations of Isaac Bickerstaff, Esq (1749).

The Manager's Pro and Con: Or, An Account of What Is Said at Child's and Tom's Coffee-House for and Against Dr. Sacheverell (1710).

Mandeville, Bernard, *The Fable of the Bees, Or, Private Vices Publick Benefits* (1714).

Mandeville, Bernard, *A Treatise of the Hypochondriack and Hysterick Diseases. In Three Dialogues* (1730).

Mandeville, Bernard, *An Enquiry into the Origin of Honour* (1732).

Matthews, William (ed.), *The Diary of Dudley Ryder, 1715–1716* (London: Methuen, 1939).

Mawson, Matthias, *The Mischiefs of Division with Respect Both to Religion and Civil Government. A Sermon Preach'd Before the House of Lords* (1746).

McLain, William, *An Essay Upon Dancing* (Edinburgh, 1711).

A Merry New Joke, on Joseph's Old Cloak (1729).

Middleton, Conyers, *Letter from Rome, Shewing an Exact Conformity between Popery and Paganism* (1713).

Mills, Benjamin, *A Sermon Preached to a Congregation of Protestant Dissenters, at Maidston, November 5, 1741* (1741).

Mirth and Wisdom in a Miscellany of Different Characters, Relating to Different Persons and Perswasions (1703).

Miscellaneous Correspondence: Containing Essays, Dissertations, &c… Sent to the Author of the Gentleman's Magazine (1742–1748).

A Narrative of the Proceedings of the Protestant Dissenters of the Three Denominations; Relating to the Repeals of the Corporation and Test Acts (1734).

Nelson, John, *The Journal of Mr John Nelson, Preacher of the Gospel … Written by Himself* (J. Mason, n.d.).

Norman, John, *Lay-Nonconformity Justified, in a Dialogue Between a Gentleman of the Town in Communion with the Church of England, and His Dissenting Friend in the Country* (1716).

Norman, John, *Remarks on a Sermon Preached at Petersfield, June the 7th, 1722, by the Reverend Mr William Louth, Rector of that Parish, and Prebendary of Winchester. In a Letter to Himself* (1723).

The Observator, Issue 2, 8 April 1702.

Of the Relation Between Church and State: Or, How Far Christian and Civil Life Affect Each Other; Being a Translation of a Book of Baron Puffendorf's, Upon This Important Subject (1719).

Ollard, Sidney Leslie, and Walker, Philip Charles (eds.), *Archbishop Herring's Visitation Returns, 1743* (Cambridge: Cambridge University Press, 5 vols., 2013), vol. 4.

Paragraph, Peter [James Makittrick Adair], *The Methodist and Mimick. A Tale, in Hudibrastick Verse* (1766).

Penn, William, *The Great Case of Liberty of Conscience Once More Briefly Debated & Defended … Which May Serve the Place of a General Reply to Such Late Discourses as Have Oppos'd a Tolleration* (n.p.., 1670).

Perkins, William, *The Whole Treatise of the Cases of Conscience Distinguished into Three Bookes* (Cambridge, 1608).

Phelps, John, *A Vindication of Free and Unprescribed Prayer: In Some Remarks Upon Dr Newton's Sermon on the Liturgy of the Church of England* (1746).

Philips, John, *The Inquisition. A Farce. As it was Acted at Child's Coffee-House, and the King's-Arms Tavern, In St Paul's Church-Yard* (London, 1717).

Pittis, William, *Aesop at Oxford: Or, a Few Select Fables in Verse* (1708).

Popery and Schism Equally Dangerous to the Church of England, as by Law Establish'd (1715).

The Procession or the Pope's Nursling Riding in Triumph (1745).

Rudd, Sayer, *A Letter to the Reverend the Ministers of the Calvinistical Baptist Persuasion, Meeting at Blackwell's Coffee-House, near Queen's-Street, London* (1735).

Sacheverell, Henry, *The Perils of False Brethren, Both in Church, and State: Set Forth in a Sermon … 5 November 1709* (1709).

Sanders, Robert, *Lucubrations of Gaffer Graybeard. Containing Many Curious Particulars Relating to the Manners of the People in England, During the Present Age* (1774).

A Scourge for the Dissenters: Or the Fanatick Vipers (1735).

Sewel, William, *The History of the Rise, Increase, and Progress of the Christian People Called Quakers, Intermixed With Several Remarkable Occurrences* (1722).

Shadwell, Charles, *The Fair Quaker of Deal, or, the Humours of the Navy. A Comedy. As it is Acted at the Theatre-Royal in Drury-Lane* (1761, first performed 1710).

Society of Friends, London Yearly Meeting, *Advice to Friends Under Prosecution, Either in the Temporal or Ecclesiastical Courts, for their Christian Testimony Against the Payment of Tithes* (1749).

Spectator, Issue 458, 15 August 1712.

Swift, Jonathan, *A Project for the Advancement of Religion and the Reformation of Manners* (1709).

Taylor, Abraham, *A Letter to the Author of An Enquiry Into the Causes of the Decay of the Dissenting Interest* (1730).

Tong, William, *An Account of the Life and Death of Mr. Matthew Henry, Minister of the Gospel at Hackney, Who Dy'd June 22. 1714. In the 52d Year of His Age. Chiefly Collected Out of His Own Papers* (London, 1716).

Tong, William, *A Funeral-Sermon on the Much Lamented Death of the Late Reverend Mr. John Shower, Preach'd at Old-Jury, July 10 1715* (1716).

Tottie, John, *Two Charges Delivered to the Clergy of the Diocese of Worcester in the Years 1763 and 1766, Being Designed as Preservatives Against the Sophistical Arts of the Papists and the Delusions of the Methodists* (Oxford, 1766).

The True Characters (1708).

Turner, Daniel, *A Compendium of Social Religion, Or the Nature and Constitution of Christian Churches* (1758).

The Turncoats (1709–10).

Ward, Ned, *The Reformer: Or, the Vices of the Age Expos'd, I. In Several Characters* (1701).

Ward, Ned, *The Modern World Disrob'd: Or, Both Sexes Stript of Their Pretended Vertue* (1708).

Watts, Isaac, *An Humble Attempt Toward the Revival of Practical Religion Among Christians, and Particularly the Protestant Dissenters* (1731).

Watts, Isaac, *Sermons on Various Subjects, Divine and Moral: With a Sacred Hymn Suited to Each Subject. In Two Volumes* (1734).

Wilkinson, Richard, *The Quaker's Wedding. A Comedy* (1723).

Wilson, William, *Charity, as a Rule of Conduct in the Affairs of a Religious Society, Explain'd and Recommended. A Sermon Preach'd to a Congregation of Protestant Dissenters in Newcastle-Upon-Tyne, November the 22nd 1733* (1734).

Withers, John, *A Defence of the True and Impartial Account of What Occurr'd at the Late Conference in Exon, and the Dissenters Vindicated from Mr. Agate's False Accusations* (Exon, 1707).

Withers, John, *A True and Impartial Account of What Occurred at the Late Conference in Exon. Publish'd to Prevent Misrepresentations* (Exon, 1707).
The World Display'd: Or Mankind Painted in Their Proper Colours (1742).

Secondary Materials

Aalders, Cynthia, '"Your Journal, My Love": Constructing Personal and Religious Bonds in Eighteenth-Century Women's Diaries', *Journal of Religious History*, 39, 3 (2014), pp. 386–98.

Acosta, Ana M., 'Spaces of Dissent and the Public Sphere in Hackney, Stoke Newington, and Newington Green', *Eighteenth-Century Life*, 27, 1 (2003), pp. 1–27.

Allen, Joan and Allen, Richard C. (eds.), *Faith of Our Fathers: Popular Culture and Belief in Post-Reformation England* (Newcastle upon Tyne: Cambridge Scholars Publishing, 2009).

Allen, Lucy Cory, 'Enchanting the Field: Where Should the History of Victorian and Edwardian Religion and Belief Go from Here?', *Cultural and Social History*, 18, 4 (2021), pp. 481–500.

Allen, Richard C., *Quaker Communities in Early Modern Wales: From Resistance to Respectability* (Cardiff: University of Wales Press, 2007).

Allen, Richard C., 'Restoration Quakerism, 1660–1691', in Stephen W. Angell and Pink Dandelion (eds.), *The Oxford Handbook of Quaker Studies* (Oxford and New York: Oxford University Press, 2013), pp. 29–45.

Allen, Richard C., and Moore, Rosemary, 'The Friends and Business in the Second Period', in Richard C. Allen and Rosemary Moore (eds.), *The Quakers, 1656–1723: The Evolution of an Alternative Community* (University Park, PA: Penn State University Press, 2018), pp. 238–62.

Alzale, Elissa B., 'From Individual to Citizen: Enhancing the Bonds of Citizenship through Religion in Locke's Political Theory', *Polity*, 46, 2 (2014), pp. 211–32.

Angell, Stephen W., and Dandelion, Pink (eds.), *The Oxford Handbook of Quaker Studies* (Oxford and New York: Oxford University Press, 2013).

Apetrei, Sarah, *Women, Feminism, and Religion in Early Enlightenment England* (Cambridge and New York: Cambridge University Press, 2010).

Arditi, Jorge, 'Hegemony and Etiquette: An Exploration on the Transformation of Practice and Power in Eighteenth-Century England', *British Journal of Sociology*, 45, 2 (1994), pp. 921–45.

Ballor, Jordan J., Systma, David, and Zuidema, Jason (eds.), *Church and School in Early Modern Protestantism* (Leiden and Boston, MA: Brill, 2013).

Bamford, Peter, '"For the Church or the Stable": A Chester Consistory Court Case of 1693–94', in Paul Middleton and Matthew Collins (eds.), *Matthew Henry: The Bible, Prayer, and Piety. A Tercentenary Celebration* (New York: T&T Clark, 2019), pp. 69–80.

Barber, Alex W., 'Censorship, Salvation and the Preaching of Francis Higgins: A Reconsideration of High Church Politics and Theology in the Early 18th Century', *Parliamentary History*, 33, 1 (2014), pp. 114–39.

Barry, Jonathan, 'Bristol Pride: Civic Identity in Bristol, c. 1640–1775', in Madge Dresser and Philip Ollerenshaw (eds.), *The Making of Modern Bristol* (Tiverton: Redcliffe Press, 1996), pp. 25–47.

Barry, Jonathan, 'Public Infidelity and Private Belief? The Discourse of Spirits in Enlightenment Bristol', in Owen Davies and Willem de Blécourt (eds.), *Beyond the Witch Trials. Witchcraft and Magic in Enlightenment Europe* (Manchester: Manchester University Press, 2004), pp. 117–43.

Barker-Benfield, G. J., *The Culture of Sensibility: Sex and Society in Eighteenth-Century Britain* (Chicago and London: Chicago University Press, 1992).

Bastow, Sarah L., *The Catholic Gentry of Yorkshire, 1536–1642: Resistance and Accommodation* (New York: Edwin Mellen Press, 2007).

Bates, Lucy, 'The Limits of Possibility in England's Long Reformation', *Historical Journal*, 53, 4 (2010), pp. 1049–70.

Beaver, Dan, 'Religion, Politics, and Society in Early Modern England: A Problem of Classification', *Journal of British Studies*, 33, 3 (July 1994), pp. 314–22.

Bebbington, David W., *Evangelicalism in Modern Britain: A History from the 1730s to the 1980s* (London: Taylor and Francis, 1989).

Berg, Maxine, *Luxury and Pleasure in Eighteenth-Century Britain* (New York: Oxford University Press, 2005).

Berman, David, *A History of Atheism in Britain: From Hobbes to Russell* (London and New York: Routledge, 1990).

Bermingham, Ann, and Brewer, John (eds.), *The Consumption of Culture, 1600–1800: Image, Object, Text* (London and New York: Routledge, 1995).

Berry, Helen, 'Rethinking Politeness in Eighteenth-Century England: Moll King's Coffee House and the Significance of "Flash Talk"', *Transactions of the Royal Historical Society*, 11 (2001), pp. 65–81.

'Creating Polite Space: The Organisation and Social Function of the Newcastle Assembly Rooms', in Helen Berry and Jeremy Gregory (eds.), *Creating and Consuming Culture in North-East England, 1660–1830* (Aldershot: Ashgate, 2004), pp. 120–40.

'The Pleasures of Austerity', *Journal for Eighteenth-Century Studies*, 37, 2 (2014), pp. 261–77.

Berry, Helen, and Gregory, Jeremy (eds.), *Creating and Consuming Culture in North-East England, 1660–1830* (Aldershot: Ashgate, 2004).

Black, Jeremy, *Charting the Past: The Historical Worlds of Eighteenth-Century England* (Bloomington, IN: Indiana University Press, 2019).

Bloomfield, Anne, and Watts, Ruth, 'Pedagogue of the Dance: The Dancing Master as Educator in the Long Eighteenth Century', *History of Education*, 37, 4 (2008), pp. 605–18.

Bolam, C. G., Goring, Jeremy, Short, H. L., and Thomas, Roger (eds.), *The English Presbyterians from Elizabethan Puritanism to Modern Unitarianism* (London: George Allen and Unwin, 1968).

Borsay, Peter, *The English Urban Renaissance. Culture and Society in the Provincial Town 1660–1770* (Oxford: Clarendon Press, 1989).

Borsay, Peter, 'The Topography of Power: Elites and the Political Landscape of the English Town, 1660–1760', in Stewart J. Brown, Frances Knight, and John Morgan-Guy (eds.), *Religion, Identity, and Conflict in Britain: From the Restoration to the Twentieth Century* (Farnham: Ashgate, 2013), pp. 47–62.

Bos, Jacques, 'The Hidden Self of the Hypocrite', in Toon van Houdt, Lan L. de Jong, Zoran Kwak, Marijke Spies, and Marc van Vaeck (eds.), *On the Edge of Truth and Honesty. Principles and Strategies of Fraud and Deceit in the Early Modern Period* (Leiden and Boston, MA: Brill, 2002), pp. 65–84.

Braddick, Michael, 'Administrative Performance: The Representation of Political Authority in Early Modern England', in Michael Braddick and John Walter (eds.), *Negotiating Power in Early Modern Society: Order, Hierarchy and Subordination in Britain and Ireland* (Cambridge and New York: Cambridge University Press, 2001), pp. 166–87.

Braddick, Michael, and Walter, John (eds.), *Negotiating Power in Early Modern Society: Order, Hierarchy and Subordination in Britain and Ireland* (Cambridge and New York: Cambridge University Press, 2001).

Bradley, James E., 'Nonconformity and the Electorate in Eighteenth-Century England', *Parliamentary History*, 6, 2 (1987), pp. 236–60.

Religion, Revolution, and English Radicalism. Nonconformity in Eighteenth-Century Politics and Society (Cambridge: Cambridge University Press, 1990).

'The Public, Parliament and the Protestant Dissenting Deputies, 1732–1740', *Parliamentary History*, 24, 1 (2005), pp. 71–90.

'Nonconformist Schools, the Schism Act, and the Limits of Toleration in England's Confessional State', in Jordan J.Ballor, David Systma, and Jason Zuidema (eds.), *Church and School in Early Modern Protestantism* (Leiden and Boston, MA: Brill, 2013), pp. 597–611.

Brewer, John, *Party Ideology and Popular Politics at the Accession of George III* (Cambridge: Cambridge University Press, 1976).

'"The Most Polite Age and the Most Vicious": Attitudes Towards Culture as a Commodity, 1600–1800', in Ann Bermingham and John Brewer (eds.), *The Consumption of Culture, 1600–1800: Image, Object, Text* (London and New York: Routledge, 1995), pp. 341–61.

Briggs, John H. Y., 'The Changing Shape of Nonconformity, 1662–2000', in Robert Pope (ed.), *T&T Clark Companion to Nonconformity* (London: Bloomsbury, 2013), pp. 3–26.

Briggs, Martin S., *Puritan Architecture and Its Future* (London and Redhill: Lutterworth Press, 1946).

Brown, Carys, 'Militant Catholicism, Interconfessional Relations, and the Rookwood Family of Stanningfield, Suffolk, c. 1689–1737', *Historical Journal*, 60, 1 (2017), pp. 21–45.

'Catholic Politics and Creating Trust in Eighteenth-Century England', *British Catholic History*, 33, 4 (2017), pp. 622–44.

'Politeness, hypocrisy, and Protestant Dissent in England after the Toleration Act, c.1689-c.1750', *Journal for Eighteenth-Century Studies*, 41, 1 (2018), pp. 61–80.

'Women and Religious Coexistence in England, c. 1689-c.1750', in Naomi Pullin and Kathryn Woods (eds.), *Negotiating Exclusion in the Early Modern England, 1550–1750* (London and New York: Routledge, 2021), pp. 68–87.

Brown, Stewart J., Knight, Frances, and Morgan-Guy, John (eds.), *Religion, Identity, and Conflict in Britain: From the Restoration to the Twentieth Century* (Farnham: Ashgate, 2013).

Burden, Mark, 'Dissent and Education', in Andrew Thompson (ed.), *The Oxford History of Protestant Dissenting Traditions, Volume II: The Long Eighteenth Century c. 1689-c. 1828* (Oxford: Oxford University Press, 2018), pp. 386–410.

Burns, William E., *An Age of Wonders. Prodigies, Politics, and Providence in England, 1657–1727* (Manchester and New York: Manchester University Press, 2002).

Burtt, Shelley, 'The Societies for the Reformation of Manners: Between John Locke and the Devil in Augustan England', in Roger D. Lund (ed.), *The Margins of Orthodoxy. Heterodox Writing and Cultural Response, 1660–1750* (Cambridge and New York: Cambridge University Press, 1995), pp. 149–69.

Capdeville, Valérie, 'Noise and Sound Reconciled: How London Clubs Shaped Conversation into a Social Art', *Etudes Epistémè*, 29 (2016), online edn: https://doi.org/10.4000/episteme.1208, accessed 30 March 2022.

Capdeville, Valérie, and Kerhervé, Alain (eds.), *British Sociability in the Long Eighteenth Century: Challenging the Anglo-French Connection* (Woodbridge: Boydell & Brewer, 2019).

Capp, Bernard, 'The Religious Marketplace: Public Disputations in Civil War and Interregnum England', *English Historical Review*, 129, 536 (2014), pp. 47–78.

Carlson, Eric, 'The Origins, Function, and Status of the Office of Churchwarden, with Particular Reference to the Diocese of Ely', in Margaret Spufford (ed.), *The World of Rural Dissenters, 1520–1725* (Cambridge: Cambridge University Press, 1995), pp. 164–207.

Clark, Brian Curtis, and Cruickshank, Joanna, 'Converting Mrs Crouch: Women, Wonders, and the Formation of English Methodism, 1738–1741', *Journal of Ecclesiastical History*, 65, 1 (2014), pp. 66–83.

Clark, J. C. D., *English Society, 1660–1832: Religion, Ideology and Politics During the Ancien Regime* (Cambridge and New York: Cambridge University Press, 2nd edn 2002).

'Secularization and Modernization: The Failure of a "Grand Narrative"', *Historical Journal*, 55, 1 (2012), pp. 161–94.

Clark, Jonathan, and Erskine-Hill, Howard (eds.), *Samuel Johnson in Historical Context* (Basingstoke: Palgrave Macmillan, 2002).

Clark, Peter, 'The Alehouse and Alternative Society', in Donald Pennington and Keith Thomas (eds.), *Puritans and Revolutionaries. Essays in Seventeenth-Century History Presented to Christopher Hill* (Oxford: Clarendon Press, 1978), pp. 47–72.

Claydon, Tony, *William III and the Godly Revolution* (Cambridge: Cambridge University Press, 1996).

Chamberlain, Jeffrey S., 'Portrait of a High Church Clerical Dynasty in Georgian England: The Frewens and Their World', in John Walsh, Colin Haydon, and Stephen Taylor (eds.), *The Church of England, c.1689–c.1833: From Toleration to Tractarianism* (Cambridge: Cambridge University Press, 1993), pp. 299–316.

'The Limits of Moderation in a Latitudinarian Parson: Or High-Church Zeal in a Low Churchman Discover'd', in Roger D. Lund (ed.), *The Margins of Orthodoxy. Heterodox Writing and Cultural Response 1660–1750* (Cambridge and New York: Cambridge University Press, 1995), pp. 195–215.

Coffey, John, 'Church and State, 1550–1750: The Emergence of Dissent', in Robert Pope (ed.), *T&T Clark Companion to Nonconformity* (London: Bloomsbury, 2013), pp. 47–78.

Coffey, John and Lim, Paul C. H. (eds.), *The Cambridge Companion to Puritanism* (Cambridge: Cambridge University Press, 2008).

Colley, Linda, 'The Loyal Brotherhood and the Cocoa Tree: The London Organization of the Tory Party, 1727–1760', *Historical Journal*, 20, 1 (1977), pp. 77–95.

In Defiance of Oligarchy. The Tory Party 1714–1760 (Cambridge: Cambridge University Press, 1982).

Britons. Forging the Nation, 1707–1837 (London: Pimlico, 1992).

Collinson, Patrick, 'Towards a Broader Understanding of the Early Dissenting Tradition', in C. Robert Cole and Michael E. Moody (eds.), *The Dissenting Tradition. Essays for Leyland H. Carlson* (Athens, OH: Ohio University Press, 1975), pp. 3–38.

'The Cohabitation of the Faithful with the Unfaithful', in Ole Peter Grell, Jonathan Israel, and Nicholas Tyacke (eds.), *From Persecution to Toleration. The Glorious Revolution and Religion in England* (Oxford: Oxford University Press, 1991), pp. 51–76.

'Antipuritanism', in John Coffey and Paul C. H. Lim (eds.), *The Cambridge Companion to Puritanism* (Cambridge: Cambridge University Press, 2008), pp. 19–33.

Cook, Alexander, Curthoys, Ned, and Konishi, Shino (eds.), *Representing Humanity in the Age of Enlightenment* (London: Pickering and Chatto, 2013).

Coolidge, John S., *The Pauline Renaissance in England. Puritanism and the Bible* (Oxford: Clarendon Press, 1970).

Connors, Richard, 'The Nature of Stability in the Augustan Age', *Parliamentary History*, 28, 1 (2009), pp. 27–40.

Copley, Stephen, 'Commerce, Conversation, and Politeness in the Early Eighteenth-Century Periodical', *Journal for Eighteenth-Century Studies*, 18, 1 (1995), pp. 63–77.

Corfield, Penelope J., '"An Age of Infidelity": Secularization in Eighteenth-Century England', *Social History*, 39, 2 (2014), pp. 229–47.

Cornwall, Robert D., 'The Church and Salvation: An Early Eighteenth-Century High-Church Anglican Perspective', *Anglican and Episcopal History*, 62, 2 (1993), pp. 175–91.

'Charles Leslie and the Political Implications of Theology', in William Gibson and Robert G. Ingram (eds.), *Religious Identities in Britain, 1660–1832* (Aldershot: Ashgate, 2005), pp. 27–42.

Cowan, Brian, 'The Rise of the Coffeehouse Reconsidered', *Historical Journal*, 47, 1 (2004), p. 21–46.

The Social Life of Coffee. The Emergence of the British Coffeehouse (New Haven and London: Yale University Press, 2005).

'"Restoration" England and the History of Sociability', in Valérie Capdeville and Alain Kerhervé (eds.), *British Sociability in the Long Eighteenth Century: Challenging the Anglo-French Connection* (Woodbridge: Boydell & Brewer, 2019), pp. 7–24.

Crawford, Patricia, *Women and Religion in England, 1500–1720* (London and New York: Routledge, 1993).

'Public Duty, Conscience, and Women in Early Modern England', in John Morrill, Paul Slack, and Daniel Woolf (eds.), *Public Duty and Private Conscience in Seventeenth-Century England: Essays Presented to G. E. Aylmer* (New York: Oxford University Press, 1993), pp. 57–76.

Cressy, David, *Birth, Marriage and Death. Ritual, Religion, and the Life-Cycle in Tudor and Stuart England*, (Oxford: Oxford University Press, 1997).

Cupples, Cynthia J., 'Pious Ladies and Methodist Madams: Sex and Gender in Anti-Methodist Writings of Eighteenth-Century England', *Critical Matrix*, 5, 2 (1990), pp. 30–60.

Cust, Richard and Hughes, Ann (eds.), *Conflict in Early Stuart England. Studies in Religion and Politics 1603–1642* (London and New York: Longman, 1989).

Daems, Jim, *Seventeenth-Century Literature and Culture* (London: Continuum, 2006).

Dasgupta, Sukanya, '"Of Polish'd Pillars or a Roofe of Gold": Authority and Affluence in the English Country-House Poem', in Matthew P. Romaniello and Charles Lipp (eds.), *Contested Spaces of Nobility in Early Modern Europe* (Farnham: Ashgate, 2011), pp. 189–212.

Davidson, Jenny, *Hypocrisy and the Politics of Politeness. Manners and Morals from Locke to Austen* (Cambridge: Cambridge University Press, 2004).

Davies, Adrian, *The Quakers in English Society* (Oxford: Oxford University Press, 2000).

Davies, Horton, *The English Free Churches* (London: Oxford University Press, 1952).

Davies, Owen, 'Urbanization and the Decline of Witchcraft: An Examination of London', *Journal of Social History*, 30, 3 (1997), pp. 597–617.

Davies, Owen and de Blécourt, Willem (eds.), *Beyond the Witch Trials. Witchcraft and Magic in Enlightenment Europe* (Manchester: Manchester University Press, 2004).

Davison, Kate, 'Occasional Politeness and Gentlemen's Laughter in Eighteenth-Century England', *Historical Journal*, 57, 4 (2014), pp. 921–45.

Daybell, James and Hinds, Peter (eds.), *Material Readings of Early Modern Culture: Texts and Social Practices, 1580–1730* (Basingstoke: Palgrave Macmillan, 2010).

Dean, Ann C., *The Talk of the Town. Figurative Publics in Eighteenth-Century Britain* (Lewisburg, NJ: Bucknell University Press, 2007).

Dickinson, H. T. (ed.), *A Companion to Eighteenth-Century Britain* (Oxford: Blackwell, 2002).

Dixon, Simon, 'The Life and Times of Peter Briggins', *Quaker Studies*, 10, 2 (2006), pp. 185–202.

'Quakers and the London Parish, 1670–1720', *The London Journal*, 32, 3 (2007), pp. 229–49.

Dresser, Madge, and Ollerenshaw, Philip (eds.), *The Making of Modern Bristol* (Tiverton: Redcliffe Press, 1996).

Dunkin, John, *The History and Antiquities of Bicester, a Market Town in Oxfordshire* (London: Richard and Arthur Taylor, 1816).

Dunn, John, 'The Claim to Freedom of Conscience, Freedom of Speech, Freedom of Thought, Freedom of Worship?', in Ole Peter Grell, Jonathan Israel, and Nicholas Tyacke (eds.), *From Persecution to Toleration: The Glorious Revolution and Religion in England* (Oxford: Oxford University Press, 1991), pp. 171–94.

Durston, Christopher, and Eales, Jacqueline, 'Introduction: The Puritan Ethos 1560–1700', in Christopher Durston and Jacqueline Eales (eds.), *The Culture of English Puritanism, 1560–1700* (Basingstoke: Macmillan, 1996), pp. 1–31.

The Culture of English Puritanism, 1560–1700 (Basingstoke: Macmillan, 1996).

Eiler, Ross E. Martinie, 'Luxury, Capitalism, and the Quaker Reformation, 1737–1798', *Quaker History*, 97, 1 (2008), pp. 11–31.

Estabrook, Carl, *Urbane and Rustic England: Cultural Ties and Social Spheres in the Provinces 1660–1780* (Manchester: Manchester University Press, 1998).

Fawcett, Trevor, 'Dance and Teachers of Dance in Eighteenth-Century Bath', *Bath History*, 2 (1988), pp. 27–48.

Fincham, Kenneth and Lake, Peter (eds.), *Religious Politics in Post-Reformation England. Essays in Honour of Nicholas Tyacke* (Woodbridge: The Boydell Press, 2006).

Fishwick, Henry, *A History of the Parish of Rochdale in the County of Lancaster* (Rochdale: J. Clegg, 1889).

Fitzpatrick, Martin Hugh, 'From Natural Law to Natural Rights? Protestant Dissent and Toleration in the Late Eighteenth Century', *History of European Ideas*, 42, 2 (2016), pp. 195–221.

Fletcher, Anthony, 'Beyond the Church: Women's Spiritual Experience at Home and in the Community 1600–1900', in R. N. Swanson (ed.), *Gender and Christian Religion* (Woodbridge: The Boydell Press, 1998), pp. 187–203.

Frijhoff, Willem, *Embodied Belief. Ten Essays on Religious Culture in Dutch History* (Hilversum: Uitgeverij Verbren, 2002).

French, Henry, *The Middle Sort of People in Provincial England, 1600–1750* (Oxford and New York: Oxford University Press, 2007).

Frost, J. William, 'From Plainness to Simplicity: Changing Quaker Ideals for Material Culture', in Emma Jones Lapsansky and Anne A. Verplanck (eds.), *Quaker Aesthetics. Reflections on a Quaker Ethic in American Design and Consumption* (Philadelphia, PA: Pennsylvania Press, 2003), pp. 16–42.

Garnett, Jane, and Matthew, Colin (eds.), *Revival and Religion Since 1700. Essays for John Walsh* (London and Rio Grande, TX: The Hambledon Press, 1993).

Gaskill, Malcolm, 'Witchcraft and Neighbourliness in Early Modern England', in Steve Hindle, Alexandra Shepard, and John Walter (eds.), *Remaking English Society. Social Relations and Social Change in Early Modern England* (Woodbridge: The Boydell Press, 2013), pp. 211–32.

Gibson, William, '"A Happy Fertile Soil Which Bringeth Forth Abundantly": The Diocese of Winchester, 1689–1800', in Jeremy Gregory and Jeffrey S. Chamberlain (eds.), *The National Church in Local Perspective: The Church of England and the Regions, 1660–1800* (Woodbridge: The Boydell Press, 2003), pp. 99–120.

Gibson, William and Ingram, Robert G. (eds.), *Religious Identities in Britain, 1660–1832* (Aldershot: Ashgate, 2005).

Gilmartin, Kevin (ed.), *Sociable Places: Locating Culture in Romantic-Period Britain* (Cambridge and New York: Cambridge University Press, 2017).

Girouard, Mark, *The English Town: A History of Urban Life* (New Haven and London: Yale University Press, 1990).

Gleadle, Katherine, '"Opinions Deliver'd in Conversation": Conversation, Politics, and Gender in the Late Eighteenth Century', in Jose Harris (ed.), *Civil Society in British History. Ideas, Identities, Institutions* (Oxford and New York: Oxford University Press, 2003), pp. 61–78.

Glickman, Gabriel, 'Political Conflict and the Memory of the Revolution in England, 1689-c.1745', in Tim Harris and Stephen Taylor (eds.), *The Final Crisis of the Stuart Monarchy: The Revolutions of 1688–91 in Their British, Atlantic, and European Contexts* (Woodbridge: The Boydell Press, 2013), pp. 243–72.

Goldie, Mark, 'The Theory of Religious Intolerance in Restoration England', in Ole Peter Grell, Jonathan Israel, and Nicholas Tyacke (eds.), *From Persecution to Toleration. The Glorious Revolution and Religion in England* (Oxford: Clarendon Press, 1991), pp. 331–68.

'The Unacknowledged Republic: Officeholding in Early Modern England', in Tim Harris (ed.) *The Politics of the Excluded* (Basingstoke: Palgrave Macmillan, 2001), pp. 153–94.

'Voluntary Anglicans', *Historical Journal*, 46, 4 (2003), pp. 977–90.

'Introduction', in Mark Goldie (ed.), *John Locke: A Letter Concerning Toleration and Other Writings* (Indianapolis, IN: Liberty Fund, 2010), pp. ix–xxiv.

Goldie, Mark, and Spurr, John, 'Politics and the Restoration Parish: Edward Fowler and the Struggle for St Giles Cripplegate', *English Historical Review*, 109, 432 (1994), pp. 572–96.

Gooch, Leo, '"The Religion for a Gentleman": The Northern Catholic Gentry in the Eighteenth Century', *Recusant History*, 23, 4 (1997), pp. 543–68.

Goring, Paul, 'Anglicanism, Enthusiasm, and Quixotism: Preaching and Politeness in Mid-Eighteenth-Century Literature', *Literature and Theology*, 15, 4 (2001), pp. 326–41.

Gowing, Laura, Hunter, Michael, and Rubin, Miri (eds.), *Love, Friendship and Faith in Europe, 1300–1800* (Basingstoke: Palgrave Macmillan, 2005).

Gray, Edward William, *The History and Antiquities of Newbury and Its Environs, Including Twenty-Eight Parishes Situate in the County of Berks* (Speenhamland: 1839).

Greaves, Richard L., 'The "Great Persecution" Reconsidered: The Irish Quakers and the Ethic of Suffering', in Muriel C. McClendon, Joseph P. Ward, and Michael MacDonald (eds.), *Protestant Identities. Religion, Society, and Self-Fashioning in Post-Reformation England* (Stanford, CA: Stanford University Press, 1999), pp. 211–33.

   'Seditious Sectaries or "Sober and Useful Inhabitants"? Changing Conceptions of the Quakers in Early Modern Britain', *Albion*, 33, 1 (Spring 2001), pp. 24–50.

Gregory, Brad S., *The Unintended Reformation. How a Religious Revolution Secularized Society* (Cambridge, MA: Harvard University Press, 2012).

Gregory, Jeremy, 'The Making of a Protestant Nation: "Success" and "Failure" in England's Long Reformation', in Nicholas Tyacke (ed.) *England's Long Reformation, 1500–1800* (London: UCL Press, 1998), pp. 307–34.

Gregory, Jeremy, 'Introduction: Transforming "the Age of Reason" into an "Age of Faiths": Or, Putting Religions and Beliefs (Back) into the Eighteenth Century', *Journal for Eighteenth-Century Studies*, 32, 3 (2009), pp. 287–305.

   '"In the Church I Will Live and Die"': John Wesley, the Church of England, and Methodism', in William Gibson and Robert G. Ingram (eds.), *Religious Identities in Britain, 1660–1832* (London and New York: Routledge, 2016 [1st edn 2005]), pp. 147–78.

   (ed.), *The Oxford History of Anglicanism, Volume II* (Oxford and New York: Oxford University Press, 2017).

Greig, Hannah, '"All Together and All Distinct": Public Sociability and Social Exclusivity in London's Pleasure Gardens, ca. 1740–1800', *Journal of British Studies*, 51, 1 (2012), pp. 50–73.

Grell, Ole Peter, Israel, Jonathan, and Tyacke, Nicholas (eds.), *From Persecution to Toleration: The Glorious Revolution and Religion in England* (Oxford: Oxford University Press, 1991).

Grell, Ole Peter, and Scribner, Bob (eds.), *Tolerance and Intolerance in the European Reformation* (Cambridge: Cambridge University Press, 1996).

Green, Adrian, and Crosbie, Barbara (eds.), *Economy and Culture in North-East England, 1500–1800* (Woodbridge: Boydell & Brewer, 2018).

Griggs, Burke W., 'Remembering the Puritan Past: John Walker and Anglican Memories of the English Civil War', in Muriel C. McClendon, Joseph P. Ward, and Michael MacDonald (eds.), *Protestant Identities. Religion, Society, and Self-Fashioning in Post-Reformation England* (Stanford, CA: Stanford University Press, 1999), pp. 158–91.

Griffiths, Paul, Fox, Adam, and Hindle, Steve (eds.), *The Experience of Authority in Early Modern England*, (Basingstoke: Palgrave Macmillan 1996).

Hailwood, Mark, 'Sociability, Work and Labouring Identity in Seventeenth-Century England', *Cultural and Social History*, 8, 1 (2011), pp. 9–29.

Alehouses and Good Fellowship in Early Modern England (Woodbridge: The Boydell Press, 2014).

Halsey, Katie, and Slinn, Jane, 'Introduction', in Katie Halsey and Jane Slinn (eds.), *The Concept and Practice of Conversation in the Long Eighteenth Century, 1688–1848* (Newcastle upon Tyne: Cambridge Scholars Publishing, 2008), pp. xi–xxvi.

Halsey, Katie, and Slinn, Jane (eds.), *The Concept and Practice of Conversation in the Long Eighteenth Century, 1688–1848* (Newcastle upon Tyne: Cambridge Scholars Publishing, 2008).

Hanlon, Gregory, *Confession and Community in Seventeenth-Century France. Catholic and Protestant Coexistence in Aquitaine* (Philadelphia, PA: University of Pennsylvania Press, 1993).

Harris, Jose (ed.), *Civil Society in British History. Ideas, Identities, Institutions* (Oxford and New York: Oxford University Press, 2003).

Harris, Tim (ed.), *Popular Culture in England, c. 1500–1800* (Basingstoke: Macmillan, 1995).

'The Legacy of the English Civil War: Rethinking the Revolution', *The European Legacy*, 5 (2000), pp. 501–14.

(ed.) *The Politics of the Excluded* (Basingstoke: Palgrave Macmillan, 2001).

Harris, Tim, and Taylor, Stephen (eds.), *The Final Crisis of the Stuart Monarchy: The Revolutions of 1688–91 in Their British, Atlantic, and European Contexts* (Woodbridge: The Boydell Press, 2013).

Harvey, Karen, 'The Substance of Sexual Difference: Change and Persistence in Representations of the Body in Eighteenth-Century England', *Gender and History*, 14, 2 (2002), pp. 202–23.

Haydon, Colin, *Anti-Catholicism in Eighteenth-Century England. A Political and Social Study* (Manchester and New York: Manchester University Press, 1993).

'"I Love My King and My Country, but a Roman Catholic I Hate": Anti-Catholicism and National Identity in Eighteenth-Century England', in Tony Claydon and Ian McBride (eds.), *Protestantism and National Identity. Britain and Ireland, c.1650-c.1850* (Cambridge: Cambridge University Press, 1998), pp. 33–52.

'Rural Religion and the Politeness of Parsons: The Church of England in South Warwickshire, c. 1689-c.1820', *Studies in Church History*, 42 (2006), pp. 282–93.

Healey, Jonathan, '"By the Charitie of Good People": Poverty and Neighbourly Support in Seventeenth-Century Lancashire', *Family and Community History*, 19, 2 (2016), pp. 83–94.

Healey, Robynne Rogers, 'Quietist Quakerism, 1692-c.1805', in Stephen W. Angell and Ben Pink Dandelion (eds.), *The Oxford Handbook of Quaker Studies* (Oxford and New York: Oxford University Press, 2013), pp. 47–62.

Hempton, David, 'Enlightenment and Faith', in Paul Langford (ed.), *The Eighteenth Century, 1688–1815* (Oxford and New York: Oxford University Press, 2002).

Methodism: Empire of the Spirit (New Haven and London: Yale University Press, 2005).

Hill II, Bracy V., 'Suffering for Their Consciences: The Depiction of Anabaptists and Baptists in the Eighteenth-Century Histories of Daniel Neal', *Welsh Journal of Religious History*, 5 (2010), pp. 84–113.

Hindle, Steve, 'The Keeping of the Public Peace', in Paul Griffiths, Adam Fox, and Steve Hindle (eds.), *The Experience of Authority in Early Modern England*, (Basingstoke: Palgrave Macmillan 1996), pp. 213–48.

On the Parish? The Micro-Politics of Poor Relief in Rural England, c. 1550–1750 (Oxford: Oxford University Press, 2004).

Hindle, Steve, Shepard, Alexandra, and Walter, John (eds.), *Remaking English Society. Social Relations and Social Change in Early Modern England* (Woodbridge: Boydell Press, 2013).

Hobsbawm, Eric, 'Methodism and the Threat of Revolution in Britain', *History Today*, 7 (1957), pp. 115–24.

Holmes, Geoffrey, *Politics, Religion and Society in England, 1679–1742* (London and Ronceverte: The Hambledon Press, 1986).

British Politics in the Age of Anne (London and Ronceverte: The Hambledon Press, 1987).

Horsley, Lee, '"Vox Populi" in the Political Literature of 1710', *Huntingdon Library Quarterly*, 38, 4 (1975), pp. 335–53.

van Houdt, Toon, de Jong, Lan L., Kwak, Zoran, Spies, Marijke, and van Vaeck, Marc (eds.), *On the Edge of Truth and Honesty. Principles and Strategies of Fraud and Deceit in the Early Modern Period* (Leiden and Boston, MA: Brill, 2002).

Houlbrooke, Ralph, *Death, Religion, and the Family in England, 1480–1750* (Oxford: Clarendon Press, 1998).

Houpt-Varner, Lindsay, 'Maintaining Moral Integrity: The Cultural and Economic Relationships of Quakers in North-East England, 1653–1700', in Adrian Green and Barbara Crosbie (eds.), *Economy and Culture in North-East England, 1500–1800* (Woodbridge: Boydell & Brewer, 2018), pp. 136–155.

Houston, R. A., *Punishing the Dead? Suicide, Lordship, and Community in Britain, 1500–1830* (Oxford: Oxford University Press, 2010).

Houston, Alan, and Pincus, Steve (eds.), *A Nation Transformed. England After the Restoration* (Cambridge: Cambridge University Press, 2001).

Howard, Skiles, 'Rival Discourses of Dancing in Early Modern England', *Studies in English Literature, 1500–1900*, 36, 1 (1996), pp. 31–56.

Hsueh, Vicki, 'Intoxicated Reasons, Rational Feelings: Rethinking the Early Modern English Public Sphere', *Review of Politics*, 78, 1 (2016), pp. 27–57.

'Puritanism and Gender', in John Coffey and Paul C. H. Lim (eds.), *The Cambridge Companion to Puritanism* (Cambridge: Cambridge University Press, 2008), pp. 294–308.

Hunt, N. C., *Two Early Political Associations. The Quakers and the Dissenting Deputies in the Age of Sir Robert Walpole* (Oxford: Clarendon Press, 1961).

Hunter, Michael, 'The Decline of Magic: Challenge and Response in Early Enlightenment England', *Historical Journal*, 55, 2 (2012), pp. 399–425.

Hurley, Alison E., 'Peculiar Christians, Circumstantial Courtiers, and the Making of Conversation in Seventeenth-Century England', *Representations*, 111, 1 (2010), pp. 33–59.

Hurwich, Judith J., '"A Fanatick Town": The Political Influence of Dissenters in Coventry, 1660–1720', *Midland History*, 4, 1 (1977), pp. 15–47.

Ingram, Martin, 'From Reformation to Toleration: Popular Religious Cultures in England, 1540–1690', in Tim Harris (ed.), *Popular Culture in England, c. 1500–1800* (Basingstoke: Macmillan, 1995), pp. 95–113.

'Church Courts in England', in Charles H.Parker and Gretchen D. Starr-LeBeau (eds.), *Judging Faith, Punishing Sin: Inquisitions and Consistories in the Early Modern World* (Cambridge: Cambridge University Press, 2017), pp. 89–103.

Ingram, Robert G., *Reformation Without End. Religion, Politics, and the Past in Post-Revolutionary England* (Manchester: Manchester University Press, 2018).

'The Church of England, 1714–1783', in Jeremy Gregory (ed.), *The Oxford History of Anglicanism, Volume II* (Oxford and New York: Oxford University Press, 2017), pp. 50–67.

Isaacs, Tina, 'The Anglican Hierarchy and the Reformation of Manners, 1688–1738', *Journal of Ecclesiastical History*, 33, 3 (1982), pp. 391–411.

Jacob, W. M., '"… This Congregation Here Present …": Seating in Parish Churches During the Long Eighteenth Century', *Studies in Church History*, 42 (2006), pp. 294–304.

Jennings, Judith, 'Mary Morris Knowles: Devout, Worldly, and "Gay"?', *Quaker Studies*, 14, 2 (2010), pp. 195–211.

Jeremy, David (ed.), *Religion, Business, and Wealth in Modern Britain* (London: Routledge, 1998).

Jones, Norman L., and Woolf, Daniel (eds.), *Local Identities in Late Medieval and Early Modern England* (Basingstoke: Palgrave Macmillan, 2007).

Kay, John, 'The Hypocrisy of Jonathan Swift: Swift's *Project* Reconsidered', *University of Toronto Quarterly*, 44, 3 (1975), pp. 213–23.

Kaplan, Benjamin, 'Fictions of Privacy: House Chapels and the Spatial Accommodation of Religious Dissent in Early Modern Europe', *American Historical Review*, 107, 4 (2002), pp. 1031–64.

Divided by Faith. Religious Conflict and the Practice of Toleration in Early Modern Europe (Cambridge, MA: Belknap Press, 2007).

Kaplan, Benjamin, Moore, Bob, van Nierop, Henk, and Pollmann, Judith (eds.), *Catholic Communities in Protestant States: Britain and the Netherlands 1580–1720* (Manchester: Manchester University Press, 2009).

Kaushik, Sandeep, 'Resistance, Loyalty and Recusant Politics: Sir Thomas Tresham and the Elizabethan State', *Midland History*, 21, 1 (1996), pp. 37–72.

Keeble, N. H., *The Literary Culture of Nonconformity in Later Seventeenth-Century England* (Leicester: Leicester University Press, 1987).

Kelleher, Paul, 'Reason, Madness, and Sexuality in the British Public Sphere', *The Eighteenth Century*, 53, 3 (2012), pp. 291–315.

Klein, Lawrence E., 'Gender, Conversation, and the Public Sphere in Early Eighteenth-Century England', in Judith Still and Michael Worton (eds.), *Textuality and Sexuality. Reading Theories and Practices* (Manchester and New York: Manchester University Press, 1993), pp. 100–15.

'Coffeehouse Civility, 1660–1714: An Aspect of Post-Courtly Culture in England', *Huntingdon Library Quarterly*, 59, 1 (1996), pp. 30–51.

'Politeness and the Interpretation of the British Eighteenth Century', *Historical Journal*, 45, 4 (2002), pp. 869–98.

Knights, Mark, 'Occasional Conformity and the Representation of Dissent: Hypocrisy, Sincerity, Moderation and Zeal', *Parliamentary History*, 24, 1 (2005), pp. 41–57.

Representation and Misrepresentation in Later Stuart Britain. Partisanship and Political Culture (Oxford and New York: Oxford University Press, 2005).

'Possessing the Visual: The Materiality of Visual Print Culture in Later Stuart Britain', in James Daybell and Peter Hinds (eds.), *Material Readings of Early Modern Culture: Texts and Social Practices, 1580–1730* (Basingstoke: Palgrave Macmillan, 2010), pp. 85–102.

The Devil in Disguise: Deception, Delusion, and Fanaticism in the Early English Enlightenment (Oxford and New York: Oxford University Press, 2011).

Kobza, Meghan, 'Dazzling or Fantastically Dull? Re-Examining the Eighteenth-Century London Masquerade', *Journal for Eighteenth-Century Studies*, 43, 2 (2020), pp. 161–81.

Lake, Peter, 'Anti-Popery: The Structure of a Prejudice', in Richard Cust and Ann Hughes (eds.), *Conflict in Early Stuart England. Studies in Religion and Politics, 1603–1642* (London and New York: Longman, 1989), pp. 72–106.

'Anti-Puritanism: The Structure of a Prejudice', in Kenneth Fincham and Peter Lake (eds.), *Religious Politics in Post-Reformation England. Essays in Honour of Nicholas Tyacke* (Woodbridge: The Boydell Press, 2006), pp. 80–97.

Langford, Paul, *A Polite and Commercial People. England 1727–1783* (Oxford: Clarendon Press, 1989).

'The Uses of Eighteenth-Century Politeness', *Transactions of the Royal Historical Society*, 12 (2002), pp. 311–31.

(ed.), *The Eighteenth Century, 1688–1815* (Oxford and New York: Oxford University Press, 2002).

Lapsansky, Emma Jones, 'Past Plainness to Present Simplicity: A Search for Quaker Identity', in Emma Jones Lapsansky and Anne A. Verplanck (eds.), *Quaker Aesthetics. Reflections on a Quaker Ethic in American Design and Consumption* (Philadelphia, PA: Pennsylvania Press, 2003), pp. 1–15.

'Plainness and Simplicity', in Stephen W.Angell and Pink Dandelion (eds.), *The Oxford Handbook of Quaker Studies* (Oxford and New York: Oxford University Press, 2013), pp. 335–46.

Lapsansky, Emma Jones and Verplanck, Anne A. (eds.), *Quaker Aesthetics. Reflections on a Quaker Ethic in American Design and Consumption* (Philadelphia, PA: Pennsylvania Press, 2003).

Laqueur, Thomas W., 'Cemeteries, Religion, and the Culture of Capitalism', in Jane Garnett and Colin Matthew (eds.), *Revival and Religion since 1700. Essays for John Walsh* (London and Rio Grande, TX: The Hambledon Press, 1993), pp. 183–200.

Laslett, Peter, *The World We Have Lost* (London: Methuen, 1965).

Lewycky, Nadine, and Morton, Adam, 'Introduction', in Nadine Lewycky and Adam Morton (eds.), *Getting Along? Religious Identities and Confessional Relations in Early Modern England – Essays in Honour of Professor W. J. Sheils* (Farnham: Ashgate, 2012), pp. 1–28.

Lewycky, Nadine, and Morton, Adam (eds.), *Getting Along? Religious Identities and Confessional Relations in Early Modern England – Essays in Honour of Professor W. J. Sheils* (Farnham: Ashgate, 2012).

Lincoln, Andrew, 'War and the Culture of Politeness: The Case of *The Tatler* and *The Spectator*', *Eighteenth-Century Life*, 36, 2 (2012), pp. 60–79.

Loveman, Kate, *Reading Fictions, 1660–1740. Deception in English Literary and Political Culture* (Farnham: Ashgate, 2008).

Lund, Roger D. (ed.), *The Margins of Orthodoxy. Heterodox Writing and Cultural Response 1660–1750* (Cambridge and New York: Cambridge University Press, 1995).

Luria, Keith P., *Sacred Boundaries. Religious Coexistence and Conflict in Early Modern France* (Washington, DC: The Catholic University of America Press, 2005).

Lynch, Jack, *Deception and Detection in Eighteenth-Century Britain* (Farnham: Ashgate, 2008).

Mackenzie, Jon, '1689 and All That. An Exploration of the Function and Form of the Second London Baptist Confession of Faith', *Baptist Quarterly*, 42, 8 (2008), pp. 555–68.

Maclear, J. F., 'Isaac Watts and the Idea of Public Religion', *Journal of the History of Ideas*, 53, 1 (1992), pp. 25–45.

Major, Emma, *Madam Britannia: Women, Church, and Nation, 1712–1812* (Oxford and New York: Oxford University Press, 2011).

McClendon, Muriel C., Ward, Joseph P., and MacDonald, Michael (eds.), *Protestant Identities: Religion, Society, and Self-Fashioning in Post-Reformation England* (Stanford, CA: Stanford University Press, 1999).

McShane, Angela, 'Roaring Royalists and Ranting Brewers: The Politicisation of Drunkenness in Political Broadside Ballads from 1640 to 1689', in Adam Smyth (ed.), *A Pleasing Sinne. Drink and Conviviality in Seventeenth-Century England* (Cambridge: D. S. Brewer, 2004), pp. 69–87.

'Material Culture and "Political Drinking" in Seventeenth-Century England', in Phil Withington and Angela McShane (eds.), *Cultures of Intoxication* (Oxford: Oxford University Press, 2014), pp. 247–76.

'Drink, Song, and Politics in Early Modern England', *Popular Music*, 35, 2 (2016), pp. 166–90.

Mee, Jon, 'Turning Things Around Together: Enlightenment and Conversation', in Alexander Cook, Ned Curthoys, and Shino Konishi (eds.), *Representing Humanity in the Age of Enlightenment* (London: Pickering and Chatto, 2013), pp. 53–63.

Mendelson, Sara, 'Neighbourhood as Female Community in the Life of Anne Dormer', in Stephanie Tarbin and Susan Broomhall (eds.), *Women, Identities and Communities in Early Modern Europe* (Aldershot: Ashgate, 2008), pp. 153–64.

Middleton, Paul, and Collins, Matthew (eds.), *Matthew Henry: The Bible, Prayer, and Piety: A Tercentenary Celebration* (New York: T&T Clark, 2019).

Miller, John, *Popery and Politics in England, 1660–1688* (Cambridge: Cambridge University Press, 1973).

'"A Suffering People": English Quakers and Their Neighbours, c. 1650-c. 1750', *Past and Present*, 188, 1 (2005), pp. 71–103.

Cities Divided. Politics and Religion in English Provincial Towns, 1660–1722 (Oxford and New York: Oxford University Press, 2007).

Miller, Stephen, *Conversation: A History of a Declining Art* (New Haven, CT: Yale University Press, 2008).

Monod, Paul Kléber, *Jacobitism and the English People, 1688–1788* (Cambridge and New York: Cambridge University Press, 1993).

'A Voyage out of Staffordshire; or Samuel Johnson's Jacobite Journey', in Jonathan Clark and Howard Erskine-Hill (eds.), *Samuel Johnson in Historical Context* (Basingstoke: Palgrave Macmillan, 2002), pp. 11–43.

Morrill, John, Slack, Paul, and Woolf, Daniel (eds.), *Public Duty and Private Conscience in Seventeenth-Century England: Essays Presented to G. E. Aylmer* (New York: Oxford University Press, 1993).

Mostefai, Ourida, 'Dissensus and Toleration: Reconsidering Tolerance in the Age of Enlightenment', *Studies in Eighteenth-Century Culture*, 47 (2018), pp. 269–73.

Mullett, Michael, 'From Sect to Denomination? Social Developments in Eighteenth-Century English Quakerism', *Journal of Religious History*, 13, 2 (1984), pp. 168–91.

Mullin, Janet E., '"We Had Carding": Hospitable Card Play and Polite Domestic Sociability Among the Middling Sort in Eighteenth-Century England', *Journal of Social History*, 42, 4 (2009), pp. 989–1008.

Neal, Daniel, *The History of the Puritans or Protestant Non-Conformists* (London: 4 vols. 1732).

Nesti, Donald S., 'Early Quaker Ecclesiology' *Quaker Religious Thought*, 47 (1978), pp. 4–34.

Neufeld, Matthew, *The Civil Wars after 1660: Public Remembering in Late Stuart England* (Woodbridge: The Boydell Press, 2013).

Nicholls, James, 'Vinum Britannicum: The "Drink Question" in Early Modern England', *Social History of Alcohol and Drugs*, 22, 2 (2008), pp. 190–208.

O'Brien, Patrick K., 'Inseparable Connections: Trade, Economy, Fiscal State, and the Expansion of Empire, 1688–1815', in P. J. Marshall and Alaine Low (eds.), *The Oxford History of the British Empire: Volume II: The Eighteenth Century* (Oxford: Oxford University Press, 1998), pp. 53–77.

Owen, Susan, *Restoration Theatre and Crisis* (Oxford: Clarendon Press, 1996).

Paul, Tawny, *The Poverty of Disaster: Debt and Insecurity in Eighteenth-Century Britain* (Cambridge: Cambridge University Press, 2019).

Peltonen, Markku, 'Politeness and Whiggism, 1688–1732', *Historical Journal*, 48, 2 (2005), pp. 391–414.

Pennington, Donald, and Thomas, Keith (eds.), *Puritans and Revolutionaries. Essays in Seventeenth-Century History Presented to Christopher Hill* (Oxford: Clarendon Press, 1978).

Phillipson, Nicholas, 'Politeness and Politics in the Reign of Anne and the Early Hanoverians', in J. G. A. Pocock, Gordon J. Schochet, and Lois Schwoerer (eds.), *The Varieties of British Political Thought, 1500–1800* (New York and Cambridge: Cambridge University Press, 1993), pp. 211–45.

Pike, Geoffrey Holden, *Ancient Meeting-Houses; Or Memorial Pictures of Nonconformity in Old London* (London: S. W. Partridge & Co., 1870).

Pinches, Sylvia, 'Women as Objects and Agents of Charity in Eighteenth-Century Birmingham', in Rosemary Sweet and Penelope Lane (eds.), *Women and Urban Life in Eighteenth-Century England* (London and New York: Routledge, 2016), pp. 65–86.

Pincus, Steve, '"Coffee Politicians Does Create": Coffeehouses and Restoration Political Culture', *Journal of Modern History*, 67, 4 (December, 1995), pp. 807–34.

Pocock, J. G. A., Schochet, Gordon J. and Schwoerer, Lois (eds.), *The Varieties of British Political Thought, 1500–1800* (New York and Cambridge: Cambridge University Press, 1993).

Pope, Robert (ed.), *T&T Clark Companion to Nonconformity* (London: Bloomsbury, 2013).

Popkin, Richard H., 'The Deist Challenge', in Ole Peter Grell, Jonathan Israel, and Nicholas Tyacke (eds.), *From Persecution to Toleration: The Glorious Revolution and Religion in England* (Oxford: Oxford University Press, 1991), pp. 195–216.

Port, M. H. (ed.), *The Commissions for Building Fifty New Churches: The Minute Book 1711–27: A Calendar* (London: London Record Society, 1986).

Porter, Roy, 'The Drinking Man's Disease: The "Pre-History" of Alcoholism in Georgian Britain', *British Journal of Addiction*, 80, 4 (1985), pp. 385–96.

Prior, Ann, and Kirby, Maurice, 'The Society of Friends and Business Culture, 1700–1830', in David Jeremy (ed.), *Religion, Business, and Wealth in Modern Britain* (London: Routledge, 1998), pp. 115–136.

Pullin, Naomi, *Female Friends and the Making of Transatlantic Quakerism, 1650–c.1750* (Cambridge: Cambridge University Press, 2018).

'Providence, Punishment, and Identity Formation in the Late-Stuart Quaker Community, c. 1650–1700', *Seventeenth Century*, 31, 4 (2016), pp. 471–94.

Pullin, Naomi, and Woods, Kathryn (eds.), *Negotiating Exclusion in the Early Modern England, 1550–1750* (London and New York: Routledge, 2021).

Raffe, Alasdair, 'Presbyterians', in Andrew Thompson (ed.), *The Oxford History of Protestant Dissenting Traditions, Volume II: The Long Eighteenth Century* (Oxford and New York: Oxford University Press, 2018), pp. 11–29.

Ramsbottom, John D., 'Presbyterians and "Partial Conformity" in the Restoration Church of England', *Journal of Ecclesiastical History*, 43, 2 (1992), pp. 249–70.

Rendell, Jane, 'Almack's Assembly Rooms: A Site of Sexual Pleasure', *Journal of Architectural Education*, 55, 3 (2002), pp. 136–49.

Rex, Richard, 'Introduction: The Morning Star or the Sunset of the Reformation?', *Bulletin of the John Rylands Library*, 90, 1 (2014), pp. 7–23.

Rivers, Isabel, *Reason, Grace, and Sentiment. A Study of the Language of Religion and Ethics in England, 1660–1780* (Cambridge: Cambridge University Press, 1991), vol. 1.

Rose, Craig, 'Providence, Protestant Union, and Godly Reformation in the 1690s', *Transactions of the Royal Historical Society*, 3 (1993), pp. 151–69.

Ross, H. S. 'Some Aspects of the Development of Presbyterian Polity in England', *Journal of the Presbyterian Historical Society of England*, 13 (1964)

Rosman, Doreen, *The Evolution of the English Churches, 1500–2000* (Cambridge: Cambridge University Press, 2003).

Rowlands, Marie B. (ed.), *English Catholics of Parish and Town, 1558–1778* (London: Catholic Record Society, 1999).

Royston, Darren, '"Filthie Groping and Uncleane Handlings": An Examination of Touching Moments in Dance of Court and Courtship', in Jackie Watson and Amy Kenny (eds.), *The Senses in Early Modern England, 1558–1660* (Manchester: Manchester University Press, 2015), pp. 55–73.

Runciman, David, *Political Hypocrisy. The Mask of Power from Hobbes to Orwell and Beyond* (Princeton and Oxford: Princeton University Press, 2008).

Russell, Gillian, '"The Place Is Not Free to You": The Georgian Assembly Room and the Ends of Sociability', in Kevin Gilmartin (ed.), *Sociable Places: Locating Culture in Romantic-Period Britain* (Cambridge and New York: Cambridge University Press, 2017), pp. 143–62.

Scammell, Lorna, 'Town Versus Country: The Property of Everyday Consumption in the Late Seventeenth and Early Eighteenth Centuries', in Jon Stobart and Alastair Owens (eds.), *Urban Fortunes: Prosperity and Inheritance in the Town, 1700–1900* (Aldershot: Ashgate, 2000), pp. 26–49.

Schochet, Gordon J. (ed.), with Tatspugh, Patricia E., and Brobeck, Carol, *Restoration, Ideology, and Revolution* (Washington, DC: The Folger Institute, 1990).

Schochet, Gordon J. '"The Tyranny of a Popish Successor" and the Politics of Religious Toleration', in Gordon J. Schochet (ed.), with Patricia E. Tatspugh and Carol Brobeck, *Restoration, Ideology, and Revolution* (Washington, DC: The Folger Institute, 1990), pp. 83–103.

Schwartz, Sally, 'William Penn and Toleration: Colonial Foundations of Pennsylvania', *Pennsylvania History*, 50, 4 (1983), pp. 284–312.

Scribner, Bob, 'Preconditions of Tolerance and Intolerance in Sixteenth-Century Germany', in Ole Peter Grell and Bob Scribner (eds.), *Tolerance and Intolerance in the European Reformation* (Cambridge: Cambridge University Press, 1996), pp. 32–47.

Seed, John, 'History and Narrative Identity: Religious Dissent and the Politics of Memory in Eighteenth-Century England', *Journal of British Studies*, 44, 1 (2005), pp. 46–63.

Sell, Alan P. F., *Dissenting Thought and the Life of the Churches. Studies in an English Tradition* (San Francisco: Mellen Research University Press, 1990).

Shagan, Ethan H., *The Rule of Moderation. Violence, Religion and the Politics of Restraint in Early Modern England* (Cambridge: Cambridge University Press, 2011).

Sheils, William, 'Catholics and Their Neighbours in a Rural Community: Egton Chapelry, 1590–1780', *Northern History*, 34, 1 (1998), pp. 109–33.

'"Getting On" and "Getting Along" in Parish and Town: English Catholics and Their Neighbours', in Benjamin J.Kaplan, Bob Moore, Henk van Nierop, and Judith Pollmann (eds.), *Catholic Communities in Protestant States: Britain and the Netherlands 1580–1720* (Manchester: Manchester University Press, 2009), pp. 67–83.

Shell, Alison, 'Sacrilege, Tractarian Fiction and the Very Long Reformation', *Reformation*, 24, 2 (2019), pp. 195–209.

Shepard, Alexandra, '"Swil-bols and Tos-pots": Drink Culture and Male Bonding in England, c. 1560–1640', in Laura Gowing, Michael Hunter, and Miri Rubin (eds.), *Love, Friendship, and Faith in Europe, 1300–1800* (Basingstoke: Palgrave Macmillan, 2005), pp. 110–30.

'Crediting Women in the Early Modern English Economy', *Historical Workshop Journal*, 79, 1 (2015), pp. 1–24.

Sirota, Brent S., *Christian Monitors: The Church of England and the Age of Benevolence, 1680–1730* (New Haven, CT: Yale University Press, 2014).

'The Occasional Conformity Controversy, Moderation, and the Anglican Critique of Modernity, 1700–1714', *Historical Journal*, 57, 1 (2014), pp. 81–105.

Sketch of the History and Proceedings of the Deputies: Appointed to Protect the Civil Rights of the Protestant Dissenters (London: 1813).

Smith, Karen E., 'Baptists', in Andrew Thompson (ed.), *The Oxford History of Protestant Dissenting Traditions, Vol. II: The Long Eighteenth Century* (Oxford and New York: Oxford University Press, 2018), pp. 54–76.

Smith, William, *A New and Compendious History, of the County of Warwick* (Birmingham: 1830).

Smyth, Adam (ed.), *A Pleasing Sinne. Drink and Conviviality in Seventeenth-Century England* (Cambridge: D. S. Brewer, 2004).

Snape, Michael Francis, 'Anti-Methodism in Eighteenth-Century England: The Pendle Forest Riots of 1748', *Journal of Ecclesiastical History*, 49, 2 (1998), pp. 257–81.

Snell, K. D. M., *Parish and Belonging. Community, Identity and Welfare in England and Wales, 1700–1950* (Cambridge: Cambridge University Press, 2006).

Southcombe, George, *The Culture of Dissent in Restoration England: The Wonders of the Lord* (Woodbridge: The Boydell Press, 2019).

Sowerby, Scott, *Making Toleration. The Repealers and the Glorious Revolution* (Cambridge, MA and London: Harvard University Press, 2013).

Spaeth, Donald, *The Church in an Age of Danger: Parsons and Parishioners, 1660–1740* (Cambridge: Cambridge University Press, 2000).

Speck, W. A., 'The Current State of Sacheverell Scholarship', *Parliamentary History*, 31, 1 (2012), pp. 16–27.

Spohnholz, Jesse, *The Tactics of Toleration. A Refugee Community in the Age of Religious Wars* (Newark, DE: University of Delaware Press, 2011).

Spufford, Margaret (ed.), *The World of Rural Dissenters, 1520–1725* (Cambridge: Cambridge University Press, 1995).

Spurr, John, 'The Church of England, Comprehension and the Toleration Act of 1689', *English Historical Review*, 104, 413 (1989), pp. 927–46.

Starkie, Andrew, *The Church of England and the Bangorian Controversy, 1716–1721* (Woodbridge: The Boydell Press, 2007).

Stevens, Ralph, *Protestant Pluralism: The Reception of the Toleration Act, 1689–1720* (Woodbridge: The Boydell Press, 2018).

Stevenson, Bill, 'The Social Integration of Post-Restoration Dissenters, 1660–1725', in Margaret Spufford (ed.), *The World of Rural Dissenters, 1520–1725* (Cambridge: Cambridge University Press, 1995), pp. 360–87.

Still, Judith, and Worton, Michael (eds.), *Textuality and Sexuality. Reading Theories and Practices* (Manchester and New York: Manchester University Press, 1993).

Stobart, Jon, 'Social and Geographical Contexts of Property Transmission in the Eighteenth Century', in Jon Stobart and Alastair Owens (eds.), *Urban Fortunes: Property and Inheritance in the Town, 1700–1900* (London and New York: Routledge, 2016), pp. 108–30.

Strivens, Robert, *Philip Doddridge and the Shaping of Evangelical Dissent* (Farnham: Ashgate, 2015).

Stubenrach, Joseph, *The Evangelical Age of Ingenuity in Industrial Britain* (Oxford and New York: Oxford University Press, 2016).

Swanson, R. N. (ed.), *Gender and Christian Religion* (Woodbridge: The Boydell Press, 1998).

Sweet, Rosemary, and Lane, Penelope (eds.), *Women and Urban Life in Eighteenth-Century England: "On the Town"* (London: Routledge, 2016).

Tadmor, Naomi, *Family and Friends in Eighteenth-Century England* (Cambridge: Cambridge University Press, 2001).

'Friends and Neighbours in Early Modern England: Biblical Translations and Social Norms', in Laura Gowing, Michael Hunter, and Miri Rubin (eds.), *Love, Friendship and Faith in Europe, 1300–1800* (Basingstoke: Palgrave Macmillan, 2005), pp. 150–76.

Tarbin, Stephanie, and Broomhall, Susan (eds.), *Women, Identities and Communities in Early Modern Europe* (Aldershot: Ashgate, 2008).

Taylor, Stephen, 'Sir Robert Walpole, the Church of England, and the Quakers Tithe Bill of 1736', *Historical Journal*, 28, 1 (1985), pp. 51–77.

'William Warburton and the Alliance of Church and State', *Journal of Ecclesiastical History*, 43, 2 (1992), pp. 271–86.

'Whigs, Tories, and Anticlericalism: Ecclesiastical Courts Legislation in 1733', *Parliamentary History*, 19, 3 (2000), pp. 329–55.

Thale, Mary, 'Deists, Papists, and Methodists at London Debating Societies, 1749–1799', *History*, 86, 283 (2001), pp. 328–47.

Thomas, Keith, *The Ends of Life: Roads to Fulfilment in Early Modern England* (Oxford and New York: Oxford University Press, 2009).

Thomas, Roger, 'The Non-Subscription Controversy Amongst Dissenters in 1719: The Salters' Hall Debate', *Journal of Ecclesiastical History*, 4, 2 (1953), pp. 162–86.

'Parties in Nonconformity', in C. G. Bolam, Jeremy Goring, H. L. Short, and Roger Thomas (eds.), *The English Presbyterians. From Elizabethan Puritanism to Modern Unitarianism* (London: George Allen and Unwin, 1968), pp. 93–112.

Thompson, Andrew, 'Contesting the Test Act: Dissent, Parliament and the Public in the 1730s', *Parliamentary History*, 24, 1 (2005), pp. 58–70.

'Introduction', in Andrew Thompson (ed.), *The Oxford History of Protestant Dissenting Traditions, Vol. II: The Long Eighteenth Century* (Oxford and New York: Oxford University Press, 2018), pp. 1–7.

(ed.), *The Oxford History of Protestant Dissenting Traditions, Vol. II: The Long Eighteenth Century* (Oxford and New York: Oxford University Press, 2018).

Thompson, E. P., *Customs in Common* (London: Penguin, 1993).

Timmons, Stephen A., 'From Persecution to Toleration in the West Country, 1672–1692', *The Historian*, 68, 3 (2006), pp. 461–88.

Trevor-Roper, Hugh, 'Toleration and Religion after 1688', in Ole Peter Grell, Jonathan Israel, and Nicholas Tyacke (eds.), *From Persecution to Toleration: The Glorious Revolution and Religion in England* (Oxford: Clarendon Press, 1991), pp. 389–410.

Tyacke, Nicholas, 'The "Rise of Puritanism" and the Legalizing of Dissent, 1571–1719', in Ole Peter Grell, Jonathan Israel, and Nicholas Tyacke (eds.), *From Persecution to Toleration: The Glorious Revolution and Religion in England* (Oxford: Oxford University Press, 1991), pp. 17–50.

Tyacke, Nicholas (ed.), *England's Long Reformation, 1500–1800* (London: UCL Press, 1998).

Wadsworth, A. P., 'The First Manchester Sunday Schools', *Bulletin of the John Rylands Library*, 33, 2 (1951), pp. 299–326.

Wahrman, Dror, 'National Society, Communal Culture: An Argument About the Recent Historiography of Eighteenth-Century Britain', *Social History*, 17, 1 (1992), pp. 43–72.

Waligore, Joseph, 'Christian Deism in Eighteenth Century England', *International Journal of Philosophy and Theology*, 75, 3 (2014), pp. 205–22.

Wallis, Patrick, Colson, Justin, and Chilosi, David, 'Structural Change and Economic Growth in the British Economy before the Industrial Revolution, 1500–1800', *The Journal of Economic History*, 78, 3 (2018), pp. 862–903.

Walsh, John, Haydon, Colin, and Taylor, Stephen (eds.), *The Church of England c.1689-c.1833: From Toleration to Tractarianism* (Cambridge: Cambridge University Press, 1993).

Walsham, Alexandra, *Charitable Hatred. Tolerance and Intolerance in England, 1500–1700* (Manchester: Manchester University Press, 2006).

'The Reformation and "the Disenchantment of the World" Reassessed', *Historical Journal*, 51, 2 (2008), pp. 497–528.

'The Godly and Popular Culture', in John Coffey and Paul C. H. Lim (eds.), *The Cambridge Companion to Puritanism* (Cambridge: Cambridge University Press, 2008), pp. 277–93.

'Cultures of Coexistence in Early Modern England: History, Literature and Religious Toleration', *The Seventeenth Century*, 28, 2 (2013), pp. 115–37.

Wanklyn, Malcolm, 'Catholics in the Village Community: Madeley, Shropshire, 1630–1770', in Marie B. Rowlands (ed.), *English Catholics of Parish and Town, 1558–1778* (London: Catholic Record Society, 1999), pp. 210–36.

Warren, Leland E., 'Turning Reality Round Together: Guides to Conversation in Eighteenth-Century England', *Eighteenth-Century Life*, 8 (1983), pp. 65–87.

Watson, Jackie, and Kenny, Amy (eds.), *The Senses in Early Modern England, 1558–1660* (Manchester: Manchester University Press, 2015).

Watts, Michael R., *The Dissenters. From the Reformation to the French Revolution* (Oxford: Clarendon Press, 1978).

White, Eryn, 'Baptisms, Burials and Brawls: Church and Community in Mid-Eighteenth Century Wales', in Joan Allen and Richard C. Allen (eds.), *Faith of our Fathers: Popular Culture and Belief in Post-Reformation England* (Newcastle upon Tyne: Cambridge Scholars Publishing, 2009), pp. 39–51.

Wilson, Kathleen, *The Sense of the People: Politics, Culture and Imperialism in England, 1715–1785* (Cambridge: Cambridge University Press, 1995).

Winship, Michael P., *Seers of God. Puritan Providentialism in the Restoration and Early Enlightenment* (Baltimore, MD: Johns Hopkins University Press, 1996).

Withington, Phil, 'Company and Sociability in Early Modern England', *Social History*, 32, 3 (2007), pp. 291–307.

'Intoxicants and Society in Early Modern England', *Historical Journal*, 54, 3 (2011), pp. 631–57.

Withington, Phil, and McShane, Angela (eds.), *Cultures of Intoxication* (Oxford: Oxford University Press, 2014).

Wood, Andy, *Faith, Hope, and Charity: English Neighbourhoods, 1500–1640* (Cambridge: Cambridge University Press, 2020).

Worden, Blair, 'The Question of Secularization', in Alan Houston and Steve Pincus (eds.), *A Nation Transformed. England After the Restoration* (Cambridge: Cambridge University Press, 2001), pp. 20–40.

Wrightson, Keith, 'Alehouses, Order, and Reformation in Rural England, 1590–1660', in Eileen Yeo and Stephen Yeo (eds.), *Popular Culture and Class Conflict 1590–1914: Explorations in the History of Labour and Leisure* (Brighton: The Harvester Press, 1981), pp. 1–27.

English Society: 1580–1680 (London: Routledge, 1993).

'The "Decline of Neighbourliness" revisited', in Norman L.Jones and Daniel Woolf (eds.), *Local Identities in Late Medieval and Early Modern England* (Basingstoke: Palgrave Macmillan, 2007), pp. 19–49.

Wykes, David, 'Religious Dissent and the Penal Laws: An Explanation of Business Success?', *History*, 75, 243 (1990), pp. 39–62.

'Quaker Schoolmasters, Toleration and the Law, 1689–1714', *Journal of Religious History*, 21 (1997), pp. 178–92.

Yeo, Eileen, and Yeo, Stephen (eds.), *Popular Culture and Class Conflict, 1590–1914: Explorations in the History of Labour and Leisure* (Brighton: The Harvester Press, 1981).

Young, B. W., 'Religious History and the Eighteenth-Century Historian', *Historical Journal*, 43, 3 (2000), pp. 849–68.

Unpublished theses

Barry, Jonathan, 'The Cultural Life of Bristol, 1640–1775' (Unpublished DPhil thesis, University of Oxford, 1985).

Jonah Miller, 'Officeholding, Patriarchy and the State in England, 1660–1750' (Unpublished PhD thesis, King's College London, 2020).

Online resources

Downie, J. A., 'Tutchin, John (1660–1707)', *Oxford Dictionary of National Biography* (Oxford University Press, 2004), www.oxforddnb.com/view/article/27899, accessed 30 May 2018.

Baggs, A. P., and Siraut, M. C., 'Lyng: Manor and other estates', in R. W. Dunning and C. R. Elrington (ed.), *A History of the County of Somerset: Volume 6, Andersfield, Cannington, and North Petherton Hundreds (Bridgwater and Neighbouring Parishes)* (London: 1992): *British History Online*, www.british-history.ac.uk/vch/som/vol6/pp56-58, accessed 18 December 2020.

Baker, Anne Pimlott, 'Kay, Richard (1716–1751)', *Oxford Dictionary of National Biography* (Oxford University Press, 2004), www.oxforddnb.com/view/article/68345, accessed 4 June 2018.

Charles II, 1662: An Act for the Uniformity of Publique Prayers and Administrac[i]on of Sacraments & Other Rites & Ceremonies and for Establishing the Form of Making Ordaining and Consecrating Bishops Priests and Deacons in the Church of England', in John Raithby (ed.), *Statutes of the Realm* (n.p., 1819), vol. V, pp. 364–370: *British History Online*, www.british-history.ac.uk/statutes-realm/vol5/pp364-370.

'EEBO N-gram Browser' created by Anupam Basu for *Early Modern Print. Text Mining Early Modern English* (Washington University, St Louis: 2014), http://earlyprint.wustl.edu/eebotcpngrambrowser.html, accessed 28 May 2018.

Gordon, Alexander, 'Gough, Strickland (*d.* 1752)', Rev. Marilyn L. Brooks, *Oxford Dictionary of National Biography* (Oxford University Press, 2004), www.oxforddnb.com/view/article/11142, accessed 30 May 2018.

Haykin, Michael A. G., 'Wallin, Benjamin (1711–1782)', *Oxford Dictionary of National Biography* (Oxford University Press, 2004), www.oxforddnb.com/view/article/71075, accessed 4 June 2018.

McNamee, Robert, et al. (eds.), *Electronic Enlightenment Scholarly Edition of Correspondence*, Vers. 3.0 (University of Oxford: 2018), https://doi.org/10.13051/ee:doc/stanphOUoo10094a1c, accessed 30 March 2022.

O'Gorman, Frank, 'Review of English Society 1688–1832: Ideology, Social Structure and Political Practice During the Ancien Regime', (review no. 41b), https://reviews.history.ac.uk/review/41b, accessed 22 March 2022.

Skidmore, Gil, 'Bownas, Samuel (1677–1753)', *Oxford Dictionary of National Biography* (Oxford University Press, 2004), www.oxforddnb.com/view/article/3083, accessed 30 May 2018.

Sox, David, 'Woolman, John (1720–1772)', *Oxford Dictionary of National Biography* (Oxford University Press, 2004), www.oxforddnb.com/view/article/29960, accessed 30 May 2018.

'William and Mary, 1688: An Act for Exempting their Majestyes Protestant Subjects Dissenting from the Church of England from the Penalties of Certaine Lawes [Chapter XVIII. Rot. Parl. pt. 5. nu. 15.]', in John Raithby (ed.), *Statutes of the Realm* (n.p., 1819), vol. VI, pp. 74–76: *British History Online*, www.british-history.ac.uk/statutes-realm/vol6/pp74-76, accessed 22 March 2022.

Williams, Shirley, 'CAREW, Thomas (1702–66), of Crowcombe, nr. Minehead, Som.', in R Sedgwick (ed.), *The History of Parliament: The House of Commons 1715–1754* (1970), via *History of Parliament Online*, www.historyofparliamentonline.org/volume/1715-1754/member/carew-thomas-1702-66, accessed 18 December 2020.

Index

For EU product safety concerns, contact us at Calle de José Abascal, 56–1°,
28003 Madrid, Spain or eugpsr@cambridge.org.

www.ingramcontent.com/pod-product-compliance
Ingram Content Group UK Ltd.
Pitfield, Milton Keynes, MK11 3LW, UK
UKHW020356140625
459647UK00020B/2511